Metaheuristic Optimization Algorithms

Metaheuristic Optimization Algorithms
Optimizers, Analysis, and Applications

Edited by

Laith Abualigah

Computer Science Department, Al al-Bayt University, Mafraq, Jordan; Hourani
Center for Applied Scientific Research, Al-Ahliyya Amman University, Amman,
Jordan; MEU Research Unit, Middle East University, Amman, Jordan; School of
Computer Sciences, Universiti Sains Malaysia, Pulau Pinang, Malaysia; School of
Engineering and Technology, Sunway University Malaysia, Petaling Jaya, Malaysia;
Department of Electrical and Computer Engineering, Lebanese American University,
Byblos, Lebanon; Artificial Intelligence and Sensing Technologies (AIST) Research
Center, University of Tabuk, Tabuk, Saudi Arabia

ELSEVIER

Publisher: Mara Conner
Acquisitions Editor: Chris Katsaropoulos
Editorial Project Manager: Manisha Rana
Production Project Manager: Neena S. Maheen
Cover Designer: Matthew Limbert

Typeset by MPS Limited, Chennai, India

Contents

List of contributors

Ashraf Ababneh University of Kwazulu-Natal, Pietermaritzburg Campus, Potchefstroom, South Africa

Laith Abualigah Artificial Intelligence and Sensing Technologies (AIST) Research Center, University of Tabuk, Tabuk, Saudi Arabia; Hourani Center for Applied Scientific Research, Al-Ahliyya Amman University, Amman, Jordan; MEU Research Unit, Middle East University, Amman, Jordan; School of Computer Sciences, Universiti Sains Malaysia, Pulau Pinang, Malaysia; School of Engineering and Technology, Sunway University Malaysia, Petaling Jaya, Malaysia; Computer Science Department, Al al-Bayt University, Mafraq, Jordan; Department of Electrical and Computer Engineering, Lebanese American University, Byblos, Lebanon

Roa'a Abualigah Luminus Technical University College, Irbid, Jordan

Eman Abu-Dalhoum University of Kwazulu-Natal, Pietermaritzburg Campus, Potchefstroom, South Africa

Aya Abusaleem School of Information Engineering, Sanming University, Sanming, P.R. China

Esraa Nasser Ahmad University of Kwazulu-Natal, Pietermaritzburg Campus, Potchefstroom, South Africa

Ahmad A. Al Turk New Engineering Industry College, Putian University, Putian, China

Laheeb Al-Abadi Computer Science Department, Al al-Bayt University, Mafraq, Jordan

Khaled Aldiabat Department of Management Information Systems, Ajloun National University, Ajloun, Jordan

Mofleh Al-diabat Computer Science Department, Al al-Bayt University, Mafraq, Jordan; Artificial Intelligence and Sensing Technologies (AIST) Research Center, University of Tabuk, Tabuk, Saudi Arabia

Ghada Al-Hilo   Unit for Data Science and Computing, North-West University, Potchefstroom, South Africa

Saif AlNajdawi   School of Computer Sciences, Universiti Sains Malaysia, Pulau Pinang, Malaysia

Faisal AL-Saqqar   Computer Science Department, Al al-Bayt University, Mafraq, Jordan

Sahar M. Alshatti   Sorbonne Center of Artificial Intelligence, Sorbonne University-Abu Dhabi, Abu Dhabi, United Arab Emirates

Mohammad Alshinwan   Faculty of Information Technology, Applied Science Private University, Amman, Jordan

Ibrahim Al-Shourbaji   Department of Computer Science, University of Hertfordshire, Hatfield, United Kingdom

Anas Ratib Alsoud   Hourani Center for Applied Scientific Research, Al-Ahliyya Amman University, Amman, Jordan

Shadi AlZu'bi   Faculty of Science and IT, Al-Zaytoonah University of Jordan, Amman, Jordan

Mohammad Al-Zyod   College of Computer Sciences and Informatics, Amman Arab University, Amman, Jordan

Mohammad El-Bashir   Computer Science Department, Al al-Bayt University, Mafraq, Jordan

El-Sayed M. El-kenawy   Department of Communications and Electronics, Delta Higher Institute of Engineering and Technology, Mansoura, Egypt

Laith Elkhalaifa   School of Computer Sciences, Universiti Sains Malaysia, Pulau Pinang, Malaysia

Diaa Salama Abd Elminaam   Information Systems Department, Faculty of Computers and Artificial Intelligence, Benha University, Benha, Egypt; Computer Science Department, Faculty of Computer Science, Misr International University, Cairo, Egypt

Absalom E. Ezugwu   Unit for Data Science and Computing, North-West University, Potchefstroom, South Africa

Sabreen Faweer   Computer Science Department, Al al-Bayt University, Mafraq, Jordan

Agostino Forestiero   Institute for High Performance Computing and Networking, National Research Council, Rende, CS, Italy

Faiza Gul   Electrical Department, Air University Aerospace and Aviation Campus, Kamra, Pakistan

Essam Said Hanandeh   Department of Computer Information System, Zarqa University, Zarqa, Jordan

Worod Hawamdeh   Sorbonne Center of Artificial Intelligence, Sorbonne University-Abu Dhabi, Abu Dhabi, United Arab Emirates

Ahmad MohdAziz Hussein   Deanship of E-Learning and Distance Education, Umm Al-Qura University, Makkah, Saudi Arabia

Abdelazim G. Hussien   Department of Computer and Information Science, Linköping University, Linköping, Sweden; Faculty of Science, Fayoum University, Faiyum, Egypt

Abiodun M. Ikotun   University of Kwazulu-Natal, Pietermaritzburg Campus, Potchefstroom, South Africa

Davut Izci   Department of Computer Engineering, Batman University, Batman, Turkey

Heming Jia   Department of Information Engineering, Sanming University, Fujian, P.R.China

Nima Khodadadi   Department of Civil, Architectural and Environmental Engineering, University of Miami, Coral Gables, FL, United States

Farah Mahadeen   Deanship of E-Learning and Distance Education, Umm Al-Qura University, Makkah, Saudi Arabia

Shubham Mahajan   Ajeenkya DY Patil University, Pune, Maharashtra, India; University Center for Research & Development (UCRD), Chandigarh University, Mohali, Punjab, India

Ala Mughaid   Department of Information Technology, Faculty of Prince Al-Hussien Bin Abdullah II for IT, The Hashemite University, Zarqa, Jordan

Mohammad Rustom Al Nasar   Department of Information Technology Management, College of Computer Information Technology (CCIT), American University in the Emirates (AUE), Academic City, Dubai, United Arab Emirates

Suhier Odah   New Engineering Industry College, Putian University, Putian, China

Mohammed Otair   Khawarizmi University Technical College, Amman, Jordan

Ali Raza   Institute of Computer Science, Khwaja Fareed University of Engineering and Information Technology, Rahim Yar Khan, Pakistan

Canan Batur Şahin   Faculty of Engineering and Natural Sciences, Malatya Turgut Ozal University, Malatya, Turkey

Batool Sbenaty   School of Computer Sciences, Universiti Sains Malaysia, Pulau Pinang, Malaysia

Mohammad Shehab   College of Computer Sciences and Informatics, Amman Arab University, Amman, Jordan

Ahlam Sheikhan   New Engineering Industry College, Putian University, Putian, China

Putra Sumari   School of Computer Sciences, Universiti Sains Malaysia, Pulau Pinang, Malaysia

Mohsen Zare   Department of Electrical Engineering, Faculty of Engineering, Jahrom University, Jahrom, Fras, Iran

Peiying Zhang   College of Computer Science and Technology, China University of Petroleum (East China), Qingdao, P.R. China; State Key Laboratory of Integrated Services Networks, Xidian University, Xi'an, P.R. China

Raed Abu Zitar   Sorbonne Center of Artificial Intelligence, Sorbonne University-Abu Dhabi, Abu Dhabi, United Arab Emirates

Particle swarm optimization algorithm: review and applications

Laith Abualigah[1,2,3,4,5,6,7], Ahlam Sheikhan[8], Abiodun M. Ikotun[9], Raed Abu Zitar[10], Anas Ratib Alsoud[2], Ibrahim Al-Shourbaji[11], Abdelazim G. Hussien[12,13], Heming Jia[14]

[1]ARTIFICIAL INTELLIGENCE AND SENSING TECHNOLOGIES (AIST) RESEARCH CENTER, UNIVERSITY OF TABUK, TABUK, SAUDI ARABIA [2]HOURANI CENTER FOR APPLIED SCIENTIFIC RESEARCH, AL-AHLIYYA AMMAN UNIVERSITY, AMMAN, JORDAN [3]MEU RESEARCH UNIT, MIDDLE EAST UNIVERSITY, AMMAN, JORDAN [4]SCHOOL OF COMPUTER SCIENCES, UNIVERSITI SAINS MALAYSIA, PULAU PINANG, MALAYSIA [5]SCHOOL OF ENGINEERING AND TECHNOLOGY, SUNWAY UNIVERSITY MALAYSIA, PETALING JAYA, MALAYSIA [6]COMPUTER SCIENCE DEPARTMENT, AL AL-BAYT UNIVERSITY, MAFRAQ, JORDAN [7]DEPARTMENT OF ELECTRICAL AND COMPUTER ENGINEERING, LEBANESE AMERICAN UNIVERSITY, BYBLOS, LEBANON [8]NEW ENGINEERING INDUSTRY COLLEGE, PUTIAN UNIVERSITY, PUTIAN, CHINA [9]UNIVERSITY OF KWAZULU-NATAL, PIETERMARITZBURG CAMPUS, POTCHEFSTROOM, SOUTH AFRICA [10]SORBONNE CENTER OF ARTIFICIAL INTELLIGENCE, SORBONNE UNIVERSITY-ABU DHABI, ABU DHABI, UNITED ARAB EMIRATES [11]DEPARTMENT OF COMPUTER SCIENCE, UNIVERSITY OF HERTFORDSHIRE, HATFIELD, UNITED KINGDOM [12]DEPARTMENT OF COMPUTER AND INFORMATION SCIENCE, LINKÖPING UNIVERSITY, LINKÖPING, SWEDEN [13]FACULTY OF SCIENCE, FAYOUM UNIVERSITY, FAIYUM, EGYPT [14]DEPARTMENT OF INFORMATION ENGINEERING, SANMING UNIVERSITY, FUJIAN, P.R. CHINA

1.1 Introduction

Particle swarm optimization (PSO) is considered as a technique for resolving global optimization problems; it belongs to the swarm intelligence methods category [1]. It is a stochastic evolutionary algorithm induced by mimicking the flocks' social behavior. The evolution of the solution swarm is compared to the movement of birds from one location to another in the process of food search. Good information shared between individual birds is compared to the most optimistic solution, and the food resource is compared to the most optimistic solution throughout the course. In PSO, candidate solutions are presented as particles to explore the search space for better solutions with reference to the local best and global best solutions [1]. Each individual's collaboration can be used to obtain the most optimum solution in the PSO.

Metaheuristic Optimization Algorithms. DOI: https://doi.org/10.1016/B978-0-443-13925-3.00019-4

This algorithm applies different sorts of operators to population's individuals, one by one, based upon the fitness information acquired from the environments [2]. The PSO has been widely employed to work out complicated nonlinear programming and optimization issues because of its superior performance in finding the global optimum [3]. Normally, optimization methods can be used to deal with many problems in science, as presented in [4−12].

PSO is simple to implement and computationally economical because of its low memory and CPU performance requirements. Nevertheless, its parameters can have a big impact on the outcome. Furthermore, it has a few drawbacks such as slow and premature convergence [13]. Various research projects have been conducted recently, and numerous PSO versions have been presented. By adjusting parameters, modifying updating rules, and constructing new techniques in the evolving process, these algorithms attempt to stabilize the local and global search abilities and achieve some gains in solution convergence [14].

This paper is a survey on the publications in the PSO algorithm. Thirty publications in the years 2017−22 are analyzed and classified into four applications categories: neural networks, feature selection (FS), data clustering, and mobile robots. Furthermore, this survey presents the inspiration and the algorithm procedure of the standard PSO, and the collected data provides those interested in the PSO algorithm adequate materials in the standard PSO, same as improved PSO implementations in neural networks, FS, data clustering, and robotics.

The remaining sections consisting this paper are arranged in this way: second section presents the standard (PSO) algorithm procedure, third section summarizes related works, and fourth section is a discussion for the proposed work. Eventually, the conclusion with some suggested future work is given in the final section.

1.2 Particle swarm optimization

Kennedy and Eberhart introduced the PSO algorithm in 1995, simulating the bird flock's or fish school's behavior [15].

1.2.1 Standard particle swarm optimization

PSO is a mechanism for optimization that is population-based, starting from a random particles population and searching for optimum through the update of generations. Assuming a search space with m dimensions, the swarm's particle j is defined with an m-dimensional vector $Y_j = (y_{j1}, y_{j2}, \ldots, y_{jm})$.

The other m-dimensional vector $Z_j = (z_{j1}, z_{j2}, \ldots, z_{jm})$ represents this particle's velocity. Each particle's fitness can be assessed using the objective function of an optimization problem. The particle j's best formerly visited position is distinguished as the best of the individual positions of the particle $K_j = (k_{j1}, k_{j2}, \ldots, k_{jn})$. The global best position is defined as the position of the best individual in the entire swarm $C = (c_1, c_2, \ldots, c_m)$. The velocity of the particle and the latest position will be allocated for each pace using Eqs. $(1{-}1)$ and $(1{-}2)$:

$$Z_j = \omega \times Z_j + b1 \times d_1 \times (K_j - Y_j) + b2 \times d_2 \times (C - Y_j) \qquad (1{-}1)$$

$$Y_{j} = Y_{j} + Z_{j} \tag{1-2}$$

wherein y is the inertia weight, a control variable for the effect of a particle's former velocity on its present one. $d1$ and $d2$ are random variables, which are distributed independently and uniformly, with range (0,1). For the purpose of controlling the maximum step size, variables $b1$ and $b2$ are used as nonnegative constant parameters and are defined as coefficients of acceleration.

Eq. (1−1) is utilized in PSO to compute the new velocity depending on the prior velocity of the particle and the distance between the particle's current position and both of its own best historical position and the best position of neighborhood or the whole population. For controlling excessive migration of particles on the outside of the search space, the value of each component in Z will be embedded in the range [− max, max]. The particle then moves toward a next position in accordance with Eq. (1−2). This iterated process will stop till that a user-defined termination criterion is attained.

1.2.2 Particle swarm optimization algorithm

The swarm of particles in this algorithm is formed at random at first, and each particle position indicates a possible solution. Every particle is placed within the search space and given a fitness value and a velocity that determines the speed and direction of its movements, as depicted in Fig. 1−1 [16]. To obtain an optimum solution, particles roam about within the search space based on their updated position and velocity [16]. The particle compares its present position to its best position in each iteration. The current position becomes the particle position if it is better than the previous position, and the swarm's best particle is selected based upon having the best value for the fitness function and the movement of the particles in the swarm lean toward this particle [16].

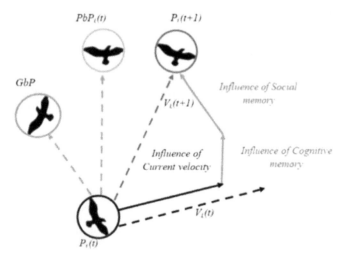

FIGURE 1–1 Graphical depiction of a particle's position and velocity update.

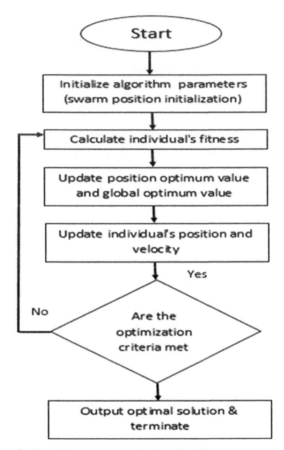

FIGURE 1–2 Flowchart of standard particle swarm optimization algorithm.

The steps of the standard PSO algorithm are demonstrated in a flowchart in Fig. 1–2.

1.3 Related works

In this section, an inspection of the 30 research studies conducted on PSO in four implementations, neural networks, FS, data clustering and mobile robots, is presented. Table 1–1 illustrates the summary of all these studies.

1.3.1 Neural networks

wA neural network (NN) is defined as a huge in-parallel dispensed processor with a naturalistic proclivity for storing and producing attainable empirical information. It is constructed of a huge number of simple processing components known as neurons. It is constructed of a single input layer, single output layer, and not less than one hidden layer, with the hidden layer acting as a conduit between the input and output layers via neurons, weights, biases,

Table 1–1 Applications summary of the particle swarm optimizer algorithm.

Application	Proposed	Problem	Year	References
NNs	ELM	Improve RSLFN's convergence performance	2019	[17]
	PSO used improved adaptive acceleration factor and inertia weight	Optimize the BP NN	2017	[18]
	A data-driven prediction method	To increase the Elman NN's prediction accuracy	2019	[19]
	A model of radial basis function NN with IPSO	Improve the accuracy of network traffic prediction	2018	[20]
	A chaos controller for rod-type plasma torch system	Modifying the search space of the parameters	2019	[21]
	BQPSO	Employing the binary encoding approach with no users domain knowledge on CNN	2019	[22]
	PSO-enhanced ensemble deep NNs for OD segmentation	OD segmentation via retinal images	2020	[23]
FS	SSA is combined with PSO	To create a hybrid optimization method for the FS problem	2019	[24]
	APSO	Enhance FS approach for image steganalysis	2019	[25]
	An intelligent decision support system for skin cancer detection	For feature optimization	2019	[26]
	ANFIS using an IPSO	Prediction model for benzene concentration in atmosphere gas	2018	[27]
	FSPSOTC	To solve the FS problem	2018	[28]
	HBBEPSO	For exploring the FS	2018	[29]
	GWO and PSO	Essential features discovery	2020	[30]
Data clustering	Kernel density estimation technique	To address the premature convergence	2018	[31]
	An improved firefly with PSO	To solve automatic data clustering problems	2019	[32]
	FCM with the QPSO	To prevent local optima stagnation	2018	[33]
	A novel SCPSO	To deal with the massive amount of text documents	2019	[34]
	IDKPSOC-k-means	To escape from local minima points	2019	[35]
	QtPSO-based FCM algorithm	To create cluster centers for a dataset	2021	[36]
Mobile robots	PSO-AWDV	For planning a mobile robots smooth path	2022	[37]
	Integration between IPSO and Bezier curve	Smooth path planning for mobile robots	2021	[38]
	MPSO	Minimizing the time and energy of a robot swarm	2021	[39]
	Integrating factors in an IPSO	Handling the problem of mobile robots' global path planning	2020	[40]
	Fringe search and PSO	Creation of a path that is collision-free	2020	[41]
	Dual-layer path planning techniques	Empowering the robot to map out a better route	2022	[42]
	MP-SAPSO	For evading premature convergence efficiently	2021	[43]
	FIMOPSO	To work out the CRPP problem	2022	[44]
	PSOMFB	To solve the path planning problem	2020	[45]
	Hybridization of JPSO and SGOA	To meet real-time multirobot path planning	2021	[46]

and activation functions [47]. Slow convergence speed and low precision are main drawbacks of the original back-propagation (BP) NN; these flaws make falling into local minimum value easier [18].

To improve random one-hidden-layer feed-forward NNs (RSLFN)'s convergence performance, an enhanced extreme learning machine (ELM) with a basis of PSO combined with input-to-output sensitivity information is proposed. PSO encoding the single-hidden-layer feed-forward NNs (SLFN)'s input-to-output susceptibility information is utilized for the input weights optimization together with hidden biases in the enhanced ELM. By lowering the network's input-to-output susceptibility, the enhanced ELM had an ability to increase the performance of generalization besides the conditioning of the SLFN [17]. For optimizing the BP NN, researchers suggested an improved PSO (IPSO) algorithm. In order to enhance the BP NN through improving the amount of initial weight and threshold of BP, PSO used a technique to improve adjustable acceleration factor and adjustable inertia weight in this new approach [18].

A data-controlled technique for prediction using condition tracking data and an Elman NN was suggested [19]. The modified particle optimization approach is applied to increase the Elman NN's forecasting accuracy. The motor deterioration index is extracted from condition monitoring data using principal component analysis. With regard to correlated theories of phase space reconstruction and network traffic, a proposed paradigm of radial basis function (NN) with IPSO is presented in [20] for the improvement of the network traffic prediction's accuracy besides the optimization of the technique of parameter and structure setting for a NN. To avoid local convergence, the modified PSO can alter learning variables besides the inertia weight, as well as make global extremum t-distribution mutations of particle positions. This improves its global searching capability.

Utilizing PSO for NN's parameters determination is widely used [21]. A torch system with rod-type plasma's chaos controller was evolved using a quantum NN, based on the value of each parameter, modifying the parameters' search space of each particle. Additionally, weaker particles will be removed, while new particles will be added in their place. These changes improved the proposed algorithm's performance by allowing for global search along with searching inside an acceptable space.

After studying the constraints of standard PSO, a quantum-acted PSO and binary encoding (BQPSO) is used. Users having domain knowledge on CNN are not required to employ the binary encoding approach. Then, to guarantee the impact of developed CNN structures, a novel quantum-acted evolving technique is provided [22]. PSO-enhanced ensemble deep NNs for optic disk (OD) segmentation via retinal images have been proposed in [23]. The PSO algorithm has been enhanced, and six search mechanisms have been added to diversify the search process.

1.3.2 Feature selection

FS is a machine learning technique for reducing datasets' high dimensionality problems. Data classifier accuracy is significantly affected by increase in the volume of data and the nature of the data characterized by large dimensionality [48]. FS allows for the extraction of the most representative information from large datasets, minimizing the computational effort required for other tasks such as classification. The FS tool removes unnecessary and irrelevant features, which negatively affect the process of data classification to reduce dataset attributes and subsequently reduce the space requirement and computational cost [49]. The slap swarm algorithm (SSA) is combined with PSO in ref [24]; the paper's aim is to create a hybridized optimization technique for resolving the FS problem. The combination of these methodologies results in an algorithm known as SSAPSO, which enhances the effectiveness of the exploration and exploitation processes.

A proposed novel FS procedure for image steganalysis with the basis of adaptive inertia weight-based PSO (APSO) is presented in [25], in which the PSO inertia weight is flexibly adjusted by the diameter of the swarm, average distance of center-encircling particles, and the average velocity of particles toward the center. The intelligence of the decision support system designed for the purpose of skin cancer detection is determined [26]. For feature optimization, two IPSO procedures are proposed. To overcome stagnation, the first procedure uses variable acceleration coefficients, multiremote leaders, detailed subdimension feature search, and resetting procedures. To increase diversity and intensification, the second procedure employs random acceleration coefficients rather than adaptive ones, which depend upon nonlinear sine, helix, and circle functions consecutively. Every base paradigm is also trained by every optimized feature subset to build ensemble classifiers. The proposed PSO models are utilized to fine-tune the hyperparameters of a deep convolutional NN.

Using an IPSO, a proposed new adaptive prediction model for benzene concentration in atmosphere gas reported in refs [2,27], the base of the model depends upon the adaptable neuro fuzzy inference system (ANFIS). In their proposed model, they suggested an ANFIS based on a new benzene prediction model. By incorporating the multiobjective fitness function-associated accuracy, the root mean squared error, the coefficient of determination (r^2), and IPSO improved ANFIS performance. The presented new FS technique [28], namely, FS utilizing the PSO method (FSPSOTC), is used in order to work out the FS problem by generating a new subset of descriptive text features. The new features subset has the potential to improve the clustering of text method's performance, while also reducing computational time.

A proposed algorithm, which is called hybrid binary bat enhanced PSO (HBBEPSO) utilized the ability of the heuristic bat algorithm in echo-locating in order to explore the FS and the ability of an IPSO variant to converge to the best global solution in the search space, for getting efficient solutions in FS [29]. Another hybrid technique was presented in ref [30], a combination of gray wolf optimization (GWO) and PSO, for discovering essential features and eliminating nonessential features from a dataset during classification.

1.3.3 Data clustering

Data clustering involves grouping of data into a number of collections or clusters based on intrinsic similarities among the data point characteristics and features [50]. In cluster analysis, the PSO algorithm is commonly utilized. For clustering performance improvement, PSO is sometimes hybridized with other metaheuristic algorithms [51]. In some cases, PSO is combined with traditional clustering algorithms such as K-means algorithm for the selection of an optimal number of clusters [52]. Nevertheless, clustering algorithms which are PSO-based face some drawbacks regarding the clustering technique such as being prone to premature convergence to suboptimal clustering solutions and requiring adjustment of learning coefficient values to figure out other solutions with better cases. These flaws might be avoided by striking the right balance between particle exploitation and exploration when searching the feature space. Furthermore, particles must consider the amount of movement in each dimension and seek the best solution in the most densely populated parts of the FS.

A new method for clustering data has been developed [31], kernel density estimation procedure combined along with novel bandwidth evaluation technique to discuss the premature convergence model is combined with estimated multidimensional gravitational learning coefficients. In order to eliminate the drawbacks of the firefly optimization algorithm, like premature convergence toward local minima on account of cluster centers' arbitrary initialization, and to optimally find out clusters' count for any presented dataset, an enhanced firefly algorithm is used in combination with the PSO to resolve automatic data clustering problems [32].

The quantum-behaved PSO is utilized in data clustering [16], in which the fuzzy C-means (FCM) clustering technique is combined with the quantum-behaved PSO (QPSO) along with a fully connected topology, and the test is conducted using UCI machine learning repository's collection of datasets. The QPSO algorithm's global search capability helps prevent local optima stagnation, while FCM's soft clustering method supports dividing data according to membership probability based. To improve the clustering of the text document, a novel spectral clustering algorithm with PSO (SCPSO) is presented [16]. The randomization is done using the initial population using global and local optimization functions to deal with the massive amount of text documents; this study intends to combine spectral clustering with swarm optimization.

The presented IDKPSOC-k-means approach [35], which is a novel hybrid partition clustering technique depending upon an enhanced self-adaptive PSO and K-means, utilizes a crossover operator for enhancement of PSO's capacity so that the escape from the local minima points is attainable. To create cluster centroids in a given dataset, a proposed quantum-inspired PSO (QtPSO)-based FCM algorithm is used. The traditional PSO method is hybridized with the effectiveness of quantum computing. The qubit (quantum bit) feature is used in conjunction with PSO to build this proposed technique [36].

1.3.4 Mobile robots

In automated industrial operations, mobile robots are becoming more common. Other applications for mobile robots include planetary exploration, monitoring, and landmine detection. The most significant issue in mobile robotics is path planning, through which collision should be avoided.

A* algorithm, artificial potential field (APF) approach, ant colony algorithm, and many other several methods for path planning have been presented. Nevertheless, these techniques have many drawbacks like search efficiency reduction, a significant number of calculations, and inefficiency in the case of large maps [53].

Recently, nature-inspired hybrid metaheuristic algorithms, like PSO and GWO algorithm, have been successfully applied to handle path planning challenges. Using metaheuristics algorithms has various advantages, including the possibility of embedding expert knowledge in a search process and [2] comprising multiple candidate solutions other than a single variable focus [54].

A novel approach for planning a mobile robots smooth path is created utilizing an enhanced PSO and a continuous high-degree Bezier curve [37] for the optimization problem of smooth path planning, and an IPSO with adaptive weighted delay velocity (PSO-AWDV) procedure is proposed, in a way that the parameter connection to ensure the convergence of PSO-AWDV is generated by the algorithm's stability analysis. On the other hand, another integration between IPSO and Bezier curve was proposed [38] for smooth path planning for mobile robots. PSO was utilized to address the issues of premature convergence and local trapping; some disruptions of the particle swarm was enforced by an adjustable fractional order velocity based on its current evolutionary state.

Mobile robot swarm is a technique that can subrogate a particle swarm in the process of exploration of the optimal solution when conducting PSO. Time and energy are significant constraints on moving distances of mobile robots, which can reduce high cost significantly when minimized. By minimizing the total distance moved by robots, the time and energy of a robot swarm are also minimized by a moving distance-minimized PSO (MPSO) [39].

Many factors like uniform distribution, cubic spline interpolation function, and learning factor of increased control are integrated in an IPSO to optimize global path planning for mobile robots [42]. The utilization of the proposed method handled the problem of mobile robots' global path planning in an indoor environment. The navigation point model is chosen as the mobile robot's working area model in the suggested algorithm.

The intelligence of classical algorithms (such as roadmap method and potential field method) is restricted in the area of mobile path planning, while the evolutionary algorithms [such as genetic algorithm (GA), the artificial NN (ANN), and PSO] have been popular in local navigation, as they overcome classical algorithms because they are more intelligent in controlling and executing a plan independently [41]. This method created a path that is collision-free between the starting and the ending point using a combination between fringe search and PSO.

A technique that empowers the robot to map out a better route [42], while avoiding moving snags efficiently in a multisnag environment, is proposed. This dual-layer path planning technique employs an optimized APF method at the global layer, whereas an improved dynamic window approach (DWA) is utilized in the local layer. PSO takes two fitness functions in this proposed method: smoothness and the length of the global path to acquire obstacle's influence range, repulsion, and the coefficients of gravitation in APF. For assessment of the danger level of mobile obstacles, a fuzzy control plan is embraced at the local path planning level based on DWA.

For evading premature convergence efficiently, a hybrid model of PSO and simulated annealing algorithm with mutation particle (MP-SAPSO) was suggested to enhance the path planning accuracy and the performance of robot working in a well-defined environment scheme [43]. A fuzzy rule-based system was utilized [43] for obstacle evasion. This proposed method combines a fuzzy-enhanced improved multiobjective PSO (FIMOPSO) algorithm, which is aimed at working out the car-like mobile robot path planning (CRPP) problem. CRPP aims to find the shortest and safest path with the minimum motor torque, path length, robot acceleration, travel time, and obstacle avoidance.

In a trimodule algorithm [45], a solution to the path planning problem was proposed by finding out the collision-free path that fulfills the shortest distance and path smoothness-selected criteria. In the first module, an optimized path is formed by a combination of PSO and a modified frequency bat (PSOMFB) algorithm for distance minimization with the following of path smoothness criteria. Any impractical points generated by PSOMFB is detected in the second module to be transformed into practical solutions. Obstacle detection and avoidance are featured in the third module.

A wireless sensor network is utilized in locating robots and obstacles for the purpose of meeting the real-time multirobot path planning besides accurate requirements in a dynamic environment [46]. The proposed method adopted a hybridization of a jumping mechanism PSO (JPSO) and a safety gap obstacle avoidance algorithm (SGOA) for path planning. Low-priority robots are trapped in a long wait and are unable to resume walking when avoiding obstacles. SGOA implementation optimizes a new safety path that is collision-free for the low-priority robot.

1.4 Discussion

The simplicity and efficiency of the PSO algorithm in optimization problems have widened its utilization in various implementation areas. Nevertheless, PSO, along with all other swarm intelligence (SI)-based optimization methods, has some limitations, such as premature convergence, high computational cost, sensitivity to parameters, and so on. These limitations opened the gate for the researchers to solve real world optimization problems by modifying PSO, through adjusting PSO parameters in searching the optimistic solution.

The findings presented in this review paper provide evidence and verification of the PSO algorithm's efficiency in a variety of applications. This confirmation is based on a review and analysis of the recommended approaches for the PSO algorithm as well as recently released optimization strategies. According to past studies, there are emerging models in the general direction of the years 2017−22.

As an optimization algorithm, PSO is utilized by researchers in NN applications for increasing NN prediction accuracy or diversifying the search space of particles in NNs, and in other proposed methods, PSO is used to overcome NN convergence issue. When used for

FS optimization problems, the hybridization of PSO with other optimization algorithms (the slap swarm, binary bat, and gray wolf) is used to enhance the FS approach. Adaptive inertia-weight PSO outperformed other approaches in optimizing FS process.

The FCM algorithm is combined with PSO to create cluster centers for a dataset and to divide data based on membership probability. To solve automatic data clustering problems, PSO is hybridized with the firefly algorithm; this hybridization overcomes the drawbacks of the firefly algorithm. PSO, along with other heuristic path planning methods, showed satisfactory results over classical methods due to their efficiency in dynamic and unknown environments.

1.5 Conclusion

Based on the research conducted in this paper, the distribution of PSO far exceeds the expectations. It is now used in almost every area that deals with optimization issues. PSO can be used to optimize in a variety of dynamic and uncertain contexts. This paper also presents the methods and procedures that aimed to adopt the improvement of PSO in various implementations, FS, NNs, and data clustering. The hybridization of IPSO with other methods overcomes many issues in the methods used in these implementations by modifying the parameters of PSO; the tested optimization approaches have clearly different traditional or evolutionary paradigms integrated with the inherent social, cooperative character of PSO. Other PSO implementations such as energy consumption, wireless networking, data mining, signal processing, cloud computing, malicious behavior detection, and collective robotic must be studied in the future.

References

[1] A.E. Ezugwu, A.K. Shukla, R. Nath, A.A. Akinyelu, J.O. Agushaka, H. Chiroma, et al., Metaheuristics: a comprehensive overview and classification along with bibliometric analysis, Artif. Intell. Rev. 54 (6) (2021) 4237−4316. Aug 16.

[2] M. Li, H. Chen, X. Wang, N. Zhong, S. Lu, An improved particle swarm optimization algorithm with adaptive inertia weights, Int. J. Inf. Technol. Decis. Mak. 18 (03) (2019) 833−866. May 10.

[3] Z. Ouyang, Y. Liu, S.-J. Ruan, T. Jiang, An improved particle swarm optimization algorithm for reliability-redundancy allocation problem with mixed redundancy strategy and heterogeneous components, Reliab. Eng. Syst. Saf. 181 (2019) 62−74. Jan.

[4] L. Abualigah, A. Diabat, C.L. Thanh, S. Khatir, Opposition-based Laplacian distribution with Prairie Dog Optimization method for industrial engineering design problems, Computer Methods Appl. Mech. Eng. 414 (2023) 116097.

[5] G. Hu, Y. Zheng, L. Abualigah, A.G. Hussien, DETDO: an adaptive hybrid dandelion optimizer for engineering optimization, Adv. Eng. Inform. 57 (2023) 102004.

[6] D. Izci, S. Ekinci, S. Mirjalili, L. Abualigah, An intelligent tuning scheme with a master/slave approach for efficient control of the automatic voltage regulator, Neural Comput. Appl. (2023) 1−17.

[7] H. Jia, C. Lu, D. Wu, C. Wen, H. Rao, L. Abualigah, An improved reptile search algorithm with ghost opposition-based learning for global optimization problems, J. Comput. Des. Eng. (2023) qwad048.

[8]   A.H. Alharbi, A.A. Abdelhamid, A. Ibrahim, S.K. Towfek, N. Khodadadi, L. Abualigah, et al., Improved dipper-throated optimization for forecasting metamaterial design bandwidth for engineering applications, Biomimetics 8 (2) (2023) 241.

[9]   S. Nama, A.K. Saha, S. Chakraborty, A.H. Gandomi, L. Abualigah, Boosting particle swarm optimization by backtracking search algorithm for optimization problems, Swarm Evolut. Comput. 79 (2023) 101304.

[10] M. Zare, M. Ghasemi, A. Zahedi, K. Golalipour, S.K. Mohammadi, S. Mirjalili, et al., A global best-guided firefly algorithm for engineering problems, J. Bionic Eng. (2023) 1−30.

[11] D. Wu, C. Wen, H. Rao, H. Jia, Q. Liu, L. Abualigah, Modified reptile search algorithm with multi-hunting coordination strategy for global optimization problems, Math. Biosci. Eng. 20 (6) (2023) 10090−10134.

[12] S. Ekinci, D. Izci, L. Abualigah, R.A. Zitar, A modified oppositional chaotic local search strategy based aquila optimizer to design an effective controller for vehicle cruise control system, J. Bionic Eng. (2023) 1−24.

[13] W.R. Abdul-Adheem, An enhanced particle swarm optimization algorithm, Int. J. Electr. Comput. Eng. 9 (6) (2019) 4904. Dec 1.

[14] F. Wang, H. Zhang, K. Li, Z. Lin, J. Yang, X.-L. Shen, A hybrid particle swarm optimization algorithm using adaptive learning strategy, Inf. Sci. (Ny.) (2018) 162−177. Apr;436−437.

[15] X. Hu, R. Eberhart, Multiobjective optimization using dynamic neighborhood particle swarm optimization, in: Proc. 2002 Congress on Evolutionary Computation CEC'02 (Cat No02TH8600), IEEE, 2002, pp. 1677−1681.

[16] S. Rengasamy, P. Murugesan, PSO based data clustering with a different perception, Swarm Evol. Comput. 64 (2021) 100895. Jul.

[17] Q.-H. Ling, Y.-Q. Song, F. Han, C.-H. Zhou, H. Lu, An improved learning algorithm for random neural networks based on particle swarm optimization and input-to-output sensitivity, Cogn. Syst. Res. 53 (2019) 51−60. Jan.

[18] T. Liu, S. Yin, An improved particle swarm optimization algorithm used for BP neural network and multimedia course-ware evaluation, Multimed. Tools Appl. 76 (9) (2017) 11961−11974. May 29.

[19] L. Yang, F. Wang, J. Zhang, W. Ren, Remaining useful life prediction of ultrasonic motor based on Elman neural network with improved particle swarm optimization, Measurement 143 (2019) 27−38. Sep.

[20] W. Zhang, D. Wei, Prediction for network traffic of radial basis function neural network model based on improved particle swarm optimization algorithm, Neural Comput. Appl. 29 (4) (2018) 1143−1152. Feb 13.

[21] E. Salahshour, M. Malekzadeh, R. Gholipour, S. Khorashadizadeh, Designing multi-layer quantum neural network controller for chaos control of rod-type plasma torch system using improved particle swarm optimization, Evol. Syst. 10 (3) (2019) 317−331. Sep 9.

[22] Y. Li, J. Xiao, Y. Chen, L. Jiao, Evolving deep convolutional neural networks by quantum behaved particle swarm optimization with binary encoding for image classification, Neurocomputing 362 (2019) 156−165. Oct.

[23] L. Zhang, C.P. Lim, Intelligent optic disc segmentation using improved particle swarm optimization and evolving ensemble models, Appl. Soft Comput. 92 (2020) 106328. Jul.

[24] R.A. Ibrahim, A.A. Ewees, D. Oliva, M. Abd Elaziz, S. Lu, Improved salp swarm algorithm based on particle swarm optimization for feature selection, J. Ambient. Intell. Humaniz.s Comput. 10 (8) (2019) 3155−3169. Aug 11.

[25] A. Adeli, A. Broumandnia, Image steganalysis using improved particle swarm optimization based feature selection, Appl. Intell. 48 (6) (2018) 1609−1622. Jun 30.

[26] T.Y. Tan, L. Zhang, C.P. Lim, Intelligent skin cancer diagnosis using improved particle swarm optimization and deep learning models, Appl. Soft Comput. 84 (2019) 105725. Nov.

[27] H.S. Pannu, D. Singh, A.K. Malhi, Improved particle swarm optimization based adaptive neuro-fuzzy inference system for benzene detection, CLEAN. − Soil, Air, Water 46 (5) (2018) 1700162. May 9.

[28] L.M. Abualigah, A.T. Khader, E.S. Hanandeh, A new feature selection method to improve the document clustering using particle swarm optimization algorithm, J. Comput. Sci. 25 (2018) 456−466. Mar.

[29] M.A. Tawhid, K.B. Dsouza, Hybrid binary bat enhanced particle swarm optimization algorithm for solving feature selection problems, Appl. Comput. Inform. 16 (1/2) (2018) 117−136. Apr 11.

[30] E.S. El-Kenawy, M. Eid, Hybrid gray wolf and particle swarm optimization for feature selection, Int. J. Innov. Comput. Inf. Control. 16 (3) (2020) 831−844.

[31] M. Alswaitti, M. Albughdadi, N.A.M. Isa, Density-based particle swarm optimization algorithm for data clustering, Expert. Syst. Appl. 91 (2018) 170−186. Jan.

[32] M.B. Agbaje, A.E. Ezugwu, R. Els, Automatic data clustering using hybrid firefly particle swarm optimization algorithm, IEEE Access. 7 (2019) 184963−184984. Dec.

[33] S. Sengupta, S. Basak, R.A. Peters, Data clustering using a hybrid of fuzzy C-means and quantum-behaved particle swarm optimization, IEEE 8th Annual Computing and Communication Workshop and Conference (CCWC), 2018, IEEE, 2018, pp. 137−142.

[34] R. Janani, S. Vijayarani, Text document clustering using spectral clustering algorithm with particle swarm optimization, Expert. Syst. Appl. 134 (2019) 192−200. Nov.

[35] L.D.S. Pacifico, T.B. Ludermir, Hybrid K-means and improved self-adaptive particle swarm optimization for data clustering, International Joint Conference on Neural Networks (IJCNN), 2019, IEEE, 2019, pp. 1−7.

[36] S. Dey, S.. De, S. Paul, A new approach of data clustering using quantum inspired particle swarm optimization based fuzzy C-means, in: 2021 11th International Conference on Cloud Computing, Data Science & Engineering (Confluence), IEEE, 2021, pp. 59−64.

[37] L. Xu, M. Cao, B. Song, A new approach to smooth path planning of mobile robot based on quartic Bezier transition curve and improved PSO algorithm, Neurocomputing 473 (2022) 98−106. Feb.

[38] B. Song, Z. Wang, L. Zou, An improved PSO algorithm for smooth path planning of mobile robots using continuous high-degree Bezier curve, Appl. Soft Comput. 100 (2021) 106960. Mar.

[39] J. Zhang, Y. Lu, L. Che, M. Zhou, Moving-distance-minimized PSO for mobile robot swarm, IEEE Trans. Cybern. 52 (9) (2022) 9871−9881. Sep.

[40] X. Li, D. Wu, J. He, M. Bashir, M. Liping, An improved method of particle swarm optimization for path planning of mobile robot, J. Control. Sci. Eng. 2020 (2020) 1−12. May 25.

[41] M.N.A. Wahab, C.M. Lee, M.F. Akbar, F.H. Hassan, Path planning for mobile robot navigation in unknown indoor environments using hybrid PSOFS algorithm, IEEE Access. 8 (2020) 161805−161815.

[42] Z. Lin, M. Yue, G. Chen, J. Sun, Path planning of mobile robot with PSO-based APF and fuzzy-based DWA subject to moving obstacles, Trans. Inst. Meas. Control. 44 (1) (2022) 121−132. Jan 4.

[43] J. Lu, Z. Zhang, An improved simulated annealing particle swarm optimization algorithm for path planning of mobile robots using mutation particles, Wirel. Commun. Mob. Comput. 2021 (2021) 1−12. Dec 6.

[44] V. Sathiya, M. Chinnadurai, S. Ramabalan, Mobile robot path planning using fuzzy enhanced improved multi-Objective particle swarm optimization (FIMOPSO), Expert. Syst. Appl. 198 (2022) 116875. Jul.

[45] F.H. Ajeil, I.K. Ibraheem, M.A. Sahib, A.J. Humaidi, Multi-objective path planning of an autonomous mobile robot using hybrid PSO-MFB optimization algorithm, Appl. Soft Comput. 89 (2020) 106076. Apr.

[46] S. Tian, Y. Li, Y. Kang, J. Xia, Multi-robot path planning in wireless sensor networks based on jump mechanism PSO and safety gap obstacle avoidance, Futur. Gener. Comput. Syst. 118 (2021) 37−47. May.

[47] R. Song, X. Zhang, C. Zhou, J. Liu, J. He, Predicting TEC in China based on the neural networks optimized by genetic algorithm, Adv. Sp. Res. 62 (4) (2018) 745−759. Aug.

[48] O.N. Oyelade, J.O. Agushaka, A.E. Ezugwu, Evolutionary binary feature selection using adaptive ebola optimization search algorithm for high-dimensional datasets, PLoS One 18 (3) (2023) e0282812. Mar 17.

[49] O.A. Akinola, A.E. Ezugwu, O.N. Oyelade, J.O. Agushaka, A hybrid binary dwarf mongoose optimization algorithm with simulated annealing for feature selection on high dimensional multi-class datasets, Sci. Rep. [Internet]. 123AD [cited 12 (2022) 14945. Available from: https://doi.org/10.1038/s41598-022-18993-0.

[50] A.E. Ezugwu, A.M. Ikotun, O.O. Oyelade, L. Abualigah, J.O. Agushaka, C.I. Eke, et al., A comprehensive survey of clustering algorithms: State-of-the-art machine learning applications, taxonomy, challenges, and future research prospects, Eng. Appl. Artif. Intell. 110 (2022) 104743. Apr.

[51] A.E. Ezugwu, Nature-inspired metaheuristic techniques for automatic clustering: A survey and performance study, SN Appl. Sci. 2 (2) (2020) 273. Feb 25.

[52] A.M. Ikotun, M.S. Almutari, A.E. Ezugwu, K-means-based nature-inspired metaheuristic algorithms for automatic data clustering problems: Recent advances and future directions, Appl. Sci. 11 (23) (2021) 11246. Nov 26.

[53] Q. Lv, D. Yang, Multi-target path planning for mobile robot based on improved PSO algorithm, IEEE 5th Information Technology and Mechatronics Engineering Conference (ITOEC), 2020, IEEE, 2020, pp. 1042−1047.

[54] F. Gul, W. Rahiman, S.S.N. Alhady, A. Ali, I. Mir, A. Jalil, Meta-heuristic approach for solving multi-objective path planning for autonomous guided robot using PSO−GWO optimization algorithm with evolutionary programming, J. Ambient. Intell. Humaniz. Comput. 12 (7) (2021) 7873−7890. Jul 16.

2

Social spider optimization algorithm: survey and new applications

Laith Abualigah[1,2,3,4,5,6,7], Ahmad A. Al Turk[8], Abiodun M. Ikotun[9],
Raed Abu Zitar[10], Anas Ratib Alsoud[2], Nima Khodadadi[11],
Abdelazim G. Hussien[12,13], Heming Jia[14]

[1]ARTIFICIAL INTELLIGENCE AND SENSING TECHNOLOGIES (AIST) RESEARCH CENTER, UNIVERSITY OF TABUK, TABUK, SAUDI ARABIA [2]HOURANI CENTER FOR APPLIED SCIENTIFIC RESEARCH, AL-AHLIYYA AMMAN UNIVERSITY, AMMAN, JORDAN [3]MEU RESEARCH UNIT, MIDDLE EAST UNIVERSITY, AMMAN, JORDAN [4]SCHOOL OF COMPUTER SCIENCES, UNIVERSITI SAINS MALAYSIA, PULAU PINANG, MALAYSIA [5]SCHOOL OF ENGINEERING AND TECHNOLOGY, SUNWAY UNIVERSITY MALAYSIA, PETALING JAYA, MALAYSIA [6]COMPUTER SCIENCE DEPARTMENT, AL AL-BAYT UNIVERSITY, MAFRAQ, JORDAN [7]DEPARTMENT OF ELECTRICAL AND COMPUTER ENGINEERING, LEBANESE AMERICAN UNIVERSITY, BYBLOS, LEBANON [8]NEW ENGINEERING INDUSTRY COLLEGE, PUTIAN UNIVERSITY, PUTIAN, CHINA [9]UNIVERSITY OF KWAZULU-NATAL, PIETERMARITZBURG CAMPUS, POTCHEFSTROOM, SOUTH AFRICA [10]SORBONNE CENTER OF ARTIFICIAL INTELLIGENCE, SORBONNE UNIVERSITY-ABU DHABI, ABU DHABI, UNITED ARAB EMIRATES [11]DEPARTMENT OF CIVIL, ARCHITECTURAL AND ENVIRONMENTAL ENGINEERING, UNIVERSITY OF MIAMI, CORAL GABLES, FL, UNITED STATES [12]DEPARTMENT OF COMPUTER AND INFORMATION SCIENCE, LINKÖPING UNIVERSITY, LINKÖPING, SWEDEN [13]FACULTY OF SCIENCE, FAYOUM UNIVERSITY, FAIYUM, EGYPT [14]DEPARTMENT OF INFORMATION ENGINEERING, SANMING UNIVERSITY, FUJIAN, P.R. CHINA

2.1 Introduction

The first idea of PSO was obtained from the behavior of a herd of birds. PSO depends on the motion of individual particles through the search space, which simulates the herd of birds or insects. Then, a huge number of versions for PSO were implemented besides modifications and enhancements [1]. There are four main parameters of PSO: two acceleration coefficients that govern the importance of cognitive and social impact, the third parameter is the inertia weight, and the fourth parameter in PSO is the swarm, which refers to the number of particles [2]. Two main concepts are self-organization and division of labor. Self-organization is the ability of a system to improve its components into a suitable form without any external help. Division of labor is the concurrent execution of different samples and tasks by individuals that agents for cooperative work [3].

Metaheuristic Optimization Algorithms. DOI: https://doi.org/10.1016/B978-0-443-13925-3.00011-X

The types of spider behavior are categorized based on the cooperation degree between members into solitary and social spiders. Solitary spiders establish their web and keep that web, while they rarely communicate with other members of the same species, whereas the social spiders establish a social connection that is strong with the other members [4]. Social spider settlement has two main parts: the members and community network. The first part is categorized based on the gender into males and females; the female gender in this community is the base, as the studies have shown that male spiders are just 30% of the total population of the settlement. As a spider society is a gender-based community, each gender will have its activities and work such as construction and other works [2]. The communication between the members is categorized into direct and indirect communication, where the direct communication is done by physical contact, which includes transferring fluids between members, whereas the indirect communication represents the medium which is the web, which transmits the information which exists in each member of different settlements

The behavior of spiders is divided based on gender. Female spiders are strong members, which rely on vibration distributed over the web, and this generated vibration relies on the weight and distance of the members which stir it, and the acceptance or rejection of the other member depends on the internal situation, which is affected by curiosity, reproduction cycle, and other random phenomena. Male spiders are a subgroup of alpha males and are classified into dominant and nondominant male spiders. Dominant male spiders have better physical features, especially in the size compared to the nondominant ones. Dominant males are attracted to the closest female spider in the web. Nondominant male spiders are found in the center of the male population in order to benefit from the resources used by dominant males [5]. Normally, optimization methods can be used to deal with many problems in science, as presented in refs [6−14].

This survey did a study on different researches, and the procedure was to compare different PSO algorithms concerning SSO (it focuses on weaknesses of the other PSO algorithms) and to show how the SSO shows a better performance based on a benchmark table, which shows the performance of each algorithm besides the SSO.

Furthermore, this survey mentioned the applications of the algorithm in different fields, especially medical, engineering, mathematics, artificial intelligence, and data science; listed the important and the latest research related to each field; then determined the fields that are familiar with this algorithm and the fields that we need to focus on in order to use this algorithm; and then indicated what fields we need more researches and improvements in to use this algorithm for the improvement and problem-solving objectives. This survey was done by dealing with a large number of researches collected from the Google Scholar engine, which helped find out the latest research; the researches that have been chosen for this survey are from 2021 onward, not earlier, to make sure that the fields included are the latest and also to take into consideration the respective authors and magazines.

This paper is organized as follows. In the second section, the related work is presented. The third section shows the procedure of the SSO algorithm and its characteristics. The fourth section shows the results of the experiment and the comparison study. The fifth section provides a discussion of the results. Finally, in the final section, the conclusion of the survey is reported.

2.2 Related work

This survey studies how particle swarm algorithm will enhance the optimization based on the social spider algorithm SSO and compares it with other PSO algorithms, including artificial bee colony algorithm (ABC), in order to prove that SSO shows the best performance among them. Besides comparing the PSO efficiency with other PSO algorithms, this survey studied different applications for the algorithm in different fields. The works related to this algorithm in different fields are summarized below in subsections.

2.2.1 Medical field

Healthcare is one of the major application areas of machine learning [15]. Optimization algorithms are used in machine learning models for a number of medical issues such as disease diagnosis, medical image processing, disease classification, and many more. The SSO has been used in cancer detection on microscopic biopsy images [16]. A neural network is controlled with the SSO algorithm to classify microscopic biopsy images of cancer. The importance of this model relies on the operative regulation of the neural network classifier weighted by the SSO. SSO is employed in prediction of lung cancer [17]. This paper proposed to detect lung cancer early, and it used a lot of methods besides SSO, which assist in detecting the disease. It used a convolutional neural network for data classification and prediction, and this classification and prediction is enhanced by using the AVHEQ method besides SSO, which will assist in distinguishing the cancer area compared with the surrounding area. Medical image denoising aims to remove the noise and maintain the original characteristics of the image [18]. The DWT method will decompose the image, and the SSO technique will do the optimal thresholding; this research shows great results in detecting lung cancer. Analysis of Cancer and Diabetes discussed in [19], enhances the SSO method to be a simplex method with the abbreviation SMSSO. The improved method has shown great results in the cancer field, including lung and breast cancer, in addition to diabetes. For breast cancer image enhancement, this paper combined the use of the SSO method with optimum wavelet-based image enhancement, which will help in removing the noises from the images and showing the targeted area clearly [20].

2.2.2 Engineering field

In hydropower generation, because the main issue is the limited amount of water resources, SSO was used to conduct a study on managing the resources of water and how it will impact hydropower generation [21]. For PID controllers with a robotic arm, the coordination of the robot arm angle was utilized by using the SSO besides the fuzzy technique, which is part of artificial intelligence [22]. In the field of heterogeneous wireless sensor networks, Cao et al. [23] focused on the issue of the coverage areas in the case where nodes of the type sensor are placed in a random manner within heterogeneous wireless sensor networks; this SSO method will enhance the coverage of the network and detraction of power consumption. For power generation in the photovoltaic system, Hou et al. [24] focused on the maximum power tracking used in order to enhance the efficiency of power conversion; thus there will be a lot of issues related to this technique, including overvoltage, overload, and frequency deviation, and the SSO method was used to reduce these issues. For hydropower station dispatch, Zhou et al. improved SSO to a quantum algorithm, which is used to optimize the hydropower station dispatch, and this method has shown that it has an advantage in the affinity, reducing the number of control parameters, accuracy, simplicity, and consistency [25]. In thermal power plants, Nguyen et al. [26]focused on thermal power plants, which are used in electrical supplements to the power systems, and it will affect the cost due to the use of the fuel; SSO was used besides the truncate swarm algorithm, which reduced the cost compared with other methods. For wind power in the restructured electricity market, Shayanfar et al. [27] focused on the challenges in controlling and monitoring the power systems, which is known as the unit commitment problem, and the SSO method was used to solve this problem, which is an interesting problem for technical and researchers, taking into consideration the wind farms. In hierarchical control of the cooperative multilift with four unmanned helicopters, Duan et al. [28] focused on the issue of nonconvex optimization in the cable layer of the multilift system and the issue of controlling the aircraft. The SSO method is used to solve these problems besides artificial intelligence methods and MATLAB®. Metaheuristics algorithms have been used in solving constrained engineering design problems [29]. For solving real-world mechanical engineering design problems, Abualigah [30] provided a deep explanation of the different optimization techniques and their relation to the mechanical engineering design problems, and it includes the SSO method. Nandwalkar and Pete [31] discussed heat management for the wet electrospun polymer fiber. This paper improved the SSO method to temperature raising SSO method, which reduces the loss of excessive light scattering by controlling the heat. For antenna designs, Oliveira et al. [32] improved SSO to a multifunctional electromagnetic SSO method, which enhances the number of parameters passed to Ansoft HFSS and reduces the computation time.

2.2.3 Mathematics field

Optimization problems are common in science, ecology, manufacturing, and businesses. They are solved using either the mathematical approach or metaheuristic approach [29]. However, the mathematical approach has some challenges such as time or computational complexity, gradient dependency, and problem dependency. The SSO was enhanced to jumping SSO for mathematical optimization [33]. This paper provided solutions for many optimization problems in terms of mathematics, and this enhanced method is compared with other optimization methods that have shown that they are able to solve mathematical problems in a specific search space. For data dissemination in VANET, Shankar et al. [34] focused on the automated industry field, which includes the communication and contact between vehicles, which enhances the duration of the contact between two vehicles using the SSO method. In financial time series prediction with feature selection, Nayak et al. [35] used the simplex method of SSO to predict time series data; this technique will facilitate analysis by decreasing the size of the data. For hyperdimensional search space,

Frimpong et al. [36] enhanced the criteria of searching by improving SSO to be social spider prey. In control of the fractional order system, Mehta and Adhyaru [37] used the SSO method to solve fractional order systems and designed computational intelligence methods.

2.2.4 Artificial intelligence field

Artificial intelligence deals with the science and engineering of achieving intelligence in machines based on computer programs receiving and controlling signals from computer hardware [15]. It provided an opportunity for replacing human capability with machine intelligence. SSO was used to control the parameters in a PD-like interval type-2 fuzzy logic controller applied to a parallel robot, adjusting the coefficients of the relative derivative versions of both IT2FLC and T1FLC, where IT2FLC tracks the path of 3-RRR, which stands for triple revolute planar parallel robot, and IT2FLC is compared with the IT2FLC from the side of robustness and path tracking properties [38]. For humanoid robotic arms control, Abulhail and Al-Faiz used the SSO method applied on the left arm and right arm of the humanoid robotic arms in order to find the angle and position with the least error possible [39]. In AI and its applications in Parkinson's disease detection, Pereira et al. used AI in detecting Parkinson's disease by using SSO to enhance the training of neural networks in order to enhance the detection of this disease [40]. This paper combined the field of AI with the medical part.

2.2.5 Data science

Extraction of valuable knowledge hidden with massive data is reportedly described as computationally expensive using traditional approaches [41]. For handling high dimensional datasets, Shanmugapriya and Meera focused on the comparison of swarm optimization algorithms in the processing speed of the data in big data and also compared the cost and accuracy of these algorithms in dealing with the big data [42]. In clustering analysis, determination of a suitable center for each cluster center is an initialization problem in classical K-means algorithm based on its random selection of initial cluster centroids [43]. Zhou et al. used the SSO method to solve the issues of determining the suitable center for each cluster in the K-mean clustering algorithm [44]. Metaheuristic algorithms have been widely applied for solving feature selection problems in machine learning applications [45]. For feature selection, Ibrahim et al. used SSO to assist in choosing the most suitable item from each data set [46]. The application of machine learning models for medical image processing makes it possible to detect medical digital image abnormalities. For multispectral image classification, Bui employed the SSO to assist fuzzy C-means clustering in finding the optimum solution for the center of each cluster [47]. Data clustering is an important tool in data mining applications and research [48]. In performing data clustering and comparison with other clustering methods, Chandran et al. enhanced the local and global search for data clustering [49]. This research used the SSO and compared it with other clustering optimization methods with the preferred results for the SSO.

2.3 Social spider optimization method

Firstly, the method determines the number of female and male spiders. The equation determines the number of females as follows [50]:

$$N_f = floor \quad [(0.9 - rand.0.25).N]$$

where N_f is the number of females, rand is a random number between zero and one, and the floor is the mathematical function that converts any number to be an integer.

In order to determine the male spider's number N_m, use the following equation:

$N_f = N - N_f$, so that the male and female can be expressed by two sets: one for males and the second for the females. The female set is expressed as $F = \{f_1, f_2, \ldots, f_{N_f}\}$, and the set of the male is expressed as $M = \{m_1, m_2, \ldots, m_{N_m}\}$, and $S = FUM(s_1, s_2, \ldots, s_N)$, such that $S = \{s_1 = f_1, s_2 = f_2, \ldots, s_{N_f} = f_{N_f}, s_{N_f+1} = m_1, \ldots, s_N = m_{N_m}\}$. The weight for each spider can be calculated by the following equation [50]:

$$W_{i,} = \frac{J(Si) - Worst_s}{best_s - Worst_s}$$

where $J(Si)$ is the fitness value obtained by the evaluation of the spider position Si concerning the objective function $J(.)$. $Worst_s$ and $best_s$ are calculated as follows:

$$best_s = \max_{k \in \{1,2,3,\ldots,N\}}(J(S_k)) \quad and \quad Worst_s = \min_{k \in \{1,2,\ldots,N\}}(J(S_k))$$

Vibrations that the agent feels i As a result of the information sent by the agent j are calculated by the following equation:

$$Vibi_{ij} = W_j.e^{-d_{ij}^2}$$

where d_{ij} is the Euclidian distance among the spiders i and j, such that $d_{ij} = |s_i - s_j|$. Theoretically conceivable to calculation of perceived vibrations using any pair of agents, the SSO approach considers three specific relationships [50]:

1. $Vibc_i = W_c.e^{-d_{i,c}^2}$: the vibration realized by the spider i and issued by individual c.

2. $Vibb_i = W_b.e^{-d_{i,b}^2}$, as $W_b = \max_{k \in \{1,2,\ldots,N\}}(W_k)$: the vibration realized by the spider i that is issued by the best spider in the web.

3. $Vibf_i = W_f.e^{-d_{i,f}^2}$: the vibration realized by individual i realized by the member cf.

The expression given below represents the initial and upper initial parameter bound P_j^{low} and P_i^{high}, respectively:

$$f_{ij}^0 = Pi^{low} + rand(0,1).\left(P_i^{high} - P_j^{low}\right) \quad m_{kj}^0 = Pi^{low} + rand.\left(P_i^{high} - P_j^{low}\right)$$

$$i = 1,2,3,\ldots\ldots,N_f, j = 1,2,\ldots,n \quad k = 1,2,3,\ldots\ldots,N_m, j = 1,2,3,\ldots\ldots,n$$

Where rand $(0,1)$ represents the generation of a random number between 0 and 1. Hence, f_{ij} is the jth parameter for the ith female spider position.

To calculate the female cooperative behavior, use the following equation:

$$f_i^{k+1} = \begin{cases} f_i^k + \alpha.Vibc_i.\left(s_c - f_i^k\right) - \beta.Vibb_i.\left(s_b - f_i^k\right) + 9.\left(rand - \dfrac{1}{2}\right) & \text{with propability } PF \\[2ex] f_i^k - \alpha.Vibc_i.\left(s_c - f_i^k\right) - \beta.Vibb_i.\left(s_b - f_i^k\right) + 9.\left(rand - \dfrac{1}{2}\right) & \text{with propability } 1 - PF \end{cases}$$

where k is the iteration number. s_c and s_b are the nearest member to i that holds a higher weight and is the best individual of the entire population S.

The median weight is indexed by $N_f + m$. The change of positions for the male spider can be calculated by the following equation [50]:

$$m_i^{k+1} = \begin{cases} m_i^{k+1} = m_i^k + \alpha.Vibf_i.\left(s_f - m_i^k\right) + \partial.\left(rand - \dfrac{1}{2}\right) & \text{if} \quad W_{N_f+i} > W_{N_f+m} \\[3ex] m_i^k + \alpha.\left(\dfrac{\sum_{h=1}^{N_m} m_n^k.W_{N_f} + h}{\sum_{h=1}^{N_m} W_{N_f} + h} - m_i^k\right) & \text{if} \quad W_{N_f+i} \leq W_{N_f+m} \end{cases}$$

where the individual s_f represents the nearest female individual to the male member i whereas $\dfrac{\sum_{h=1}^{N_m} m_n^k.W_{N_f} + h}{\sum_{h=1}^{N_m} W_{N_f} + h}$ correspond to the weighted mean of the male population M.

The radius of the range r is determined by the size of the search space. The radius r is calculated using the following equation:

$$r = \frac{\sum_{j=1}^{n} Pj^{high} - Pj^{low}}{2.n}$$

The roulette approach, which assigns each member's influence probability P_{s_i}, can be calculated as the following equation:

$$P_{s_i} = \frac{W_i}{\sum_{j \in T^k} W_j}$$

where $i \in T^g$

The suggested algorithm's computational approach can be stated as follows:

First step: Define the number of male Nm and females N_f spiders in the entire population S:

$$N_f = floor \quad [(0.9 - rand.0.25).N] \quad \text{and} \quad N_f = N - N_f$$

Second step: Initialize randomly the female $(F = \{f1, f2, \ldots, f(N_f)\})$ and male $(M = \{m1, m2, \ldots, m(Nf)\})$ members (where $S = \{s1 = f1, s2 = f2, \ldots, S(N_f) = f(N_f),$ $S(N_f + 1) = m1, \ldots, SN = m(Nm)\})$ and calculate the radius of mating [50]:

$$r = \frac{\sum_{j=1}^{n} Pj^{high} - Pj^{low}}{2.n}$$

$$for(i = 1; i < N_f + 1; i++)$$

$$for(i = 1; i < n + 1; j++)$$

$$f_{ij}^{0} = Pi^{low} + rand(0,1).\left(P_i^{high} - P_j^{low}\right)$$

$$end \quad for$$

$$end \quad for$$

$$for(i = 1; i < N_m + 1; k++)$$

$$for(i = 1; j < n + 1; j++)$$

$$m_{kj}^{0} = Pi^{low} + rand.\left(P_i^{high} - P_j^{low}\right)$$

$$end \quad for$$

$$end \quad for$$

Third step: Calculate the weight of every spider of S:

$$for \quad (i = 1; i < N; i++)$$

$$wi = \frac{J(Si) - Worst_s}{best_s - Worst_s}$$

where $bests = \max \ k \in (1, 2, \ldots, N)$

$$end \quad for$$

Fourth step: Move female spiders according to the female cooperative operator

$$for(i = 1; i < N_f + 1; i++)$$

Calculate $Vibc_i$ and $Vibb_i$
If $(r_m < PF)$; where $r_m \in$ rand $(0,1)$

$$f_i^{k+1} = f_i^{k} + \alpha.Vibc_i.\left(s_c - f_i^{k}\right) + \beta.Vibb_i.\left(s_b - f_i^{k}\right) + 9.\left(rand - \frac{1}{2}\right)$$

$$else \quad if$$

$$f_i^{k+1} = f_i^k + \alpha.Vibc_i.\left(s_c - f_i^k\right) - \beta.Vibb_i.\left(s_b - f_i^k\right) + \vartheta.\left(rand - \frac{1}{2}\right) end \; if \; end \; for$$

Fifth step: Move the male spiders according to the male cooperative operator. Find the median male individual $(W_{N_f} + m)$ from M.

$$for(i = 1; i < N_m + 1; i++)$$

Calculate $Vibf_i$

$$if\left(W_{N_f} + i\right) < (W_{N_f} + m)$$

$$m_i^{k+1} = m_i^k + \alpha.Vibf_i.\left(s_f - m_i^k\right) + \partial.\left(rand - \frac{1}{2}\right)$$

$$else \quad if$$

$$m_i^{k+1} = m_i^k + \alpha.\left(\frac{\sum_{h=1}^{N_m} m_n^k.W_{N_f} + h}{\sum_{h=1}^{N_m} W_{N_f} + h} - m_i^k\right)$$

$$end \quad if$$

$$end \quad for$$

Sixth step: Perform the mating operation.

$$for(i = 1; i < N_m + 1; i++)$$

$$if(m_i \in D)$$

Find E^i

$$if\left(E^i \quad is \quad not \quad empty\right)$$

$$From \quad s_{new} \quad using \quad the \quad roulette \quad method$$

$$if(W_{new} > W_{wo})$$

$$s_{wo} = W_{wo}$$

$$end \quad if$$

$$end \quad if$$

$$end \quad if$$

$$end \quad for$$

Seventh step: If the stop criteria are met, the process is finished; otherwise, go back to the third step.

In this experiment, the SSO algorithm was applied to 19 functions, the population has been fixed at 50 people in all comparisons. The maximum number of iterations has been set at 1000.

The parameter setting for each algorithm in the comparison is described as follows:

1. PSO: The parameters are set to c1 = 2 and c2 = 2; besides, the weight factor decreases linearly from 0.9 to 0.2.
2. ABC: The algorithm has been implemented using the guidelines provided by its reference, using the parameter limit = 100.
3. SSO: Once it has been determined experimentally, the parameter PF has been set to 0.7. It is kept for all experiments in this section.

2.4 Experiment result

This survey achieved two parts: the first part is studying the research published since 2021 and checking how SSO affected these researches and what field was improved by using this algorithm. Table 2−1 shows the comparison among different optimization methods: SSO, ABC, and PSO. The performance indexes taken into consideration in this table are Average Best So Far (AB), Median Best So Far, and Standard Deviation (SD). This table applied 30 runs with 1000 maximum number of iterations. "The dataset was collected from Cuevas et al. [50].

The functions mentioned in Table 2−1 are Sphere, Schwefel 2.22, Schwefel 1.2, F4, Rosenbrock, Step, Quartic, Dixon & price, Levy, Sum of squares, Zakharov, Penalized, Penalized 2, Schwefel, Rastrigin, Ackley, Griewank, Powell I, and Salomon, noting that each function has a dimension of 10 and minimum $x^* = (0, \ldots, 0); f(x^*) = 0$.

The second part is an experiment that compares SSO with other optimization algorithms: ABC and PSO; this comparison was done by using three performance indexes: AB, MB, and SD. Based on this experiment, SSO has shown the best performance results compared with the two algorithms.

2.5 Discussion

This survey focused on experimental and theoretical parts. The experimental part applied the SSO to 19 functions with maximum iterations of 1000 and $n = 10$, and three performance indexes applied to each function are AB, MB, and SD; then the result of SSO was compared with the two other optimization algorithms: ABC and PSO. The technical result has shown that SSO outperforms the other algorithms, and applying the benchmark of 19 functions provided evidence that the results are not coincidental.

Table 2–1   Results of applying functions with n = 30 with the maximum number of iterations = 1000.

		SSO	ABC	PSO
$f(x)_1$	AB	0.00196	0.0029	1000
	MB	0.00281	0.0015	0.000000000208
	SD	0.000996	0.00144	
$f(x)_2$	AB	0.0137	0.135	51.7
	MB	0.0134	0.105	50
	SD	0.0311	0.0801	20.2
$f(x)_3$	AB	0.0427	1.13	86300
	MB	0.0349	0.611	80000
	SD	0.0311	1.57	55600
$f(x)_4$	AB	0.054	5820	1470
	MB	0.0543	5920	1510
	SD	0.0101	7020	3130
$f(x)_5$	AB	114	138	33400
	MB	58.6	132	403
	SD	390	155	43800
$f(x)_6$	AB	0.00268	0.00406	1000
	MB	0.00268	0.00374	0.0000000016
	SD	0.000605	0.00298	630600
$f(x)_7$	AB	12	12.1	15
	MB	12	12.3	13.7
	SD	57.6	0.9	4.75
$f(x)_8$	AB	214	3.6	31200
	MB	364	0.804	208
	SD	1.26	3.54	57400
$f(x)_9$	AB	0.0000692	0.000144	2.47
	MB	0.000068	0.0000809	0.909
	SD	0.0000402	0.000169	3.27
$f(x)_{10}$	AB	0.000444	0.11	2.47
	MB	0.0000405	0.0497	0.909
	SD	0.000029	0.198	3.27
$f(x)_{11}$	AB	68.1	312	411
	MB	61.2	313	431
	SD	30	43.1	156
$f(x)_{12}$	AB	0.0000534	0.000118	42700000
	MB	0.000054	0.000105	0.104
	SD	0.0000154	0.0000888	47000000
$f(x)_{13}$	AB	0.00176	0.00187	0.574
	MB	0.0012	0.00169	0.0000108
	SD	0.00675	0.00147	2.36
$f(x)_{14}$	AB	-936	-960	-963
	MB	-936	-960	-992
	SD	16.1	65.5	66.6
$f(x)_{15}$	AB	8.59	26.4	135

(Continued)

Table 2−1 (Continued)

		SSO	ABC	PSO
	MB	8.78	22.4	136
	SD	1.11	10.6	37.3
$f(x)_{16}$	AB	0.0136	0.653	11.4
	MB	0.0139	0.639	14.3
	SD	0.00236	0.309	88.6
$f(x)_{17}$	AB	0.00329	0.0522	12
	MB	0.00321	0.046	0.0135
	SD	0.00544	0.0342	31.2
$f(x)_{18}$	AB	1.87	2.13	1260
	MB	1.61	2.14	5670
	SD	1.2	1.22	1120
$f(x)_{19}$	AB	0.274	4.14	1.53
	MB	0.3	4.10	0.55
	SD	0.0517	0.464	2.94

For the theoretical part, this survey did a study for several types of research fetched using Google scholar and based on publishing date after 2021, in order to keep up with the latest results of the SSO algorithm. These researches can be classified based on the field that focuses on medical, engineering, mathematics, artificial intelligence, and data science fields. Some of these researches are hybrid of two fields such as artificial intelligence in the medical field, artificial intelligence with engineering, and mathematics with artificial intelligence. These researches are summarized in Fig. 2−1.

From Fig. 2−1, the engineering field took the highest number of researches, and this field combines a lot of majors including networking, mechanical, and power and finding the largest number of researches in the engineering field gives a sign that SSO is used to optimize various issues which integrate the design and mathematics to satisfy engineering concept. The lowest number of researches regarding the SSO is the artificial intelligence, and the reason is that the researchers usually combine the AI with other fields such as the medical field with AI, so that to find a pure AI research that used SSO is not as frequent as in the other fields. In the medical field, the cancer disease took the most research with its various identification methods, by images or classification. SSO and data science fields focus on data classification, so the number of SSO researches in the data field is concentrated on classification.

From the fetched researches that are related to the engineering field, we find that most of the researches are focusing on power engineering such as hydropower engineering, wind power, thermal power, and so forth, whereas the rest of the engineering fields are distributed with other fields. Fig. 2−2 shows the distribution of the fields of engineering fetched in this research:

For the medical field where SSO is applied, in this survey, five types of research were collected for the medical field; four of them are related to cancer detection and one is related to

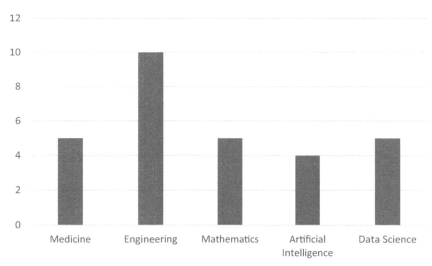

FIGURE 2–1 Number of researches per field.

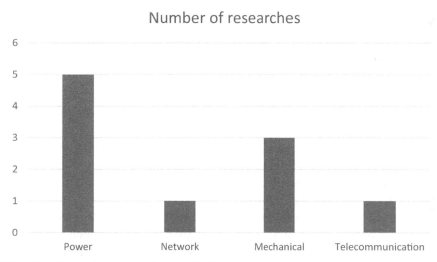

FIGURE 2–2 Number of researches per engineering field.

diagnosis of the medical images and research focused on Parkinson's disease integrated with AI, which is classified in this research as AI application, as shown in Fig. 2–3.

From the collected researches, three researches integrated two fields together and used the SSO method: integrating AI with engineering, AI and medicine, and mathematics and AI. Thus, it gives an indication that SSO can optimize a group of fields together without focusing on only one field at a time.

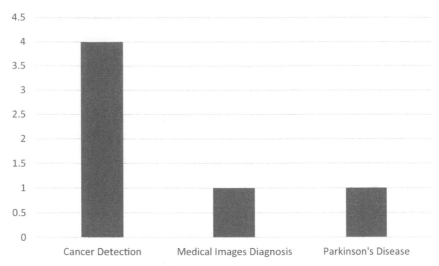

FIGURE 2–3 Number of researches per medical field.

2.6 Conclusion

This survey indicates a comparison between different optimization algorithms in front of SSO: ABC and PSO; SSO has shown the preference in the performance between 19 functions. Then, this survey has discussed how the SSO researches gave value to the different fields, including medical, engineering, mathematics, AI, and data science. Also, engineering and medical fields have distributed majors, and this survey mentioned the fields related to the engineering and medical fields.

From the collected research, it can be determined that SSO has a big intervention in engineering and medical fields in all their different majors, and in the engineering field, the power engineering with its all specifications is popular among the researchers, and the cancer detection is popular in the medical part.

This survey indicates the future work that can be done on SSO algorithms; as noticed from the collected papers, there is a possibility of working on enhancing the AI algorithms and methods purely using SSO, as most SSO researches in AI are used in the third-party fields such as engineering. Furthermore, SSO can be used in telecommunication and networking fields with more research, so that it can provide enhancements in these fields.

References

[1] I. Alharkan, M. Saleh, M.A. Ghaleb, H. Kaid, A. Farhan, A. Almarfadi, Tabu search and particle swarm optimization algorithms for two identical parallel machines scheduling problem with a single server, J. King Saud. Univ. - Eng. Sci. 32 (5) (2020) 330–338. Available from: https://doi.org/10.1016/j.jksues.2019.03.006.

[2] A.P. Piotrowski, J.J. Napiorkowski, A.E. Piotrowska, Population size in particle swarm optimization, Swarm Evol. Comput. 58 (2020) 100718. Available from: https://doi.org/10.1016/J.SWEVO.2020.100718.

[3] A. Gupta, S. Srivastava, Comparative analysis of ant colony and particle swarm optimization algorithms for distance optimization, Procedia Comput. Sci. 173 (2020) 245−253. Available from: https://doi.org/10.1016/J.PROCS.2020.06.029.

[4] S. Pervaiz, Z. Ul-Qayyum, W.H. Bangyal, L. Gao, J. Ahmad, A systematic literature review on particle swarm optimization techniques for medical diseases detection, Comput. Math. Methods Med. 2021 (2021) 1−10. Available from: https://doi.org/10.1155/2021/5990999.

[5] G. Uetz, Colonial web-building spiders: balancing the costs and benefits of group-living, Evol. Soc. Behav. insects Arachn. 1997 (2023)Accessed: Jun. 06. Available from: https://cir.nii.ac.jp/crid/1571980075199154816.bib?lang = en.

[6] L. Abualigah, A. Diabat, C.L. Thanh, S. Khatir, Opposition-based Laplacian distribution with Prairie Dog Optimization method for industrial engineering design problems, Comput. Methods Appl. Mech. Eng. 414 (2023) 116097.

[7] G. Hu, Y. Zheng, L. Abualigah, A.G. Hussien, DETDO: An adaptive hybrid dandelion optimizer for engineering optimization, Adv. Eng. Inform. 57 (2023) 102004.

[8] D. Izci, S. Ekinci, S. Mirjalili, L. Abualigah, An intelligent tuning scheme with a master/slave approach for efficient control of the automatic voltage regulator, Neural Comput. Appl. (2023) 1−17.

[9] H. Jia, C. Lu, D. Wu, C. Wen, H. Rao, L. Abualigah, An improved reptile search algorithm with ghost opposition-based learning for global optimization problems, J. Computational Des. Eng. (2023) qwad048.

[10] A.H. Alharbi, A.A. Abdelhamid, A. Ibrahim, S.K. Towfek, N. Khodadadi, L. Abualigah, et al., Improved dipper-throated optimization for forecasting metamaterial design bandwidth for engineering applications, Biomimetics 8 (2) (2023) 241.

[11] S. Nama, A.K. Saha, S. Chakraborty, A.H. Gandomi, L. Abualigah, Boosting particle swarm optimization by backtracking search algorithm for optimization problems, Swarm Evolut. Computation 79 (2023) 101304.

[12] M. Zare, M. Ghasemi, A. Zahedi, K. Golalipour, S.K. Mohammadi, S. Mirjalili, et al., A global best-guided firefly algorithm for engineering problems, J. Bionic Eng. (2023) 1−30.

[13] D. Wu, C. Wen, H. Rao, H. Jia, Q. Liu, L. Abualigah, Modified reptile search algorithm with multi-hunting coordination strategy for global optimization problems, Math. Biosci. Eng. 20 (6) (2023) 10090−10134.

[14] S. Ekinci, D. Izci, L. Abualigah, R.A. Zitar, A modified oppositional chaotic local search strategy based Aquila optimizer to design an effective controller for vehicle cruise control system, J. Bionic Eng. (2023) 1−24.

[15] A.E. Ezugwu, O.N. Oyelade, A.M. Ikotun, J.O. Agushaka, Y.-S. Ho, Machine learning research trends in Africa: a 30 years overview with bibliometric analysis review, Arch. Comput. Methods Eng. (2023). Available from: https://doi.org/10.1007/s11831-023-09930-z.

[16] P. Balaji, K. Chidambaram, Cancer diagnosis of microscopic biopsy images using a social spider optimisation-tuned neural network, Diagnostics 12 (1) (2021) 11. Available from: https://doi.org/10.3390/diagnostics12010011.

[17] P. Brindha, Prediction of lung cancer using FSSO optimization and deep learning based CNN algorithm, Turkish J. Comput. Math. Educ. Res. Artic. 12 (12) (2021) 3376−3389.

[18] N.E. Benhassine, A. Boukaache, D. Boudjehem, Medical image denoising using optimal thresholding of wavelet coefficients with selection of the best decomposition level and mother wavelet, Int. J. Imaging Syst. Technol. 31 (4) (2021) 1906−1920. Available from: https://doi.org/10.1002/ima.22589.

[19] M. Nayak, S. Das, U. Bhanja, M.R. Senapati, Predictive analysis for cancer and diabetes using simplex method based social spider optimization algorithm, IETE J. Res. (2022) 1−15. Available from: https://doi.org/10.1080/03772063.2022.2027276.

[20] T.V.S. Vivek, C. Raju, D.G. Kumar, Breast cancer image enhancement with the aid of optimum wavelet-based image enhancement using social spider optimisation, Int. J. Biomed. Eng. Technol. 38 (1) (2022) 29. Available from: https://doi.org/10.1504/IJBET.2022.120861.

[21] X. Ren, Y. Zhao, D. Hao, Y. Sun, S. Chen, F. Gholinia, Predicting optimal hydropower generation with help optimal management of water resources by developed wildebeest herd optimization (DWHO), Energy Rep. 7 (2021) 968−980. Available from: https://doi.org/10.1016/J.EGYR.2021.02.007.

[22] N. Basil, H. Kasim, PID controller with robotic arm using optimization algorithm, Int. J. Mech. Eng. 7 (2) (2022) 3746−3751.

[23] L. Cao, Y. Yue, Y. Cai, Y. Zhang, A novel coverage optimization strategy for heterogeneous wireless sensor networks based on connectivity and reliability, IEEE Access. 9 (2021) 18424−18442. Available from: https://doi.org/10.1109/ACCESS.2021.3053594.

[24] G. Hou, Y. Ke, C. Huang, A flexible constant power generation scheme for photovoltaic system by error-based active disturbance rejection control and perturb & observe, Energy 237 (2021) 121646. Available from: https://doi.org/10.1016/J.ENERGY.2021.121646.

[25] G. Zhou, R. Zhao, Q. Luo, Y. Zhou, Optimal hydropower station dispatch using quantum social spider optimization algorithm, Concurr. Comput. Pract. Exp. 34 (9) (2022). Available from: https://doi.org/10.1002/cpe.5782.

[26] V.B. Nguyen, T.S. Doan, K.H. Do, H.S. Le, V.D. Phan, Power generation cost optimization for Thermal power plants considering prohibited operation zones and power losses, AIP Conf. Proc. 2406 (1) (2021) 020013. Available from: https://doi.org/10.1063/5.0066464.

[27] H.A. Shayanfar, H. Shayeghi, L. Bagherzadeh, Application of modified social spider algorithm on unit commitment solution considering the uncertainty of wind power in restructured electricity market, 2021, pp. 437−448. doi:10.1007/978-3-030-70296-0_33.

[28] D. Duan, H. Zhao, T. Yu, C. Zhang, J. Li, Application of social spider optimization and improved active disturbance rejection controller in hierarchical control of cooperative multi-lift with four unmanned helicopters, Proc. Inst. Mech. Eng. Part. G. J. Aerosp. Eng. 236 (4) (2022) 671−684. Available from: https://doi.org/10.1177/09544100211018108.

[29] J.O. Agushaka, A.E. Ezugwu, O.N. Olaide, O. Akinola, R.A. Zitar, L. Abualigah, Improved dwarf mongoose optimization for constrained engineering design problems, J. Bionic Eng. (2022). Available from: https://doi.org/10.1007/s42235-022-00316-8.

[30] L. Abualigah, et al., Meta-heuristic optimization algorithms for solving real-world mechanical engineering design problems: a comprehensive survey, applications, comparative analysis, and results, Neural Comput. Appl. 34 (6) (2022) 4081−4110. Available from: https://doi.org/10.1007/s00521-021-06747-4.

[31] J.R. Nandwalkar, D.J. Pete, Social spider optimization based optimized heat management for <scp > wet-electrospun < /scp> polymer fiber, Microw. Opt. Technol. Lett. 63 (2) (2021) 670−678. Available from: https://doi.org/10.1002/mop.32607.

[32] P.S. Oliveira, A.G. D'Assunção, E.A.M. Souza, C. Peixeiro, A fast and accurate technique for FSS and antenna designs based on the social spider optimization algorithm, Microw. Opt. Technol. Lett. 58 (8) (2016) 1912−1917. Available from: https://doi.org/10.1002/mop.29941.

[33] H. Peraza-Vázquez, A. Peña-Delgado, P. Ranjan, C. Barde, A. Choubey, A.B. Morales-Cepeda, A bio-inspired method for mathematical optimization inspired by *Arachnida salticidade*, Mathematics 10 (1) (2021) 102. Available from: https://doi.org/10.3390/math10010102.

[34] A. Shankar, R. Dayalan, C. Chakraborty, C. Dhasarathan, M. Kumar, A modified social spider algorithm for an efficient data dissemination in VANET, Environ. Dev. Sustain. (2022). Available from: https://doi.org/10.1007/s10668-021-01994-w.

[35] M. Nayak, S. Das, U. Bhanja, M.R. Senapati, Financial time-series prediction with feature selection using simplex method based social spider optimization algorithm, Indian. J. Comput. Sci. Eng. 12 (2) (2021) 326−347. Available from: https://doi.org/10.21817/indjcse/2021/v12i2/211202036.

[36] S.O. Frimpong, R.C. Millham, I.E. Agbehadji, J.J. Jung, Social spider and the prey search method for global optimization in hyper dimensional search space, Informatics and Intelligent Applications, Springer, 2022, pp. 214−226. Available from: 10.1007/978-3-030-95630-1_15.

[37] S.A. Mehta, D.M. Adhyaru, Social spider optimisation based identification and optimal control of fractional order system, Int. J. Model. Identif. Control. 37 (1) (2021) 80. Available from: https://doi.org/10.1504/IJMIC.2021.119033.

[38] A.J. Humaidi, H.T. Najem, A.Q. Al-Dujaili, D.A. Pereira, I.K. Ibraheem, A.T. Azar, Social spider optimization algorithm for tuning parameters in PD-like interval type-2 fuzzy logic controller applied to a parallel robot, Meas. Control. 54 (3−4) (Mar. 2021) 303−323. Available from: https://doi.org/10.1177/0020294021997483.

[39] S.F. Abulhail, M.Z. Al-Faiz, Social spider optimization for solving inverse kinematics for both humanoid robotic arms, in: 2021 IEEE International Conference on Automatic Control & Intelligent Systems (I2CACIS), June 2021, pp. 46−51. doi:10.1109/I2CACIS52118.2021.9495922.

[40] L.A.M. Pereira, D.Rodrigues, P.B. Ribeiro, J.P. Papa, S.A.T. Weber, Social-spider optimization-based artificial neural networks training and its applications for Parkinson's disease identification, in: 2014 IEEE 27th International Symposium on Computer-Based Medical Systems, May 2014, pp. 14−17. doi:10.1109/CBMS.2014.25.

[41] A.M. Ikotun, A.E. Ezugwu, L. Abualigah, B. Abuhaija, J. Heming, K-means clustering algorithms: a comprehensive review, variants analysis, and advances in the era of big data, Inf. Sci. (Ny). 622 (2023) 178−210. Available from: https://doi.org/10.1016/j.ins.2022.11.139.

[42] B. Shanmugapriya, S. Meera, A survey of parallel social spider optimization algorithm based on swarm intelligence for high dimensional datasets, Int. J. Comput. Intell. Res. 13 (9) (2017) 2259−2265.

[43] A.M. Ikotun, A.E. Ezugwu, Improved SOSK-means automatic clustering algorithm with a three-part mutualism phase and random weighted reflection coefficient for high-dimensional datasets, Appl. Sci. 12 (24) (2022) 13019. Available from: https://doi.org/10.3390/app122413019.

[44] Y. Zhou, Y. Zhou, Q. Luo, M. Abdel-Basset, A simplex method-based social spider optimization algorithm for clustering analysis, Eng. Appl. Artif. Intell. 64 (2017) 67−82. Available from: https://doi.org/10.1016/J.ENGAPPAI.2017.06.004.

[45] O.O. Akinola, et al., Multiclass feature selection with metaheuristic optimization algorithms: a review, Neural Comput. Appl. 34 (2022). Available from: https://doi.org/10.1007/s00521-022-07705-4.

[46] R.A. Ibrahim, M.A. Elaziz, D. Oliva, E. Cuevas, S. Lu, An opposition-based social spider optimization for feature selection, Soft Comput. 23 (24) (2019) 13547−13567. Available from: https://doi.org/10.1007/s00500-019-03891-x.

[47] Q.-T. Bui, et al., A novel method for multispectral image classification by using social spider optimization algorithm integrated to fuzzy C-mean clustering, Can. J. Remote. Sens. 45 (1) (2019) 42−53. Available from: https://doi.org/10.1080/07038992.2019.1610369.

[48] A.E. Ezugwu, et al., A comprehensive survey of clustering algorithms: state-of-the-art machine learning applications, taxonomy, challenges, and future research prospects, Eng. Appl. Artif. Intell. 110 (2022) 104743. Available from: https://doi.org/10.1016/j.engappai.2022.104743.

[49] T.R. Chandran, A. V. Reddy, B. Janet, Performance comparison of social spider optimization for data clustering with other clustering methods, in: 2018 Second International Conference on Intelligent Computing and Control Systems (ICICCS), June 2018, pp. 1119−1125. Available from: https://doi.org/10.1109/ICCONS.2018.8662994.

[50] E. Cuevas, M. Cienfuegos, D. Zaldívar, M. Pérez-Cisneros, A swarm optimization algorithm inspired in the behavior of the social-spider, Expert. Syst. Appl. 40 (16) (2013) 6374−6384. Available from: https://doi.org/10.1016/J.ESWA.2013.05.041.

3

Animal migration optimization algorithm: novel optimizer, analysis, and applications

Laith Abualigah[1,2,3,4,5,6,7], Esraa Nasser Ahmad[8], Abiodun M. Ikotun[8], Raed Abu Zitar[9], Anas Ratib Alsoud[2], Nima Khodadadi[10], Absalom E. Ezugwu[11], Heming Jia[12]

[1]ARTIFICIAL INTELLIGENCE AND SENSING TECHNOLOGIES (AIST) RESEARCH CENTER, UNIVERSITY OF TABUK, TABUK, SAUDI ARABIA [2]HOURANI CENTER FOR APPLIED SCIENTIFIC RESEARCH, AL-AHLIYYA AMMAN UNIVERSITY, AMMAN, JORDAN [3]MEU RESEARCH UNIT, MIDDLE EAST UNIVERSITY, AMMAN, JORDAN [4]SCHOOL OF COMPUTER SCIENCES, UNIVERSITI SAINS MALAYSIA, PULAU PINANG, MALAYSIA [5]SCHOOL OF ENGINEERING AND TECHNOLOGY, SUNWAY UNIVERSITY MALAYSIA, PETALING JAYA, MALAYSIA [6]COMPUTER SCIENCE DEPARTMENT, AL AL-BAYT UNIVERSITY, MAFRAQ, JORDAN [7]DEPARTMENT OF ELECTRICAL AND COMPUTER ENGINEERING, LEBANESE AMERICAN UNIVERSITY, BYBLOS, LEBANON [8]UNIVERSITY OF KWAZULU-NATAL, PIETERMARITZBURG CAMPUS, POTCHEFSTROOM, SOUTH AFRICA [9]SORBONNE CENTER OF ARTIFICIAL INTELLIGENCE, SORBONNE UNIVERSITY-ABU DHABI, ABU DHABI, UNITED ARAB EMIRATES [10]DEPARTMENT OF CIVIL, ARCHITECTURAL AND ENVIRONMENTAL ENGINEERING, UNIVERSITY OF MIAMI, CORAL GABLES, FL, UNITED STATES [11]UNIT FOR DATA SCIENCE AND COMPUTING, NORTH-WEST UNIVERSITY, POTCHEFSTROOM, SOUTH AFRICA [12]DEPARTMENT OF INFORMATION ENGINEERING, SANMING UNIVERSITY, FUJIAN, P.R. CHINA

3.1 Introduction

In recent years, optimization algorithms have played a significant role in solving numerous problems in many science and engineering domains. These algorithms are applied to find the optimal solution from several suggested solutions to solve the underlying problem [1]. Until now, no algorithm performs the best for all problem fields; some algorithms perform better than others in some fields and worse in other fields. However, proposing a new optimization algorithm is always an open issue.

Like many other optimization algorithms, the animal migration optimization (AMO) algorithm was inspired by the natural system observed from the animal behavior in migration seasons. Animal migration can be summarized as the movement of the animal groups from one place to another to find warmer weather and better food, which may be found in a wide range of animal species, including birds, mammals, insects, and fish. Animal behavior in migration is based on three main rules: (1) coordinate your movement with your neighbors which means stay in the same direction, (2) try to stay close to your neighbors, and (3) stay away from collisions with neighbors [2].

AMO contains two main steps: the first step is the simulation of how the animals move from one place to another; in this step, animals should follow the three mentioned rules. The second step is the simulation of how animals are entering and leaving the group during this movement [2].

In recent years, some researchers have proposed approaches to improve the AMO algorithm. A new version of AMO called elitist animal migration optimization (ELAMO) was proposed in 2018 by Ülker to improve the solution quality of AMO for solving the traveling salesman problem [3]. Another approach was proposed in 2020 called improved animal migration optimization (IAMO), which is an improved version of AMO with an interactive learning mechanism that deals with high dimensional benchmark functions [4]. In 2021, an extended version of AMO called multimodal animal migration optimization (MAMO) was proposed to find all or most of local or global optima in the problem domain [5]. Another improved version of AMO was proposed in 2021 and tested with a larger variety of benchmark functions to train a multilayer perceptron neural network [6].

Optimization algorithms are used in many domains to find the optimal solution for a specific problem; one of the most important domains is image segmentation, which used the AMO algorithm to find the optimal thresholds values for multilevel image thresholding [7]. Data mining is also an important and trendy domain that uses optimization algorithms like AMO to limit and reduce the results of association rule mining (ARM) and find the most useful and necessary rules [8]. Normally, optimization methods can be used to deal with many problems in science, as presented in [9–17].

In this paper, we present the procedure of the AMO algorithm and show some of the most recent related works and applications that used AMO algorithms in their research. The related works were classified in many majors based on the application domain that the AMO was used in, and finally, some future works and study domains were suggested for upcoming studies and researches.

The remaining sections in this paper are presented as follows: In Section 3.2, we describe the algorithm procedure; in Section 3.3, we present some related researches that used the AMO algorithm; in Section 3.4, we discuss the algorithm advantages, disadvantages, and the related works; and in Section 3.5, we conclude our work in this chapter.

3.2 Animal migration optimization algorithm procedure

AMO is based on two typical suppositions:

1. The head animal that has a high-quality position will be preserved for the next migration.
2. The number of animals that join the group equals the number of animals that leave the group so the number of all animals is fixed.

AMO contains two main procedures:

1. The migration procedure: in this part, the algorithm simulates the animal migration process, which is the movement of the animal group from one place to another with the obeisance to the three rules: (1) avoid crashing your neighbors, (2) stay in the exact direction as your neighbors, and (3) stay near your neighbors. To apply the first rule, the algorithm assumed that every animal has a specific position, and for the next two rules, the algorithm assumed that the animal should move from the current position to another based on its neighbors.

For each individual dimension, they set the neighborhood length to five and represent the neighborhood concept using ring schema, which is shown in Fig. 3–1. The neighborhood topology is fixed and is represented on the set of indices of vectors. If the animal index is k, then the neighborhood animal indices are $k-2$, $k-1$, k, $k+1$, and $k+2$, as presented in Fig. 3–1. The neighboring indices will be $P-1$, P, 1, 2, 3, and so on if the animal index is 1, where P presents the size of the population.

As soon as the neighborhood topology has been built, the algorithm will choose one neighbor erratically and then update the individual position according to this neighbor, as shown by the following formula:

$$X_{k,G+1} = X_{k,G} + \delta \left(X_{\text{neighborhood},G} - X_{k,G} \right)$$

where $X_{\text{neighborhood},G}$ indicates the neighborhood position and δ indicates a random number generated by Gaussian distribution represents some factors that depend on real-world problems.

2. The population updating procedure: in this part, the algorithm simulates the leaving and joining process of animals during migration; the algorithm assumes that animal numbers

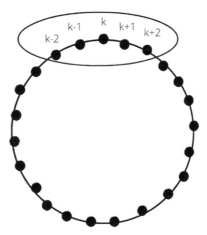

FIGURE 3–1 The concept of the local neighborhood of an individual.

are fixed, so the leaving animals during migration are replaced with the same number in the next population. The probability P_a is used to assess the fitness quality; the probability P_a for the best fitness is 1. For the worst fitness, the probability is $1/P$.

This process's procedure is explained as

For $k = 1$ to P
    For $y = 1$ to D
        If rand $> P_a$
            $X_{k,\ G+1} = X_{r1,\ G} + \text{random}\ (X_{\text{best},\ G} - X_{k,\ G}) + \text{random}\ (X_{r2,\ G} - X_{k,\ G})$
        End if
    End for
End for

$r_1, r_2 \in [1, \ldots, P]$ are random numbers, and $r_1 \neq r_2 \neq k$. After calculating the new solution $X_{k,\ G+1}$, it should be calculated and compared to the $X_{k,\ G}$, If the objective fitness of $X_{k,\ G+1}$ is less than the fitness of $X_{k,\ G}$, and $X_{k,\ G+1}$ is obtained as a replacement solution; otherwise, $X_{k,\ G}$ is obtained.

3.3 Related works

This section summarizes the related works into several application domains as follows.

3.3.1 Image processing

Image segmentation is a very important step in image processing, and thresholding has become one of the most famous techniques used for image segmentation. Applying multilevel thresholding and determining the thresholds values is a very expensive process, so the AMO algorithm has been used to determine the optimum thresholds values in multilevel thresholding [7].

3.3.2 Data clustering

In data clustering, data objects are grouped distinctly into clusters such that data objects that are in the same cluster share common characteristics and are different from data objects in other clusters [18]. AMO has achieved very high performance in solving numeric optimization problems. A modified AMO algorithm has been proposed with an entropy-based heuristic approach for data clustering.

The major contribution in the proposed method is that in each step of the algorithm (migration and update), the method can automatically adjust the conjunction speed and global search efforts by computing the information entropy per element for a particular dataset and suggesting an adaptive process for this balance [19].

It is difficult for conventional clustering algorithms to effectively handle clustering analysis of real-world data characterized with high complexity, and metaheuristic optimization algorithms have been used to resolve these issues [20]. An enhanced AMO method has been proposed [21] to solve clustering issues with high complexity.

3.3.3 Data mining

A new mining method has been proposed based on the AMO algorithm to reduce the number of rules generated by ARM and limit the results extracted by data mining. The proposed method contains two main steps; firstly, the rules are generated by the a priori algorithm, and then the unnecessary rules are deleted from the data using an AMO algorithm with a new fitness function.

The proposed algorithm minimizes the number of rules generated by ARM, the computing time, and the memory used to generate these rules. Another mining algorithm was proposed for the ARM, which resembles that reported in Ref. [8], except that the proposed method in Ref. [22] is used especially for the crime analysis department.

3.3.4 Benchmark functions

Metaheuristic optimization algorithms have been used in optimizing a number of engineering benchmark functions [23]. AMO shows great results in benchmark functions with low dimensions (30 and less), and its performance gets worse with benchmark functions with high dimensions. To overwhelm this weakness, an enhanced AMO with the reacting learning technique has been proposed. The main function of the learning technique is to make the AMO more intelligent by passing the information between individuals during the search step [4,24].

Another improved method has been suggested to enhance the investigation and exploitation ability of the AMO; the proposed method was applied on 23 benchmark test functions and shows better results than the original AMO. For magnifying the search area and improving the search capability, a new algorithm has been proposed [25] based on the opposition-based learning.

3.3.5 Computer networks

In quantum computing, the classical computing two states 0 and 1 are replaced with the quantum bit to allow for many different computational paths that execute simultaneously [26]. A new approach was suggested based on the AMO algorithm using quantum representation and chaotic map to resolve the multicast routing issue. The proposed method shows better performance and efficiency compared with the original AMO [27]. The optimal power flow (OPF) problem used a new mechanism based on AMO to find the optimal parameters for the OPF [28].

The AMO algorithm was used to find the best placement of the unmanned aerial vehicles (UAVs), which act as a wireless station when the building mobile network falls down [29]. The wireless networks also used AMO to propose a new group mobility model based on the AMO concept [30]. The suggested model covered some of the limitations and weaknesses in the current models of mobility so that it can be more realistic.

3.3.6 Neural networks

Neural networks are also an important domain that uses optimization algorithms, and an enhanced AMO was proposed with the Lévy flight feature to improve the training process of neural network multilayer perceptron [6].

3.3.7 Other applications

An enhanced AMO was proposed in 2018 to solve the traveling salesperson problem [3]; the proposed method is based on the idea of rebuilding the community topology of each individual through the migration process. Multimodal optimization problems were covered in [5] by proposing a new method called memetic AMO; the method does not face the difficulty of having previous knowledge of the problem area, and it also does not need to set the niching parameter.

Some of the AMO limitations and weaknesses such as the individuals' fixed growing limitations, moving possibility, and duplication constraints were taken into consideration in Ref. [29] to improve the original AMO. The proposed method can be applied to multiple schemas and can work with numerous operators. The AMO was used to find the optimal organization and size for the bridge hangers for solving the bridge falling problem [30]. A mixed AMO and random forest approach was proposed in Ref. [31] to indicate the ECM protein ordering with four different features designing approaches.

Table 3−1 presents the related works, their authors, published year, and its proposed methods.

Fig. 3−2 presents the number of researches included in this paper for each category.

3.4 Discussion

As presented in this paper, the AMO algorithm has many advantages such as simplicity, flexibility, and a few controlling parameters; these advantages make it widely used in many majors and applications to solve various optimization problems. On the other hand, the AMO algorithm has many limitations and weaknesses such as the individuals' fixed growing limitations, moving possibility, and duplication constraints. Many of the related works presented in this paper proposed improved AMO methods to cover these limitations and weaknesses.

The AMO algorithm has been used in several domains to find the optimal solution for many problems; new methods based on AMO have been suggested to enhance the performance of the algorithm and get better result in these domains. Some of these methods were used to solve problems in a specific domain such as image processing [7], data mining [8,22], data clustering [19], and neural networks [6].

Other methods were focused on improving the algorithm itself such as improving the performance of the algorithm for high dimensional optimization problems [4,24], designing a MAMO algorithm [5], and enhancing the algorithm search capability [25].

Table 3–1   Related works.

No.	Years	References	Authors	Method name	Proposed methods
1.	2013	[25]	Cao, Li, and Wang	AMO	Opposition-based animal migration optimization (AMO).
2.	2015	[21]	Ma et al.	IAMO	Improved AMO for solving clustering issues.
3.	2016		Luo, Ma, and Zhou	AMO	A new migration method has been suggested to enhance the investigation and exploitation ability of the AMO algorithm.
4.	2016	[19]	Hou, Gao, and Chen	AMO	Enhanced AMO version with an entropy-based heuristic technique was used for data clustering.
5.	2016	[32]	Zhou et al.	FCAMO	Enhanced AMO has been proposed to increase the converging speed and accuracy of regular AMO.
6.	2017	[31]	Guan, Zhang, and Xu	BAMORF	Mixed AMO algorithm and random forest approach to indicate the ECM protein ordering.
7.	2018	[28]	Chinta, Subhashini, and Satapathy	AMO	New technique to solve the OPF.
8.	2018	[27]	Mahseur, Boukra, and Meraihi	AMO	Enhanced quantum chaotic AMO algorithm to solve the multicast routing problem.
9.	2018	[8]	Chiclana et al.	AMO	AMO for association rules mining from a given database.
10.	2018	[3]	Ülker	ELAMO	ELAMO for solving the traveling salesperson problem.
11.	2018	[7]	Farshi	AMO	AMO algorithm for multilevel thresholding.
12.	2018	[33]	Rai and Kushwah	AMO	Improved version of AMO to cover the weakness and limitations.
13.	2019	[24]	Lai, Feng, and Yu	IAMO	Enhanced version of AMO for high dimensional problems with interactive learning mechanism.
14.	2019	[30]	Morales et al.	AMO	AMO for finding the optimal organization and size for the bridge hangers for solving the bridge falling problem.
15.	2019	[34]	Verma and Kesswani	AMIGM	Group mobility sample based on AMO for mobile ad hoc networks.
16.	2019	[35]	Subhashini and Chinta	AAMO-DE	Expanded AMO algorithm in the environment of differential growth.
17.	2019	[36]	Othman, Ismail, and Isa	AMO	AMO has been used to extract solar cell model variables values.
18.	2020	[37]	Ridhor et al.	AMO	AMO has been used to gain the parameters of the photovoltaic cell model.
19.	2020	[4]	Lai, Hu, and Jiang	IAMO	Improved AMO with the interactive learning technique.
20.	2020	[29]	Duraki, Demirci, and Aslan	AMO	AMO for solving the mobile network falling down problem by using UAVs.
21.	2020	[22]	Jagadeesh, and Kumanan	AMO	A novel mining approach based on AMO for reducing the Association rules.
22.	2021	[38]	Prakash, Sangeetha, and Informatics	AMO	AMO has been used to extract features for RNN which is used in breast cancer early detection.
23.	2021	[5]	Farshi	MAMO	MAMO for finding multiple solutions.
24.	2021	[6]	Gülcü	IAMO-MLP	Enhanced AMO with the Lévy flight feature.
25.	2022	[39]	Dash, Subhashini, and China	BA-AMO	To investigate the OPF problem in IEEE bus systems, a new version of AMO algorithm has been developed.

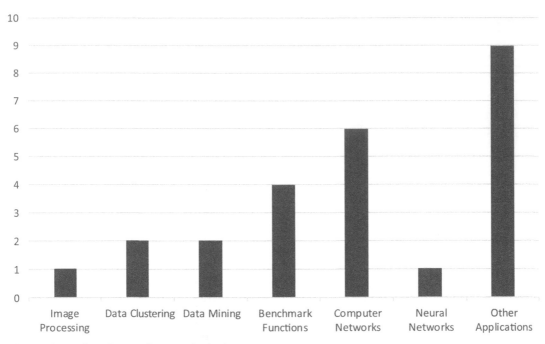

FIGURE 3–2 Number of research papers for each category.

3.5 Conclusion

AMO is an optimization algorithm based on the animal's behavior in migration seasons. It contains two main processes: the migration process, which represents the movement of the animals from one place to a new place, and the updating process, which simulates how the animals enter and leave the group. AMO has solved many optimization problems since it was proposed in 2013 and can be applied to solve optimization problems in many domains such as engineering problems, text clustering problems, feature selection problems, text summarization problems, and image segmentation problems. In this paper, we analyze and review the AMO algorithm, present and classify some of the recent related works that use this algorithm, and suggest several application domains that can use the AMO in it.

References

[1] L. Abualigah, A. Diabat, A comprehensive survey of the Grasshopper optimization algorithm: results, variants, and applications, Neur. Comput. Appl. 32 (19) (2020) 15533–15556. Available from: https://doi.org/10.1007/s00521-020-04789-8.

[2] X. Li, J. Zhang, M. Yin, Animal migration optimization: an optimization algorithm inspired by animal migration behavior, Neur. Comput. Appl. 24 (7–8) (2014) 1867–1877. Available from: https://doi.org/10.1007/s00521-013-1433-8.

[3] E. ÜLKER, An elitist approach for solving the traveling salesman problem using an animal migration optimization algorithm, Turkish J. Electr. Eng. Comput. Sci. 26 (2018) 605−617. Available from: https://doi.org/10.3906/elk-1705-61.

[4] Z. Lai, X. Hu, C. Jiang, An intelligent algorithm with interactive learning mechanism for high-dimensional optimization problem based on improved animal migration optimization, Concurr. Comput. Pract. Exp. 34 (12) (2022). Available from: https://doi.org/10.1002/cpe.5774.

[5] T.R. Farshi, A memetic animal migration optimizer for multimodal optimization, Evol. Syst. 13 (1) (2022) 133−144. Available from: https://doi.org/10.1007/s12530-021-09368-3.

[6] Gülcü, An improved animal migration optimization algorithm to train the feed-forward artificial neural networks, Arab. J. Sci. Eng. 47 (8) (2022) 9557−9581. Available from: https://doi.org/10.1007/s13369-021-06286-z.

[7] T. Rahkar Farshi, A multilevel image thresholding using the animal migration optimization algorithm, Iran J. Comput. Sci. 2 (1) (2019) 9−22. Available from: https://doi.org/10.1007/s42044-018-0022-5.

[8] L.H. Son, et al., ARM−AMO: an efficient association rule mining algorithm based on animal migration optimization, Knowl.-based Syst. 154 (2018) 68−80. Available from: https://doi.org/10.1016/j.knosys.2018.04.038.

[9] L. Abualigah, A. Diabat, C.L. Thanh, S. Khatir, Opposition-based Laplacian distribution with Prairie Dog Optimization method for industrial engineering design problems, Comput. Meth. Appl. Mech. Eng. 414 (2023) 116097.

[10] Y. Zheng, L. Abualigah, A.G. Hussien, DETDO: an adaptive hybrid dandelion optimizer for engineering optimization, Adv. Eng. Inform. 57 (2023) 102004.

[11] D. Izci, S. Ekinci, S. Mirjalili, L. Abualigah, An intelligent tuning scheme with a master/slave approach for efficient control of the automatic voltage regulator, Neur. Comput. Appl. (2023) 1−17.

[12] H. Jia, C. Lu, D. Wu, C. Wen, H. Rao, L. Abualigah, An improved reptile search algorithm with ghost opposition-based learning for global optimization problems, J. Comput. Design Eng. (2023). qwad048.

[13] A.H. Alharbi, A.A. Abdelhamid, A. Ibrahim, S.K. Towfek, N. Khodadadi, L. Abualigah, et al., Improved dipper-throated optimization for forecasting metamaterial design bandwidth for engineering applications, Biomimetics 8 (2) (2023) 241.

[14] S. Nama, A.K. Saha, S. Chakraborty, A.H. Gandomi, L. Abualigah, Boosting particle swarm optimization by backtracking search algorithm for optimization problems, Swarm Evolution. Comput. 79 (2023) 101304.

[15] M. Zare, M. Ghasemi, A. Zahedi, K. Golalipour, S.K. Mohammadi, S. Mirjalili, et al., A global best-guided firefly algorithm for engineering problems, J. Bionic Eng (2023) 1−30.

[16] D. Wu, C. Wen, H. Rao, H. Jia, Q. Liu, L. Abualigah, Modified reptile search algorithm with multi-hunting coordination strategy for global optimization problems, Math. Biosci. Eng. 20 (6) (2023) 10090−10134.

[17] S. Ekinci, D. Izci, L. Abualigah, R.A. Zitar, A modified oppositional chaotic local search strategy based Aquila optimizer to design an effective controller for vehicle cruise control system, J. Bionic Eng. (2023) 1−24.

[18] A.M. Ikotun, A.E. Ezugwu, Boosting k-means clustering with symbiotic organisms search for automatic clustering problems, PLoS One 17 (8) (2022) e0272861. Available from: https://doi.org/10.1371/journal.pone.0272861.

[19] L. Hou, J. Gao, R. Chen, An information entropy-based animal migration optimization algorithm for data clustering, Entropy 18 (5) (2016) 185. Available from: https://doi.org/10.3390/e18050185.

[20] A.E. Ezugwu, et al., A comprehensive survey of clustering algorithms: State-of-the-art machine learning applications, taxonomy, challenges, and future research prospects, Eng. Appl. Artif. Intell. 110 (2022) 104743. Available from: https://doi.org/10.1016/j.engappai.2022.104743.

[21] M. Ma, Q. Luo, Y. Zhou, X. Chen, L. Li, An improved animal migration optimization algorithm for clustering analysis, Discr. Dynam. Nat. Soc. 2015 (2015) 1–12. Available from: https://doi.org/10.1155/2015/194792.

[22] K.R. Jagadeesh, T. Kumanan, An efficient association rule mining algorithm based on animal migration optimization processing of unknown incidents in crime analysis brance, IOP Conf. Ser. Mater. Sci. Eng. 925 (1) (2020) 012013. Available from: https://doi.org/10.1088/1757-899X/925/1/012013.

[23] J.O. Agushaka, A.E. Ezugwu, O.N. Olaide, O. Akinola, R.A. Zitar, L. Abualigah, Improved dwarf mongoose optimization for constrained engineering design problems, J. Bionic Eng. (2022). Available from: https://doi.org/10.1007/s42235-022-00316-8.

[24] Z. Lai, X. Feng, & H. Yu, An improved animal migration optimization algorithm based on interactive learning behavior for high dimensional optimization problem, in: 2019 International Conference on High Performance Big Data and Intelligent Systems (HPBD&IS), May 2019, pp. 110–115. doi:10.1109/HPBDIS.2019.8735450.

[25] Y. Cao, X. Li, J. Wang, Opposition-based animal migration optimization, Math. Probl. Eng. 2013 (2013) 1–7. Available from: https://doi.org/10.1155/2013/308250.

[26] A.E. Ezugwu, O.N. Oyelade, A.M. Ikotun, J.O. Agushaka, Y.-S. Ho, Machine learning research trends in Africa: a 30 years overview with bibliometric analysis review, Arch. Comput. Methods Eng. (2023). Available from: https://doi.org/10.1007/s11831-023-09930-z.

[27] M. Mahseur, A. Boukra, Y. Meraihi, Improved quantum chaotic animal migration optimization algorithm for QoS multicast routing problem, Computational Intelligence and Its Applications, 2018, pp. 128–139. Available from: https://doi.org/10.1007/978-3-319-89743-1_12.

[28] P. Chinta, K.R. Subhashini, J.K. Satapathy, Optimal power flow using a new evolutionary approach: animal migration optimization, Int. Conf. Innov. Technol. Eng., 2018, 2018.

[29] S. Duraki, S. Demirci, & S. Aslan, UAV placement with animal migration optimization algorithm, in: 2020 28th Telecommunications Forum (TELFOR), November 2020, pp. 1–4. Available from: https://doi.org/10.1109/TELFOR51502.2020.9306631.

[30] A. Morales et al., Correction to: optimization of bridges reinforcement by conversion to tied arch using an animal migration algorithm, 2021, pp. C1–C1. Available from: https://doi.org/10.1007/978-3-030-22999-3_74.

[31] L. Guan, S. Zhang, H. Xu, BAMORF: a novel computational method for predicting the extracellular matrix proteins, IEEE Access 5 (2017) 18498–18505. Available from: https://doi.org/10.1109/ACCESS.2017.2751499.

[32] Y. Zhou, Q. Luo, M. Ma, S. Qiao, Z. Bao, animal migration optimization algorithm for constrained engineering optimization problems, J. Comput. Theor. Nanosci. 13 (1) (2016) 539–546. Available from: https://doi.org/10.1166/jctn.2016.4838.

[33] R. Rai, & V.S. Kushwah, New approach for animal migration optimization algorithm, 2018, pp. 509–516. Available from: https://doi.org/10.1007/978-981-10-8198-9_54.

[34] J. Verma, N. Kesswani, AMIGM: animal migration inspired group mobility model for mobile ad hoc networks, Scalable Comput. Pract. Exp. 20 (3) (2019) 577–590. Available from: https://doi.org/10.12694/scpe.v20i3.1574.

[35] K.R. Subhashini, P. Chinta, An augmented animal migration optimization algorithm using worst solution elimination approach in the backdrop of differential evolution, Evol. Intell. 12 (2) (2019) 273–303. Available from: https://doi.org/10.1007/s12065-019-00223-8.

[36] M.N. Othman, B. Ismail, Z.M. Isa, Performance analysis of animal migration optimization algorithm in extracting solar cell double diode model parameters, Univers. J. Electr. Electron. Eng. 6 (5A) (2019) 23–30. Available from: https://doi.org/10.13189/ujeee.2019.061503.

[37] S.I.A. Ridhor, Z.M. Isa, N.M. Nayan, Parameter extraction of PV cell single diode model using animal migration optimization, Int. J. Electr. Eng. Appl. Sci. 3 (2) (2020) 1−6 [Online]. Available. Available from: https://ijeeas.utem.edu.my/ijeeas/article/view/5853.

[38] S. Prakash, K. Sangeetha, An early breast cancer detection system using recurrent neural network (RNN) with animal migration optimization (AMO) based classification method, J. Med. Imag. Heal. Inform. 11 (12) (2021) 2950−2965. Available from: https://doi.org/10.1166/jmihi.2021.3885.

[39] S.P. Dash, K.R. Subhashini, P. Chinta, Development of a boundary assigned animal migration optimization algorithm and its application to optimal power flow study, Exp. Syst. Appl. 200 (2022)116776. Available from: https://doi.org/10.1016/J.ESWA.2022.116776.

4

A Survey of cuckoo search algorithm: optimizer and new applications

Laith Abualigah[1,2,3,4,5,6,7], Ashraf Ababneh[8], Abiodun M. Ikotun[8], Raed Abu Zitar[9], Anas Ratib Alsoud[2], Nima Khodadadi[10], Absalom E. Ezugwu[11], Essam Said Hanandeh[12], Heming Jia[13]

[1]ARTIFICIAL INTELLIGENCE AND SENSING TECHNOLOGIES (AIST) RESEARCH CENTER, UNIVERSITY OF TABUK, TABUK, SAUDI ARABIA [2]HOURANI CENTER FOR APPLIED SCIENTIFIC RESEARCH, AL-AHLIYYA AMMAN UNIVERSITY, AMMAN, JORDAN [3]MEU RESEARCH UNIT, MIDDLE EAST UNIVERSITY, AMMAN, JORDAN [4]SCHOOL OF COMPUTER SCIENCES, UNIVERSITI SAINS MALAYSIA, PULAU PINANG, MALAYSIA [5]SCHOOL OF ENGINEERING AND TECHNOLOGY, SUNWAY UNIVERSITY MALAYSIA, PETALING JAYA, MALAYSIA [6]COMPUTER SCIENCE DEPARTMENT, AL AL-BAYT UNIVERSITY, MAFRAQ, JORDAN [7]DEPARTMENT OF ELECTRICAL AND COMPUTER ENGINEERING, LEBANESE AMERICAN UNIVERSITY, BYBLOS, LEBANON [8]UNIVERSITY OF KWAZULU-NATAL, PIETERMARITZBURG CAMPUS, POTCHEFSTROOM, SOUTH AFRICA [9]SORBONNE CENTER OF ARTIFICIAL INTELLIGENCE, SORBONNE UNIVERSITY-ABU DHABI, ABU DHABI, UNITED ARAB EMIRATES [10]DEPARTMENT OF CIVIL, ARCHITECTURAL AND ENVIRONMENTAL ENGINEERING, UNIVERSITY OF MIAMI, CORAL GABLES, FL, UNITED STATES [11]UNIT FOR DATA SCIENCE AND COMPUTING, NORTH-WEST UNIVERSITY, POTCHEFSTROOM, SOUTH AFRICA [12]DEPARTMENT OF COMPUTER INFORMATION SYSTEM, ZARQA UNIVERSITY, ZARQA, JORDAN [13]DEPARTMENT OF INFORMATION ENGINEERING, SANMING UNIVERSITY, FUJIAN, P.R. CHINA

4.1 Introduction

Optimization seeks to discover the optimal solution among population of solutions, and it naturally occurs in most human endeavors [1]. Most structural design optimization issues are nonlinear and involve several variables with severe limitations. This constraint can be expressed as a simple limit, such as a range of material characteristics or a nonlinear relationship that includes the maximum stress, minimum load-carrying capacity, maximum deflection, and shape. This nonlinearity frequently leads to a state of multimodal responsiveness.

Metaheuristic Optimization Algorithms. DOI: https://doi.org/10.1016/B978-0-443-13925-3.00018-2

Therefore, local search approaches such as Hill Climbing and Nelder-Mead Downhill Simplex are ineffective; only global algorithms may produce optimal answers. A metaheuristic is a broad, high-level method (template) that can be employed as a heuristic strategy to create low-level reasoning to solve a particular optimization problem [2]. Diversity and abundance are two key aspects of metascience [3], which enhances the current search for the optimal solution and choose the optimal candidate or option. Diversification ensures that the algorithm can efficiently explore the search area, typically via randomness. Cuckoo search (CS) is a revolutionary algorithm for metaheuristic searching. The algorithm depends on some cuckoo species' forced reproductive parasitic behavior and the flight pattern of certain birds and fruit flies. The CS algorithm imitates the special female cuckoo species' obligate parasitic nature, which mimics the pattern and color of the host bird [4]. According to preliminary research, the algorithm is intriguing and can outperform the existing algorithms [5].

Normally, optimization methods can be used to deal with many problems in the sciences, as presented in [6−15]. The CS algorithm is further validated for various technical optimization issues in this article. A comparison is made between the proposed search technique and other standard optimization techniques. The article concludes with a discussion of computer science fundamentals and a proposal of future study subjects.

The remainder of the chapter is formatted as follows. Section 4.2 reviews the basic CS algorithm. Section 4.3 discusses related work. Methodology and discussion are, respectively, discussed in Sections 4.4 Sections 4.5. Lastly, Section 4.6 summarizes the entire work, while Section 4.7 outlines the work to come.

4.2 Cuckoo search algorithm

Natural phenomena have been successfully used by researchers to develop metaheuristic algorithms [16]. Metaheuristic algorithms inspired by nature are becoming increasingly complex and gaining popularity. Particle swarm optimization (PSO), for example, was inspired by the swarm intelligence of birds and fish, while the flashing rhythm of tropical fireflies influenced the firefly algorithm [17,18]. Various optimization issues, particularly NP-hard problems like the traveling salesman problem, have been solved using nature-inspired metaheuristic algorithms. Practically all modern metaheuristics derive their power from their capacity to imitate the most advantageous characteristics of nature, especially biological systems that evolved through natural processes over millennia. The choices of the best and environmental adaptation are two essential characteristics. It can be transformed into two contemporary metaheuristic characteristics: intensification and diversification [17]. Diversification guarantees that the algorithm can traverse the search space efficiently [19]. Intensification tries to explore the existing best solutions and recruit the best alternatives.

CS is a metaheuristic optimization approach that was recently designed to handle optimization problems. This metaheuristic strategy relies on the brood parasitism of several species of cuckoo, Lévy flights, and randomized walks. Typically, the CS's characteristics are held constant for a long time, affecting the algorithm's efficiency [20].

The CS algorithm is a new swarm intelligence optimization algorithm developed by Yang and Deb [21] after observing the behavior of cuckoos, such as investigating various hosts' nests and laying one or more eggs. As in fundamental CS, locating other hosts' nests is represented by the Lévy flight, a random process with short step lengths in the short term but potentially large step lengths in the long run. Due to this sporadic jump, the CS has low local search precision and convergence efficiency, and the optimal global position of the solution oscillates in subsequent rounds. Various upgraded CS, such as the parameters, step length, and site of the bird's nest, are intensively investigated to address the primary CS's fundamental challenges. The multispecies cuckoo method was presented by Yang et al. [22] to promote the coevolution of the cuckoo host in competitive contexts. By combining annex and cooperation operators, both the population's variety and the CS algorithm's optimization capability were increased. Zhang et al. [23] proposed a hybrid CS-DE technique to address the need for extreme precision in constrained problems when solving this kind of problems. The simulation results demonstrated that the suggested algorithm's solution to global optimization is more precise and competitive. Cheng et al. [24] suggested an adaptive hybrid cuckoo algorithm (AHCS) for resolving a CEC2017 optimization issue utilizing the mutation operator, evolution strategy, and Lévy flying. The test results demonstrated the AHCS's resilience and advantages. Abdelbaset et al. [25] created a CS-GA, and simulation results indicated that the CS-GA resolves nonconstrained optimization problems with improved precision and robustness. Ikotun et al. [4] reviewed some of the articles that combined CS with *K*-means algorithm for data clustering.

To understand this algorithm, we will look at the reproductive pattern of some cuckoo species. After that, we will define the concepts and phases of the CS algorithm.

Cuckoo search algorithm

```
begin
    Objective function f(x), x = (x1,..., xd)T;
    Initial a population of n host nests xi (i = 1,2,...,n); while (t<Maximum Generation) or
    (stop criterion);
        Get a cuckoo (say i) randomly
    and generate a new solution by Lévy flights;
        Evaluate its quality/fitness; Fi
        Choose a nest among n (say j) randomly; if (Fi > Fj),
            Replace j by the new solution; end
        Abandon a fraction (Pa) of worse nests
[and build new ones at new locations via Lévy flights];
        Keep the best solutions (or nests with quality solutions);
        Rank the solutions and find the current best; end while
        Postprocess results and visualization; end
```

The next flow chart explains the main idea of the algorithm:

```
                          ┌──────────┐
                          │  Begin   │
                          └────┬─────┘
                               │            ┌──────────────────────┐
                               ▼            │ Determine egg laying  │
   ┌───────────────────────────────┐       │ radius for each cuckoo│
   │ Initialize the random solution │      └──────────┬───────────┘
   │   (Cuckoos) to the Kapur's     │                 ▲
   │      entropy function          │      ┌──────────┴───────────┐
   └──────────────┬─────────────────┘      │   Move all cuckoo's  │
                  ▼                         │ toward best environment│
   ┌──────────────────────────┐            └──────────┬───────────┘
   │ Lay eggs in different nests│                      ▲
   └──────────────┬───────────┘            ┌──────────┴───────────┐
                  ▼                         │  Determine cuckoo    │
   ┌──────────────────────────┐            │     societies        │
   │Some eggs are detected and killed│     └──────────┬───────────┘
   └──────────────┬───────────┘                       ▲
                  ▼                         ┌──────────┴───────────┐
            ◇ Population is less            │  Find nests with best │
              than the max value? ◇         │    survival rate      │
                  │                         └──────────┬───────────┘
                  ▼                                    ▲
   ┌──────────────────────────┐            ┌──────────┴───────────┐
   │Check the values of fitness function│  │    Let eggs grow     │
   └──────────────┬───────────┘            └──────────────────────┘
                  ▼                                    ▲
            ◇ Stop condition ◇ ─────────────────────────┘
              satisfied?
                  │
                  ▼
   ┌──────────────────────────┐
   │Get threshold values to the image│
   └──────────────┬───────────┘
                  ▼
             ┌──────────┐
             │   End    │
             └──────────┘
```

4.2.1 Cuckoo rearing conduct

To simplify the explanation of the cuckoo hunting technique, we will first describe the primary characteristics of the cuckoo host system as accumulations of cuckoos with nesting. In typical cuckoo host systems, there are usually three or more eggs per nest, and each cuckoo can attack a large number of nests by laying eggs in these nests [26]. Assuming that only one egg might be laid by each cuckoo and contaminate one nest at the same time, the number of eggs matches the number of nests and cuckoo nests. Therefore, we can represent the egg's position as the optimization problem's solution vector x. In this manner, there should be no differentiation between eggs, cuckoos, and nests. Therefore, the following equation holds true: "egg = cuckoo = nest."

- Each cuckoo deposits an egg in the nest of a randomly selected host. In the interest of simplicity, the number of eggs, nests, and cuckoos are all the same.

- Each egg placed by the cuckoo has a probability of being discovered and discarded equally to P_a a. This equates to a modified fraction P_a of the entire population at each iteration t.
- The appropriateness of an egg or a solution is determined by its objective value. The next generation inherits the optimal solution with the lowest target value (for minimization). Thus, the optimal solution is kept.

The optimal layout achieved by CS is often much better than the optimal layout achieved by the current strategy. Finally, the details of specific searches used in CS and consequences for future searches are thoroughly examined. The introduction of a planning scheduling problem in low-level design is exceptionally nonlinear, including various planning factors under complex requirements [2]. Simple restrictions (e.g., material property ranges) or non-linear relationships, such as maximum stress, maximum deflection, minimum stress limits, and mathematical permutations, can be used as constraints. Multimodal response scenarios usually result from this nonlinearity. In this sense, close search calculations, such as the simple climb strategies and the nailer med regression, are not suitable; Only global accounts can get the desired permutation. Metaheuristic computation can be described as a general, high-level process (planning) that can be used as a heuristic method for planning basic empirical methods for solving explicit optimization problems. The main properties of metaproperties are enhancement and amplification: add a plan, find the best arrangement, and choose the best climber or arrangement. The search space can be explored efficiently utilizing scaling, usually through randomization. Today's metaheuristic computing is designed to perform global research with three key objectives: tackle problems faster, solve big problems, and get meaningful computations. Genetic computation (GA) and PSO are common examples of such computations. The effectiveness of metacalculations can be attributed to how it mimics the best elements of nature, especially the selection of the most suitable features within an organic framework that has evolved over millions of years of natural selection [3].

4.2.2 Lévy trips in nature

Creatures seek for their food randomly or semirandomly. Overall, a successful mob robbery path is erratic; the next step depends on the existing region/state and the odds of advancing to the next area. The probability that the numbers can determine the direction he takes. For instance, it was proven that the flight behavior of various fearsome creatures and reptiles could maneuver in daily flight. A recent report by Reynolds and Frye [27] showed that the organophilic or drosophila melanogaster explored its scene in a series of straight paths with unexpected 90-degree turns, resulting in Le's paradoxes: continuous, scale-free search for flight mode. Studies of human behavior also show the natural elements of Lévy's voyage. The lights can be customized for Levi's trips. Therefore, this behavior was applied to rationalization and ideal search, and the results of the primers showed their promising capabilities [5]. The results obtained using CS outperform the best possible solutions previously reported using other algorithms.

4.3 Related works

Cuckoo-seeking account (CSA) is another approach that integrates biomimicry into the optimization process and iteratively replicates the breeding method recently proposed by Yang and Depp [28] [29] for the most common parasitic bird, the cuckoo. The cuckoo is perhaps the scariest and most dangerous of all birds. He secretly lays eggs in the homes of other host birds, relieving them of their parental obligations to raise the young. Cuckoo is constantly practicing duality in his new life. They mimic the shadows and examples of their host eggshells to hide their eggs from host birds. The cuckoo sneaks into the house and takes the owner's egg to give the chicks more space and food. However, the link between the host species and the cuckoo is often an ongoing arms race. The owner figures out how to warn the scam, throw the parasite eggs or leave the house.

Parasites develop mimetic abilities that make their eggs more similar to their hosts. In the pioneering work of Yang and Deb, CSA effectively improved some normative skills, and their results showed that CSA is more suitable for global research than GA and PSO [30]. On the other hand, CSA has been used in various fields from the very beginning. This includes designing the planning process [30], interference frameworks, and remote sensing networks and addressing potential improvement issues, remediation procedures, and billing issues. More sophisticated inductive methods are emerging, being heavily promoted, and becoming more popular.

Numerous applications exist for CS; however, theoretical research is minimal. This section will draw attention to the need for more research into the theoretical components of CS. It can be difficult to classify research into theoretical or nontheoretical categories, as the content may contain simulations and computer analyses. Consequently, the classification that follows may not be stringent. Nevertheless, we may characterize certain CS studies as follows:

Three novel CS algorithms with dynamically increasing switching parameters have been developed by Mareli and Twala [31]. By utilizing 10 mathematical test functions, three novel CS methods are validated. Their results are compared to those of CS algorithms with static and decrementing parameter values for switching. Experiments in this chapter show that the CS algorithm with exponentially growing switching parameters beats other CS methods.

The CS yielded the most effective results compared to other tactics found in the literature. Baskan [32] employed the CS algorithm to alleviate traffic congestion by enhancing the operation of transportation route networks. The aim function was the sum of travel expenses and the time required to invest in 16 link capacity expansions. The CS algorithm maintained the fault level and voltage changes within reasonable ranges in a smart grid, lowering actual power losses [33].

By implementing random operators and changing the Lévy Flight search step length optimization framework, a modified CS (MCS) algorithm that boosts the method's convergence accuracy was suggested [34]. Experiments show that MCS can modify the search approach to optimize high-dimensional functions and converge on the ideal global value.

4.4 Method

CS is an innovative heuristic algorithm motivated by certain birds' parasitic behavior when they lay eggs in host bird nests. Some cuckoos specialize in imitating the colors and patterns of the eggs of a limited number of host species. This decreases the likelihood of eggs being abandoned. When the host bird discovers a strange egg, it discards or leaves it. Parasitic cuckoos choose nests where their hosts deposit eggs. Cuckoo eggs hatch before their host eggs, propelling the host eggs out of the nest when they do.

Cuckoo chicks receive a large amount of food as a result, and more often they replicate the sounds of host chicks to obtain additional food. The majority of cuckoos utilize a simple random wandering to get food. The random walk is a Markov chain in which the following location is decided by the current position and the transition probability. Employing Lévy flights instead of random walks improves the search capability. The Lévy flight is a random walk with a strong tail probability distribution [21]. Each cuckoo indicates a possible resolution to the current problem. The fundamental purpose is to replace a poor solution with a novel and potentially superior alternative (cuckoo). There are three fundamentally idealized CS rules. In accordance with the first rule, each cuckoo lays a single egg in a random nest. The second rule says that only the healthiest nest will be handed on to future generations. Each nest has a single egg, but as the complexity of the problem increases, numerous eggs may be utilized to represent a set of keys.

On the contrary, the final rule specifies that the amount of the available host nests remains constant, and the probability that the cuckoo's egg would be detected by the host bird is $p \in [0, 1]$. Depending on the value of p, the host bird either discards the egg or neglects the nest. It is expected that new nests replace only a percentage p of nests.

The CS has been conducted according to the three rules. To generate a new solution x_i^{t+1} for ith cuckoo, Lévy flight is utilized. This step is known as the global random walk, and it is determined by

$$x_i^{t+1} = x_i^t + \alpha \otimes \text{Lévy}(\lambda)(x_{\text{best}} - x_i^t)$$

The local random walk is presented by

$$x_i^{t+1} = x_i^t + \alpha \otimes H(P - \epsilon) \otimes (x_j^t - x_k^t)$$

where

Parameter	Value
x_i^t	The previous solution
$\alpha > 0$	The step size related to problem scales
$\otimes$	Entry-wise multiplication
x_j^t, x_k^t	Randomly selected solutions
x_{best}	Current best solution

Due to the greater effectiveness of Lévy flights in discovering the search space, the randomized step length via Lévy flight is examined in the current work and is derived from a Lévy distribution with an unlimited variation and mean.

$$\text{Lévy} \sim \left\{ \frac{\lambda\Gamma(\lambda)\sin(\pi\lambda/2)}{\pi} \quad \frac{1}{S^{1+\lambda}}(S''S_0 > 0) \right.$$

As Lévy flights produce fractions of new solutions, the local search accelerates. Here, a portion of the solutions must be created using far-field randomization to prevent the system shape from becoming locally optimal.

Parameter	Value
$\Gamma(\lambda)$	Gamma function
p	Switch probability
ε	Random number
$(1 < \lambda \leq 3)$	

Due to wide-scale randomization, any huge step is feasible in the CS, where the length of each step is heavy-tailed.

4.5 Discussion

With Lévy flight, a unique CS method is employed to solve structural optimization issues. The effectiveness of the CS algorithm was initially verified against various standard structural construction challenges. Extensive comparative studies demonstrate that CS outperforms all the existing techniques. In part, this is due to the fact that in CS, fewer parameters are fine-tuned than in other algorithms like GA and PSO. Besides the population size n, there is primarily a Pa coefficient. The CS algorithm consists of three major components: optimal choice, random walking paths, and randomized exploration of Lévy's global excursion. Selecting the correct solution by retaining the best solution or nest compatible with a typical elitism in GA guarantees that the best solution is brought over to the subsequent iteration. There is no better way to eliminate population-related dangers. A local random walk utilizes the most advantageous solutions.

$$x^{t+1} = x^t + \alpha\varepsilon_t$$

In particular, if ε_t follows a Gaussian distribution, it becomes a typical random path. This corresponds to the basic adjustment step in finding harmony. When ε_t comes from the Lévy distribution, the transfer step is larger and more efficient. Nevertheless, if the stride is too large, it may go too far. Fortunately, elitism brings exploitation movements closer to local ideals by maintaining optimal solutions. Another way to slightly improve this search is to replace x^t with the current best value, so that the broad local use phase concentrates on the local search for the best available value at the time, and the radius or locale size of the search step is a reflective question. Alternatively, to rapidly test the entire search space to check that newly developed solutions are sufficiently diverse, it is sufficient to ensure that the generated search terms/solutions are evenly spread throughout the search space. However, this quasi-standard method is not always effective. The most efficient and effective approach to conducting research is to fly with Levi. In contrast, the majority of descriptive measures use normal or Gaussian algorithms to produce new research approaches. Frequently, retaliation flights are more successful when the search space is expansive.

Consequently, an efficient CS-like algorithm can be developed by combining the three components listed above. This uniformity also eliminates the need to tailor these parameters to a particular problem. Consequently, CS is more universal and potent than other descriptive features of most optimization problems. Similar to population-based algorithms like PSO and genetic algorithms, this potentially powerful optimization technique can be extended to investigate generic optimization applications with varied restrictions, including difficult NP problems. It can also be combined with other prominent algorithms, such as PSO. Further research could investigate the relationship between the algorithmic approach's speed and its sensitivity and parameters.

As with the majority of metaheuristics, there is an urgent need for mathematical examination of computational systems from an analytical standpoint. Currently, there is no indicative generic framework for metaanalysis. Path-based algorithms, such as simulated annealing, are investigated within the context of Markov chain Monte Carlo. On the one hand, CS can be considered an evolutionary system in which many interacting Markov chains are selected and aligned to achieve a global optimum. Creating a distinct kind of CS to address combinatorial optimization problems, such as travel providers and booking schedules, is another possible but simple expansion. Any advancement in the discipline may yield fresh insights into how and why metaheuristic algorithms function. It will also aid in developing more effective and frequent hybrid optimization techniques.

The algorithm should be verified employing test functions with analytical or known solutions after it has been implemented. To illustrate, consider the bivariate Michaelwicz function:

$$f(x, y) = -\sin(4)\sin^{2m}\left(\frac{x^2}{\pi}\right) - \sin(y)\sin^{2m}\left(\frac{2y^2}{\pi}\right)$$

where

Parameter	Value
m	10
(x, y)	$\in [0, 5] \times [0, 5]$

The topography of this function is depicted in Fig. 4−1. This global optimum may be easily identified using CS, and the findings are depicted in Fig. 4−2, where the ultimate nest locations are also noted ⊠ in the figure.

As the globally optimal approach, the graph depicts the majority of nests converging toward it. In the case of multimodal functions, the nests are also spread at various

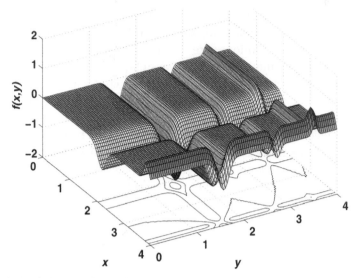

FIGURE 4–1 The landscaped of Michaelwicz's function.

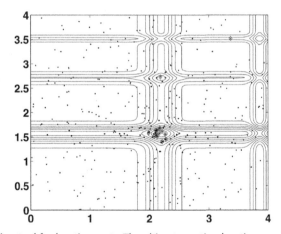

FIGURE 4–2 Cuckoo search is a tool for locating nests. The ultimate nesting locations are highlighted ⊗ in the figure.

optimums. This shows that CS can simultaneously locate all optimum solutions if the number of nests is much more than the optimal local solution. This benefit may become increasingly large when addressing multimodal and multiobjective optimization situations.

4.6 Advanced work

A new CSA based on the Gaussian distribution (GCSA) has recently been proposed. The research finds the best solution in a simple CSA, but everything depends on the random walk. However, the speed and accuracy of convergence cannot be guaranteed. To this end, GCSA was introduced to overcome the low base affinity of CSA. GCSA is used to handle standard test functions and design improvements. The results show that GCSA proves its effectiveness by providing a better solution than traditional CSA. Chandrasekaran and Simon [18] proposed a hybrid algorithm combining CSA and fuzzy systems to solve the generic cell problem. A successful energy system requires a reliable operation, environmental protection, and economic protection. However, these three points contradict each other because fuel prices do not match emission levels and system reliability. The authors use fuzzy group theory to construct a fuzzy membership search domain for all possible solutions. They also use CSA to find optimal solutions in unclear areas of research. The proposed technique begins with a fundamental CSA by initializing a predetermined number of host sockets; each nest includes cuckoo eggs. After each generation, the host nest grows in size. Then Mystery Fitness began searching for the optimal answer, but the host bird's destruction of the alien egg was by no means the optimal solution. Otherwise, the egg will survive to the next generation because of the fitness function. The proposed method is validated compared to a conventional system of single- and multipurpose optimization tasks.

The findings of the suggested method indicate that it outperforms other strategies discussed in the literature. It also can solve common smoothing problems in power systems. A Voronoi Centroid Tessellation (CVT) is a series of Voronoi tessellations, in which Voronoi generators establish a common centroid, all running simultaneously (in parallel). Integrating CSA and CVT has been proposed to improve the base CSA (CSA and CVT). The CVT is a uniformly distributed problem area, and the authors use the CVT as a starting point for the disturbance. Then, the CSA was used to derive the Voronoi score. Experimental results demonstrate the effectiveness, durability, and feasibility of CSA compared to CVT-based CSA.

4.7 Conclusion

This article gives an overview of the CS algorithm and its variants. It provides a quick overview of almost all the vital research we can find on CS (e.g., Google Scholar, Scopus, and Web of Science). Cuckoo hunting is a very hot topic right now, and we look forward to more articles on this topic in the near future. Further theoretical analysis and mathematical proofs are urgently needed to understand the performance, parameter tuning, and control of algorithms such as cuckoo hunting. In addition, there are many unanswered questions about improving cuckoo research, including designing adaptive cuckoo studies, effectively managing parameters, and controlling them for optimal performance. Various practical applications in technology and industry are of great benefit. As we have seen, cuckoo hunting is used in many areas, such as technological improvement and various applications. Additionally, many industries use CS to simplify tasks and improve industrial processes. However, there is still a lot of room for improvement. Based on our research and feedback, we anticipate that further research on cuckoo hunting will be useful in the following areas:

- large-scale global optimization, like in Ref. [35],
- combinatorial optimization, for example, graph coloring [36], scheduling, and traveling salesmen problems,
- hybridization with other algorithms, for example, Krill herd by Gandomi and Alavi [37].

References

[1] J.O. Agushaka, A.E. Ezugwu, O.N. Olaide, O. Akinola, R.A. Zitar, L. Abualigah, Improved dwarf Mongoose optimization for constrained engineering design problems, J. Bionic Eng. (2022). Available from: https://doi.org/10.1007/s42235-022-00316-8. May.

[2] A.H. Gandomi, X.-S. Yang, A.H. Alavi, Cuckoo search algorithm: a metaheuristic approach to solve structural optimization problems, Eng. Comput. 29 (1) (2013) 17−35. Available from: https://doi.org/10.1007/s00366-011-0241-y. Jan.

[3] C.A. Coello, Use of a self-adaptive penalty approach for engineering optimization problems, Comput. Ind. 41 (2) (2000) 113−127. Available from: https://doi.org/10.1016/S0166-3615(99)00046-9. Mar.

[4] A.M. Ikotun, M.S. Almutari, A.E. Ezugwu, K-means-based nature-inspired metaheuristic algorithms for automatic data clustering problems: recent advances and future directions, Appl. Sci. 11 (23) (2021) 11246. Available from: https://doi.org/10.3390/app112311246. Nov.

[5] P. Kim, J. Lee, An integrated method of particle swarm optimization and differential evolution, J. Mech. Sci. Technol. 23 (2) (2009) 426−434. Available from: https://doi.org/10.1007/s12206-008-0917-4. Feb.

[6] M. Hadni, H. Hassane, New model of feature selection based chaotic firefly algorithm for Arabic text categorization, Int. Arab. J. Inf. Technol. 20 (3A) (2023) 461−468.

[7] G. Hu, Y. Zheng, L. Abualigah, A.G. Hussien, DETDO: an adaptive hybrid dandelion optimizer for engineering optimization, Adv. Eng. Inform. 57 (2023) 102004.

[8] D. Izci, S. Ekinci, S. Mirjalili, L. Abualigah, An intelligent tuning scheme with a master/slave approach for efficient control of the automatic voltage regulator, Neural Comput. Appl. (2023) 1−17.

[9] H. Jia, C. Lu, D. Wu, C. Wen, H. Rao, L. Abualigah, An improved reptile search algorithm with ghost opposition-based learning for global optimization problems, J. Comput. Des. Eng. qwad0 (2023) 48.

[10] A.H. Alharbi, A.A. Abdelhamid, A. Ibrahim, S.K. Towfek, N. Khodadadi, L. Abualigah, et al., Improved dipper-throated optimization for forecasting metamaterial design bandwidth for engineering applications, Biomimetics 8 (2) (2023) 241.

[11] S. Nama, A.K. Saha, S. Chakraborty, A.H. Gandomi, L. Abualigah, Boosting particle swarm optimization by backtracking search algorithm for optimization problems, Swarm Evolut. Comput. 79 (2023) 101304.

[12] M. Zare, M. Ghasemi, A. Zahedi, K. Golalipour, S.K. Mohammadi, S. Mirjalili, et al., A global best-guided firefly algorithm for engineering problems, J. Bionic Eng. (2023) 1−30.

[13] D. Wu, C. Wen, H. Rao, H. Jia, Q. Liu, L. Abualigah, Modified reptile search algorithm with multi-hunting coordination strategy for global optimization problems, Math. Biosci. Eng. 20 (6) (2023) 10090−10134.

[14] S. Ekinci, D. Izci, L. Abualigah, R.A. Zitar, A modified oppositional chaotic local search strategy based Aquila optimizer to design an effective controller for vehicle cruise control system, J. Bionic Eng. (2023) 1−24.

[15] L. Abualigah, D. Falcone, A. Forestiero, Swarm intelligence to face IoT challenges, Comput. Intell. Neurosci. (2023) 2023.

[16] J.O. Agushaka, A.E. Ezugwu, L. Abualigah, Dwarf Mongoose optimization algorithm, Comput. Methods Appl. Mech. Eng. (2022) 391. Available from: https://doi.org/10.1016/j.cma.2022.114570. Mar.

[17] B. Webb, Swarm intelligence: from natural to artificial systems, Conn. Sci. 14 (2) (2002) 163−164. Available from: https://doi.org/10.1080/09540090210144948.

[18] C. Blum, A. Roli, Metaheuristics in combinatorial optimization, ACM Comput. Surv. 35 (3) (2003) 268−308. Available from: https://doi.org/10.1145/937503.937505. Sep.

[19] A. Mesa, K. Castromayor, C. Garillos-Manliguez, V. Calag, Cuckoo search via Lévy flights applied to uncapacitated facility location problem, J. Ind. Eng. Int. 14 (3) (2018) 585−592. Available from: https://doi.org/10.1007/s40092-017-0248-0. Sep.

[20] A.S. Joshi, O. Kulkarni, G.M. Kakandikar, V.M. Nandedkar, Cuckoo search optimization—a review, Mater. Today Proc. 4 (8) (2017) 7262−7269. Available from: https://doi.org/10.1016/J. MATPR.2017.07.055. Jan.

[21] X.-S. Yang, & S. Deb, Cuckoo search via Levy flights, in: 2009 World Congress on Nature & Biologically Inspired Computing (NaBIC), 2009, pp. 210−214. Available from: https://doi.org/10.1109/ NABIC.2009.5393690.

[22] X.-S. Yang, S. Deb, S.K. Mishra, Multi-species cuckoo search algorithm for global optimization, Cognit. Comput. 10 (6) (2018) 1085−1095. Available from: https://doi.org/10.1007/s12559-018-9579-4. Dec.

[23] Z. Zhang, S. Ding, W. Jia, A hybrid optimization algorithm based on cuckoo search and differential evolution for solving constrained engineering problems, Eng. Appl. Artif. Intell. 85 (2019) 254−268. Available from: https://doi.org/10.1016/j.engappai.2019.06.017. Oct.

[24] Z. Cheng, et al., Improvement and application of adaptive hybrid cuckoo search algorithm, IEEE Access. 7 (2019) 145489−145515. Available from: https://doi.org/10.1109/ACCESS.2019.2944981.

[25] M. Abdel-Baset, I. Hezam, Cuckoo search and genetic algorithm hybrid schemes for optimization problems, Appl. Math. Inf. Sci. 10 (3) (2016) 1185−1192. Available from: https://doi.org/10.18576/amis/100337. May.

[26] A. Kaveh, S. Talatahari, An improved ant colony optimization for constrained engineering design problems, Eng. Comput. (Swansea, Wales) 27 (1) (2010) 155−182. Available from: https://doi.org/10.1108/ 02644401011008577.

[27] A.M. Reynolds, M.A. Frye, Free-flight odor tracking in drosophila is consistent with an optimal intermittent scale-free search, PLoS One 2 (4) (2007) e354. Available from: https://doi.org/10.1371/journal. pone.0000354. Apr.

[28] M. Shatnawi, & M.F. Nasrudin, Starting configuration of cuckoo search algorithm using Centroidal Voronoi Tessellations, in: 2011 11th International Conference on Hybrid Intelligent Systems (HIS), Dec. 2011, pp. 40−45. Available from: https://doi.org/10.1109/HIS.2011.6122077.

[29] S. Walton, O. Hassan, K. Morgan, Reduced order mesh optimisation using proper orthogonal decomposition and a modified cuckoo search, Int. J. Numer. Methods Eng. 93 (5) (2013) 527−550. Available from: https://doi.org/10.1002/nme.4400. Feb.

[30] H. Zheng, Y. Zhou, A novel cuckoo search optimization algorithm base on gauss distribution, J. Comput. Inf. Syst. 8 (10) (2012) 4193−4200.

[31] M. Mareli, B. Twala, An adaptive cuckoo search algorithm for optimisation, Appl. Comput. Inform. 14 (2) (2018) 107−115. Available from: https://doi.org/10.1016/j.aci.2017.09.001. Jul.

[32] O. Baskan, Determining optimal link capacity expansions in road networks using cuckoo search algorithm with Lévy flights, J. Appl. Math. 2013 (2013) 1−11. Available from: https://doi.org/10.1155/2013/718015.

[33] W. Buaklee, & K. Hongesombut, Optimal DG allocation in a smart distribution grid using cuckoo search algorithm, in: 2013 10th International Conference on Electrical Engineering/Electronics, Computer, Telecommunications and Information Technology, May 2013, pp. 1−6. Available from: https://doi.org/ 10.1109/ECTICon.2013.6559624.

[34] S.Q. Ye, F.L. Wang, K.Q. Zhou, A modified cuckoo search algorithm and its applications in function optimization, J. Phys. Conf. Ser. 2129 (1) (2021) 012025. Available from: https://doi.org/10.1088/1742-6596/ 2129/1/012025. Dec.

[35] I. Fister, I.J. Fister, & J.B. Zumer, Memetic artificial bee colony algorithm for large-scale global optimization, in: 2012 IEEE Congress on Evolutionary Computation, June 2012, pp. 1−8. Available from: https://doi.org/ 10.1109/CEC.2012.6252938.

[36] I. Fister, X.S. Yang, J. Brest, D. Fister, A brief review of nature-inspired algorithms for optimization, Elektroteh. Vestnik/Electrotechnical Rev. 80 (3) (2013) 116−122.

[37] A.H. Gandomi, A.H. Alavi, Krill herd: a new bio-inspired optimization algorithm, Commun. Nonlin. Sci. Numer. Simul. 17 (12) (2012) 4831−4845. Available from: https://doi.org/10.1016/j.cnsns.2012.05.010. Dec.

Teaching–learning-based optimization algorithm: analysis study and its application

Laith Abualigah[1,2,3,4,5,6,7], Eman Abu-Dalhoum[8], Abiodun M. Ikotun[8], Raed Abu Zitar[9], Anas Ratib Alsoud[2], Nima Khodadadi[10], Absalom E. Ezugwu[11], Essam Said Hanandeh[12], Heming Jia[13]

[1]ARTIFICIAL INTELLIGENCE AND SENSING TECHNOLOGIES (AIST) RESEARCH CENTER, UNIVERSITY OF TABUK, TABUK, SAUDI ARABIA [2]HOURANI CENTER FOR APPLIED SCIENTIFIC RESEARCH, AL-AHLIYYA AMMAN UNIVERSITY, AMMAN, JORDAN [3]MEU RESEARCH UNIT, MIDDLE EAST UNIVERSITY, AMMAN, JORDAN [4]SCHOOL OF COMPUTER SCIENCES, UNIVERSITI SAINS MALAYSIA, PULAU PINANG, MALAYSIA [5]SCHOOL OF ENGINEERING AND TECHNOLOGY, SUNWAY UNIVERSITY MALAYSIA, PETALING JAYA, MALAYSIA [6]DEPARTMENT OF ELECTRICAL AND COMPUTER ENGINEERING, LEBANESE AMERICAN UNIVERSITY, BYBLOS, LEBANON [7]COMPUTER SCIENCE DEPARTMENT, AL AL-BAYT UNIVERSITY, MAFRAQ, JORDAN [8]UNIVERSITY OF KWAZULU-NATAL, PIETERMARITZBURG CAMPUS, POTCHEFSTROOM, SOUTH AFRICA [9]SORBONNE CENTER OF ARTIFICIAL INTELLIGENCE, SORBONNE UNIVERSITY-ABU DHABI, ABU DHABI, UNITED ARAB EMIRATES [10]DEPARTMENT OF CIVIL, ARCHITECTURAL AND ENVIRONMENTAL ENGINEERING, UNIVERSITY OF MIAMI, CORAL GABLES, FL, UNITED STATES [11]UNIT FOR DATA SCIENCE AND COMPUTING, NORTH-WEST UNIVERSITY, POTCHEFSTROOM, SOUTH AFRICA [12]DEPARTMENT OF COMPUTER INFORMATION SYSTEM, ZARQA UNIVERSITY, ZARQA, JORDAN [13]DEPARTMENT OF INFORMATION ENGINEERING, SANMING UNIVERSITY, FUJIAN, P.R. CHINA

5.1 Introduction

In general, the optimization issue can be defined as the issue of selecting the optimum solution from a variety of solutions, given constraints that define which solutions are viable, and a goal function that determines which of the feasible solutions is the best. Optimization seeks for the optimal solution among a population of solutions and are commonly found in manufacturing, science, ecology, and businesses problems [1].

Constrained and unconstrained optimization problems are commonly associated with many issues, such as multimodality, differentiability, and high-dimensionality. Traditional

Metaheuristic Optimization Algorithms. DOI: https://doi.org/10.1016/B978-0-443-13925-3.00016-9

optimization techniques, especially with nonlinear objective functions, frequently fail to address such problems. To solve these challenges, more powerful optimization techniques are needed. Accordingly, various effective nature-inspired metaheuristic optimization strategies have been suggested to fix many of the difficult optimization problems including butterfly optimization algorithm [2], particle swarm optimization (PSO) [3], Krill Herd approach [4], social spider optimization [5], artificial bee colony [6], dwarf mongoose optimization [7], prairie dog optimization [8], ebola search optimization [9], gazelle optimization [100], and teaching—learning-based optimization [11]. Further research is ongoing to find more effective optimization approaches in many scientific applications.

The TLBO algorithm was proposed as one of the latest heuristic optimization strategies in ref [12] with some special characteristics, like reduced computational endeavor, higher uniformity, and fewer variables. The working principle of TLBO is derived from a classroom's natural teaching—learning process. According to this approach, students gain knowledge both from teachers and the interaction between them. When compared to other heuristic algorithms, the TLBO is straightforward and easy to construct and implement. Furthermore, the TLBO method has fewer parameters, excellent accuracy, fast convergence, and good resistance to optimization difficulties. Because of this, TLBO had received much attention from researchers and scientists in the last few years. The TLBO algorithm has not only been considerably enhanced, but it is now widely employed in a variety of applications areas. TLBO was first developed for the mechanical design difficulties, but later its applications are observed in a wide range of scientific, engineer sectors, manufacturing processes, and also systems that have a huge number of parameters.

Normally, optimization methods can be used to deal with many problems in the sciences [39—48]. The major objectives of this chapter are to provide an introduction to the TLBO algorithm, show how it works, describe the implementation procedures of the algorithm, and summarize several previous studies that used the TLBO algorithm as well as its results in different fields.

The chapter is divided into five sections as follows: Section 5.1 gives a brief introduction about the TLBO algorithm, while Section 5.2 presents the structure and the phases of the TLBO algorithm. Section 5.3 summarizes the relevant research that has been done by many researchers in order to strengthen the algorithm, with the description of the algorithm's ability to address various optimization problems presented in Section 5.4. Section 5.5 concludes the chapter.

5.2 Teaching—learning-based optimization

As we mentioned earlier, the TLBO algorithm is based on the classroom teaching—learning process. The algorithm consists of two elements, learners and teacher, where the learners are the potential answers to the issue and then optimal solution is chosen as a new teacher. In each iteration, the population size refers to the number of learners, and the subjects that the learners study indicate the design features or parameters of the problem. The learner's understanding of that particular subject is said to be the value of the parameters.

The algorithm's objective is to improve the learners' knowledge and, as a result, improve the worth of the arguments to reach the optimal solution.

The TLBO procedure is split into two sections: "Teacher section" where the learners learn from the teacher and "Learner section" where the learners learn by the interaction between them. First and foremost is the randomly created population. Suppose the population size is represented by p (i.e., $P = 1, 2, 3, \ldots, n$), and t is the number of topics (i.e., $T = 1, 2, 3, \ldots, m$), the mean for the jth topic is calculated during any iteration and is indicated as Mi,j. XpBest$_i$ represents the teacher for each iteration. The mean and the teacher change at the start of each iteration.

5.2.1 Teacher section

During this section, students learn from their teacher; the most well-informed person in the group is the teacher who works hard to bring students up to his or her level. Assume that at any iteration, Mi represents the average of the grades, and the teacher Ti who will work hard to get the average to its proper level. In this step, learners will refresh their information using Eq. (5–1):

$$X_{\text{new},i} = X_{\text{old},i} + r_i \, (T_i - T_f M_i) \tag{5-1}$$

where old X_i represents the grade of the ith learner before updating, and new X_i represents the grade after the learning. E_i represents the education indicator that governs the change in average, and r_i is a set of uniform random values ranging from 0 to 1.

5.2.2 Learner section

At this section, learners expand their information by working together to study. They interact randomly with each other, through discussions, presentations, and lectures, which can help the learners to enhance their information that they get from someone who has a greater expertise and experience. The following Eq. (5–2) describes the learner's modification process:

Choose two learners X_i, X_j randomly where $i \neq j$ from any random iteration:

$$X_{\text{new},i} = \begin{cases} X_{\text{old},i} + r_i & (X_i - X_j) \quad \text{if} \quad (X_i) < (X_j) \\ X_{\text{old},i} + r_i & (X_j - X_i) \quad \text{if} \quad (X_i) > (X_j) \end{cases} \tag{5-2}$$

5.3 Literature review

This section of the chapter presents some related work on the TLBO algorithm, the hybrid methods using TLBO, and some applications that are based on the algorithm. Table 5–1 shows a summary of the related work.

Table 5–1 Summary about teaching–learning-based optimization application.

No	Year	References	Method name	Contribution
1	2020	8	TLNNA	A new model called TLNNA is suggested to solve four complex engineering issues
2	2020	9	TLBO	Adaptive algorithm using TLBO using to solve global optimization problems
3	2013	10	I-TLBO	Improved the TLBO algorithm into I-TLBO for solving linear, nonlinear, and multidimensional issues
4	2016	11	ITLBO	Proposed ITLBO algorithm as a new version of basic TLBO
5	2019	16	TLBO	Using the TLBO strategy to solve the ELD issue for a network with six power plant units
6	2020	17	TLBO	Use of TLBO to minimize the cost of an excellent design of a PV system connected to the grid.
7	2018	18	TLBO	Using the teaching learning-based optimization TLBO to enhance the pair-wise comparative matrix consistency in the AHP using TLBO
8	2014	19	DGSTLBO	An improved TLBO approach called DGSTLBO based on DGS
9	2019	23	FFWNN	Employed TLBO to solve the classification issue of five medical datasets
10	2018	25	FSBTLBO	The development of an algorithm FS-BTLBO using TLBO to solve the problem of data analysis and classification
11	2017	24	TLBO	Using the TLBO approach for solving brain problems in MRI by screening based on the segmentation concept of disease assessment
12	2016	12	ETLBO	ETLBO is a hybrid method (ETLBO-K-means) to solve data clustering problem
13	2019	27	TLBO-ELM	A hybrid model based on the TLBO approach and ELM to solve the issue of classification data
14	2016	28	Ms-TLBO	Modified a new approach, Ms-TLBO, based on TLBO to enhance the capacity of exploitation and exploration
15	2016	29	TLBO	Introduced SBO for shape and size optimization issues by rate limitations
16	2018	30	SVM–TLBO	A hybrid model called SVM–TLBO for analyzing and predicting financial time-series data to improve investment decisions
17	2021	13	LebTLBO	LebTLBO is an improvement, which used in many engineering and science applications
18	2021	14	MTLBO	MTLBO is a modified algorithm developed to lower the NOx emissions concentration of a circulation fluidized bed boiler
19	2022	15	RLTLBO	RLTLBO is an enhanced TLBO algorithm, which is used to solve optimization issues
20	2021	20	BTLBO	BTLBO is a BTLBO algorithm, which used a weighted mean rather of a mean value to maintain diversification
21	2021	21	HTLBO	HTLBO is a HTLBO, which makes use of the strengthening of TLBO algorithm's exploitation and exploration skills
22	2021	22	WOA-TLBO	WOA-TLBO is a new hybrid algorithm based on a TLBO and WOA that is used in global search
23	2021	31	TLBO-Color	TLBO-color has been developed to solve the GCP using the fewest colors possible
24	2022	26	ETLBO	ETLBO an algorithm extracted from the TLBO approach that used to solve complex problems

5.3.1 Optimization problem

Zhang, Jin, and Chen [13] proposed a new hybrid method called TLNNA which is based on TLBO and neural network algorithm (NNA) to solve some difficult engineering optimization issues. The new method examines 30 popular benchmarks and has successfully resolved four complex engineering issues. The outcomes of TLNNA were compared with other algorithms like SSA, SCA, PSO, and whale optimization algorithm (WOA), which showed that the proposed method of TLNNA is capable of achieving the best solutions for all the problems. The results of these comparatives showed that TLNNA does not have excellent global searching capability of the NNA, but it has the quick converging time of the TLBO, and it is more effective in conditions of solution characteristic and computing effectiveness for most test cases.

This research offers solution for global optimization problems (constant or discrete) by an adaptive approach built on an improved TLBO, which works by generating a scattered population to increase the characteristic for the current population. This was confirmed by the efficiency of the suggested approach when tested on gene expression datasets and three classifications. Because of the high costs of computational experiments required to discover error rates, which need a long time to discover, the application employed metaheuristic algorithms to solve such problems. This experiment recorded the highest accuracy rate of 100% [14].

Rao and Patel [15] improved the TLBO algorithm by proposing I-TLBO. In this research, the exploring and utilization capabilities of the TLBO algorithm are enhanced by showing the conception about the number of teachers, education worker, seminar learning, and learning on its own. The I-TLBO performance was evaluated by executing it on many unrestricted benchmark problems, which have special features. To validate the results of using the I-TLBO algorithm, it was compared with the standard TLBO algorithm and some other existing algorithms used for optimization in other papers.

The ITLBO algorithm was proposed in ref [16] as a new edition of basic TLBO, with the feedback phase added to improve the students' learning methods and the TLBO's exploration potential. The ITLBO algorithm's performance was assessed using 10 traditional unrestricted benchmark functions ranging from lower to higher dimensional distance. The outcomes of the tests show that ITLBO bypassed the rest of algorithms considered from the literature. To test the ITLBO algorithm's performance in addressing real constrained engineering issues, five popular engineering optimization problems were chosen; the proposed ITLBO algorithm outperforms other algorithms in terms of robustness, effectiveness, and high standard of quality based on the experimental results and comparisons.

A unique evolutionary algorithm called ETLBO extracted from the TLBO approach with a big capabilities in solving complex problems to improve the design of space frame in real-size structures was proposed [17]. Although there are other ways in the literature, the ETLBO approach can be used to create a wide space framework due to its high speed and accuracy. The results reveal that the TLBO algorithm is superior to other algorithms in solving the problem and outperformed them in the majority of cases. So, using a machine learning technique and combination operators, an attempt was made to improve the algorithm. In the instructor phase, an algorithm enhancement is created by adding a junction operation among the new solutions and the best solution. This adjustment leads the algorithm to move abruptly and escape from its local minima. Convergence speed and ideal response quality also increased as a result of the new algorithm. Finally, several new practical cases have been optimized using this technique.

Learning enthusiasm based on TLBO in the teaching—learning approach LebTLBO [18] is recently used in many engineering and science applications. In LebTLBO, most of the learners can get the same opportunity to obtain the knowledge from others as with the original TLBO. The paper focused on making use of the TLBO algorithm and improving the performance algorithm to achieve the enhanced performance by balancing the exploitation with exploration abilities. The algorithm was examined and assessed on CEC2019 benchmark functions, and the results show that the LebTLBO offers promising results over other algorithms, and it has opportunities in real-world problems like wireless sensor networks.

A modified TLBO (MTLBO) algorithm is developed to lower the NO_x emissions concentration of a circulation fluidized bed boiler [19]. The MTLBO is also divided into two stages: teaching and learning. In the teaching stage, all students are divided into two sections depending on the class's mean marks, and each section offers a distinct solution update strategy, and in the learning stage, all students were also divided into two sections with the top half of the students in the first group and the other students in the second. In addition, the two organizations have different methodologies for updating their solutions. The proposed MTLBO algorithm's performance was tested on 14 unconstrained numerical functions. The results revealed that the MTLBO has superior solution quality and faster convergence speed when compared to TLBO and other state-of-the-art optimization techniques. The MTLBO is an excellent method for lowering NOx emissions, according to experimental results.

A research proposed an enhanced TLBO algorithm named RLTLBO to solve optimization issues [20]. This approach came in two steps: the first one is based on the effect of what the teacher gives, where the second is based on the Q-learning approach in reinforced learning (RL), which is created to switch the mechanism among the learning ways in the learner stage. These two steps successfully increase the accuracy and convergence speed of the new algorithm. RLTLBO is examined on eight CEC2017 test functions and 23 standard benchmark functions to check the optimization efficiency. The outcomes show that the new algorithm offers efficient and powerful performance in solving benchmark test functions, and it has the ability of solving eight manufacturing engineering design problems. Comparing it to the original TLBO and seven state-of-the-art algorithms, it demonstrated high performance ability in dealing with real-world optimization issues.

5.3.2 Technoeconomic analysis

The TLBO technique is employed to solve some specific economic issue-like load dispatch (ELD), which is discussed in ref [21]. To assess the suggested method's performance, the authors investigate the ELD on a network that has six power station units. The outcomes of the simulation are done by comparing them with some other algorithms such as EMA, GA, PSO, and SA. So the outcomes show that the approach of the TLBO achieves greater computational ability and effectiveness than other optimization methods, which had a stronger ability to generate global solution.

An improved algorithm using TLBO was proposed to reduce the cost of an excellent design of a photovoltaic (PV) system connected to the grid [22]. This paper shows how using spare (PV) batteries systems may minimize electricity cost. In comparison with other optimization algorithms such as GA and PSO, the outcomes show that the batteries connected to the network are more efficient. This confirm that the proposed algorithm displays high accuracy.

5.3.3 Analytical process

Borkar and Sarode aimed to enhance the pair-wise comparative matrix consistency in the analytic hierarchical order approach (AHP) using the TLBO approach [23]. The goal of this paper is to reduce the consistency ratio to 0 and maintain the value of pair-wise comparative matrix. Consistency assessment on the pair-wise comparison matrix by the AHP system is examined carefully using TLBO, but these methods are very complex and not easy. This approach has been applied on two true situations, which are selection of the product design and selection of the material. The experiment shows that this method is very effective and proved to be of high precision in meeting the AHP problem of consistency.

5.3.4 Global optimization

For global optimization problems, Zou et al. [24] suggested an improved TLBO approach based on the dynamic group scheme (DGS) called DGSTLBO. In this study, unlike the original TLBO, the DGSTLBO approach allows the learner in the teacher stage base its learning on the correspondent group instead of learning based on the classroom. In this study, the algorithm was tested on 18 benchmarks using different dimensions 10, 30, and 50 to assess the efficiency and the cost of the suggested approach. The outcomes suggest that the proposed DGSTLBO approach is a good solution to solve global optimization issues. DGSTLBO uses regional knowledge more effectively, resulting in better quality solutions.

Taheri et al. [25] proposed a balanced TLBO (BTLBO) algorithm based on TLBO, which came in four stages: teacher stage, which uses a weighted mean instead of a mean value to maintain diversification; learner stage, which is like the original TLBO algorithm; tutoring stage, which is based on founding the optimal solutions; and restarting stage, which exchanges nonworking learners randomly with new learners. The BTLBO algorithm proves its efficiency with sufficient balancing among exploitation and exploration abilities.

The evolutionary computing is a fascinating subfield of the soft computing. A lot of progressing approaches based on Darwinian natural selection principles have been created based on the EC cover, which can deliver many optimal solutions in one simulation. One of the most recently developed EA is the TLBO to solve global optimization search problems.

Mashwani et al. [26] produced a hybrid TLBO (HTLBO) based on the strengthening of TLBO algorithm's exploitation and exploration skills. The efficiency of the proposed HTLBO algorithm was evaluated on freshly constructed benchmark functions. In terms of proximity and diversity, the suggested algorithm outperforms some well-known evolutionary algorithms.

Vijaya Lakshmi and Mohanaiah [27] proposed a new hybrid algorithm based on a TLBO algorithm and the WOA. The WOA is inspired by the whale hunting characterized with a high global search ability, but it has a slow rate so it is difficult to apply it in the real problems. Combining it with the features of TLBO, the new algorithm proves itself in solving global optimization issues. In facial expression research, a majority of typical techniques which are based on the motions of sections of the human face fail to distinguish expressions accurately as expressions. This research presents FER's productive process using the WOA-TLBO-based multisupport vector neural network. In terms of accuracy, the investigational outcomes provide an indication of the enhancement of the recommended technique resolutions.

5.3.5 Medical disease diagnosis

A new classification technology called FFWNN has been suggested to improve a new hybrid method using the TLBO approach with fuzzy wavelet neural network strategy (FWNN) and functional link neural network [28]. This method is applied on five datasets, which are related to some important illness like breast diseases, heart illness, liver disease, Indian diabetes (pima), and appendicitis. The test results prove that the efficacy of the new hybrid approach is 98.309%, 91.1%, 91.39%, 88.67%, and 93.51% in precision for the datasets after 30 epochs for all the dataset with less computing complication. It shows that the new method shows effective performance compared with the other methods mentioned in other papers.

Rajinikanth et al. [29] proposed a new TLBO-based approach to solve brain problems in magnetic resonance imaging (MRI), in which this approach works for MRI tumor detection while integrating education-based learning and other factors demonstrated by screening based on the segmentation concept of disease assessment. The efficiency of the algorithm was tested using two types of datasets, BRAINIX, CEREBRIX, and BRATS, and it achieved good results for accuracy, efficiency and privacy indicators.

5.3.6 Data clustering

Allam and Nandhini [30] took advantage of some of the features of improved algorithms to solve the problem of data analysis and classification. Since most algorithms that use parameters have difficulty controlling the value of the parameter and thus finding it difficult to reach an optimal solution, this paper proposed an algorithm (FS-BTLBO) using TLBO, which only needs a set of specific values such as population and specific classifications to evaluate the system in terms of efficiency. The results of the research found that the new algorithm produced the most accurate results on the lowest number of features and was able to detect certain diseases such as cancers.

An attempt [31] was made to cluster data using a lately discovered metaheuristic model, which is dependent on population known as elitist using TLBO called ETLBO to solve the data clustering issue [32], by combining it with the K-means method. The experiments are examined on typical real-life and specific synthetic datasets; the suggested method's efficiency was compared with other techniques like PSO, IPSO, and GA. The suggested method's effectiveness and efficiency are demonstrated through simulation and comparative findings. Other combinations of TLBO with K-means algorithm can be found in ref [33].

To solve the issue of classification of data, Sevinç and Dökeroğlu [34] suggested a hybrid model based on the TLBO approach and extreme learning machines (ELM) that proposed a new improved approach (TLBO-ELM). To test the proposed algorithm, UCI datasets were used. For both multiclass and binary data classification issues, the efficiency of TLBO-ELM was found to be competitive. For the ELM, the TLBO-ELM employs (near-) optimal parameter settings.

5.3.7 Shape and size optimization

Tejani et al. [35] proposed a new modified approach (Ms-TLBO) based on TLBO to enhance the capacity of exploitation and exploration depending on the total number of teachers, adapted teaching element, learning based on tutoring, and learning based on their own through the TLBO approach. However, this research had many issues because of the increased parameters, and sometimes, it leads to different results. Nevertheless, the outcomes show that the modified approach is more efficient than the other TLBO-based algorithms.

For shape and size optimization issues by rate limitations, a new metaheuristic technique is proposed in ref [36]. A MTLBO is used in a collaborating frame in this study, and a high level of TLBO approach dubbed school-based optimization (SBO) is introduced. SBO is presented as a school that has numerous independence classes and different schoolteachers, as well as class cooperation and teacher reassignment based on fitness. TLBO's exploration and exploitation capabilities are considerably improved by SBO without increasing the complexity of the algorithms. Five benchmark optimization issues by rate limitations are solved using the SBO technique. The efficacy of the suggested SBO algorithm is demonstrated by the high quality and consistency of the findings.

5.3.8 Investment decisions

In [37], the authors designed a model that combined support vector machine (SVM) and TLBO in a hybrid model named SVM–TLBO for analyzing and predicting financial time-series data to improve investment decisions. The TLBO is a tool that may be used to find the best characteristics for an SVM retrogression model. The author tested the hybrid model viability and efficiency by projecting the close prices of COMDEX commodities future tense index, which is traded in India by Multi Commodity Exchange.

5.3.9 Large graph coloring problems

A new algorithm named TLBO-Color is proposed in ref [38] to solve the graph coloring problem (GCP) using the fewest colors possible when the academics are still working on solving this critical NP hard problem for huge figures at a considerably faster rate and with better results. Because of its algorithm-specific parameter-less concept and great performance, the TLBO algorithm has piqued the interest of numerous researchers. For painting 43 benchmark figures with a huge number of vertices and edging, a modular parallel version of TLBO-Color is also being created, which has very fast optimization times, and the perfect outcomes with 33 of the figures, and the outcomes with a few extra colors are presented. In comparison to the top solutions, there are only 1.77% more colors on average. The collected results show that the suggested approach is competitive with the existing latest techniques.

5.4 Discussion and future works

With reference to the wide range of studies carried out on TLBO, we found that the TLBO algorithm is universally acceptable for various purposes and that the method has garnered attention from researchers all over the world. Moreover, the large amount of variables and the dynamic group of applications demonstrate where the TLBO proves itself with a strong potential for solving optimization problems and other issues. Many authors have helped to enhance the TLBO performance. Even though the algorithm has proved to be really effective, there is still space between the most advanced TLBO algorithm and consumers' hopes, which indicates that the TLBO method still needs more studies for some optimization issues. This provides a wide area for future research such as reducing the TLBO algorithm complexity and settings of phases as well as usage in increasingly difficult optimization situations.

5.5 Conclusion

The major objectives of this survey are to provide an overview of the TLBO algorithm, show how it works, describe the implementation procedures of the TLBO algorithm, and summarize several previous studies that used the TLBO and their results in various application areas such as engineering, electrical engineering, technology and science, mechanical design, artificial intelligence, classification problem, healthcare, and economics. A simple systematic approach was used for the past 5 years to survey the TLBO algorithm successful research. Moreover, the TLBO algorithm structure was described, and the application of TLBO and the enhanced TLBO was examined and discussed in various listed areas.

References

[1] J.O. Agushaka, A.E. Ezugwu, O.N. Olaide, O. Akinola, R.A. Zitar, L. Abualigah, Improved dwarf Mongoose optimization for constrained engineering design problems, J. Bionic Eng. (2022). Available from: https://doi.org/10.1007/s42235-022-00316-8. May.

[2] S. Arora, S. Singh, Butterfly optimization algorithm: a novel approach for global optimization, Soft Comput 23 (3) (2019) 715–734. Available from: https://doi.org/10.1007/s00500-018-3102-4.

[3] F. Marini, B. Walczak, Particle swarm optimization (PSO). A tutorial, Chemom. Intell. Lab. Syst. 149 (2015) 153–165. Available from: https://doi.org/10.1016/j.chemolab.2015.08.020. Dec.

[4] G.-G. Wang, A.H. Gandomi, A.H. Alavi, Stud krill herd algorithm, Neurocomputing 128 (2014) 363−370. Available from: https://doi.org/10.1016/j.neucom.2013.08.031. Mar.

[5] A. Luque-Chang, E. Cuevas, F. Fausto, D. Zaldívar, M. Pérez, Social spider optimization algorithm: modifications, applications, and perspectives, Math. Probl. Eng. 2018 (2018) 1−29. Available from: https://doi.org/10.1155/2018/6843923. Dec.

[6] D. Karaboga, B. Gorkemli, C. Ozturk, N. Karaboga, A comprehensive survey: artificial bee colony (ABC) algorithm and applications, Artif. Intell. Rev. 42 (1) (2014) 21−57. Available from: https://doi.org/10.1007/s10462-012-9328-0.

[7] J.O. Agushaka, A.E. Ezugwu, L. Abualigah, Dwarf Mongoose optimization algorithm, Comput. Methods Appl. Mech. Eng. 391 (2022). Available from: https://doi.org/10.1016/j.cma.2022.114570. Mar.

[8] A.E. Ezugwu, J.O. Agushaka, L. Abualigah, S. Mirjalili, A.H. Gandomi, Prairie Dog optimization algorithm, Neural Comput. Appl. 34 (22) (2022) 20017−20065. Available from: https://doi.org/10.1007/s00521-022-07530-9.

[9] O.N. Oyelade, A.E.-S. Ezugwu, T.I.A. Mohamed, L. Abualigah, Ebola optimization search algorithm: a new nature-inspired metaheuristic optimization algorithm, IEEE Access. 10 (2022) 16150−16177. Available from: https://doi.org/10.1109/ACCESS.2022.3147821.

[10] J.O. Agushaka, A.E. Ezugwu, L. Abualigah, Gazelle optimization algorithm: a novel nature-inspired metaheuristic optimizer, Neural Comput. Appl. 35 (5) (2023) 4099−4131. Available from: https://doi.org/10.1007/s00521-022-07854-6.

[11] R. Venkata Rao, Review of applications of TLBO algorithm and a tutorial for beginners to solve the unconstrained and constrained optimization problems, Decis. Sci. Lett. (2016) 1−30. Available from: https://doi.org/10.5267/j.dsl.2015.9.003.

[12] R.V. Rao, V.J. Savsani, D.P. Vakharia, Teaching−learning-based optimization: a novel method for constrained mechanical design optimization problems, Comput. Des 43 (3) (2011) 303−315. Available from: https://doi.org/10.1016/j.cad.2010.12.015.

[13] Y. Zhang, Z. Jin, Y. Chen, Hybrid teaching−learning-based optimization and neural network algorithm for engineering design optimization problems, ” Knowl. Syst 187 (2020) 104836. Available from: https://doi.org/10.1016/j.knosys.2019.07.007. Jan.

[14] A.K. Shukla, P. Singh, M. Vardhan, An adaptive inertia weight teaching-learning-based optimization algorithm and its applications, Appl. Math. Model. 77 (2020) 309−326. Available from: https://doi.org/10.1016/j.apm.2019.07.046. Jan.

[15] R.V. Rao, V. Patel, An improved teaching-learning-based optimization algorithm for solving unconstrained optimization problems, Sci. Iran. (2012). Available from: https://doi.org/10.1016/j.scient.2012.12.005. Dec.

[16] K. Yu, X. Wang, Z. Wang, An improved teaching-learning-based optimization algorithm for numerical and engineering optimization problems, J. Intell. Manuf. 27 (4) (2016) 831−843. Available from: https://doi.org/10.1007/s10845-014-0918-3.

[17] D.P. Kanungo, J. Nayak, B. Naik, H.S. Behera, Hybrid clustering using elitist teaching learning-based optimization, Int. J. Rough. Sets Data Anal. 3 (1) (2016) 1−19. Available from: https://doi.org/10.4018/IJRSDA.2016010101.

[18] N. Mittal, A. Garg, P. Singh, S. Singh, H. Singh, Improvement in learning enthusiasm-based TLBO algorithm with enhanced exploration and exploitation properties, Nat. Comput. 20 (3) (2021) 577−609. Available from: https://doi.org/10.1007/s11047-020-09811-5.

[19] Y. Ma, X. Zhang, J. Song, L. Chen, A modified teaching−learning-based optimization algorithm for solving optimization problem, ” Knowl. Syst 212 (2021) 106599. Available from: https://doi.org/10.1016/j.knosys.2020.106599. Jan.

[20] D. Wu, S. Wang, Q. Liu, L. Abualigah, H. Jia, An improved teaching-learning-based optimization algorithm with reinforcement learning strategy for solving optimization problems, Comput. Intell. Neurosci. 2022 (2022) 1−24. Available from: https://doi.org/10.1155/2022/1535957. Mar.

[21] R. Ghanizadeh, S.M. Hojber kalali, & H. Farshi, Teaching−learning-based optimization for economic load dispatch, in: 2019 5th Conference on Knowledge Based Engineering and Innovation (KBEI), February 2019, pp. 851−856. Available from: https://doi.org/10.1109/KBEI.2019.8734963.

[22] M. Najafi Ashtiani, A. Toopshekan, F. Razi Astaraei, H. Yousefi, A. Maleki, Techno-economic analysis of a grid-connected PV/battery system using the teaching-learning-based optimization algorithm, Sol. Energy 203 (2020) 69−82. Available from: https://doi.org/10.1016/j.solener.2020.04.007. Jun.

[23] P. Borkar, M.V. Sarode, Modality of teaching learning based optimization algorithm to reduce the consistency ratio of the pair-wise comparison matrix in analytical hierarchy processing, Evol. Syst. 9 (2) (2018) 169−180. Available from: https://doi.org/10.1007/s12530-017-9185-9.

[24] F. Zou, L. Wang, X. Hei, D. Chen, D. Yang, Teaching−learning-based optimization with dynamic group strategy for global optimization, Inf. Sci. (Ny). 273 (2014) 112−131. Available from: https://doi.org/10.1016/j.ins.2014.03.038. Jul.

[25] A. Taheri, K. RahimiZadeh, R.V. Rao, An efficient balanced teaching-learning-based optimization algorithm with individual restarting strategy for solving global optimization problems, Inf. Sci. (Ny). 576 (2021) 68−104. Available from: https://doi.org/10.1016/j.ins.2021.06.064. Oct.

[26] W.K. Mashwani, H. Shah, M. Kaur, M.A. Bakar, M. Miftahuddin, Large-scale bound constrained optimization based on hybrid teaching learning optimization algorithm, Alex. Eng. J. 60 (6) (2021) 6013−6033. Available from: https://doi.org/10.1016/j.aej.2021.04.002.

[27] A. Vijaya Lakshmi, P. Mohanaiah, WOA-TLBO: whale optimization algorithm with teaching-learning-based optimization for global optimization and facial emotion recognition, Appl. Soft Comput. 110 (2021) 107623. Available from: https://doi.org/10.1016/j.asoc.2021.107623. Oct.

[28] J.S. Majeed Alneamy, Z. A. Hameed Alnaish, S.Z. Mohd Hashim, R.A. Hamed Alnaish, Utilizing hybrid functional fuzzy wavelet neural networks with a teaching learning-based optimization algorithm for medical disease diagnosis, Comput. Biol. Med. 112 (2019) 103348. Available from: https://doi.org/10.1016/j.compbiomed.2019.103348. Sep.

[29] V. Rajinikanth, S.C. Satapathy, S.L. Fernandes, S. Nachiappan, Entropy based segmentation of tumor from brain MR images − a study with teaching learning based optimization, Pattern Recognit. Lett. 94 (2017) 87−95. Available from: https://doi.org/10.1016/j.patrec.2017.05.028. Jul.

[30] M. Allam, M. Nandhini, Optimal feature selection using binary teaching learning based optimization algorithm, J. King Saud. Univ. - Comput. Inf. Sci 34 (2) (2022) 329−341. Available from: https://doi.org/10.1016/j.jksuci.2018.12.001.

[31] M.S. Es-Haghi, A. Salehi, A. Strauss, Enhanced teacher-learning based algorithm in real size structural optimization, J. Civ. Eng. Manag 28 (4) (2022) 292−304. Available from: https://doi.org/10.3846/jcem.2022.16387.

[32] A.E. Ezugwu, et al., A comprehensive survey of clustering algorithms: state-of-the-art machine learning applications, taxonomy, challenges, and future research prospects, Eng. Appl. Artif. Intell. 110 (2022) 104743. Available from: https://doi.org/10.1016/j.engappai.2022.104743. Apr.

[33] A.M. Ikotun, M.S. Almutari, A.E. Ezugwu, K-means-based nature-inspired metaheuristic algorithms for automatic data clustering problems: recent advances and future directions, Appl. Sci. 11 (23) (2021) 11246. Available from: https://doi.org/10.3390/app112311246.

[34] E. Sevinç, T. Dökeroğlu, A novel hybrid teaching-learning-based optimization algorithm for the classification of data by using extreme learning machines, Turkish J. Electr. Eng. Comput. Sci. (2019) 1523−1533. Available from: 10.3906/elk-1802-40.

[35] G.G. Tejani, V.J. Savsani, V.K. Patel, Modified sub-population teaching-learning-based optimization for design of truss structures with natural frequency constraints, Mech. Based Des. Struct. Mach. 44 (4) (2016) 495−513. Available from: https://doi.org/10.1080/15397734.2015.1124023.

[36] M. Farshchin, C.V. Camp, M. Maniat, Optimal design of truss structures for size and shape with frequency constraints using a collaborative optimization strategy, Expert. Syst. Appl. 66 (2016) 203−218. Available from: https://doi.org/10.1016/j.eswa.2016.09.012. Dec.

[37] S.P. Das, S. Padhy, A novel hybrid model using teaching—learning-based optimization and a support vector machine for commodity futures index forecasting, Int. J. Mach. Learn. Cybern. 9 (1) (2018) 97—111. Available from: https://doi.org/10.1007/s13042-015-0359-0.

[38] T. Dokeroglu, E. Sevinc, Memetic teaching—learning-based optimization algorithms for large graph coloring problems, Eng. Appl. Artif. Intell. 102 (2021) 104282. Available from: https://doi.org/10.1016/j.engappai.2021.104282. Jun.

[39] L. Abualigah, A. Diabat, C.L. Thanh, S. Khatir, Opposition-based Laplacian distribution with Prairie Dog optimization method for industrial engineering design problems, Computer Methods Appl. Mech. Eng. 414 (2023) 116097.

[40] G. Hu, Y. Zheng, L. Abualigah, A.G. Hussien, DETDO: an adaptive hybrid dandelion optimizer for engineering optimization, Adv. Eng. Inform. 57 (2023) 102004.

[41] D. Izci, S. Ekinci, S. Mirjalili, L. Abualigah, An intelligent tuning scheme with a master/slave approach for efficient control of the automatic voltage regulator, Neural Comput. Appl. (2023) 1—17.

[42] H. Jia, C. Lu, D. Wu, C. Wen, H. Rao, L. Abualigah, An improved reptile search algorithm with ghost opposition-based learning for global optimization problems, J. Comput. Design Eng. (2023).

[43] A.H. Alharbi, A.A. Abdelhamid, A. Ibrahim, S.K. Towfek, N. Khodadadi, L. Abualigah, et al., Improved dipper-throated optimization for forecasting metamaterial design bandwidth for engineering applications, Biomimetics 8 (2) (2023) 241.

[44] S. Nama, A.K. Saha, S. Chakraborty, A.H. Gandomi, L. Abualigah, Boosting particle swarm optimization by backtracking search algorithm for optimization problems, Swarm Evolut. Computation 79 (2023) 101304.

[45] M. Zare, M. Ghasemi, A. Zahedi, K. Golalipour, S.K. Mohammadi, S. Mirjalili, et al., A global best-guided firefly algorithm for engineering problems, J. Bionic Eng. (2023) 1—30.

[46] D. Wu, C. Wen, H. Rao, H. Jia, Q. Liu, L. Abualigah, Modified reptile search algorithm with multi-hunting coordination strategy for global optimization problems, Math. Biosci. Eng. 20 (6) (2023) 10090—10134.

[47] S. Ekinci, D. Izci, L. Abualigah, R.A. Zitar, A modified oppositional chaotic local search strategy based Aquila optimizer to design an effective controller for vehicle cruise control system, J. Bionic Eng. (2023) 1—24.

[48] M. Hadni, H. Hassane, New model of feature selection based chaotic firefly algorithm for Arabic text categorization, Int. Arab. J. Inf. Technol. 20 (3A) (2023) 461—468.

6

Arithmetic optimization algorithm: a review and analysis

Laith Abualigah[1,2,3,4,5,6,7], Aya Abusaleem[8], Abiodun M. Ikotun[9], Raed Abu Zitar[10], Anas Ratib Alsoud[2], Nima Khodadadi[11], Absalom E. Ezugwu[12], Essam Said Hanandeh[13], Heming Jia[14]

[1]ARTIFICIAL INTELLIGENCE AND SENSING TECHNOLOGIES (AIST) RESEARCH CENTER, UNIVERSITY OF TABUK, TABUK, SAUDI ARABIA [2]HOURANI CENTER FOR APPLIED SCIENTIFIC RESEARCH, AL-AHLIYYA AMMAN UNIVERSITY, AMMAN, JORDAN [3]MEU RESEARCH UNIT, MIDDLE EAST UNIVERSITY, AMMAN, JORDAN [4]SCHOOL OF COMPUTER SCIENCES, UNIVERSITI SAINS MALAYSIA, PULAU PINANG, MALAYSIA [5]SCHOOL OF ENGINEERING AND TECHNOLOGY, SUNWAY UNIVERSITY MALAYSIA, PETALING JAYA, MALAYSIA [6]COMPUTER SCIENCE DEPARTMENT, AL AL-BAYT UNIVERSITY, MAFRAQ, JORDAN [7]DEPARTMENT OF ELECTRICAL AND COMPUTER ENGINEERING, LEBANESE AMERICAN UNIVERSITY, BYBLOS, LEBANON [8]SCHOOL OF INFORMATION ENGINEERING, SANMING UNIVERSITY, SANMING, P.R. CHINA [9]UNIVERSITY OF KWAZULU-NATAL, PIETERMARITZBURG CAMPUS, POTCHEFSTROOM, SOUTH AFRICA [10]SORBONNE CENTER OF ARTIFICIAL INTELLIGENCE, SORBONNE UNIVERSITY-ABU DHABI, ABU DHABI, UNITED ARAB EMIRATES [11]DEPARTMENT OF CIVIL, ARCHITECTURAL AND ENVIRONMENTAL ENGINEERING, UNIVERSITY OF MIAMI, CORAL GABLES, FL, UNITED STATES [12]UNIT FOR DATA SCIENCE AND COMPUTING, NORTH-WEST UNIVERSITY, POTCHEFSTROOM, SOUTH AFRICA [13]DEPARTMENT OF COMPUTER INFORMATION SYSTEM, ZARQA UNIVERSITY, ZARQA, JORDAN [14]DEPARTMENT OF INFORMATION ENGINEERING, SANMING UNIVERSITY, FUJIAN, P.R. CHINA

6.1 Introduction

Optimization techniques are commonly used in solving complex problems in various domains, such as data mining, energy, machine learning, and others. They are mainly focused on getting the optimal solution by getting the most out of the decisions made by the users [1]. The purpose of an optimization problem is to find the best solution that fits its various objectives. Unfortunately, many solutions are not ideal [2]. Local and global optimization are the two main types of optimization problems. The former is interested in finding the optimal solution for specific search spaces, and the latter is interested in finding optimal solutions for local optima problems [3]; Fig. 6−1 specifies the meaning of local and global optimization. Due to real-world problems and their close relation to

Metaheuristic Optimization Algorithms. DOI: https://doi.org/10.1016/B978-0-443-13925-3.00012-1

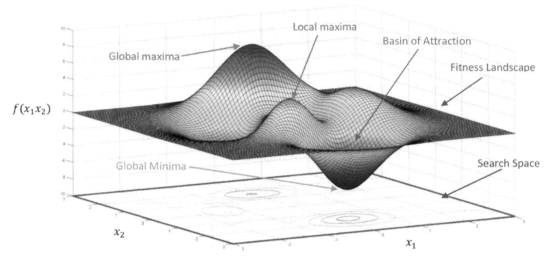

FIGURE 6–1 Local and global optimization search space [4].

optimization fields, many of the studies conducted in this area have been successful [5]. In addition, there are different kinds of optimization problems that can be studied in real-world situations. These include drug design, power quality problems, and engineering design [6].

Metaheuristic optimization is a process that involves taking into account the optimal value of a given function and then optimizing it to achieve the best result [1]. Over the past 10 years, several metaheuristic algorithms for optimization have been developed [7−10]. These are capable of tackling complex nonlinear problems [11]. In addition, it has solved a wide range of real-life issues in engineering, network, image processing, and many more, but traditional optimization techniques usually focus on solving problems involving the local optima and the lack of search space. Therefore, they cannot effectively address the other issues such as exploitation and exploration [12,13]. Normally, optimization methods can be used to deal with many problems in the sciences, as presented in refs [14−23,55].

A new metaheuristic algorithm known as the arithmetic optimization algorithm (AOA) was presented in 2021 by Abualigah et al. [24]. It features four essential operators: subtraction, addition, division, and multiplication [24]. The AOA is straightforward to implement and performs better than other metaheuristic algorithms because it has a framework that consists of only a few parameters [25]. As a result, the AOA has been widely used in various applications, such as network, engineering, artificial intelligence, and others. However, it can also be used for real-world multiobjective problems such as optimization problems, engineering problems, and many more to test its performance [26,27]. This paper presents the AOA method, procedure, and papers published about it in 2022. In addition, it also includes a survey of research, which uses the AOA in various applications. Some of these include network and image processing, engineering, and others.

The paper structure is divided into four sections. Section 6.2 focuses on the algorithm procedure, while Section 6.3 covers the related work. Section 6.4 introduces the discussion. Finally, Section 6.5 presents the possible future work.

6.2 Arithmetic optimization algorithm

The AOA provides a framework for exploring and exploiting various mechanisms in mathematics. These include, but are not limited to, multiplication ($\times$), division ($\div$), subtraction ($-$), and addition ($+$). The proposed algorithm can solve optimization problems without taking into account the derivatives [24].

6.2.1 Initialization

The optimization process in AOA begins with the selection of candidate solutions (x). The solutions generated randomly are considered to be the best performing in each iteration. See matrix (6−1).

$$x = \begin{bmatrix} x_{1,1} & \cdots & \cdots & x_{1,n} \\ x_{2,1} & \cdots & \cdots & x_{2,n} \\ \vdots & \ddots & \ddots & \vdots \\ x_{n,1} & \cdots & \cdots & x_{n,n} \end{bmatrix} \tag{6−1}$$

The AOA should start selecting the search phase before it can start working (i.e., exploration or exploitation). It is essential to allow the system to identify the areas of interest. The Math Optimizer Accelerated function is a calculated coefficient shown in Eq. (6−2).

$$\text{MOA}(C_{\text{Iter}}) = \text{Min} + C_{Iter} \times \left(\frac{\text{Max} - \text{Min}}{M_{Iter}} \right) \tag{6−2}$$

The function value is also shown by the number of iterations it has been in MOA(*C_Iter*). The *C_Iter* value indicates the current iteration, while the (*M_Iter*) value is the maximum iteration number that the function can take.

6.2.2 Exploration

The AOA's exploration operators explore the area randomly and develop a better solution by implementing the various search strategies. These strategies are divided into two main categories: division (D) and multiplication (M), as shown in Eq. (6−3).

$$x_{ij}(C\_Iter + 1) = \begin{cases} \text{best}(x_j) \div (\text{MOP} + \epsilon) \times ((UB_j - LB_j) \times \mu + LB_j), & r2 < 0.5 \\ \text{best}(x_j) \times \text{MOP} \times ((UB_j - LB_j) \times \mu + LB_j), & \text{otherwise} \end{cases} \tag{6−3}$$

In the next iteration, $x_{ij}(C\_Iter + 1)$ indicates the ith solution, and $x_{ij}(C\_Iter)$ denotes the current iteration of the jth position of the ith solution. The best-known solution for best(x_j) is the jth position. A small integer number is referred to ϵ. LB_j and UB_j represent the lower and upper bound values, respectively. The control μ is used to modify the search process. It can be used to make the search process more efficient.

$$MOP(C\_Iter) = 1 - \frac{C\_Iter^1/\alpha}{M\_iter^1/\alpha} \qquad (6-4)$$

The probability of a given outcome is computed by math optimizer probability (MOP), and the $MOP(C\_Iter)$ is a function that indicates the value of the ith iteration. The value of the current iteration is also known as C_Iter.[1] The maximum number of iterations that can be performed is also known as M_Iter^1. This parameter α defines the accuracy of the exploitation over the iterations. It is fixed at 5 by the experiments.

6.2.3 Exploitation

The AOA strategy is introduced to help operators perform calculations with either addition or subtraction. Due to their low dispersion, these operators can usually reach the target easily. The exploitation search algorithm then finds the optimal solution by running various operators.

Therefore, this phase of searching is dependent on the math optimizer accelerated (MOA) function (see Eq. 6−2). In AOA, the exploitation operators look for the best possible solution by exploring the various dense regions in the search area. They then use the two main search strategies, namely, subtraction and addition, to find a better solution, as introduced in Eq. (6−5).

$$x_{ij}(C\_Iter + 1) = \begin{cases} \text{best}(x_j) - \text{MOP} \times ((UB_j - LB_j) \times \mu + LB_j), & r3 < 0.5 \\ \text{best}(x_j) + \text{MOP} \times ((UB_j - LB_j) \times \mu + LB_j), & \text{otherwise} \end{cases} \qquad (6-5)$$

The first operator is conditioned by $r3 < 5$, while the other operator will be ignored until the end of the current task. If the other operator finishes its task, then it will be ignored. This procedure is similar to the previous phase.

The complexity of AOA is mainly due to the various steps involved in its development. These include evaluating fitness function solutions, updating solutions, and creating new computational models.

6.3 Related Works

The following subsections present the various improvement of the AOA commonly used to solve multiple problems.

6.3.1 Engineering application

The use of arithmetic optimization in solving various optimization problems has been studied. However, this method was mainly utilized in solving engineering problems. The following research aims to explain the effectiveness of this algorithm in performing various tasks in engineering.

A couple of years ago, Ridha et al. [28] proposed a new algorithm that combines the advantages of the third-order method known as GCAOA$_{EmNR}$ with the optimization techniques of the AOA strategy. This method is designed to solve the problems of PV models based on the collected data. This method can also help identify the unknown parameters of a model. The results of the exploitation search algorithm show that the error in the model can be zero under different environmental conditions. Khodadadi, Snasel, and Mirjalili [29] suggest a dynamic version of the DAOA algorithm, which allows developers to introduce new solutions during an optimization process without performing any fine-tuning. This system eliminates the need for developers to modify the existing parameters.

Zhang, Yang, and Chen [30] used an algorithm known as the AOA algorithm to enhance the efficiency and utilization of a thermoelectric power plant by identifying and implementing the optimal solution for each LMPP. The AOA algorithm considers the distribution mechanism of the various arithmetic operators during the computation process. In experiments, it could harvest the optimal amount of power with minimal power fluctuations. Abualigah et al. [31] developed an algorithm that improves the exploitation capabilities of the AOA. The paper presents a set of experiments designed to test the algorithm's efficiency. These tests show that the method can improve the convergence rate of the solutions and reduce the chances of getting stuck at the local point.

Kharrich et al. [32] proposed a new hybrid energy system that combines various technologies, such as wind turbines, batteries, and diesel generators. It is called HRES and uses the aquila optimizer to perform optimization on various aspects of the project. A recent study on the optimal sizes and allocations of battery energy storage in a radial distribution system revealed that a hybrid algorithm that combines an AOA and a sine-cosine approach (AOA-SCA) achieves better performance. The method proposed by Abdel-Mawgoud, Fathy, and Kamel [33] is mainly used to minimize the network's active power loss. The study was performed on two different networks: IEEE 69-bus and modified 30-bus.

Hu et al. [34] presented an enhanced hybrid AOA called the CSOAOA, which combines the point set strategy and the crisscross strategy features. It achieves a better convergence speed by adding a good initialization strategy. The algorithm is then improved to guide the search behavior of the individual. It also avoids the algorithm falling into its current local optimum. Finally, the optimization capabilities of the crisscross algorithm are integrated into the AOA. Kaveh and Hamedani [35] proposed an improved version of the AOA called IAOA that can perform better optimization tasks for skeletal structures. This variant is mainly used for performing discrete design optimization tasks. Two significant improvements distinguish the proposed IAOA from the standard AOA. One of these is the addition of a new exploration and exploitation feature. The other is reducing the number of algorithm-specific parameters, making the IAOA very easy to implement. In the paper, three benchmark problems were used to test the efficiency and performance of the proposed IAOA.

A mathematical model for a hybrid power system that combines cooling and heating was presented by Li et al. [36]. The system includes various components such as batteries, micro-turbines, and solar thermal collectors. A multiobjective AOA was proposed to improve the hybrid system's performance by implementing various optimization techniques. The method is based on mutation operations, sorting operations, and an external archive mechanism. Devan et al. [37] presented a hybrid algorithm that combines the advantages of an arithmetic-trigonometric optimization method and a conventional trigonometric algorithm. It considers the various trigonometric functions, namely, cos, tan, and sin, and combines them with the AOA to improve the search area and convergence rate in complex real-time problems. The proposed algorithm shows the effectiveness of the ATOA in 33 optimization test problems.

Hao et al. [38] proposed an algorithm for solving the CEED problem based on the order of variable penalty function. It can reduce energy consumption and save money by efficiently solving the problem. The energy-attenuated version of the AOA was also proposed to replace the MOA in the original algorithm.

6.3.2 Artificial intelligence

One of the main advantages of artificial intelligence is its ability to reduce the computational costs associated with optimization by developing various algorithms based on their assumptions.

Abualigah et al. [39] proposed a new version of the AOA for the text document cluster problem. First, it combines the advantages of the traditional AOA with the features of the opposition-based learning and Levy flight distribution methods. Next, it is evaluated with various UCI datasets and global optimization benchmarks. Bahmanyar, Razmjooy, and Mirjalili [40] proposed a multiobjective version of the original AOA. This new version, called the MOA, can find the optimal schedule for various home appliances. The HEMS algorithm finds the optimal schedule pattern for electricity consumption by considering the various factors that affect its cost. It also reduces the peak to average ratio and increases user comfort.

Abualigah and Diabat [41] proposed a new search algorithm that combines the AOA algorithm with the MCAOA. The goal of the new algorithm is to find optimal results in terms of both performance and ensemble mutation strategy. The paper tests the proposed method on various benchmark functions and engineering design cases. An improved algorithm for solving economic load dispatch problems was proposed by Hao et al. [42] to use the elementary function disturbance in the AOA. The algorithm's two crucial parameters are the math optimizer accelerator and the MOP. Ten elementary functions were considered for the algorithm, including the power function, arc-cosine function, the tangent function, the power function, the hyperbolic secant function, and the sine function. The addition of six elementary functions to the MOP and MOA parameters can improve the efficiency of AOA and enhance global search capabilities.

Aydemir [43] presented a new algorithm that combines the AOA and the chaotic maps for performing optimization tasks. It produces promising results when done efficiently. The statistical significance of the proposed algorithm is studied.

6.3.3 Chemistry

Almalawi et al. [44] presented a novel algorithm for forecasting the size-fractionated airborne metal-bound matter using a multihead attention model called MABLSTM.

The AOA-MABLSTM algorithm combines the advantages of an AOA and long-/short-term memory. The paper aims to develop a model that can predict the concentration of PM and the size-fractionated airborne metal-bound matter in an atmosphere. The proposed model can then be used to analyze the temporal trend of heavy metals.

6.3.4 Machine learning

Abualigah et al. [45] proposed a new algorithm called FDAOA that improves the performance of the flow direction algorithm when used in combination with other optimization techniques. It is mainly used for solving various optimization problems. The proposed FDAOA aims to avoid the common weaknesses in the current methods. These include the lack of equilibrium between the exploitation and exploration mechanisms, the stuck in the local area, and premature convergence. Pashaei and Pashaei [46] presented a hybrid gene selection method called mRMR-BAOAC-SA, minimum redundancy maximum relevance (mRMR), a first-stage filter that aims to identify the most relevant genes. The proposed method is powered by the BAOA, a multistep algorithm that combines the simulated annealing and the crossover operator.

6.3.5 Network

Several network applications have used optimization techniques to improve their performance. Bhat and KV [47] proposed a localization and deployment model that uses the AOA algorithm. The goal of this method is to develop a network that is completely connected. Through this algorithm, the network can be accurately localized and can identify coverage holes. Furthermore, the AOA can achieve a rate of error of less than 0.27% when the average localization error is within 5 m.

6.3.6 Other applications

The use of metaheuristic algorithms allows them to perform random strategies and come up with methods that can improve the efficiency of the models. Some of the most commonly used optimization methods include population-based and nature-inspired approaches.

Mahajan et al. [48] proposed an aquila optimizer with AOA (AO-AOA). The approach is evaluated against the existing procedures to determine its effectiveness. The algorithm results are compared with the results of the previous studies. In optimization tests, the impact of varying dimensions is a standard procedure to improve the efficiency of the AOA. This method can be used for low-dimensional and high-dimensional problems. Mahajan, Abualigah, and Pandit [49] proposed a hybrid method (AOA-HGS), based on the different dimensions of the functions of the hunger games search. It shows that varying dimensions can improve the efficiency of AOA-HGS for both standard and high-dimensional problems. In previous studies, the effects of varying dimensions have been shown to improve the efficiency of various test functions.

Zhang et al. [25] proposed a hybrid algorithm that combines the AOA and aquila optimizer. The performance of the AOAAO was compared with that of the Harris Hawk algorithm. An energy parameter was also introduced to balance the exploration and exploitation procedures of the AOAAO members. On the other hand, a piecewise linear map was introduced to reduce the randomization of the energy. The AOAAO is efficient in optimization. It also exhibited higher convergence accuracy and a faster convergence rate. Elkasem et al. [50] proposed an algorithm, which is known as the eagle strategy optimization algorithm. It addresses the shortcomings of the previous algorithm. It also improves the parameters of the controllers of a hybrid power system. The paper reveals that the proposed algorithm is superior to the other controllers based on its performance on 23 benchmark functions. It also outperforms the other controllers in various operating conditions.

Çetınbaş, Tamyürek, and Demırtaş [51] presented a hybrid algorithm that combines the capabilities of the AOA and the Harris Hawks optimizer. It is designed to improve the accuracy of the solution when it comes to designing and optimizing autonomous microgrids. This algorithm was developed through a cooperative process. The main objective of this algorithm is to develop a more diverse set of solutions that can be used during the optimization process. Mahajan et al. [52] proposed a fusion method that combines the advantages of GOA and AOA for global optimization tasks known as AOA-GOA. The proposed method can be used for various tasks, such as image processing, wireless networks, and engineering design.

A novel metaheuristic optimization algorithm called Ls-AOA was proposed by Ekinci et al. [53] to be used in biomedical applications. The proposed algorithm is constructed using a combination of whale optimization and greedy selection schemes. In addition, it utilizes the logarithmic spiral search mechanism to find optimal solutions. The proposed algorithm was tested against various benchmark functions and demonstrated superior capabilities compared to other metaheuristic methods. Implementing a proportional-integrative design for a functional electrical stimulation system was then proposed. Maleknasab Ardakani, Tabarzad, and Shayegan's [54] framework and fuzzy logic-based solutions are designed to implement in roadside units. The first step in the process is to analyze the various factors that affect the performance of the set. The second step is to consider the other factors, such as the signal strength indication, the number of neighbors, and the network entry time. Finally, the AOA algorithm is used to perform a better analysis of the set's performance.

Zheng et al. [55] presented an improved AOA powered by the forced switching mechanism. This algorithm aims to improve the quality of the search results by increasing the number of people involved in the process. The proposed algorithm also helps the search agents exit the local optima. Turgut, Turgut, and Abualigah [56] proposed a novel computational optimization algorithm known as the COAOA to improve the efficiency of a tube and shell condenser system using a combination of different refrigerant mixtures. Its results are compared with those of the original AOA. An overview of the presented papers is given in Table 6−1.

Table 6–1   Related work summarization.

No.	Method name	Author	Application	Year	References
1.	GCAOAEmNR	Ridha et al.	Engineering	2022	[28]
2.	DAOA	Khodadadi, Snasel, and Mirjalili	Engineering	2022	[29]
3.	MPPT	Zhang, Yang, and Chen	Engineering	2022	[30]
4.	AOASC	Abualigah et al.	Engineering	2022	[31]
5.	HRES - IAOA	Kharrich, Abualigah, Kamel, AbdEl-Sattar, and Tostado-Véliz	Engineering	2022	[32]
6.	AOA-SCA	Abdel-Mawgoud, Fathy, and Kamel	Engineering	2022	[33]
7.	CSOAOA	Hu, Zhong, Du, and Wei	Engineering	2022	[34]
8.	IAOA	Kaveh and Hamedani	Engineering	2022	[35]
9.	Multiobjective AOA	Li, Ren, Tseng, Wu, and Lim	Engineering	2022	[36]
10	ATOA	Devan et al.	Engineering	2022	[37]
11.	AOA	Hao, Wang, Li, Song, and Bao	Engineering	2022	[38]
12.	AO-AOA	Mahajan, Abualigah, Pandit, and Altalhi	Other applications	2022	[48]
13.	AOA-HGS	Mahajan, Abualigah, and Pandit	Other applications	2022	[49]
14.	AOAAO	Y.-J. Zhang, Yan, Zhao, and Gao	Other applications	2022	
15.	ESAOA	Elkasem, Kamel, Hassan, Khamies, and Ahmed	Other applications	2022	[50]
16.	hHHO-AOA	Çetınbaş, Tamyürek, and Demırtaş	Other applications	2022	[51]
17.	AOA-GOA	Mahajan, Abualigah, Pandit, Nasar, et al.	Other applications	2022	[52]
18.	Ls-AOA	Ekinci et al.	Other applications	2022	[53]
19.	AOA	Maleknasab Ardakani, Tabarzad, and Shayegan	Other applications	2022	[54]
20.	IAOA	Zheng et al.	Other applications	2022	[55]
21.	COAOA	Turgut, Turgut, and Abualigah	Other applications	2022	[56]
22.	IAOA	Abualigah, Almotairi, et al.	Artificial intelligence	2022	[39]
23.	MOAOA	Bahmanyar, Razmjooy, and Mirjalili	Artificial intelligence	2022	[40]
24.	MCAOA	Abualigah and Diabat	Artificial intelligence	2022	[41]
25.	AOA	Hao, Wang, Li, Wang, and Zhang	Artificial intelligence	2022	[42]
26.	CAOA	Aydemir	Artificial intelligence	2022	[43]
27.	AOA-MABLSTM	Almalawi et al.	Chemistry	2022	[44]
28.	FDAOA	Abualigah, Almotairi, Abd Elaziz, Shehab, and Altalhi	Machine learning	2022	[45]
29.	mRMR-BAOAC-SA	Pashaei and Pashaei	Machine learning	2022	[46]
30.	AOA	Bhat and KV	Network	2022	[47]

6.4 Discussion

Due to the increasing complexity of global numerical problems, such as test functions, developing new and powerful stochastic methods is becoming more critical. These methods give near-optimal solutions for various optimization tasks, such as engineering and real-world problems. The rapid emergence and evolution of local search have resulted in losing the powerful local search strategy. Developing a procedure that can help maintain the diversification of the search methods is solved by the AOA. Furthermore, new metaheuristic optimization techniques have been widely used in addressing various real-world optimization problems. These techniques have addressed various aspects of the problem by providing various advantages, such as their ability to avoid the local optima and adaptability.

Despite the widespread use of metaheuristic optimization techniques, the most common shortcomings of these techniques are still found in local searches because the techniques are usually not able to deliver near-global solutions. The advantages of metaheuristic techniques are shown in various ways. One of these is their ability to avoid getting stuck in local exploitation. Another reason is their simplicity, which allows them to focus on the near-optimal solution.

The AOA has become a powerful tool for solving complex problems since it was first proposed in 2021. It combines the multiple mathematical operations commonly used in optimization with one-dimensional and multidimensional functions to find the ideal solution. It can be easily implemented and used in a wide range of domains and applications. Fig. 6–2 shows the number of AOA used in different applications in 2022, as presented in the previous section. Fig. 6–3 shows the number of published AOA papers in 2021 and 2022 in different publishers such IEEE, Elsevier, Springer, Hindawi, and MDPI.

6.5 Conclusion and future work

This paper aims to review the various variants and applications of the AOA algorithm. It is mainly focused on reviewing the literature on the subject. In addition, some of the papers that were presented featured AOA in various applications, such as machine learning and engineering networks. Many researchers believe that the AOA can be used to solve various optimization problems, such as clustering optimization [57–60] and unconstrained optimization. Moreover, it is efficient in all the tested problems. In conclusion, future researchers can enhance the algorithm's performance and use it in different optimization problems.

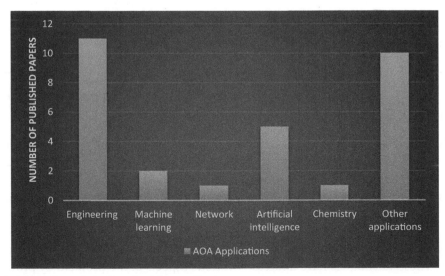

FIGURE 6–2 Arithmetic optimization algorithm applications.

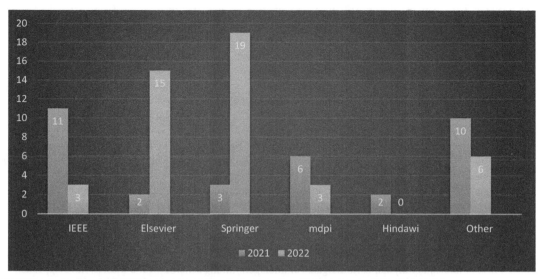

FIGURE 6–3 Number of published arithmetic optimization algorithm papers in different publishers.

References

[1] L. Abualigah, A. Diabat, A comprehensive survey of the Grasshopper optimization algorithm: results, variants, and applications, Neural Comput. Appl. 32 (19) (2020) 15533–15556. Available from: https://doi.org/10.1007/s00521-020-04789-8.

[2] R.R. Ihsan, S.M. Almufti, B.M.S. Ormani, R.R. Asaad, R.B. Marqas, A survey on cat swarm optimization algorithm, Asian J. Res. Comput. Sci. (2021) 22–32. Available from: https://doi.org/10.9734/ajrcos/2021/v10i230237.

[3] R. Xue, Z. Wu, A survey of application and classification on teaching-learning-based optimization algorithm, IEEE Access 8 (2020) 1062–1079. Available from: https://doi.org/10.1109/ACCESS.2019.2960388.

[4] J.M. Bryan, Global Optimization Of Mga-Dsm Problems Using The Interplanetary Gravity Assist Trajectory Optimizer (Igato), California Polytechnic State University, San Luis Obispo, California, 2011. Available from: https://doi.org/10.15368/theses.2011.218.

[5] L. Abualigah, M. Shehab, M. Alshinwan, H. Alabool, Salp swarm algorithm: a comprehensive survey, Neural Comput. Appl. 32 (15) (2020) 11195–11215. Available from: https://doi.org/10.1007/s00521-019-04629-4.

[6] H.M. Alabool, D. Alarabiat, L. Abualigah, A.A. Heidari, Harris hawks optimization: a comprehensive review of recent variants and applications, Neural Comput. Appl. 33 (15) (2021) 8939–8980. Available from: https://doi.org/10.1007/s00521-021-05720-5.

[7] J.O. Agushaka, A.E. Ezugwu, L. Abualigah, Dwarf Mongoose optimization algorithm, Comput. Methods Appl. Mech. Eng. 391 (2022). Available from: https://doi.org/10.1016/j.cma.2022.114570.

[8] A.E. Ezugwu, J.O. Agushaka, L. Abualigah, S. Mirjalili, A.H. Gandomi, Prairie Dog optimization algorithm, Neural Comput. Appl. 34 (22) (2022) 20017–20065. Available from: https://doi.org/10.1007/s00521-022-07530-9.

[9] O.N. Oyelade, A.E.-S. Ezugwu, T.I.A. Mohamed, L. Abualigah, Ebola optimization search algorithm: a new nature-inspired metaheuristic optimization algorithm, IEEE Access 10 (2022) 16150–16177. Available from: https://doi.org/10.1109/ACCESS.2022.3147821.

[10] J.O. Agushaka, A.E. Ezugwu, L. Abualigah, Gazelle optimization algorithm: a novel nature-inspired meta-heuristic optimizer, Neural Comput. Appl. 35 (5) (2023) 4099−4131. Available from: https://doi.org/10.1007/s00521-022-07854-6.

[11] L. Abualigah, et al., Nature-inspired optimization algorithms for text document clustering—a comprehensive analysis, Algorithms 13 (12) (2020) 345. Available from: https://doi.org/10.3390/a13120345.

[12] S. Khatir, S. Tiachacht, C. Le Thanh, E. Ghandourah, S. Mirjalili, M. Abdel Wahab, An improved artificial neural network using arithmetic optimization algorithm for damage assessment in FGM composite plates, Compos. Struct. 273 (2021)114287. Available from: https://doi.org/10.1016/j.compstruct.2021.114287.

[13] E.H. Houssein, M.R. Saad, F.A. Hashim, H. Shaban, M. Hassaballah, Lévy flight distribution: a new metaheuristic algorithm for solving engineering optimization problems, Eng. Appl. Artif. Intell. 94 (2020) 103731. Available from: https://doi.org/10.1016/j.engappai.2020.103731.

[14] L. Abualigah, A. Diabat, C.L. Thanh, S. Khatir, Opposition-based Laplacian distribution with Prairie Dog optimization method for industrial engineering design problems, Comput. Meth. Appl. Mech. Eng. 414 (2023) 116097.

[15] G. Hu, Y. Zheng, L. Abualigah, A.G. Hussien, DETDO: an adaptive hybrid dandelion optimizer for engineering optimization, Advanced Engineering Informatics 57 (2023) 102004.

[16] D. Izci, S. Ekinci, S. Mirjalili, L. Abualigah, An intelligent tuning scheme with a master/slave approach for efficient control of the automatic voltage regulator, Neur. Computi. Appl. (2023) 1−17.

[17] H. Jia, C. Lu, D. Wu, C. Wen, H. Rao, L. Abualigah, An improved reptile search algorithm with ghost opposition-based learning for global optimization problems, J. Comput. Design Eng (2023). qwad048.

[18] A.H. Alharbi, A.A. Abdelhamid, A. Ibrahim, S.K. Towfek, N. Khodadadi, L. Abualigah, et al., Improved dipper-throated optimization for forecasting metamaterial design bandwidth for engineering applications, Biomimetics 8 (2) (2023) 241.

[19] S. Nama, A.K. Saha, S. Chakraborty, A.H. Gandomi, L. Abualigah, Boosting particle swarm optimization by backtracking search algorithm for optimization problems, Swarm and Evol. Comput. 79 (2023) 101304.

[20] M. Zare, M. Ghasemi, A. Zahedi, K. Golalipour, S.K. Mohammadi, S. Mirjalili, et al., A global best-guided firefly algorithm for engineering problems, J. Bionic Eng. (2023) 1−30.

[21] D. Wu, C. Wen, H. Rao, H. Jia, Q. Liu, L. Abualigah, Modified reptile search algorithm with multi-hunting coordination strategy for global optimization problems, Math. Biosci. Eng. 20 (6) (2023) 10090−10134.

[22] S. Ekinci, D. Izci, L. Abualigah, R.A. Zitar, A modified oppositional chaotic local search strategy based Aquila optimizer to design an effective controller for vehicle cruise control system, J. Bionic Eng. (2023) 1−24.

[23] L. Abualigah, D. Falcone, A. Forestiero, Swarm intelligence to face IoT challenges, Comput. Intell. Neurosci. (2023) 2023.

[24] L. Abualigah, A. Diabat, S. Mirjalili, M. Abd Elaziz, A.H. Gandomi, The arithmetic optimization algorithm, Comput. Methods Appl. Mech. Eng. 376 (2021)113609. Available from: https://doi.org/10.1016/j.cma.2020.113609.

[25] Y.-J. Zhang, Y.-X. Yan, J. Zhao, Z.-M. Gao, AOAAO: the hybrid algorithm of arithmetic optimization algorithm with Aquila optimizer, IEEE Access 10 (2022) 10907−10933. Available from: https://doi.org/10.1109/ACCESS.2022.3144431.

[26] R.A. Ibrahim, et al., An electric fish-based arithmetic optimization algorithm for feature selection, Entropy 23 (9) (2021) 1189. Available from: https://doi.org/10.3390/e23091189.

[27] J.O. Agushaka, A.E. Ezugwu, Advanced arithmetic optimization algorithm for solving mechanical engineering design problems, PLoS One 16 (8) (2021) e0255703. Available from: https://doi.org/10.1371/journal.pone.0255703.

[28] H.M. Ridha, H. Hizam, S. Mirjalili, M.L. Othman, M.E. Ya'acob, M. Ahmadipour, Parameter extraction of single, double, and three diodes photovoltaic model based on guaranteed convergence arithmetic optimization algorithm and modified third order Newton Raphson methods, Renew. Sustain. Energy Rev. 162 (2022)112436. Available from: https://doi.org/10.1016/j.rser.2022.112436.

[29] N. Khodadadi, V. Snasel, S. Mirjalili, Dynamic arithmetic optimization algorithm for truss optimization under natural frequency constraints, IEEE Access 10 (2022) 16188−16208. Available from: https://doi.org/10.1109/ACCESS.2022.3146374.

[30] R. Zhang, B. Yang, N. Chen, Arithmetic optimization algorithm based MPPT technique for centralized TEG systems under different temperature gradients, Energy Reports 8 (2022) 2424−2433. Available from: https://doi.org/10.1016/j.egyr.2022.01.185.

[31] L. Abualigah, et al., Boosting arithmetic optimization algorithm by sine cosine algorithm and levy flight distribution for solving engineering optimization problems, Neural Comput. Appl. 34 (11) (2022) 8823−8852. Available from: https://doi.org/10.1007/s00521-022-06906-1.

[32] M. Kharrich, L. Abualigah, S. Kamel, H. AbdEl-Sattar, M. Tostado-Véliz, An improved arithmetic optimization algorithm for design of a microgrid with energy storage system: case study of El Kharga Oasis, Egypt, J. Energy Storage 51 (2022)104343. Available from: https://doi.org/10.1016/j.est.2022.104343.

[33] H. Abdel-Mawgoud, A. Fathy, S. Kamel, An effective hybrid approach based on arithmetic optimization algorithm and sine cosine algorithm for integrating battery energy storage system into distribution networks, J. Energy Storage 49 (2022)104154. Available from: https://doi.org/10.1016/j.est.2022.104154.

[34] G. Hu, J. Zhong, B. Du, G. Wei, An enhanced hybrid arithmetic optimization algorithm for engineering applications, Comput. Methods Appl. Mech. Eng. 394 (2022)114901. Available from: https://doi.org/10.1016/j.cma.2022.114901.

[35] A. Kaveh, K. Biabani Hamedani, Improved arithmetic optimization algorithm and its application to discrete structural optimization, Structures 35 (2022) 748−764. Available from: https://doi.org/10.1016/j.istruc.2021.11.012.

[36] L.-L. Li, X.-Y. Ren, M.-L. Tseng, D.-S. Wu, M.K. Lim, Performance evaluation of solar hybrid combined cooling, heating and power systems: A multi-objective arithmetic optimization algorithm, Energy Convers. Manag. 258 (2022)115541. Available from: https://doi.org/10.1016/j.enconman.2022.115541.

[37] P.A.M. Devan, F.A. Hussin, R.B. Ibrahim, K. Bingi, M. Nagarajapandian, M. Assaad, An arithmetic-trigonometric optimization algorithm with application for control of real-time pressure process plant, Sensors 22 (2) (2022) 617. Available from: https://doi.org/10.3390/s22020617.

[38] W.-K. Hao, J.-S. Wang, X.-D. Li, H.-M. Song, Y.-Y. Bao, Probability distribution arithmetic optimization algorithm based on variable order penalty functions to solve combined economic emission dispatch problem, Appl. Energy 316 (2022)119061. Available from: https://doi.org/10.1016/j.apenergy.2022.119061.

[39] L. Abualigah, et al., Efficient text document clustering approach using multi-search arithmetic optimization algorithm, Knowledge-Based Syst 248 (2022)108833. Available from: https://doi.org/10.1016/j.knosys.2022.108833.

[40] D. Bahmanyar, N. Razmjooy, S. Mirjalili, Multi-objective scheduling of IoT-enabled smart homes for energy management based on arithmetic optimization algorithm: a node-RED and NodeMCU module-based technique, Knowledge-Based Syst 247 (2022)108762. Available from: https://doi.org/10.1016/j.knosys.2022.108762.

[41] L. Abualigah, A. Diabat, Improved multi-core arithmetic optimization algorithm-based ensemble mutation for multidisciplinary applications, J. Intell. Manuf. 34 (4) (2023) 1833−1874. Available from: https://doi.org/10.1007/s10845-021-01877-x.

[42] W.-K. Hao, J.-S. Wang, X.-D. Li, M. Wang, M. Zhang, Arithmetic optimization algorithm based on elementary function disturbance for solving economic load dispatch problem in power system, Appl. Intell. 52 (10) (2022) 11846−11872. Available from: https://doi.org/10.1007/s10489-021-03125-4.

[43] S.B. Aydemir, A novel arithmetic optimization algorithm based on chaotic maps for global optimization, Evol. Intell. 16 (3) (2022) 981−996. Available from: https://doi.org/10.1007/s12065-022-00711-4.

[44] A. Almalawi, et al., Arithmetic optimization algorithm with deep learning enabled airborne particle-bound metals size prediction model, Chemosphere 303 (2022)134960. Available from: https://doi.org/10.1016/j.chemosphere.2022.134960.

[45] L. Abualigah, K.H. Almotairi, M.A. Elaziz, M. Shehab, M. Altalhi, Enhanced flow direction arithmetic optimization algorithm for mathematical optimization problems with applications of data clustering, Eng. Anal. Bound. Elem. 138 (2022) 13−29. Available from: https://doi.org/10.1016/j.enganabound.2022.01.014.

[46] E. Pashaei, E. Pashaei, Hybrid binary arithmetic optimization algorithm with simulated annealing for feature selection in high-dimensional biomedical data, J. Supercomput. 78 (13) (2022) 15598−15637. Available from: https://doi.org/10.1007/s11227-022-04507-2.

[47] S.J. Bhat, S.K. V, A localization and deployment model for wireless sensor networks using arithmetic optimization algorithm, Peer-to-Peer Netw. Appl. 15 (3) (2022) 1473−1485. Available from: https://doi.org/10.1007/s12083-022-01302-x.

[48] S. Mahajan, L. Abualigah, A.K. Pandit, M. Altalhi, Hybrid Aquila optimizer with arithmetic optimization algorithm for global optimization tasks, Soft Comput 26 (10) (2022) 4863−4881. Available from: https://doi.org/10.1007/s00500-022-06873-8.

[49] S. Mahajan, L. Abualigah, A.K. Pandit, Hybrid arithmetic optimization algorithm with hunger games search for global optimization, Multimed. Tools Appl. 81 (20) (2022) 28755−28778. Available from: https://doi.org/10.1007/s11042-022-12922-z.

[50] A.H.A. Elkasem, S. Kamel, M.H. Hassan, M. Khamies, E.M. Ahmed, An eagle strategy arithmetic optimization algorithm for frequency stability enhancement considering high renewable power penetration and time-varying load, Mathematics 10 (6) (2022) 854. Available from: https://doi.org/10.3390/math10060854.

[51] I. Cetinbas, B. Tamyurek, M. Demirtas, The hybrid harris hawks optimizer-arithmetic optimization algorithm: a new hybrid algorithm for sizing optimization and design of microgrids, IEEE Access 10 (2022) 19254−19283. Available from: https://doi.org/10.1109/ACCESS.2022.3151119.

[52] S. Mahajan, L. Abualigah, A.K. Pandit, M.R. Al Nasar, H.A. Alkhazaleh, M. Altalhi, Fusion of modern meta-heuristic optimization methods using arithmetic optimization algorithm for global optimization tasks, Soft Comput 26 (14) (2022) 6749−6763. Available from: https://doi.org/10.1007/s00500-022-07079-8.

[53] S. Ekinci, D. Izci, M.R. Al Nasar, R. Abu Zitar, L. Abualigah, Logarithmic spiral search based arithmetic optimization algorithm with selective mechanism and its application to functional electrical stimulation system control, Soft Comput 26 (22) (2022) 12257−12269. Available from: https://doi.org/10.1007/s00500-022-07068-x.

[54] M. Maleknasab Ardakani, M.A. Tabarzad, M.A. Shayegan, Detecting sybil attacks in vehicular ad hoc networks using fuzzy logic and arithmetic optimization algorithm, J. Supercomput. 78 (14) (2022) 16303−16335. Available from: https://doi.org/10.1007/s11227-022-04526-z.

[55] R. Zheng, H. Jia, L. Abualigah, Q. Liu, S. Wang, An improved arithmetic optimization algorithm with forced switching mechanism for global optimization problems, Math. Biosci. Eng. 19 (1) (2022) 473−512. Available from: https://doi.org/10.3934/mbe.2022023.

[56] M.S. Turgut, O.E. Turgut, L. Abualigah, Chaotic quasi-oppositional arithmetic optimization algorithm for thermo-economic design of a shell and tube condenser running with different refrigerant mixture pairs, Neural Comput. Appl. 34 (10) (2022) 8103−8135. Available from: https://doi.org/10.1007/s00521-022-06899-x.

[57] A.E. Ezugwu, et al., A comprehensive survey of clustering algorithms: state-of-the-art machine learning applications, taxonomy, challenges, and future research prospects, Eng. Appl. Artif. Intell. 110 (2022) 104743. Available from: https://doi.org/10.1016/j.engappai.2022.104743.

[58] A.M. Ikotun, M.S. Almutari, A.E. Ezugwu, K-means-based nature-inspired metaheuristic algorithms for automatic data clustering problems: recent advances and future directions, Appl. Sci. 11 (23) (2021) 11246. Available from: https://doi.org/10.3390/app112311246.

[59] A.M. Ikotun, A.E. Ezugwu, Enhanced firefly-k-means clustering with adaptive mutation and central limit theorem for automatic clustering of high-dimensional datasets, Appl. Sci. 12 (23) (2022) 12275. Available from: https://doi.org/10.3390/app122312275.

[60] M. Hadni, H. Hassane, New model of feature selection based chaotic firefly algorithm for Arabic text categorization, Int. Arab J. Inf. Technol. 20 (3A) (2023) 461−468.

Aquila optimizer: review, results and applications

Laith Abualigah[1,2,3,4,5,6,7], Batool Sbenaty[4], Abiodun M. Ikotun[8],
Raed Abu Zitar[9], Anas Ratib Alsoud[2], Nima Khodadadi[10],
Absalom E. Ezugwu[11], Essam Said Hanandeh[12], Heming Jia[13]

[1]ARTIFICIAL INTELLIGENCE AND SENSING TECHNOLOGIES (AIST) RESEARCH CENTER,
UNIVERSITY OF TABUK, TABUK, SAUDI ARABIA [2]HOURANI CENTER FOR APPLIED SCIENTIFIC
RESEARCH, AL-AHLIYYA AMMAN UNIVERSITY, AMMAN, JORDAN [3]MEU RESEARCH UNIT,
MIDDLE EAST UNIVERSITY, AMMAN, JORDAN [4]SCHOOL OF COMPUTER SCIENCES, UNIVERSITI
SAINS MALAYSIA, PULAU PINANG, MALAYSIA [5]SCHOOL OF ENGINEERING AND
TECHNOLOGY, SUNWAY UNIVERSITY MALAYSIA, PETALING JAYA, MALAYSIA [6]COMPUTER
SCIENCE DEPARTMENT, AL AL-BAYT UNIVERSITY, MAFRAQ, JORDAN [7]DEPARTMENT OF
ELECTRICAL AND COMPUTER ENGINEERING, LEBANESE AMERICAN UNIVERSITY, BYBLOS,
LEBANON [8]UNIVERSITY OF KWAZULU-NATAL, PIETERMARITZBURG CAMPUS,
POTCHEFSTROOM, SOUTH AFRICA [9]SORBONNE CENTER OF ARTIFICIAL INTELLIGENCE,
SORBONNE UNIVERSITY-ABU DHABI, ABU DHABI, UNITED ARAB EMIRATES [10]DEPARTMENT
OF CIVIL, ARCHITECTURAL AND ENVIRONMENTAL ENGINEERING, UNIVERSITY OF MIAMI,
CORAL GABLES, FL, UNITED STATES [11]UNIT FOR DATA SCIENCE AND COMPUTING, NORTH-
WEST UNIVERSITY, POTCHEFSTROOM, SOUTH AFRICA [12]DEPARTMENT OF COMPUTER
INFORMATION SYSTEM, ZARQA UNIVERSITY, ZARQA, JORDAN [13]DEPARTMENT OF
INFORMATION ENGINEERING, SANMING UNIVERSITY, FUJIAN, P.R. CHINA

7.1 Introduction

Optimization helps to reduce damage and increase the benefits by finding the optimal result of the objective function. In recent times, there have been numerous proposed innovative optimization approaches. They have been used to solve a variety of issues [1]. Metaheuristic (MH) is one of the approaches that have received a lot of attention and been utilized to solve many optimization problems. MH can be classified into four classes: swarm intelligent algorithm, which has a series of algorithms that suggest swarm and animal behavior; evolutionary algorithms, which is inspired by biological evolutionary behavior; physics-based algorithm, which is proposed by the simulating physical law; and human-based methods, which are influenced by human behavior.

Metaheuristic Optimization Algorithms. DOI: https://doi.org/10.1016/B978-0-443-13925-3.00001-7

The AO algorithm is a natural strategy that was inspired by aquila's hunting behavior. The aquila is one of the predatory birds, and four known hunting methods can be used. The difference between them is according to the situation of aquila and prey. When the aquila is being so far from the ground, it uses the high rise and vertical downhill method; when it is at a low level over the ground, it uses reconnoitering from a close search area by outlining aviation with the low slip pounce method, which is the most used method by aquila. The third one is reconnoitering from a close search area by short aviation with slow going down pounce; this is used when the aquila is low to the ground and the prey is slow; finally, attack by the walk and seize victim method is used when the prey is young and large.

Normally, optimization methods can be used to deal with many problems in the sciences, as presented in [2–12,55]. This survey presents the AO algorithm, its utilization, and analysis of some papers that used the MH algorithm to solve several real-world problems.

The remainder of this work is divided into sections as follows. Section 7.2 presents the procedure of the AO optimizer. Section 7.3 shows the related work and brief of this paper. Section 7.4 discusses the outcoming of this survey. Finally, Section 7.5 lists some benefits of the algorithm and future work.

7.2 Procedure

The aquila is one of the smartest predatory birds; AO is obtained from the hunting methods mentioned above. In this section, we present the mathematical standard of the AO techniques as follows:

7.2.1 Step1: (X_1)

This step is presented as in Eq. (7–3). Aquila is being so far from the ground that it uses the high rise and vertical downhill method

$$X_1(t+1) = X_{\text{best}}(t) \times \left(1 - \frac{t}{T}\right) + (X_M(t) - X_{\text{best}}(t) * rand) \qquad (7-1)$$

where $X_1(t+1)$ is indicated as the solution following iteration of t, created by (X_1) procedure of the first search. The ($X_{\text{best}}(t)$) is the optimal solution; this considers the convergent area of the prey. $\left(\frac{1-t}{T}\right)$ denotes the number of repetitions controlling the expanded search; $M(t)$ presents the location center value of the current solution studied by Eq. (7–1); *rand* represents a random number between 0 and 1; t and T denote the current repetition and the extreme number of repetitions, respectively.

$$X_m(t) = \frac{1}{N} \sum_{i=1}^{N} X_i(t), \ \forall j = 1, 2, \ldots, Dim. \qquad (7-2)$$

where *Dim* is the depth of the issue, and N is the number of filter solutions.

7.2.2 Step 2: (X_2)

In this procedure (X_2), the aquila strictly selects the area of the objective victim in planning for the raid; this is present in Eq. (7−5).

$$X_2(t + 1) = X_{best}(t) \times \text{Levy}(D) + X_R(t) + (y - x) * rand \qquad (7-3)$$

where X_2 $(t + 1)$ denotes the solution of the following repetition of t, produced by (X_2), the second search procedure, D is the distance area, and Levy (D) is denoted by the distribution function of levy flight, which is calculated by Eq. (7−2). $x_R(t)$ is a random solution taken in [1 *N*] at the *i*th repetition.

$$\text{Levy}(D) = s \times \frac{\mu \times \sigma}{|v|^{\frac{1}{\beta}}} \qquad (7-4)$$

$S = 0.01$, u, and v are random numbers from 0 and 1, σ is calculated using Eq. (7−4).

$$\sigma = \left(\frac{\Gamma(1 + \beta) \times \sin\left(\frac{\pi\beta}{2}\right)}{\Gamma\left(\frac{1+\beta}{2}\right) \times \beta \times 2^{\left(\frac{\beta-1}{2}\right)}} \right) \qquad (7-5)$$

where $\beta = 1.5$, and in Eq. (7−5), y and x display the spiral form in the search, which is calculated using Eqs. (7−6) and (7−7).

$$y = r \times \cos(\theta) \qquad (7-6)$$

$$x = r \times \sin(\theta) \qquad (7-7)$$

where

$$r = r_1 + U \times D_1 \qquad (7-8)$$

$$\theta = -\omega \times D_1 + \theta_1 \qquad (7-9)$$

$$\theta_1 = \frac{3 \times \pi}{2} \qquad (7-10)$$

r_1 takes a value between 1 and 20 for specifying the number of studying cycles, and U is a little value set to 0.00565. D_1 is an integer number from 1 to the length of the (Dim), and ω is a little value set to 0.005.

7.2.3 Step 3: (X_3)

After selecting a specific area of the prey and the aquila is prepared to raid, it goes down vertically to take feedback from the prey. This method is called reconnoitering from a close search area by short aviation with slow going down pounce, and it is presented mathematically in Eq. (7−11).

$$X_3(t+1) = (X_{best}(t) - X_M(t)) \times \alpha - rand + ((UB - LB) \times rand + LB) \times \delta. \qquad (7-11)$$

where $X_3(t+1)$ is the answer of the next repetition of t, which is calculated by the third search procedure ($X_{best}(t)$), indicating the convergent place of the prey until ith repetition (the best-obtained solution), and $X_M(t)$ presents the median value of the present answer at $t$threpetition, which is presented by Eq. (7−1). rand's value is between 0 and 1. α and δ are the exploitation adjustment parameters set to a small value in this paper (0.1). LB represents the minimum limit, and the maximum limit of the given problem is represented by UB.

7.2.4 Step 4: (X_4)

In the fourth procedure (X_4), the aquila is ready to attack the prey; this method is presented in Eq. (7−12).

$$X_4(t+1) = QF \times X_{best}(t) - (G_1 \times X(t) \times rand) - G_2 \times \text{Levy}(D) + rand \times G_1 \qquad (7-12)$$

where $X_4(t+1)$ is the answer to the following iteration of t, which is generated by (X_4). QF presents a quality process used to equilibrium the search techniques that are produced by Eq. (7−13). G1 presents different actions of the AO that are tracked to the target as it flees, which is calculated by Eq. (7−14). G2 shows lowering values between 2 and 0, which indicates the flight pitch of the AO that is used to follow the prey during the escape from the first place (1) to the last place (t), which is calculated by Eq. (7−15). (X_t) represents the existing solution at the $t$thiteration.

$$QF(t) = t^{\frac{2 \times rand - 1}{(1-T)^2}} \qquad (7-13)$$

$$G_1 = 2 \times rand - 1 \qquad (7-14)$$

$$G_2 = 2 \times \left(1 - \frac{t}{T}\right) \qquad (7-15)$$

7.2.5 Aquila Optimizer Pseudocode

To summarize, in AO, the enhancement method begins by creating an accidental group of elect solutions, named population. Over the track of iteration, the plans of the AO reconnoiter the best solution and near-best solution; each solution improves its position depending on the optimal solution obtained from the AO algorithm. Finally, the search method ended when the end standard is met. The Algorithm 7−1 shows pseudocode of the AO.

Algorithm 7–1 Aquila optimizer.

1: **Initialization phase:**
2: Initialize the population X of the AO.
3: Initialize the parameters of the AO (i.e., α, δ, etc).
4: **WHILE** (The end condition is not met) **do**
5:   Calculate the fitness function values.
6:   $X_{best}(t)=$ Determine the best obtained solution according to the fitness values.
7:   **for** $(i = 1,2...,N)$ **do**
8:     Update the mean value of the current solution $X_M(t)$.
9:     Update the x, y, G_1, G_2, Levy(D), etc.
10:       **If** $t \leqslant (\frac{2}{3}) \cdot T$ **then**
11:       **if** $rand \leqslant 0.5$ **then**
12:         ▷ Step 1: Expanded exploration (X_1)
13:         Update the current solution using Eq. (3).
14:         **If** Fitness$(X_1(t + 1)) <$ Fitness$(X(t))$ **then**
15:         $X(t) = (X_1(t + 1))$
16:         **If** Fitness$(X_1(t + 1)) <$ Fitness$(X_{best}(t))$ **then**
17:             $X_{best}(t) = X_1(t + 1)$
18:         **end if**
19:       **end if**
20:     **else**
21:         {▷ Step 2: Narrowed exploration (X_2)}
22:         Update the current solution using Eq. (5).
23:         **If** Fitness$(X_2(t + 1)) <$ Fitness$(X(t))$ **then**
24:             $X(t) = (X_2(t + 1))$
25:             **If** Fitness$(X_2(t + 1)) <$ Fitness$(X_{best}(t))$ **then**
26:                 $X_{best}(t) = X_2(t + 1)$
27:             **end if**
28:         **end if**
29:       **end if**
30:     **else**
31:       **if** $rand \leqslant 0.5$ **then**
32:         {▷ Step 3: Expanded exploitation (X_3)}
33:         Update the current solution using Eq. (13).
34:         **If** Fitness$(X_3(t + 1)) <$ Fitness$(X(t))$ **then**
35:             $X(t) = (X_3(t + 1))$
36:             **If** Fitness$(X_3(t + 1)) <$ Fitness$(X_{best}(t))$ **then**
37:         $X_{best}(t) = X_3(t + 1)$
38:             **end if**
39:       **end if**
40:     **else**
41:       ▷ Step 4: Narrowed exploitation (X_4)
42:       Update the current solution using Eq. (14).
43:       **If** Fitness$(X_4(t + 1)) <$ Fitness$(X(t))$ **then**
44:           $X(t) = (X_4(t + 1))$
45:             **If** Fitness$(X_4(t + 1)) <$ Fitness$(X_{best}(t))$ **then**
46:                 $X_{best}(t) = X_4(t + 1)$
47:             **end if**
48:         **end if**
49:       **end if**
50:         **end if**
51:   **end for**
52: **end while**
53: **return** The best solution (X_{best}).

7.3 Related works

In this section, we briefly present MH and their categories, and how the algorithms are applied to solve several problems. The increasing size of data due to industrial IoT, digitization, social media, and wireless communication technology required storage and treatment, for which cloud computing and fog computing are the best solutions. Transferring data from the cloud to it required a lot of time and high network bandwidth; while there is a sufficient amount of the fog layer's energy, the main challenge in saving energy is the listing of the mission. Based on a MH known as Harris Hawks optimization, the researcher suggested a new energy-saving task scheduling technique; the reader can read more about the listing mission and how to apply the MH algorithm in [13].

The reptile search algorithm (RSA) is a new nature-inspired MH optimizer inspired by the crocodile's behavior in hunting; the optimization (RSA) procedure is represented in two steps: surrounded, which is implemented by rise walk or low walk, and hunting, which is implemented by coordination hunting or collaboration hunting; this optimizer comparing with another one and Excellence was her ally [14].

Wang et al. [15] merged the AO and Harris Hawks optimizer (HHO) to make a hybrid optimizer containing the most successful feature from both optimizers and to solve some technical issues and add random opposition-based learning in the utilization stage to enhance native optimal release. The result was the best when applying the optimizer to 23 standard benchmark functions and four industrial engineering issues.

Using the MH algorithm for fixing the optimal power flow (OPF) by three methods presented in [16], which treat the problem of the MH algorithm, required a long time to execute a great number of load/power flows required to process; it maintains the original advantages of MH such as stopping in the target operation, detached variables treatment, capability of handling difficult nonlinearities, and multiobjective optimization; the result of these techniques was better than other MH algorithms. However, it is more generic to use in several types of MH algorithm-based OPF. In a recent study, to fix the OPF problem, a defined objective function was optimized by changing parameters of control; while pleased all constraints, depends on artificial ecosystem optimization (AEO) [17] proposed method to improve the problem of OPF.

Communication required large energy since energy efficiency is a challenge in the growing wireless sensor networks (WSNs), and effective routing is a great solution to solve these issues. Therefore, lifetime advancement is an effective situation, but the main WSN procedure in an ignored climate cannot be accessed by a human. A strong approach to organizing system operation is to reduce the energy used, improve the lifetime of the network, and improve power efficiency and network expansion. The researchers proposed an energy-efficient collection for WSN using the enhancement of the LEACH protocol. It is used to pick an ideal cluster head by energy-efficient clustering, and it combines two MH techniques, the salp swarm algorithm and the grasshopper optimization method, into a hybrid algorithm called salp-swarm grasshopper optimization, which was evaluated in many different conditions and found to increase the network lifetime compared to other protocols [18].

Many MH algorithms were developed in several different domains [19–23]; one of these algorithms is the predator–prey optimization (PPO) algorithm [24], which is taken by the biological phenomenon. The body mass of predators and prey and the interplay among predators and their mutual prey are affected by energy gains for both predators and prey. The PPO was improved in three steps: the first one tested different characteristics of the PPO algorithm on a group of 16 mathematical functions as an optimizer, and the second one was estimated by seven datasets to solve the feature selection problem. Also, PPO has a higher performance index of about 5%−10% than competitor techniques concerning exploration−exploitation, equilibrium, and a big grade of constancy.

In the application of the MH algorithm, a novel hybrid FA, called CVRP-FA [25], was proposed to resolve the vehicle routing challenges caused by overcapacity using construction of two types of native search and original factor to increase the quality of the answer and speed up convergence, thus overcoming the original FA's disadvantage.

The cell division optimizer (CDO) is a unique MH method proposed in [26]. The CDO algorithm is based on cellular reproduction mechanisms, defined by the cell division process known as mitosis; it is an application to solve classical engineering optimization problems.

There is an important situation of the community structure to clarify and explore inherent functions in real networks; while it's hard to detect the community structure whether the current algorithms depend on optimization or heuristic that need to be improved. Especially, a physarum-based network model (PNM) was used to determine interedges of the community in a network to improve previous knowledge of the existing evolutional algorithms [27].

Mahajan et al. [28] suggested a hybrid method of AO and arithmetic optimization algorithm (AOA) to be applied in different applications such as image processing, wireless network, power system, and engineering design. It is proven that it works effectively with high-dimensional and low-dimensional situations.

Many proposed algorithms are used to enhance mathematical equations, but there is none of them that solves all the problems, and most of them often have weaknesses in some parts. Zhang et al. [29] proposed a hybrid algorithm that combined AO and AOA with the improved efficiency of the Harris Hawk optimization (HHO) algorithm. An energy parameter E was added to balance the exploration and exploitation procedures of individuals in AOAAO swarms, as well as a piecewise linear map to reduce the energy parameter's randomness.

Moreover, AOA is modified by the basic operators of AO to propose an improved algorithm (IAOA) [30]. The modified version aims to improve the original AOA's search capabilities, while avoiding flaws such as becoming stuck in a local search. The collected findings show that the proposed IAOA outperforms other well-known algorithms. It is widely acknowledged that the proposed IAOA is a promising alternative for solving hybrid renewable energy systems.

Researchers developed adaptive neuro-fuzzy inference system (ANFIS) using AO to generate an AO_ANFIS. The AO_ANFIS is superior to the traditional ANFIS and different modified models in terms of numerical returns and statistics [31].

Also, AO was used [32] to improve search and opposition-based learning (AOOBL) to enhance the achievement of ANFSI. Several performance criteria are used to evaluate the proposed model using real-world oil production information acquired from various oilfields.

Although the AO performs well in different situations, it suffers from some limitations in its search mechanism, such as local optima stagnation and slow convergence time, similar to other optimization techniques. That is a general difficulty that practically all optimization problems have, and it can be handled by boosting an optimizer's search process with the help of an assistant search tool [33,34]. The improved AO (IAO) takes advantage of both the AO and the whale optimization algorithm (WOA) [35]. It avoids the restrictions of local searches and the loss of solution variety in the search process.

Abd Elaziz et al. [36] proposed frames for classification images depending on deep learning and AO algorithm. This method improves precision and reduces the dimensionality during attribute extraction and chosen level.

Multilevel inverters (MLIs) can generate high-quality output voltage and handle enormous amounts of power; to reduce losses, device quantity and device ratings and a variety of MLI topologies have been identified. In a paper [37], a seven-level modified H-bridge inverter with a lower component count and lower THD was presented. To generate seven-level output voltage, two DC sources with six IGBTs were employed, and AO was used to get the regulated output.

A new WSP system was proposed [38], which integrates data preprocessing, benchmark model selection, and a sophisticated AO based optimizer for point and interval forecast. The experimental results show that the created model outperforms the tested models in all circumstances for point forecasting, as well as obtaining a forecasting interval with high coverage and low width error, which is a critical directive for ensuring the power system's security and stability.

Many MH algorithms were improved by combining two or more algorithms into one [34]. These improve the algorithm's convergence speed and accuracy [39,40]. The AO algorithm was combined with the piecewise linear map-enabled Harris Hawk optimization (HHO) strategy in CHHOAO and the AO algorithm's advantages were employed to compensate for the piecewise linear map-enabled HHO algorithm's weaknesses [41].

The AO algorithm is used to estimate the parameters of a proportional integral derivative (PID) controller used to control the speed of a DC motor [42]. The proposed AO technique is used to solve unimodal and multimodal benchmark optimization problems. The findings indicate that the AO is both promising and effective. The AO approach for determining PID parameters for a dc motor speed control system exhibits higher performance.

Zhao and Gao [43] introduced the multiple updating principle, and the heterogeneous AO (HAO) was proposed, taking into account the improved performance and slow later convergence rates of the AO method in optimization. Both unimodal and multimodal benchmark functions were used in simulation trials. The majority of the results backed the superior performance.

The AO was applied to estimate the parameters of the control autoregressive (CAR) model in [44]. The experiment shows the strength and accuracy of AO in different situations for CAR identification.

Four distinct stages were proposed [45] using a deep neural network (DNN)-based AO for detection and classification to resolve the problems of high execution time in the latest research in automatic diabetic retinopathy classification, which was also found to be cheap. A new reduction method was recommended [46], which focuses on the gray wolf's exploitation skill and aquila's exploring capacity for balancing two stages of exploration and exploitation. The approach was tested on four real-world engineering issues, and the findings suggest that it is suitable for challenging problems with unknown search spaces. Table 7−1 presents the summary of the related work.

Table 7–1 Summary of the related works.

References	Algorithm	Date	Journal	Application
[13]	Harries Hawks optimization algorithm	2021	Springer	Task scheduling in fog computing
[14]	RSA	2022	Elsevier	Searching
[15]	Hybrid of aquila and Harris Hawks optimization	2021	MDPI	The industrial engineering optimization problem
[47]	Hybrid of CSA and WOA	2022	Elsevier	Prediction of landslides
[16]	Evolutionary algorithm	2016	Elsevier	Solve OPF problem
[17]	AEO	2021	Intelligent Engineering and System	Solve OPF problem
[18]	Hybrid of salp swarm and grasshopper optimization algorithm	2021	Springer	Energy-efficient clustering protocols in the sensor network
[24]	PPO algorithm	2021	Springer	To solve the feature selection problem
[25]	Firefly algorithm	2019	Elsevier	For the capacitated vehicle routing problem
[26]	CDO	2021	Springer	Classical engineering optimization problems
[27]	PNM	2021	Springer	For community discovery in complex networks
[28]	Hybrid of AO and AOA	2022	Springer	Image processing, wireless network, power system, and engineering design
[29]	Hybrid of AOA and AO	2022	IEEE	To solve the mathematical equations that explain the real-world issues
[30]	IAOA	2022	Elsevier	New hybrid renewable energy systems design
[31]	ANFIS using AO	2021	MDPI	Oil production forecasting
[32]	AOOBL_ANFIS	2022	Taylor & Francis Online	Oil production
[35]	IAO	2022	MDPI	Feature selection technique using different benchmark functions
[36]	MobileNe-V3 and AO algorithm	2021	MDPI	Classification of COVID-19 images
[37]	DC with six IGBTs used with AO	2022	MDPI	Modified H-bridge inverter
[38]	Forecasting system based on multiobjective AO	2022	Elsevier	Wind speed forecasting
[41]	CHHOAO	2022	SPIE	To increase the algorithm's convergence speed and accuracy
[42]	AO algorithm to determine the parameters of the PID	2022	(IJPEDS)	To regulate the speed of a dc motor, determine the parameters of the PID controller.
[43]	HAO	2022	MBE	Optimizing three real-world engineering benchmark problems
[44]	AO estimation	2022	Mathematics	Design CAR identification
[45]	DNN-based AO	2022	IEEE	Automatic diabetic retinopathy detection and classification

(Continued)

Table 7–1 (Continued)

References	Algorithm	Date	Journal	Application
[46]	GWO and AO	2022	Elsevier	Four practical engineering problems, challenging problems with unknown search space
[21]	DMOA	2022	Elsevier	A new MH algorithm inspired by the foraging behavior of dwarf mongoose for solving engineering optimization problems
[20]	GAOA	2023	Springer	benchmark optimization test functions and selected engineering design problems
[48]	Initialization methods of population-based MH algorithms	2023	Springer	CEC2020 test functions
[23]	IDMOA	2023	Springer	For constrained engineering design problems
[49]	Multiclass feature selection	2022	Springer	Review of MH-based feature selection algorithms
[50]	Big data classification technique for healthcare applications	2022	Springer	Big data classification
[51]	Differential evolution and its applications in image processing problems	2023	Springer	Image processing
[52]	Prairie dog optimization algorithm	2022	Springer	A new MH algorithm
[53]	Survey of the clustering algorithm	2022	Elsevier	Survey on clustering algorithms
[54]	Image processing identification	2022	Springer	Image processing
[55]	Enhanced MapReduce performance	2022	Springer	Parallel computing on big data
[22]	Ebola optimization	2022	IEEE	A new MH algorithm
[56]	A generative adversarial network for synthesis	2022	Scientific reports	Synthetization of regions of interest
[57]	Artocarpus classification technique	2022	Springer	CNN-based classification technique
[58]	Moth flame optimization	2023	Springer	A new MH algorithm
[59]	Review on K-means clustering	2023	Elsevier	A comprehensive review

7.4 Discussion

This section discusses an estimate of the AO algorithm. The improvement of effective random techniques becomes more sensitive, necessary, and serious than before because the complexity of the optimization is growing. In recent decades, different optimization techniques have been suggested for solving complex problems by applying different aspects of natural life. The optimization algorithm is split into two classes: individual-based optimization method and population-based optimization method, which use the initial random state from the available search area and improved by repetitions, one by one.

The AO algorithm is a population-based algorithm with two main parameters. The effect of value change was tested on its performance [1]. The AO algorithm was applied to a series of experiments, such as finding solutions to well-known 23 functions, solving a group of seven real-world engineering issues, and more difficult problems like 30 CEC2017 test functions and 10 CEC2019 test functions; they noticed that AO is stronger and lower in weight by the population size. However, its superiority was compared with another MH algorithm.

7.5 Conclusion

In this survey, we present a population-based method called AO, inspired by the actions of each step in Aquila hunting. The main aim of this paper is to discuss and analyze the outcomes, applications, and results of the AO algorithm in solving different problems; it creates new opportunities for future works. AO has been used in different applications such as PV parameter estimation, neural network, image processing applications, text and data mining applications, big data applications, network applications, industry and engineering applications, solving benchmark test functions, smart home applications, feature selection, image segmentation, task scheduling, and others [1].

Finally, the researchers can improve and enhance this algorithm by mixing it with other MH algorithms to obtain a more effective result.

References

[1] L. Abualigah, D. Yousri, M. Abd Elaziz, A.A. Ewees, M.A.A. Al-qaness, A.H. Gandomi, Aquila optimizer: a novel meta-heuristic optimization algorithm, Comput. Ind. Eng. 157 (2021) 107250. Available from: https://doi.org/10.1016/j.cie.2021.107250.

[2] L. Abualigah, A. Diabat, C.L. Thanh, S. Khatir, Opposition-based Laplacian distribution with Prairie Dog optimization method for industrial engineering design problems, Comput. Methods Appl. Mech. Eng. 414 (2023) 116097.

[3] G. Hu, Y. Zheng, L. Abualigah, A.G. Hussien, DETDO: an adaptive hybrid dandelion optimizer for engineering optimization, Adv. Eng. Inform. 57 (2023) 102004.

[4] D. Izci, S. Ekinci, S. Mirjalili, L. Abualigah, An intelligent tuning scheme with a master/slave approach for efficient control of the automatic voltage regulator, Neural Comput. Appl. (2023) 1−17.

[5] H. Jia, C. Lu, D. Wu, C. Wen, H. Rao, L. Abualigah, An improved reptile search algorithm with ghost opposition-based learning for global optimization problems, J. Comput. Des. Eng. (2023) qwad048.

[6] A.H. Alharbi, A.A. Abdelhamid, A. Ibrahim, S.K. Towfek, N. Khodadadi, L. Abualigah, et al., Improved dipper-throated optimization for forecasting metamaterial design bandwidth for engineering applications, Biomimetics 8 (2) (2023) 241.

[7] S. Nama, A.K. Saha, S. Chakraborty, A.H. Gandomi, L. Abualigah, Boosting particle swarm optimization by backtracking search algorithm for optimization problems, Swarm Evolut. Comput. 79 (2023) 101304.

[8] M. Zare, M. Ghasemi, A. Zahedi, K. Golalipour, S.K. Mohammadi, S. Mirjalili, et al., A global best-guided firefly algorithm for engineering problems, J. Bionic Eng. (2023) 1−30.

[9] D. Wu, C. Wen, H. Rao, H. Jia, Q. Liu, L. Abualigah, Modified reptile search algorithm with multi-hunting coordination strategy for global optimization problems, Math. Biosci. Eng. 20 (6) (2023) 10090−10134.

[10] S. Ekinci, D. Izci, L. Abualigah, R.A. Zitar, A modified oppositional chaotic local search strategy based aquila optimizer to design an effective controller for vehicle cruise control system, J. Bionic Eng. (2023) 1−24.

[11] L. Abualigah, D. Falcone, A. Forestiero, Swarm intelligence to face IoT challenges, Comput. Intell. Neurosci. (2023) 2023.

[12] M. Hadni, H. Hassane, New model of feature selection based chaotic firefly algorithm for Arabic text categorization, Int. Arab. J. Inf. Technol. 20 (3A) (2023) 461−468.

[13] S. AL-Amodi, S.S. Patra, S. Bhattacharya, J.R. Mohanty, V. Kumar, R.K. Barik, Meta-heuristic algorithm energy-efficient task, Sched. Fog Comput (2022) 915−925. Available from: https://doi.org/10.1007/978-981-16-2761-3_80.

[14] L. Abualigah, M.A. Elaziz, P. Sumari, Z.W. Geem, A.H. Gandomi, Reptile search algorithm (RSA): a nature-inspired meta-heuristic optimizer, Expert. Syst. Appl. 191 (2022) 116158. Available from: https://doi.org/10.1016/j.eswa.2021.116158.

[15] S. Wang, H. Jia, L. Abualigah, Q. Liu, R. Zheng, An improved hybrid aquila optimizer and Harris Hawks algorithm for solving industrial engineering optimization problems, Processes 9 (9) (2021) 1551. Available from: https://doi.org/10.3390/pr9091551.

[16] S. Surender Reddy, P.R. Bijwe, Efficiency improvements in meta-heuristic algorithms to solve the optimal power flow problem, Int. J. Electr. Power Energy Syst. 82 (2016) 288−302. Available from: https://doi.org/10.1016/j.ijepes.2016.03.028.

[17] T.L. Duong, N.A. Nguyen, T.T. Nguyen, Application of meta-heuristic algorithm for finding the best solution for the optimal power flow problem, Int. J. Intell. Eng. Syst. 14 (6) (2021) 528−538. Available from: https://doi.org/10.22266/ijies2021.1231.47.

[18] Y.A. Rani, E.S. Reddy, A novel energy-efficient clustering protocol in wireless sensor network: multi-objective analysis based on hybrid meta-heuristic algorithm, J. Reliab. Intell. Environ. 8 (4) (2022) 415−432. Available from: https://doi.org/10.1007/s40860-021-00159-w.

[19] A.E. Ezugwu, J.O. Agushaka, L. Abualigah, S. Mirjalili, A.H. Gandomi, Prairie Dog optimization algorithm, Neural Comput. Appl. 34 (22) (2022) 20017−20065. Available from: https://doi.org/10.1007/s00521-022-07530-9.

[20] J.O. Agushaka, A.E. Ezugwu, L. Abualigah, Gazelle optimization algorithm: a novel nature-inspired meta-heuristic optimizer, Neural Comput. Appl. 35 (5) (2023) 4099−4131. Available from: https://doi.org/10.1007/s00521-022-07854-6.

[21] J.O. Agushaka, A.E. Ezugwu, L. Abualigah, Dwarf Mongoose optimization algorithm, Comput. Methods Appl. Mech. Eng. 391 (2022). Available from: https://doi.org/10.1016/j.cma.2022.114570.

[22] O.N. Oyelade, A.E.-S. Ezugwu, T.I.A. Mohamed, L. Abualigah, Ebola optimization search algorithm: a new nature-inspired metaheuristic optimization algorithm, IEEE Access. 10 (2022) 16150−16177. Available from: https://doi.org/10.1109/ACCESS.2022.3147821.

[23] J.O. Agushaka, A.E. Ezugwu, O.N. Olaide, O. Akinola, R.A. Zitar, L. Abualigah, Improved dwarf Mongoose optimization for constrained engineering design problems, J. Bionic Eng. (2022). Available from: https://doi.org/10.1007/s42235-022-00316-8.

[24] B. Mohammad Hasani Zade, N. Mansouri, PPO: a new nature-inspired metaheuristic algorithm based on predation for optimization, Soft Comput. 26 (3) (2022) 1331−1402. Available from: https://doi.org/10.1007/s00500-021-06404-x.

[25] A.M. Altabeeb, A.M. Mohsen, A. Ghallab, An improved hybrid firefly algorithm for capacitated vehicle routing problem, Appl. Soft Comput. 84 (2019) 105728. Available from: https://doi.org/10.1016/j.asoc.2019.105728.

[26] S. Jain, K.K. Bharti, A novel meta-heuristic optimization algorithm based on cell division: cell division optimizer, Res. Sq. (2021) 1−37.

[27] X. Li, C. Gao, S. Wang, Z. Wang, C. Liu, X. Li, A new nature-inspired optimization for community discovery in complex networks, Eur. Phys. J. B 94 (7) (2021) 137. Available from: https://doi.org/10.1140/epjb/s10051-021-00122-x.

[28] S. Mahajan, L. Abualigah, A.K. Pandit, M. Altalhi, Hybrid aquila optimizer with arithmetic optimization algorithm for global optimization tasks, Soft Comput. 26 (10) (2022) 4863−4881. Available from: https://doi.org/10.1007/s00500-022-06873-8.

[29] Y.-J. Zhang, Y.-X. Yan, J. Zhao, Z.-M. Gao, AOAAO: the hybrid algorithm of arithmetic optimization algorithm with aquila optimizer, IEEE Access. 10 (2022) 10907−10933. Available from: https://doi.org/10.1109/ACCESS.2022.3144431.

[30] M. Kharrich, L. Abualigah, S. Kamel, H. AbdEl-Sattar, M. Tostado-Véliz, An improved arithmetic optimization algorithm for design of a microgrid with energy storage system: case study of El Kharga Oasis, Egypt, J. Energy Storage 51 (2022) 104343. Available from: https://doi.org/10.1016/j.est.2022.104343.

[31] A.M. AlRassas, et al., Optimized ANFIS model using aquila optimizer for oil production forecasting, Processes 9 (7) (2021) 1194. Available from: https://doi.org/10.3390/pr9071194.

[32] M.A.A. Al-qaness, A.A. Ewees, H. Fan, A.M. AlRassas, M. Abd Elaziz, Modified aquila optimizer for forecasting oil production, Geo-spatial Inf. Sci. 25 (4) (2022) 519−535. Available from: https://doi.org/10.1080/10095020.2022.2068385.

[33] A.M. Ikotun, M.S. Almutari, A.E. Ezugwu, K-means-based nature-inspired metaheuristic algorithms for automatic data clustering problems: recent advances and future directions, Appl. Sci. 11 (23) (2021) 11246. Available from: https://doi.org/10.3390/app112311246.

[34] A.M. Ikotun, A.E. Ezugwu, Boosting k-means clustering with symbiotic organisms search for automatic clustering problems, PLoS One 17 (8) (2022) e0272861. Available from: https://doi.org/10.1371/journal.pone.0272861.

[35] A.A. Ewees, et al., A Cox proportional-hazards model based on an improved aquila optimizer with whale optimization algorithm operators, Mathematics 10 (8) (Apr. 2022) 1273. Available from: https://doi.org/10.3390/math10081273.

[36] M. Abd Elaziz, A. Dahou, N.A. Alsaleh, A.H. Elsheikh, A.I. Saba, M. Ahmadein, Boosting COVID-19 image classification using MobileNetV3 and aquila optimizer algorithm, Entropy 23 (11) (2021) 1383. Available from: https://doi.org/10.3390/e23111383.

[37] M.R. Hussan, et al., Aquila Optimization based harmonic elimination in a modified H-bridge inverter, Sustainability 14 (2) (2022) 929. Available from: https://doi.org/10.3390/su14020929.

[38] Q. Xing, J. Wang, H. Lu, S. Wang, Research of a novel short-term wind forecasting system based on multi-objective aquila optimizer for point and interval forecast, Energy Convers. Manag. 263 (2022) 115583. Available from: https://doi.org/10.1016/j.enconman.2022.115583.

[39] A.M. Ikotun, A.E. Ezugwu, Improved SOSK-means automatic clustering algorithm with a three-part mutualism phase and random weighted reflection coefficient for high-dimensional datasets, Appl. Sci. 12 (24) (2022) 13019. Available from: https://doi.org/10.3390/app122413019.

[40] A.M. Ikotun, A.E. Ezugwu, Enhanced firefly-K-means clustering with adaptive mutation and central limit theorem for automatic clustering of high-dimensional datasets, Appl. Sci. 12 (23) (2022) 12275. Available from: https://doi.org/10.3390/app122312275.

[41] Y.-J. Zhang, J. Zhao, Z.-M. Gao, Hybridized improvement of the chaotic Harris Hawk optimization algorithm and aquila optimizer, in: International Conference on Electronic Information Engineering and Computer Communication (EIECC 2021), May 2022, p. 7. Available from: https://doi.org/10.1117/12.2634395.

[42] W. Aribowo, Supari, B. Suprianto, Optimization of PID parameters for controlling DC motor based on the aquila optimizer algorithm, Int. J. Power Electron. Drive Syst. 13 (1) (2022) 216–222. Available from: https://doi.org/10.11591/ijpeds.v13.i1.pp216-222.

[43] J. Zhao, Z.-M. Gao, The heterogeneous Aquila optimization algorithm, Math. Biosci. Eng. 19 (6) (2022) 5867–5904. Available from: https://doi.org/10.3934/mbe.2022275.

[44] K. Mehmood, N.I. Chaudhary, Z.A. Khan, M.A.Z. Raja, K.M. Cheema, A.H. Milyani, Design of aquila optimization heuristic for identification of control autoregressive systems, Mathematics 10 (10) (2022) 1749. Available from: https://doi.org/10.3390/math10101749.

[45] V.D. Vinayaki, R. Kalaiselvi, Aquila optimizer based deep neural network for automatic diabetic retinopathy detection and classification, in: 2022 IEEE International Conference on Signal Processing, Informatics, Communication and Energy Systems (SPICES), March. 2022, pp. 55–60. doi: 10.1109/SPICES52834.2022.9774065.

[46] C. Ma, H. Huang, Q. Fan, J. Wei, Y. Du, W. Gao, Grey wolf optimizer based on Aquila exploration method, Expert. Syst. Appl. 205 (2022) 117629. Available from: https://doi.org/10.1016/j.eswa.2022.117629.

[47] A. Jaafari, et al., Swarm intelligence optimization of the group method of data handling using the cuckoo search and whale optimization algorithms to model and predict landslides, Appl. Soft Comput. 116 (2022) 108254. Available from: https://doi.org/10.1016/j.asoc.2021.108254.

[48] J.O. Agushaka, A.E. Ezugwu, L. Abualigah, S.K. Alharbi, H.A.E.-W. Khalifa, Efficient initialization methods for population-based metaheuristic algorithms: a comparative study, Arch. Comput. Methods Eng. 30 (3) (2023) 1727–1787. Available from: https://doi.org/10.1007/s11831-022-09850-4.

[49] O.O. Akinola et al., Multiclass feature selection with metaheuristic optimization algorithms: a review. Available from: https://doi.org/10.1007/s00521-022-07705-4.

[50] H. Al-Manaseer, L. Abualigah, A.R. Alsoud, R.A. Zitar, A.E. Ezugwu, H. Jia, A novel big data classification technique for healthcare application using support vector machine, random forest and J48, 2023, pp. 205–215. Available from: https://doi.org/10.1007/978-3-031–17576-3_9.

[51] S. Chakraborty, A.K. Saha, A.E. Ezugwu, J.O. Agushaka, R.A. Zitar, L. Abualigah, Differential evolution and its applications in image processing problems: a comprehensive review, Arch. Comput. Methods Eng. 30 (2) (2023) 985–1040. Available from: https://doi.org/10.1007/s11831-022-09825-5.

[52] T. Amudha, Artificial intelligence: a complete insight, in artificial intelligence theory, models, and applications, Auerb. Publ. (2021) 1–24.

[53] A.E. Ezugwu, et al., A comprehensive survey of clustering algorithms: State-of-the-art machine learning applications, taxonomy, challenges, and future research prospects, Eng. Appl. Artif. Intell. 110 (2022) 104743. Available from: https://doi.org/10.1016/j.engappai.2022.104743.

[54] A. Khazalah et al., Image processing identification for sapodilla using convolution neural network (CNN) and transfer learning techniques, 2023, pp. 107–127. Available from: https://doi.org/10.1007/978-3-031–17576-3_5.

[55] N. Milhem, L. Abualigah, M.H. Nadimi-Shahraki, H. Jia, A.E. Ezugwu, A.G. Hussien, Enhanced MapReduce performance for the distributed parallel computing: application of the big data, 2023, pp. 191–203. Available from: https://doi.org/10.1007/978-3-031-17576-3_8.

[56] O.N. Oyelade, A.E. Ezugwu, M.S. Almutairi, A.K. Saha, L. Abualigah, H. Chiroma, A generative adversarial network for synthetization of regions of interest based on digital mammograms, Sci. Rep. 12 (1) (2022) 6166. Available from: https://doi.org/10.1038/s41598-022-09929-9.

[57] L.Z. Pen et al., Artocarpus classification technique using deep learning based convolutional neural network, 2023, pp. 1−21. Available from: https://doi.org/10.1007/978-3-031-17576-3_1.

[58] M. Ghasemi, M. Zare, A. Zahedi, P. Trojovský, L. Abualigah, E. Trojovská, Optimization based on performance of lungs in body: Lungs performance-based optimization (LPO), Comput. Methods Appl. Mech. Eng. 419 (2024) 116582.

[59] S.K. Sahoo, et al., Moth flame optimization: theory, modifications, hybridizations, and applications, Arch. Comput. Methods Eng. 30 (1) (2023) 391−426. Available from: https://doi.org/10.1007/s11831-022-09801-z.

8

Whale optimization algorithm: analysis and full survey

Laith Abualigah[1,2,3,4,5,6,7], Roa'a Abualigah[8], Abiodun M. Ikotun[9], Raed Abu Zitar[10], Anas Ratib Alsoud[2], Nima Khodadadi[11], Absalom E. Ezugwu[12], Essam Said Hanandeh[13], Heming Jia[14]

[1]ARTIFICIAL INTELLIGENCE AND SENSING TECHNOLOGIES (AIST) RESEARCH CENTER, UNIVERSITY OF TABUK, TABUK, SAUDI ARABIA [2]HOURANI CENTER FOR APPLIED SCIENTIFIC RESEARCH, AL-AHLIYYA AMMAN UNIVERSITY, AMMAN, JORDAN [3]MEU RESEARCH UNIT, MIDDLE EAST UNIVERSITY, AMMAN, JORDAN [4]SCHOOL OF COMPUTER SCIENCES, UNIVERSITI SAINS MALAYSIA, PULAU PINANG, MALAYSIA [5]SCHOOL OF ENGINEERING AND TECHNOLOGY, SUNWAY UNIVERSITY MALAYSIA, PETALING JAYA, MALAYSIA [6]DEPARTMENT OF ELECTRICAL AND COMPUTER ENGINEERING, LEBANESE AMERICAN UNIVERSITY, BYBLOS, LEBANON [7]COMPUTER SCIENCE DEPARTMENT, AL AL-BAYT UNIVERSITY, MAFRAQ, JORDAN [8]LUMINUS TECHNICAL UNIVERSITY COLLEGE, IRBID, JORDAN [9]UNIVERSITY OF KWAZULU-NATAL, PIETERMARITZBURG CAMPUS, POTCHEFSTROOM, SOUTH AFRICA [10]SORBONNE CENTER OF ARTIFICIAL INTELLIGENCE, SORBONNE UNIVERSITY-ABU DHABI, ABU DHABI, UNITED ARAB EMIRATES [11]DEPARTMENT OF CIVIL, ARCHITECTURAL AND ENVIRONMENTAL ENGINEERING, UNIVERSITY OF MIAMI, CORAL GABLES, FL, UNITED STATES [12]UNIT FOR DATA SCIENCE AND COMPUTING, NORTH-WEST UNIVERSITY, POTCHEFSTROOM, SOUTH AFRICA [13]DEPARTMENT OF COMPUTER INFORMATION SYSTEM, ZARQA UNIVERSITY, ZARQA, JORDAN [14]DEPARTMENT OF INFORMATION ENGINEERING, SANMING UNIVERSITY, FUJIAN, P.R. CHINA

8.1 Introduction

In many optimization problems, detecting the optimal solution for a given problem within complex restrictions is very important [1]. There are various strategies that can be used to get better optimization process performance, but they are not efficient to get the desired results [2,3]. Most optimization techniques try to find a way for solving a specific problem in order to minimize the amount of resources required to perform the task, so there are various effective search algorithms that are based on computational simulations and mathematical formulae. In the last few years, researchers have been working on developing new metaheuristic optimization algorithms that are designed to solve various complex optimization

Metaheuristic Optimization Algorithms. DOI: https://doi.org/10.1016/B978-0-443-13925-3.00015-7

problems [4–10]. The WOA was proposed by Lewis and Mirjalili using a swarm-based method known as molecular metaheuristics, which is a type of computational design that imitates the behavior of certain animals. It was noted that the whales are highly emotional and smart; they specially simulated the humpback whales' hunting behavior. These whales can hunt either by chasing the animal using a random or the best search agent or by using a bubble net.

Normally, optimization methods can be used to deal with many problems in the sciences, as presented in [11–21]. This paper proposed a survey of papers that were published between 2017 and 2022, which used the WOA in combination with other algorithm techniques to solve problems in several fields like computer networks, engineering, clustering, and so on.

The remaining sections of this paper are organized as follows: Section 8.2 describes WOA in detail, while Section 8.3 shows the related works that were applied in several areas (computer networks, networks Security, clustering, image processing, feature selection, and electrical power and energy systems). Discussion is provided in Section 8.4, while the conclusion as well as suggestion for the future work is presented in Section 8.5.

8.2 The whale optimization algorithm

8.2.1 Inspiration

Whales are very intelligent and emotional animals, although they never sleep. Therefore, the study of the behavior of these animals has received great attention from scientists. The whales use an amazing way to hunt by creating a spiral of bubbles wrapping around the prey and then swimming toward the surface of the sea, as shown in Fig. 8–1 [22].

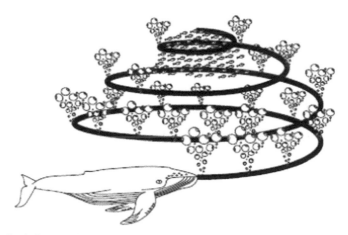

FIGURE 8–1 Humpback whale's spiral way.

8.2.2 Mathematical model and the optimization algorithm

8.2.2.1 Encircling prey

For finding the best possible search agent, the other search agents will try to update their locations after the best one has been defined [23]:

$$D = \left| \vec{C} . \vec{X} *(t) - \vec{X}(t) \right| \tag{8-1}$$

$$\vec{X}(t+1) = \vec{X} *(t) - \vec{A} . \vec{D} \tag{8-2}$$

where t is the immediate iteration, $\vec{C}$ and $\vec{A}$ are the coefficient vectors, X* indicates the position vector during the best solution that has already been obtained, and this should be frequently updated during each iteration if it finds a better solution, $\vec{X}$ represents position vector, "." indicates one element by one element multiplication, and | | is the absolute value.

The vectors $\vec{C}$ and $\vec{A}$ are computed as follows [23]:

$$\vec{A} = 2\vec{a} \cdot \vec{r} - \vec{a} \tag{8-3}$$

$$\vec{C} = 2.r \tag{8-4}$$

A linear decrease starting from 2 until reaching 0 over the course of iterations is represented by $\vec{a}$, and a random vector in the range [0, 1] is represented by $\vec{r}$.

8.2.2.2 Bubble-net attacking method

1. The mechanism of shrinking encircling: In order to achieve the behavior diminishing, the $\vec{a}$ value, which is shown in Eq. (8–3), is needed, where $\vec{A}$ represents a random value in the [− a, a] range; a is diminishing, starting from 2 to 0 within the course of iterations. The search agent's new location can be defined somewhere between the position of the immediate best agent and the agent's original position [23].

2. Updating position spirally: The first step is defined by computing the distance between the whales that are located in (X, Y) and the prey that is located in (X*, Y*); Eq. (8–5) represents the position of the prey and whale in order to simulate the humpback whales' helix-shaped motion [23].

$$\vec{X}(t+1) = \vec{D}'\_\cdot e^{bl} \cdot \cos(2\pi l) + \vec{X} * (t) \tag{8-5}$$

where $\vec{D} = \left| \vec{X} *(t) - \vec{X}(t) \right|$ and represents the distance of the *ith* whale to the prey, b is a constant for determining the logarithmic spiral shape, l is a random number in the range [− 1, 1], and "." is a one element by one element multiplication.

The humpback whales swim using a shortening circle and along a spiral-shaped path around the prey, a probability of 50% to pick either the shrinking encircling mechanism or the spiral model to model this behavior.

$$\vec{X}(t+1) = \begin{cases} \vec{X}*(t) - A.D & \text{if } p < 0.5 \\ D'.e^{lb}.\cos(2\pi l) + \vec{X}*(t) & \text{if } p \geq 0.5 \end{cases} \qquad (8-6)$$

where p presents a random number within the range [0, 1].

8.2.2.3 Exploration phase: searching for a prey

Remember that the humpback whale searches in a random way depending on the location of each other, so vector $\vec{A}$ is used when the random value is more than 1 or smaller than -1 to make the search agent to move far away regarding the reference whale. The mathematical model is shown as follows [23]:

$$\vec{D} = \left| \vec{C} \cdot \vec{X} rand - \vec{X} \right| \qquad (8-7)$$

$$\vec{X}(t+1) = \vec{X} rand - \vec{A}.\vec{D} \qquad (8-8)$$

where vector $\vec{X}$ rand represents a random whale (random position) that is chosen from the current population.

The WOA algorithm pseudocode is shown in Fig. 8–2.

8.3 Related work

8.3.1 Computer networks

A properly allocated resource is a crucial component of wireless networks' performance. It is typically considered as a nonlinear programming problem approach, and due to the complexity of the problem, it usually requires a special type of approach to solve it. This is usually performed through a combination of global optimization and machine learning. The usual method is not feasible due to the lack of guarantees of performance optimality and the large training time involved. It was proved that the WOA can be used to help in solving many problems regarding the resource allocation in 5G networks [24].

Aljarah et al. [25] proposed a new training algorithm that combines the functions of the WOA and the stochastic optimization method. After comparing various techniques used in the development of a trainer with six evolutionary techniques and the back-propagation algorithm, the results show that the proposed trainer outperforms the current algorithms in terms of both local optima avoidance and convergence speed.

The creation of a vehicle communication network using the help of a roadside unit is carried out through the use of a vehicle ad hoc network; the enhanced WOA is used in the

```
Initialize the whales population X_i (i = 1, 2, ..., n)
Calculate the fitness of each search agent
X*=the best search agent
while (t < maximum number of iterations)
    for each search agent
    Update a, A, C, l, and p
        if1 (p<0.5)
            if2 (|A| < 1)
                Update the position of the current search agent by the Eq. (2.1)
            else if2 (|A| ≥ 1)
                Select a random search agent (X_rand)
                Update the position of the current search agent by the Eq. (2.8)
            end if2
        else if1 (p≥0.5)
                Update the position of the current search by the Eq. (2.5)
        end if1
    end for
    Check if any search agent goes beyond the search space and amend it
    Calculate the fitness of each search agent
    Update X* if there is a better solution
    t=t+1
end while
return X*
```

FIGURE 8–2 Pseudocode of the whale optimization algorithm [23].

routing protocol for vehicle network mobility to analyze the motion of each vehicle in order to help in solving issues related to the mobility management of the system [26].

WOA combined with other algorithms helped in identifying the optimal cluster head of a vehicle-based network based on various factors such as the transmission range, node density, and grid size; they were also able to increase the cluster lifetime by 46% [27].

A routing problem called the two-dimensional loading open vehicle was solved using WOA to get a good quality solution after searching the solution space, by designing and performing a search method based on vehicle and fleet in the high-quality solution region [28].

Due to the continuous efforts being made to bring down the electrical distribution network's line losses, proper allocation of capacitors is very important. This will help in maintaining the system's stability and prevent its failure. Prakash and Lakshminarayana [29] presented a WOA that is designed to find the optimal placement and size of ideal distribution system's capacitors. It was validated on two different test systems: the IEEE 34 bus and the IEEE 85 bus.

One of the most challenging issues that wireless sensor networks face is the optimization of their connections; this process can help them reduce the intrusion between their nodes and expand the lifetime of the network. The WOA can be used to perform a simple and efficient optimization of the networks [30].

The rise of the internet of things and the emergence of new technology like the wireless sensors and distributed data processing have created a greater focus on remote operations. Due to the low cost and reduction in size of sensor nodes, they have become widely used in various applications, such as monitoring forest fires and remote surveillance. A hybridized version of the WOA was used to help in solving the challenges in the design and implementation of wireless sensor networks, which are usually related to the location of the nodes [31].

A study proves that the WOA has an active role in improving the artificial neural networks and in solving the problem of easy entrapment in local optima and a slow convergence rate; this also improves the process of acquiring Brillouin frequency shift information [32].

8.3.2 Network security

Due to the rapid emergence and evolution of new communication technologies, it is now important that the confidentiality of the information transmitted through the internet is maintained. This is especially true in the fields of e-mail, e-commerce, and medicine, so a modified version of the WOA known as the MWOA was used for improving the current cryptosystems for powerful and secure systems [33].

The importance of the WOA has also been acknowledged in the medical field due to its role in protecting and securing the data in the cloud; a study proposed the adaptive fractional brain storm integrated with WOA, which is the hybridization of WOA and the adaptive fractional brain storm optimization, to solve the problem of data leakages and attacks [34].

The smart grid is a revolutionary technology that aims to improve the efficiency and security of the system with the ability to prevent and detect cyber attacks. Through the use of the artificial neural network, they were able to train a system to analyze and predict the failure of a system [35].

8.3.3 Clustering

Data mining techniques known as clustering are very powerful tools that involve identifying groups of objects based on their attributes [36–38], and due to the emergence of metaheuristic algorithms, such as those used for artificial bee colony optimization, clustering is becoming more prevalent. WOA has proven its worth in data clustering after it was tested against seven real data sets [39].

WOA also played an important role in solving clustering problems like exploration and late convergence of results by increasing the ability to deal with unbalanced and outlier clusters [40]. WOA also left a good imprint in solving the weak exploration mechanisms regarding data clustering [41].

8.3.4 Image processing

WOA was used for the segmentation of the liver in magnetic resonance imaging (MRI) images; it took into account the various clusters in the image to perform the process of segmentation. A statistical image is then prepared for revealing the potential liver position, so its worth has been proven after validating the resulting images by performing a collection of 70 MRI images [42].

It was revealed that WOA showed better results and also provided a faster convergence rate to improve the multilevel threshold values for image segmentation [43].

8.3.5 Feature selection

A new approach to feature selection [44] was presented using the improved version of WOA, an amalgamation of the concepts of the classical and quantum models, which allows for the exploitation of the inherent power of the classical WOA. The improved algorithm utilizes modified crossover and mutation operators to explore the spiral and shrinking movements of whales, so the statistical tests show that the improved version of WOA performs significantly better than eight well-known algorithms [45].

A novel WOA was proposed [46], which takes into account the features of a whale and generates a set of binary solutions that are ideal for reducing the classification and dimensionality problems. The novel WOA was evaluated against 11 different datasets; the results revealed that the new algorithm was able to find the optimal feature more efficiently [46].

8.3.6 Electrical power and energy systems

The WOA was modified and applied in the power system stability scope in order to calculate the variable parameters of the overhead AC transmission line, and it was proved that the modified WOA technique gives reliability and good accuracy to gain global optimal settings of these control variables [47].

The increasing number of solar power plants globally has led to high penetration of the electric grid. To maintain their optimal operation, it is important that the systems are maintained at their optimal conditions. A strategy based on the WOA was presented to improve the performance of PV systems by implementing a proportional integral [48].

WOA also was improved with a special encoding scheme, which positively influenced the control strategy process for safeguarding neighboring structures from earthquake excitations. The simulation results verify that WOA provides good results [49].

8.4 Discussion

According to the obtained results in the literature, we found that the algorithm got comparative results for solving several problems. Fig. 8−3 displays the number of papers that were reviewed in this study against the study areas. Fig. 8−4 displays the number of papers that were reviewed in this study against the publishing year (2017−22).

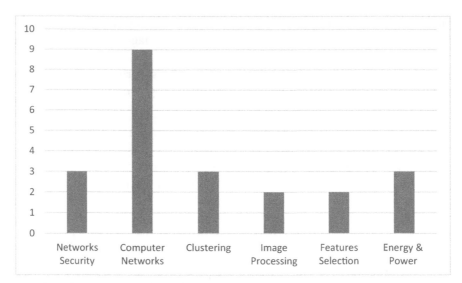

FIGURE 8–3 Number of papers against the study areas.

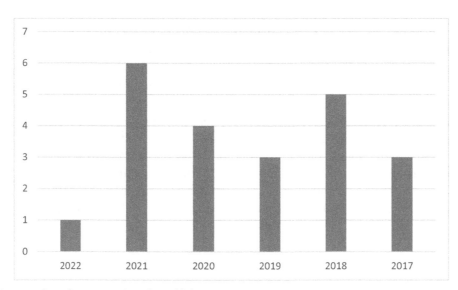

FIGURE 8–4 Number of papers against the publishing year.

8.5 Conclusion and future work

This study is focused on summarizing the WOA and its applications of in all categories. It proves that WOA improves the optimization problem results, and it is very efficient in most of the test problems. Also, the applications prove that WOA is a widely applicable in several fields like networking, clustering, image processing, and many other problems. For future works, this algorithm can be applied in solving more engineering problems.

References

[1] H. Shayanfar, F.S. Gharehchopogh, Farmland fertility: a new metaheuristic algorithm for solving continuous optimization problems, Appl. Soft Comput. 71 (2018) 728−746. Available from: https://doi.org/10.1016/j.asoc.2018.07.033.

[2] Y. Miao, M. Zhao, V. Makis, J. Lin, Optimal swarm decomposition with whale optimization algorithm for weak feature extraction from multicomponent modulation signal, Mech. Syst. Signal. Process. 122 (2019) 673−691. Available from: https://doi.org/10.1016/j.ymssp.2018.12.034.

[3] J. Ghahremani-Nahr, R. Kian, E. Sabet, A robust fuzzy mathematical programming model for the closed-loop supply chain network design and a whale optimization solution algorithm, Expert. Syst. Appl. 116 (2019) 454−471. Available from: https://doi.org/10.1016/j.eswa.2018.09.027.

[4] B. He, Y. Huang, D. Wang, B. Yan, D. Dong, A parameter-adaptive stochastic resonance based on whale optimization algorithm for weak signal detection for rotating machinery, Measurement 136 (2019) 658−667. Available from: https://doi.org/10.1016/j.measurement.2019.01.017.

[5] D. Yousri, D. Allam, M.B. Eteiba, Chaotic whale optimizer variants for parameters estimation of the chaotic behavior in permanent magnet synchronous motor, Appl. Soft Comput. 74 (2019) 479−503. Available from: https://doi.org/10.1016/j.asoc.2018.10.032.

[6] O.N. Oyelade, A.E.-S. Ezugwu, T.I.A. Mohamed, L. Abualigah, Ebola optimization search algorithm: a new nature-inspired metaheuristic optimization algorithm, IEEE Access. 10 (2022) 16150−16177. Available from: https://doi.org/10.1109/ACCESS.2022.3147821.

[7] A.E. Ezugwu, J.O. Agushaka, L. Abualigah, S. Mirjalili, A.H. Gandomi, Prairie Dog optimization algorithm, Neural Comput. Appl. 34 (22) (2022) 20017−20065. Available from: https://doi.org/10.1007/s00521-022-07530-9.

[8] J.O. Agushaka, A.E. Ezugwu, L. Abualigah, Dwarf Mongoose optimization algorithm, Comput. Methods Appl. Mech. Eng. 391 (2022). Available from: https://doi.org/10.1016/j.cma.2022.114570.

[9] J.O. Agushaka, A.E. Ezugwu, O.N. Olaide, O. Akinola, R.A. Zitar, L. Abualigah, Improved dwarf Mongoose optimization for constrained engineering design problems, J. Bionic Eng. (2022). Available from: https://doi.org/10.1007/s42235-022-00316-8.

[10] J.O. Agushaka, A.E. Ezugwu, L. Abualigah, Gazelle optimization algorithm: a novel nature-inspired metaheuristic optimizer, Neural Comput. Appl. 35 (5) (2023) 4099−4131. Available from: https://doi.org/10.1007/s00521-022-07854-6.

[11] L. Abualigah, A. Diabat, C.L. Thanh, S. Khatir, Opposition-based Laplacian distribution with Prairie Dog optimization method for industrial engineering design problems, Comput. Methods Appl. Mech. Eng. 414 (2023) 116097.

[12] G. Hu, Y. Zheng, L. Abualigah, A.G. Hussien, DETDO: an adaptive hybrid dandelion optimizer for engineering optimization, Adv. Eng. Inform. 57 (2023) 102004.

[13] D. Izci, S. Ekinci, S. Mirjalili, L. Abualigah, An intelligent tuning scheme with a master/slave approach for efficient control of the automatic voltage regulator, Neural Comput. Appl. (2023) 1−17.

[14] H. Jia, C. Lu, D. Wu, C. Wen, H. Rao, L. Abualigah, An improved reptile search algorithm with ghost opposition-based learning for global optimization problems, J. Comput. Des. Eng. (2023). qwad048.

[15] A.H. Alharbi, A.A. Abdelhamid, A. Ibrahim, S.K. Towfek, N. Khodadadi, L. Abualigah, et al., Improved dipper-throated optimization for forecasting metamaterial design bandwidth for engineering applications, Biomimetics 8 (2) (2023) 241.

[16] S. Nama, A.K. Saha, S. Chakraborty, A.H. Gandomi, L. Abualigah, Boosting particle swarm optimization by backtracking search algorithm for optimization problems, Swarm Evolut. Comput. 79 (2023) 101304.

[17] M. Zare, M. Ghasemi, A. Zahedi, K. Golalipour, S.K. Mohammadi, S. Mirjalili, et al., A global best-guided firefly algorithm for engineering problems, J. Bionic Eng. (2023) 1–30.

[18] D. Wu, C. Wen, H. Rao, H. Jia, Q. Liu, L. Abualigah, Modified reptile search algorithm with multi-hunting coordination strategy for global optimization problems, Math. Biosci. Eng. 20 (6) (2023) 10090–10134.

[19] S. Ekinci, D. Izci, L. Abualigah, R.A. Zitar, A modified oppositional chaotic local search strategy based Aquila optimizer to design an effective controller for vehicle cruise control system, J. Bionic Eng. (2023) 1–24.

[20] L. Abualigah, D. Falcone, A. Forestiero, Swarm intelligence to face IoT challenges, Comput. Intell. Neurosci. (2023) 2023.

[21] M. Hadni, H. Hassane, New model of feature selection based chaotic firefly algorithm for Arabic text categorization, Int. Arab. J. Inf. Technol. 20 (3A) (2023) 461–468.

[22] J.A. Goldbogen, A.S. Friedlaender, J. Calambokidis, M.F. McKenna, M. Simon, D.P. Nowacek, Integrative approaches to the study of baleen whale diving behavior, feeding performance, and foraging ecology, Bioscience 63 (2) (2013) 90–100. Available from: https://doi.org/10.1525/bio.2013.63.2.5.

[23] S. Mirjalili, A. Lewis, The whale optimization algorithm, Adv. Eng. Softw. 95 (2016) 51–67. Available from: https://doi.org/10.1016/j.advengsoft.2016.01.008.

[24] Q.-V. Pham, S. Mirjalili, N. Kumar, M. Alazab, W.-J. Hwang, Whale optimization algorithm with applications to resource allocation in wireless networks, IEEE Trans. Veh. Technol. 69 (4) (2020) 4285–4297. Available from: https://doi.org/10.1109/TVT.2020.2973294.

[25] I. Aljarah, H. Faris, S. Mirjalili, Optimizing connection weights in neural networks using the whale optimization algorithm, Soft Comput. 22 (1) (2018) 1–15. Available from: https://doi.org/10.1007/s00500-016-2442-1.

[26] S.R. Valayapalayam Kittusamy, M. Elhoseny, S. Kathiresan, An enhanced whale optimization algorithm for vehicular communication networks, Int. J. Commun. Syst. 35 (12) (2022). Available from: https://doi.org/10.1002/dac.3953.

[27] G. Husnain, S. Anwar, An intelligent cluster optimization algorithm based on whale optimization algorithm for VANETs (WOACNET), PLoS One 16 (4) (2021) e0250271. Available from: https://doi.org/10.1371/journal.pone.0250271.

[28] N.K. Yu, W. Jiang, R. Hu, B. Qian, L. Wang, Learning whale optimization algorithm for open vehicle routing problem with loading constraints, Discret. Dyn. Nat. Soc. 2021 (2021) 1–14. Available from: https://doi.org/10.1155/2021/8016356.

[29] D.B. Prakash, C. Lakshminarayana, Optimal siting of capacitors in radial distribution network using whale optimization algorithm, Alex. Eng. J. 56 (4) (2017) 499–509. Available from: https://doi.org/10.1016/j.aej.2016.10.002.

[30] M.M. Ahmed, E.H. Houssein, A.E. Hassanien, A. Taha, & E. Hassanien, Maximizing lifetime of wireless sensor networks based on whale optimization algorithm, 2018, pp. 724–733. Available from: https://doi.org/10.1007/978-3-319-64861-3_68.

[31] N. Bacanin, E. Tuba, M. Zivkovic, I. Strumberger, & M. Tuba, Whale optimization algorithm with exploratory move for wireless sensor networks localization, 2021, pp. 328–338. Available from: https://doi.org/10.1007/978-3-030-49336-3_33.

[32] Liu Ya-nan, Guo Nan, Zhao Yang, Yu Kuang-lu, et al., BOTDA sensing information extraction based on artificial neural network using whale optimization algorithm, Comput. Mod. 0 (12) (2021) 19–26.

[33] M. Abdel-Basset, D. El-Shahat, I. El-henawy, A.K. Sangaiah, S.H. Ahmed, A novel whale optimization algorithm for cryptanalysis in Merkle-Hellman cryptosystem, Mob. Netw. Appl. 23 (4) (2018) 723−733. Available from: https://doi.org/10.1007/s11036-018-1005-3.

[34] S. Thanga Revathi, A. Gayathri, J. Kalaivani, M.S. Christo, D. Pelusi, M. Azees, Cloud-assisted privacy-preserving method for healthcare using adaptive fractional brain storm integrated whale optimization algorithm, Secur. Commun. Netw. 2021 (2021) 1−10. Available from: https://doi.org/10.1155/2021/6210054.

[35] L. Haghnegahdar, Y. Wang, A whale optimization algorithm-trained artificial neural network for smart grid cyber intrusion detection, Neural Comput. Appl. 32 (13) (2020) 9427−9441. Available from: https://doi.org/10.1007/s00521-019-04453-w.

[36] A.E. Ezugwu, et al., A comprehensive survey of clustering algorithms: state-of-the-art machine learning applications, taxonomy, challenges, and future research prospects, Eng. Appl. Artif. Intell. 110 (2022) 104743. Available from: https://doi.org/10.1016/j.engappai.2022.104743.

[37] A.M. Ikotun, M.S. Almutari, A.E. Ezugwu, K-means-based nature-inspired metaheuristic algorithms for automatic data clustering problems: recent advances and future directions, Appl. Sci. 11 (23) (2021) 11246. Available from: https://doi.org/10.3390/app112311246.

[38] A.M. Ikotun, A.E. Ezugwu, L. Abualigah, B. Abuhaija, J. Heming, K-means clustering algorithms: a comprehensive review, variants analysis, and advances in the era of big data, Inf. Sci. (Ny). 622 (2023) 178−210. Available from: https://doi.org/10.1016/j.ins.2022.11.139.

[39] J. Nasiri, Farzin, M. Khiyabani, & F.M. Khiyabani, A whale optimization algorithm (WOA) approach for clustering under a creative commons attribution (CC-BY) 4.0 license, 2018, Available from: https://doi.org/10.1080/25742558.2018.1483565.

[40] N. Rahnema, F.S. Gharehchopogh, An improved artificial bee colony algorithm based on whale optimization algorithm for data clustering, Multimed. Tools Appl. 79 (43−44) (2020) 32169−32194. Available from: https://doi.org/10.1007/s11042-020-09639-2.

[41] T. Singh, A novel data clustering approach based on whale optimization algorithm, Expert. Syst. 38 (3) (2021). Available from: https://doi.org/10.1111/exsy.12657.

[42] A. Mostafa, A.E. Hassanien, M. Houseni, H. Hefny, Liver segmentation in MRI images based on whale optimization algorithm, Multimed. Tools Appl. 76 (23) (2017) 24931−24954. Available from: https://doi.org/10.1007/s11042-017-4638-5.

[43] M.A. El Aziz, A.A. Ewees, A.E. Hassanien, M. Mudhsh, & S. Xiong, Multi-objective whale optimization algorithm for multilevel thresholding segmentation, 2018, pp. 23−39. Available from: https://doi.org/10.1007/978-3-319-63754-9_2.

[44] O.O. Akinola et al., Multiclass feature selection with metaheuristic optimization algorithms: a review, Available from: https://doi.org/10.1007/s00521-022-07705-4.

[45] R.K. Agrawal, B. Kaur, S. Sharma, Quantum based whale optimization algorithm for wrapper feature selection, Appl. Soft Comput. 89 (2020)106092. Available from: https://doi.org/10.1016/j.asoc.2020.106092.

[46] A.G. Hussien, A.E. Hassanien, E.H. Houssein, S. Bhattacharyya, & M. Amin, S-shaped binary whale optimization algorithm for feature selection, 2019, pp. 79−87. Available from: https://doi.org/10.1007/978-981-10-8863-6_9.

[47] M. Suhail Shaikh, et al., Optimal parameter estimation of 1-phase and 3-phase transmission line for various bundle conductor's using modified whale optimization algorithm, Int. J. Electr. Power Energy Syst. 138 (2022)107893. Available from: https://doi.org/10.1016/j.ijepes.2021.107893.

[48] H.M. Hasanien, Performance improvement of photovoltaic power systems using an optimal control strategy based on whale optimization algorithm, Electr. Power Syst. Res. 157 (2018) 168−176. Available from: https://doi.org/10.1016/j.epsr.2017.12.019.

[49] X. Lin, W. Lin, Optimal allocation and control of magnetorheological dampers for enhancing seismic performance of the adjacent structures using whale optimization algorithm, Shock. Vib. 2021 (2021) 1−16. Available from: https://doi.org/10.1155/2021/1218956.

9

Spider monkey optimizations: application review and results

Laith Abualigah[1,2,3,4,5,6,7], Sahar M. Alshatti[8], Abiodun M. Ikotun[9], Raed Abu Zitar[8], Anas Ratib Alsoud[2], Nima Khodadadi[10], Absalom E. Ezugwu[11], Essam Said Hanandeh[12], Heming Jia[13], Mohsen Zare[14]

[1]ARTIFICIAL INTELLIGENCE AND SENSING TECHNOLOGIES (AIST) RESEARCH CENTER, UNIVERSITY OF TABUK, TABUK, SAUDI ARABIA [2]HOURANI CENTER FOR APPLIED SCIENTIFIC RESEARCH, AL-AHLIYYA AMMAN UNIVERSITY, AMMAN, JORDAN [3]MEU RESEARCH UNIT, MIDDLE EAST UNIVERSITY, AMMAN, JORDAN [4]SCHOOL OF COMPUTER SCIENCES, UNIVERSITI SAINS MALAYSIA, PULAU PINANG, MALAYSIA [5]SCHOOL OF ENGINEERING AND TECHNOLOGY, SUNWAY UNIVERSITY MALAYSIA, PETALING JAYA, MALAYSIA [6]DEPARTMENT OF ELECTRICAL AND COMPUTER ENGINEERING, LEBANESE AMERICAN UNIVERSITY, BYBLOS, LEBANON [7]COMPUTER SCIENCE DEPARTMENT, AL AL-BAYT UNIVERSITY, MAFRAQ, JORDAN [8]SORBONNE CENTER OF ARTIFICIAL INTELLIGENCE, SORBONNE UNIVERSITY-ABU DHABI, ABU DHABI, UNITED ARAB EMIRATES [9]UNIVERSITY OF KWAZULU-NATAL, PIETERMARITZBURG CAMPUS, POTCHEFSTROOM, SOUTH AFRICA [10]DEPARTMENT OF CIVIL, ARCHITECTURAL AND ENVIRONMENTAL ENGINEERING, UNIVERSITY OF MIAMI, CORAL GABLES, FL, UNITED STATES [11]UNIT FOR DATA SCIENCE AND COMPUTING, NORTH-WEST UNIVERSITY, POTCHEFSTROOM, SOUTH AFRICA [12]DEPARTMENT OF COMPUTER INFORMATION SYSTEM, ZARQA UNIVERSITY, ZARQA, JORDAN [13]DEPARTMENT OF INFORMATION ENGINEERING, SANMING UNIVERSITY, FUJIAN, P.R. CHINA [14]DEPARTMENT OF ELECTRICAL ENGINEERING, FACULTY OF ENGINEERING, JAHROM UNIVERSITY, JAHROM, FRAS, IRAN

9.1 Introduction

Since the Stone Age, nature has been a major source of inspiration for human society's evolution. The algorithms that are produced based on nature are widely used in computer simulations to comprehend nature using several optimization algorithms [1]. The optimization algorithm is a procedure which is executed iteratively by comparing various solutions till an optimum or a satisfactory solution is found. With the advent of computers, optimization has become a part of computer-aided design activities.

Metaheuristic Optimization Algorithms. DOI: https://doi.org/10.1016/B978-0-443-13925-3.00003-0

There are three distinct types of optimization algorithms widely used today, which are classified into evolutionary, swarm, and local search algorithms. Using the swarm intelligence-based algorithms is a metaheuristic approach based on the smart attitude and adaption of different animals like birds, whale, hawk, bats, monkeys, and wolves, which is employed to solve optimization issues [2].

Lately, a number of algorithms have been proposed based on nature to solve optimization issues to find a near solution to the best target in real applications in different areas [3–6]. One of these algorithms is spider monkey optimization (SMO), which is being reviewed in this work. The SMO was proposed by Bansal [7] based on the spider monkey's behavior in looking for food in different places.

The spider monkey fission–fusion social structure (FFSS) is split into larger (unit groups) and smaller groups (subgroups) and vice versa from smaller groups into larger groups in order to search for food according to food shortage and availability in forest. The SMO algorithm was inspired by the spider monkeys' social activity to create a numerical optimization algorithm as one of common algorithms in the field of nature-inspired computing for decision-making [8].

Normally, optimization methods can be used to deal with many problems in the sciences, as presented in [9–19]. The main aim of this paper is to review related papers that used SMO in different applications and then classified them. Besides an overview of SMO applications, we present and explain the main steps of the SMO algorithm. The papers about SMO that were gathered for review were those published between 2020 and 2021, as shown in Fig. 9–1.

Over 30 papers in this collection are from a number of well-known computer science publishers (IEEE, Springer, Elsevier, Wiley library, and others). Fig. 9–2 shows the number of journal papers ordered by the publisher. Fig. 9–3 shows the distribution of these papers published according to the type of application.

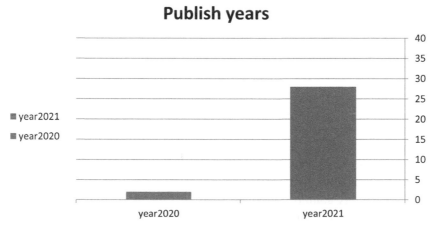

Publish years

FIGURE 9–1 Number of papers published of spider monkey optimization per year.

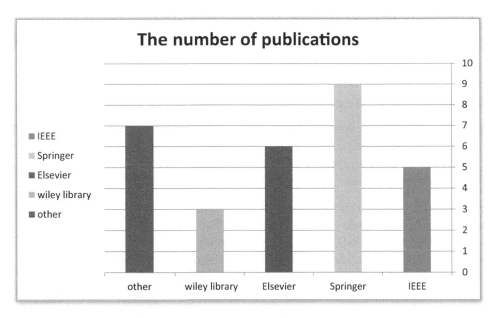

FIGURE 9–2 Spider monkey optimization papers published per publisher.

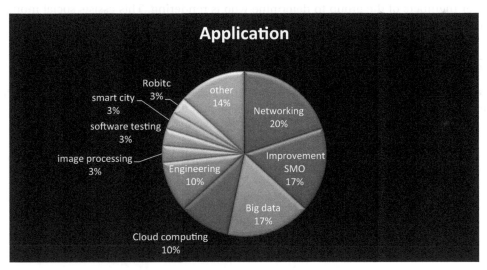

FIGURE 9–3 Applications areas of published spider monkey optimization papers.

We organized this work as follows: the main steps to SMO are presented in Section 9.2. Section 9.3 presents related work and applications, while the discussion on related works is presented in Section 9.4 The conclusion and future works are presented in Section 9.5.

9.2 Spider monkey optimization algorithm

In this part, we show the behavior of the SMO algorithm and the main steps of the SMO algorithm.

9.2.1 The behavior of spider monkey optimization

The spider monkey FFSS is split into bigger, unit groups and smaller, subgroups to seek food according to food shortage and availability. The algorithm was inspired by spider monkeys' social activity to create a numerical optimization approach that simulates spider monkeys' FFSS-based foraging behavior [1,8]. The main characteristics are as follows:

1. Spider monkeys with a FFSS arrangement are sociable in a set of 50−60 independent ones, to make foraging less competitive to seek food.
2. The set is led by a female (First leader) who is in charge of locating food sources. When she is unable to locate enough food for the set, she divides the set into tiny subsets (ranging from 2 to 7 independent) so as to forage alone.
3. Female-directed (Second leader) subsets make the choice and design a fully organized foraging path every day. In this scenario, the leader is referred to as the Second leader.
4. The members of the set communicate across vast distances by employing a specific call among themselves. Each one has a characteristic voice that can be simply recognized by other members of the group to determine who is rendering. This assists social monkeys in maintaining social connections. (Fig. 9−4).

9.2.2 The spider monkey optimization algorithm

The algorithm has six stages: first stage, second stage, second leader learning stage, first leader learning stage, second leader decision stage, and first leader decision stage.

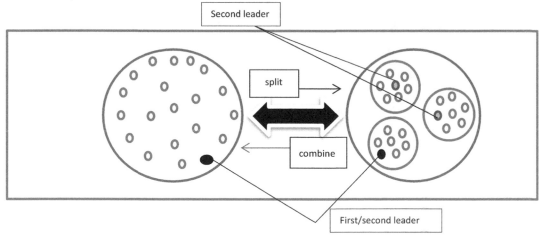

FIGURE 9–4 Fission−fusion social structure means split or combine.

9.2.2.1 Preparation of the community

First, it starts with a uniformly divided starting community of C spider monkeys, each of which is a D-dimensional vector $SM_n = (n = 1, 2, \ldots, C)$. SM_n represents the nth SM in the community. Every SM represents a possible solution to an issue under investigation. Every SM_{nj} is set up as follows:

$$SMnj = SMminj + rand(1, 0)(SMmaxj - SMminj)$$

9.2.2.2 Second leader stage

During the second leader stage (SLS), every SM adjusts its present location depending on data from the second leader's and local set experiences. The new position's appropriateness amount is determined. Whether or not the late position's appropriateness amount is higher than the old one, the SM switches to it. During this stage, the up-to-date position equation for the nth SM (an one of the zth local group) is:

$$SMnewnj = SMnj + rand(0, 1)x(SLzj - SMnj) + rand(1, -1)x(SMwj - SMnj)$$

SM_{wj} is late position's new path, and SL_z is the second leader position.

9.2.2.3 First leader stage

Following the end of the SLS, the first leader stage begins by the expertise of the FL and members of the local set; all of SMs reevaluate their positions. For this level, the up-to-date position equation is

$$SMnewnj = SMnj + rand(1, 0)(FLj - SMnj) + rand(1, -1)(SMwj - SMnj)$$

During this stage, the placements of (SM_n) are modified depending on probabilities (P) derived by their appropriateness amount. As a result, a superior nominee will have a better opportunity of succeeding. The p_n is determined by the following statement:

$$p_n = 00.9 \, x \, \frac{fitness \ n}{max\_fitness \ n} + 00.1$$

the fitness$_n$ is the appropriateness amount (value) of the nth SM. Further, the fitness of the freshly created SMs' position is computed and compared to the previous one, with the superior position being accepted.

9.2.2.4 First leader learning

Using greedy selection (GS), the location of the SM with the top appropriateness amount in the community is chosen as up to date in the stage. Furthermore, the place of first leader is checked to see if it is updated or not, the First End Count is increased by 1.

9.2.2.5 Second leader learning

By employing GS in that set, the status of the second leader is updated at this stage. Whether or not the second leader position is updated, the Second End Count is increased by 1.

9.2.2.6 Second leader decision

When any SL position is not changed to a pre-second leader limit (SLLimit), the place of all SM of that smaller group is changed through random choice or by using collective data from FL and SL by the statement:

$$SMnewnj = SMnj + rand(0, 1)(FLj - SMnj) + rand(1, 0)(SMnj - SLzj)$$

9.2.2.7 First leader decision

The first leader's place is reviewed at this step; whether or not it has been altered for a predefined number of repetitions, called the first leader limit (FLLimit), the community is split into smaller sets by the first leader. The community is split into two sets, then three sets, and so forth until the maximum number of sets (MaxSets) are created, and the SLL begins to select the second leader for the recently created sets. When MaxSets are produced, the first leader merges every smaller set into one set; also, the first leader place does not change.

9.2.3 Control parameters in spider monkey optimization

According to the preceding description, the SMO technique has four control parameters: the value of the SLLimit, FLLimit, max set, and the deviation average (DV). The following settings are proposed:

- Ms $= H/20$, the minimum number of sets should be 20
- FLLimit must be between $(H/2)$ and $(2 \times H)$.
- SLLimit must be $H \times T$.
- DV between 0.1 and 0.9.

    Note that T is the overall size of the set, and H is the swarm size.

9.3 Related work

Recently, there have been many papers about SMO. Bansal et al. [1] proposed a novel algorithm for numerical optimization called spider monkey. It had been classified as animals with a FFSS. Animals with FFSS divide themselves into larger and smaller sets depending on food shortage or availability. The proposed swarm smart technique is known as the SMO algorithm.

9.3.1 Optimization problems

SMO algorithm's local leader phase was modified using a suggested algorithm, termed changed second leader (CSLP-SMO), which balanced the seek process during the SLS by giving every spider monkey chosen by upgrading the opportunity to have a best place based on the strength of its preceding value [8]. On nine benchmark issues, the new algorithm was compared with the SMO and its enhancement, adaptive step-size-based SMO algorithm.

Kwegyir et al. [20] upgraded the SMO algorithm by trainer-modified SLS SMO to propose the improved form (MLLP-SMO). Modifying the SMO's local leader phase allowed it to be improved. Each spider monkey selected for updating has an opportunity to upgrade to a best place as a result of the alteration.

Singh et al. [21] presented a new solution alternative to the SMO algorithm, namely, the mutual learning-based (MuLSMO), which was inspired by the Mutual Learning concept between members in order to overcome restrictions common with SMO such as slowdown convergence and standstill and establishing a choice between exploration and exploitation. It was compared with regular SMO as well as other newer versions, including (MLSMO), Fibonacci-based (FSMO), PLSMO, and LFSMO. An in-depth statistical examination of the findings reveals that MuLSMO performed much better in confirming the newly proposed algorithm.

Menon et al. [22] developed a new algorithm to handle the problem of computing complexity and resource allocation. The Taylor series method and associated prediction theory were used with SMO to develop the Taylor SMO (TaySMO). By the SLS and the first leader stage, the proposed TaySMO calculates the swarm's updated location.

9.3.2 Deep learning

Chugh et al. [23] proposed a classification model (sentiment), called the SMO crow technique (SMC), for training (DeepRNN). The telecom review is used in this approach to delete stop words and stemming to delete irrelevant material and shorten the user's search time.

9.3.3 Data clustering

Patel et al. [24] proposed an LNSMO local neighbor SMO algorithm for data clustering [25]. A chaotic operator is used to improve the first search global leader stage SMO.

9.3.4 Big data problems

Shekhawat et al. [26] developed the MeSMO algorithm used to fix a large data challenge [27], specifically, the spam review detection problem. A comparison of the data revealed that the new algorithm is a good approach for solving this identification problem, with a 3.68% improvement in precision.

9.3.5 Networking problems

Ramalingam and Joseph and Samiayya and Joseph [28,29] reported a multiobjective-based SMO algorithm for energy-efficient load balancing, optimal routing, and clustering by integrating both the shortest path crossed by the gateways and the least number of hops. The simulation results indicate that the new SMO-based clustering and routing strategy outperforms the existing methods in terms of energy consumption, delivery ratio, throughput, and network lifetime.

Sivagar and Prabakaran and Al-Quh et al. [30,31] reported new algorithms based on SMO to create solution for the load balancing problem in the long-term evolution network. Sivagar and Prabakaran [30] proposed the opposition-based spider monkey optimization algorithm (OSMOA) through the optimal cell selection method. Al-Quh et al. [31] presented the chosen optimal cluster head-based SMO (OCHSMO) to settle the issues of cluster routing in the WSNs.

Jabbar and Alshawi [32] proposed the SMO routing protocol (SMORP). In comparison to well-known routing protocols, simulation results have proven the efficiency of the proposed protocol in terms of minimizing end-to-end delay and lowering energy usage.

9.3.6 Cloud computing

Cloud computing field issues are presented in [33–35]. Work scheduling was discussed as one of the key challenges in the cloud environment [33]. The goal of the scheduling is to distribute jobs across the virtual machine (VM) and balance the load such that no VM is overburdened while others are underutilized. The scheduling problem is regarded as an NP-hard optimization problem. The paper presented a novel SMO load balancing technique dubbed SMO inspired load balancing (SMO-LB), which is based on spider monkeys' searching for food. The goal to distribute workload evenly among VMs in order to improve performance by shortening the makespan and reaction time. The proposed solution decreases the rate of response time of jobs to 10.7 from 30.8 seconds for another methods.

Rizvi et al. [34] reported that workflows in the cloud are bound by quality of service (QoS) criteria when they are scheduled. For the QoS-restricted workflow scheduling problem, several heuristic and metaheuristic algorithms had been studied. The hybrid spider monkey optimization (HSMO) algorithm was introduced in this study as a solution to this challenge. The suggested algorithm reduces the time and expense of a project while staying within budget and meeting deadlines. The suggested algorithm is a combination of two prominent heuristic algorithms: SMO and BDSD. HSMO is guided by the BDSD algorithm. The results demonstrate that the performance of HSMO is better than that of other algorithms in this study.

Chicken-based deep belief network (ChicSMO-based DBN) is presented in [35] as an effective technique to execute the violation detection mechanism in the cloud environment since breach of the service level agreement is a key problem in the research of SaaS cloud. The suggested technique improved performance based on the assessment metrics such as accuracy, coverage rate, and *F*-value. It improves the reliability of the prediction model, while also addressing QoS guarantee problems.

9.3.7 Scheduling issues

Zhang et al. and Mohanty et al. [36,37] discussed scheduling issues. Zhang et al. [36] reported that the existing Hadoop scheduling methods fail to account for performance changes across nodes in heterogeneous Hadoop clusters [38], resulting in issues such as inconsistent task distribution and soft resource exploitation. To address the issue, the researchers presented an SMO scheduling (SMOSA) for heterogeneous Hadoop. When compared with the existing scheduling methods, the SMOSA greatly enhances scheduling efficiency and task execution speed.

A binary SMO approach is used to schedule numbers of user multiple-input multiple-output broadcasts [37]. For common user and antenna scheduling problem, the researchers used a newly created binary SMO optimization technique to increase the overall rate performance of the system.

9.3.8 Privacy problems

Priya et al. [39] discussed crowdsourcing as a method of exhibiting data outsourcing to a large number of individuals rather than a single agency or business. By employing human knowledge, crowdsourcing has created a variety of opportunities for certain difficult problems that required collection of data on the position of all workers in order to achieve an optimal global assignment approach. During the acquisition of information, a few security issues arise that pose a serious hazard to all workers, To resolve the issue, the authors provided a privacy-preserving approach based on fuzzy with the black widow (BW-SMO) to address privacy problems. The query solution can be clustered using the fuzzy.

9.3.9 Image processing

Baneamoon and Sama [40] suggested an effective approach for analyzing satellite pictures 1 to optimize all parameters in a fuzzy system to improve the accuracy of the contrast and brightness improvement of satellite images. A variety of satellite images are used to test the suggested method. LANDSAT was received from the earth explorer site and the global land survey, and the results demonstrate that the analysis is better and more effective, and that the image has enough contrast and brightness enhancement.

9.3.10 Software engineering field

Agrawal et al. [41] offered a regression test suite optimization algorithm based on hybrid SMO. Experiments are carried out to compare the suggested algorithm to the existing search-based approaches under investigation, employing statistical tests such as m-way analysis of variance. The proposed algorithm, according to the findings, is superior in most circumstances and comparable to others.

9.3.11 Other applications

SMO based on sine–cosine algorithm (SCNWSMO) was developed by Yin and Zhang [42] to increase spectrum allocation optimization and optimal convergence accuracy. Individual spider monkeys are optimized by the sine-cosine algorithm during the decision-making stages of the first leader and second leader. SCNWSMO's performance is compared to the overall system and average network benefit of various methods. SCNWSMO outperforms other algorithms in terms of network efficiency, according to simulation data.

An urban transport network for the optimal location of bus stops in a smart city was designed by Montalvo-Martel et al. [43] by using big data and the SMO. The vehicle routing problem with stochastic demands (VRPSDs) was proposed by Liao et al. [44], in which client demands follow a known probability distribution. Lan et al. [45] presented interleaved parallel bidirectional DC–DC converter model predictive control based on SMO algorithm in electric vehicles.

Lattice optimization by the SMO grid synchronization control strategy was presented for a three-phase PV system based on Levenberg–Marquardt recursive least squares. Das and Namrata [46] reported that using an optimization technique based on the SMO principle, the performance analysis of a PV generation system's MPPT controller unit (SMO) was improved.

A machine learning model improved by the SMO optimization technique was used to evaluate and analyze irrigation water consumption efficiency [47]. An adaptive ageist SMO model was used for optimizing a convolutional neural network for detecting maize leaf illnesses [48].

Firgiawan et al. [49] carried out performance comparison between SMO and genetic algorithm for the traveling salesman problem for finding the minimum tour cost. Based on the results of these comparison, it was possible to infer that SMO gave the optimum solution for TSP.

Agrawal et al. [50] used fuzzy logic to create an efficient and durable controller that efficiently controls the end position of a single link robotic manipulator to follow the intended trajectory. The results show that the fuzzy proportional integral derivative controller optimized using the SMO technique is more accurate, quick, and resilient than the proportional integral derivative controller and the controllers optimized with the genetic algorithm techniques. Furthermore, when the integral absolute error values of all the controllers were compared, it was discovered that the controller improved with the SMO outperforms the genetic algorithm technique by 99%.

9.4 Discussion

SMO is one of the metaheuristic algorithms inspired by the characteristics of monkeys when they are looking for food in the forest/mountains and is helpful in obtaining the optimal location from a large search space. According to the literature, one can say that the SMO replicates the FFSS behavior of spider monkeys,

The researchers made various improvements in the essential adaptation of SMO with the objective goal of eliminating some of disadvantages, for example, stagnation and low utilization capacities. Many differences are proposed by utilizing a different perturbation rate, a variation chaotic operator, a change in local search ability, a changed place update technique, and so on. The strong point of the SMO is that it is a **competitive** swarm-based algorithm that is utilized to resolve complicated real-life situations.

SMO has a wide range of applications that have been documented in a multitude of sectors. SMO has been used to handle performance optimization and real-world challenges. Table 9−1 presents a quick review of the main proposed methods that use the SMO in specific fields.

Table 9–1 Summary of the optimization algorithm proposed based on the spider monkey optimization algorithm.

Category	Published year	Ref.	Proposed algorithm
Networking problems	2021	[21]	Energy-efficient node clustering and routing using multiobjective SMO
	2021	[22]	Multiobjective SMO for energy-efficient clustering and routing in wireless sensor networks
	2021	[23]	OSMOA
	2021	[24]	OCHSMO
	2021	[25]	SMORP
Optimization problems	2021	[3]	Changed second leader (CSLP-SMO)
	2021	[4]	Modified SLS (MLLP-SMO)
	2021	[5]	Mutual learning-based (MuLSMO)
	2021	[6]	Taylor (TaySMO)
Data clustering	2021	[8]	Local neighbor LNSMO
Big data	2021	[20]	MeSMO
Image processing	2021	[32]	Analyzing satellite pictures that use SMO
Software engineering	2021	[33]	A regression test suite optimization algorithm based on hybrid SMO
Scheduling problems	2021	[30]	Binary SMO optimization technique
	2021	[29]	SMOSA
Security issues (privacy)	2021	[31]	BW-SMO
Smart city	2021	[35]	The optimal location of bus stops in a smart city by SMO
Deep learning	2021	[7]	SMC
Cloud computing	2021	[26]	SMO-LB
	2021	[27]	HSMO
	2021	[28]	Chicken-based deep belief network (ChicSMO-based DBN)
Other applications	2021	[34]	SMO based on sine-cosine (SCNWSMO)
	2021	[36]	VRPSD
	2021	[37]	Predictive control by SMO in electric vehicles
	2021	[38]	Lattice optimization by SMO for a three-phase PV system
	2021	[39]	A PV generation system's MPPT controller unit (SMO)
	2021	[40]	Irrigation water consumption efficiency
	2020	[42]	Traveling salesman problem
	2021	[43]	Robotic (best path)

9.5 Conclusion and future works

In this paper, we present an overview of the recent related works that uses SMO to solve specific problems in different computer science fields and classify the related works in the same category and the problems that they try to solve such as routing in networks, big data, data clustering, and deep learning, image processing, scheduling problems, and smart city. Researchers can help to improve this algorithm by incorporating some special features of the other algorithms into the SMO. The monkey algorithm is efficient in solving the optimization of multivariate systems.

References

[1] J.C. Bansal, H. Sharma, S.S. Jadon, M. Clerc, Spider monkey optimization algorithm for numerical optimization, Memetic Comput. 6 (1) (2014) 31−47. Available from: https://doi.org/10.1007/s12293-013-0128-0.

[2] S.K. Sahoo, et al., Moth flame optimization: theory, modifications, hybridizations, and applications, Arch. Comput. Methods Eng. 30 (1) (2023) 391−426. Available from: https://doi.org/10.1007/s11831-022-09801-z.

[3] J.O. Agushaka, A.E. Ezugwu, L. Abualigah, Dwarf Mongoose optimization algorithm, Comput. Methods Appl. Mech. Eng. 391 (2022). Available from: https://doi.org/10.1016/j.cma.2022.114570. Mar.

[4] J.O. Agushaka, A.E. Ezugwu, L. Abualigah, Gazelle optimization algorithm: a novel nature-inspired metaheuristic optimizer, Neural Comput. Appl. 35 (5) (2023) 4099−4131. Available from: https://doi.org/10.1007/s00521-022-07854-6.

[5] A.E. Ezugwu, J.O. Agushaka, L. Abualigah, S. Mirjalili, A.H. Gandomi, Prairie Dog optimization algorithm, Neural Comput. Appl. 34 (22) (2022) 20017−20065. Available from: https://doi.org/10.1007/s00521-022-07530-9.

[6] O.N. Oyelade, A.E.-S. Ezugwu, T.I.A. Mohamed, L. Abualigah, Ebola optimization search algorithm: a new nature-inspired metaheuristic optimization algorithm, IEEE Access. 10 (2022) 16150−16177. Available from: https://doi.org/10.1109/ACCESS.2022.3147821.

[7] A. Chakraborty, A.K. Kar, Swarm intelligence: A review of algorithms, 2017, pp. 475−494. Available from: https://doi.org/10.1007/978-3-319-50920-4_19.

[8] D. Kwegyir, E.A. Frimpong, Modified local leader phase spider monkey optimization algorithm, ADRRI J. Eng. Technol. 5 (2) (2021) 4.

[9] L. Abualigah, A. Diabat, C.L. Thanh, S. Khatir, Opposition-based Laplacian distribution with Prairie Dog optimization method for industrial engineering design problems, Comput. Methods Appl. Mech. Eng. 414 (2023) 116097.

[10] G. Hu, Y. Zheng, L. Abualigah, A.G. Hussien, DETDO: An adaptive hybrid dandelion optimizer for engineering optimization, Adv. Eng. Inform. 57 (2023) 102004.

[11] D. Izci, S. Ekinci, S. Mirjalili, L. Abualigah, An intelligent tuning scheme with a master/slave approach for efficient control of the automatic voltage regulator, Neural Comput. Appl. (2023) 1−17.

[12] H. Jia, C. Lu, D. Wu, C. Wen, H. Rao, L. Abualigah, An improved reptile search algorithm with ghost opposition-based learning for global optimization problems, J. Comput. Des. Eng. (2023) qwad048.

[13] A.H. Alharbi, A.A. Abdelhamid, A. Ibrahim, S.K. Towfek, N. Khodadadi, L. Abualigah, et al., Improved dipper-throated optimization for forecasting metamaterial design bandwidth for engineering applications, Biomimetics 8 (2) (2023) 241.

[14] S. Nama, A.K. Saha, S. Chakraborty, A.H. Gandomi, L. Abualigah, Boosting particle swarm optimization by backtracking search algorithm for optimization problems, Swarm Evolut. Comput. 79 (2023) 101304.

[15] M. Zare, M. Ghasemi, A. Zahedi, K. Golalipour, S.K. Mohammadi, S. Mirjalili, et al., A global best-guided firefly algorithm for engineering problems, J. Bionic Eng. (2023) 1−30.

[16] D. Wu, C. Wen, H. Rao, H. Jia, Q. Liu, L. Abualigah, Modified reptile search algorithm with multi-hunting coordination strategy for global optimization problems, Math. Biosci. Eng. 20 (6) (2023) 10090−10134.

[17] S. Ekinci, D. Izci, L. Abualigah, R.A. Zitar, A modified oppositional chaotic local search strategy based aquila optimizer to design an effective controller for vehicle cruise control system, J. Bionic Eng. (2023) 1−24.

[18] L. Abualigah, D. Falcone, A. Forestiero, Swarm intelligence to face IoT challenges, Comput. Intell. Neurosci. 2023 (2023).

[19] M. Hadni, H. Hassane, New model of feature selection based chaotic firefly algorithm for Arabic text categorization, Int. Arab. J. Inf. Technol. 20 (3A) (2023) 461−468.

[20] D. Kwegyir, E.A. Frimpong, D. Opoku, Optimization of feedforward neural network training using modified local leader phase spider monkey optimization, Int. Res. J. Eng. Technol. (2021) [Online]. Available from: http://www.irjet.net.

[21] M. Singh, N. Sharma, H. Sharma, Mutual learning-based spider monkey optimization for constraint optimization, 2021, pp. 745−758. Available from: https://doi.org/10.1007/978-981-16-1089-9_58.

[22] R. Menon, A. Kulkarni, D. Singh, M. Venkatesan, Hybrid multi-objective optimization algorithm using Taylor series model and spider monkey optimization, Int. J. Numer. Methods Eng. 122 (10) (2021) 2478−2497. Available from: https://doi.org/10.1002/nme.6628.

[23] A. Chugh, et al., Spider monkey crow optimization algorithm with deep learning for sentiment classification and information retrieval, IEEE Access. 9 (2021) 24249−24262. Available from: https://doi.org/10.1109/ACCESS.2021.3055507.

[24] V.P. Patel, M.K. Rawat, A.S. Patel, Local neighbour spider monkey optimization algorithm for data clustering, Evol. Intell. 16 (1) (2023) 133−151. Available from: https://doi.org/10.1007/s12065-021-00647-1.

[25] A.E. Ezugwu, et al., A comprehensive survey of clustering algorithms: state-of-the-art machine learning applications, taxonomy, challenges, and future research prospects, Eng. Appl. Artif. Intell. 110 (2022) 104743. Available from: https://doi.org/10.1016/j.engappai.2022.104743. Apr.

[26] S.S. Shekhawat, H. Sharma, S. Kumar, Memetic spider monkey optimization for spam review detection problem, Big Data 11 (2) (2023) 137−149. Available from: https://doi.org/10.1089/big.2020.0188.

[27] A.M. Ikotun, A.E. Ezugwu, L. Abualigah, B. Abuhaija, J. Heming, K-means clustering algorithms: a comprehensive review, variants analysis, and advances in the era of big data, Inf. Sci. (Ny). 622 (2023) 178−210. Available from: https://doi.org/10.1016/j.ins.2022.11.139. Apr.

[28] A. Ramalingam, S. Joseph, Energy efficient nodes clustering and routing using multi-objective spider monkey optimization algorithm in wireless sensor network energy, 2021. Available from: https://doi.org/10.21203/rs.3.rs-618230/v1.

[29] D. Samiayya, S. Joseph, Multi-objective spider monkey optimization for energy eecient clustering and routing in wireless sensor networks multi-objective spider monkey optimization for energy efficient clustering and routing in wireless sensor networks, 2021. Available from: https://doi.org/10.21203/rs.3.rs-412238/v1.

[30] M.R. Sivagar, N. Prabakaran, Opposition based spider monkey optimization algorithm for load balancing in LTE network, Webology 18 (Special Issue 01) (2021) 211−229. Available from: https://doi.org/10.14704/WEB/V18SI01/WEB18055.

[31] A.H. Al-Quh, K. Al-Hussaini, F. Abdulrazzak, OCHSMO: selection optimal of cluster head based spider monkey optimization, in: 2021 International Conference of Technology, Science and Administration (ICTSA), March 2021, pp. 1−6. Available from: https://doi.org/10.1109/ICTSA52017.2021.9406526.

[32] A.H. Jabbar, I.S. Alshawi, Spider monkey optimization routing protocol for wireless sensor networks, Int. J. Electr. Comput. Eng. 11 (3) (2021) 2432. Available from: https://doi.org/10.11591/ijece.v11i3.pp2432-2442.

[33] S. Alshattnawi, M. AL-Marie, Spider monkey optimization algorithm for load balancing in cloud computing environments, Int. Arab. J. Inf. Technol. 18 (5) (2021). Available from: https://doi.org/10.34028/iajit/18/5/13.

[34] N. Rizvi, R. Dharavath, D.R. Edla, Cost and makespan aware workflow scheduling in IaaS clouds using hybrid spider monkey optimization, Simul. Model. Pract. Theory 110 (2021) 102328. Available from: https://doi.org/10.1016/j.simpat.2021.102328. Jul.

[35] P. Pradeepa, R. PushpaLakshmi, Violation detection in service level agreement to ensure the privacy in cloud community using chicken spider monkey optimization-based deep belief network, Wirel. Pers. Commun. 117 (2) (2021) 1659−1683. Available from: https://doi.org/10.1007/s11277-020-07940-9.

[36] C. Zhang, S. Guan, Y. Li, W. Sun, SMOSA: spider monkey optimization-based scheduling algorithm for heterogeneous Hadoop, Concurr. Comput. Pract. Exp. 33 (20) (2021). Available from: https://doi.org/10.1002/cpe.6368.

[37] J. Mohanty, P. Pattanayak, A. Nandi, K.L. Baishnab, D.S. Gurjar, M. Mandloi, MIMO broadcast scheduling using binary spider monkey optimization algorithm, Int. J. Commun. Syst. 34 (17) (2021). Available from: https://doi.org/10.1002/dac.4975.

[38] N. Milhem, L. Abualigah, M.H. Nadimi-Shahraki, H. Jia, A.E. Ezugwu, A.G. Hussien, Enhanced MapReduce performance for the distributed parallel computing: application of the big data, 2023, pp. 191−203. Available from: https://doi.org/10.1007/978-3-031-17576-3_8.

[39] J.S. Priya, N. Bhaskar, S. Prabakeran, Fuzzy with black widow and spider monkey optimization for privacy-preserving-based crowdsourcing system, Soft Comput. 25 (7) (2021) 5831−5846. Available from: https://doi.org/10.1007/s00500-021-05657-w.

[40] S.M. Baneamoon, A.S.B. Sama, Satellite image analysis enhancement based on spider monkey optimization, J. Xidian Univ. 14 (7) (2020). Available from: https://doi.org/10.37896/jxu14.7/067.

[41] A.P. Agrawal, A. Choudhary, P. Nand, An efficient regression test suite optimization approach using hybrid spider monkey optimization algorithm, Int. J. Swarm Intell. Res. 12 (4) (2021) 57−80. Available from: https://doi.org/10.4018/IJSIR.2021100104.

[42] D. Yin, D. Zhang, Spectrum allocation based on spider monkey optimization algorithm with nonlinear inertia weight and sine-cosine algorithm, in: 2020 IEEE 6th International Conference on Computer and Communications (ICCC), December 2020, pp. 776−780. Available from: https://doi.org/10.1109/ICCC51575.2020.9345294.

[43] M. Montalvo-Martel, A. Ochoa-Zezzatti, E. Carrum, D. Barzaga, Design of an urban transport network for the optimal location of bus stops in a smart city based on a big data model and spider monkey optimization algorithm, 2021, pp. 167−201, Available from: https://doi.org/10.1007/978-3-030-68655-0_9.

[44] X. Xia, W. Liao, Y. Zhang, X. Peng, A discrete spider monkey optimization for the vehicle routing problem with stochastic demands, Appl. Soft Comput. 111 (2021) 107676. Available from: https://doi.org/10.1016/j.asoc.2021.107676. Nov.

[45] Y. Lan, Q. Chen, L. Zhang, R. Long, Model predictive control based on spider monkey optimization algorithm of interleaved parallel bidirectional DC-DC converter, in: 2020 16th International Conference on Control, Automation, Robotics and Vision (ICARCV), December 2020, pp. 50−55. Available from: https://doi.org/10.1109/ICARCV50220.2020.9305361.

[46] S. Das, K. Namrata, Improving the performance analysis of MPPT controller unit of a PV generation system using optimization technique based on spider monkey principle (SMO), 2021, pp. 553−564, Available from: https://doi.org/10.1007/978-981-16-0182-8_41.

[47] D. Liu, et al., Evaluation and analysis of irrigation water use efficiency based on an extreme learning machine model optimized by the spider monkey optimization algorithm, J. Clean. Prod. 330 (2022) 129935. Available from: https://doi.org/10.1016/j.jclepro.2021.129935. Jan.

[48] S. Arjunagi, N.B. Patil, Optimized convolutional neural network for identification of maize leaf diseases with adaptive ageist spider monkey optimization model, Int. J. Inf. Technol. 15 (2) (2023) 877−891. Available from: https://doi.org/10.1007/s41870-021-00657-3.

[49] W. Firgiawan, S. Cokrowibowo, A. Irianti, A. Gunawan, Performance comparison of spider monkey optimization and genetic algorithm for traveling salesman problem, in: 2021 3rd International Conference on Electronics Representation and Algorithm (ICERA), July 2021, pp. 191−195. Available from: https://doi.org/10.1109/ICERA53111.2021.9538795.

[50] A. Agrawal, V. Goyal, P. Mishra, Comparative study of fuzzy PID and PID controller optimized with spider monkey optimization for a robotic manipulator system, Recent. Adv. Comput. Sci. Commun. 14 (4) (2021) 1173−1181. Available from: https://doi.org/10.2174/2213275912666191107104635.

10

Marine predator's algorithm: a survey of recent applications

Laith Abualigah[1,2,3,4,5,6,7]**, Suhier Odah**[8]**, Abiodun M. Ikotun**[9]**,**
Anas Ratib Alsoud[2]**, Agostino Forestiero**[10]**, Absalom E. Ezugwu**[11]**,**
Essam Said Hanandeh[12]**, Heming Jia**[13]**, Mohsen Zare**[14]

[1]*ARTIFICIAL INTELLIGENCE AND SENSING TECHNOLOGIES (AIST) RESEARCH CENTER, UNIVERSITY OF TABUK, TABUK, SAUDI ARABIA* [2]*HOURANI CENTER FOR APPLIED SCIENTIFIC RESEARCH, AL-AHLIYYA AMMAN UNIVERSITY, AMMAN, JORDAN* [3]*MEU RESEARCH UNIT, MIDDLE EAST UNIVERSITY, AMMAN, JORDAN* [4]*SCHOOL OF COMPUTER SCIENCES, UNIVERSITI SAINS MALAYSIA, PULAU PINANG, MALAYSIA* [5]*SCHOOL OF ENGINEERING AND TECHNOLOGY, SUNWAY UNIVERSITY MALAYSIA, PETALING JAYA, MALAYSIA* [6]*DEPARTMENT OF ELECTRICAL AND COMPUTER ENGINEERING, LEBANESE AMERICAN UNIVERSITY, BYBLOS, LEBANON* [7]*COMPUTER SCIENCE DEPARTMENT, AL AL-BAYT UNIVERSITY, MAFRAQ, JORDAN* [8]*NEW ENGINEERING INDUSTRY COLLEGE, PUTIAN UNIVERSITY, PUTIAN, CHINA* [9]*UNIVERSITY OF KWAZULU-NATAL, PIETERMARITZBURG CAMPUS, POTCHEFSTROOM, SOUTH AFRICA* [10]*INSTITUTE FOR HIGH PERFORMANCE COMPUTING AND NETWORKING, NATIONAL RESEARCH COUNCIL, RENDE, CS, ITALY* [11]*UNIT FOR DATA SCIENCE AND COMPUTING, NORTH-WEST UNIVERSITY, POTCHEFSTROOM, SOUTH AFRICA* [12]*DEPARTMENT OF COMPUTER INFORMATION SYSTEM, ZARQA UNIVERSITY, ZARQA, JORDAN* [13]*DEPARTMENT OF INFORMATION ENGINEERING, SANMING UNIVERSITY, FUJIAN, P.R. CHINA* [14]*DEPARTMENT OF ELECTRICAL ENGINEERING, FACULTY OF ENGINEERING, JAHROM UNIVERSITY, JAHROM, FRAS, IRAN*

10.1 Introduction

MPA is a nature-inspired metaheuristic that simulates predator behaviors when hunting prey. The improved marine predator's algorithm (MPA) is used in image processing like image segmentation. In addition, the ranking-based updating strategy (RUS) is focused on a new updating scheme, which finds the most effective solutions in the most recent iterations [1].

Improving accuracy when studying an image may be cluttered with items that are not useful for the analysis, and as a result, the accuracy will suffer from paying attention to certain unnecessary regions [1]. Therefore, for various photovoltaic (PV) models, the enhanced MPA (EMPA) was presented to find unknown parameters. EMPA includes both dynamic and static PV models (single-diode and double-diode) [2].

Normally, optimization methods can be used to deal with many problems in the sciences, as presented in [3−12]. In this survey paper, MPA is presented with details in related works published since 2020, which are divided into four parts: engineering problems, image processing, benchmark function, and feature selection. This survey paper can help the researchers in this field to determine the different areas where MPA is used in order to explore the best agents. Therefore, the primary goal of this survey is to review the recent work of the MPA algorithm. Table 10−1 presents an overview of the related work on the MPA algorithm published from 2020 to 2022. Fig. 10−1 displays the number of researches depending on the classes of MPA applications.

Table 10–1 The overview of the presented survey.

No.	Years	References	Proposed
1.	2021	[1]	Based on the MPA, a new image segmentation technique has been developed (MPA).
2.	2021	[2]	The parameters of single-diode and double-diode PV models which are unknown were identified using an algorithm.
3.	2020	[13]	EMPA and IMPAPSO are strong and adaptive algorithms for optimization for dealing with ORPD nonlinearity that has the fewest variable parameters.
4.	2020	[14]	Uses 29 test functions, the CEC-BC-2017 test suite, a randomly generated landscape, two real-world engineering designs, and three engineering benchmarks to evaluate MPA's performance in the fields of building energy and ventilation performance.
5.	2021	[15]	MMPA.
6.	2020	[16]	For extracting the parameters of the PV module/cells, many stochastic approaches have been presented.
7.	2020	[17]	The unknown parameters of PEMFC models have also been successfully evaluated using new metaheuristic optimization tools, particularly the MPA and political optimizer methodologies.
8.	2020	[18]	MPA is being used for the first time to identify the electrical parameters of a PV panel's TDPV model.
9.	2021	[19]	A modified marine predator's optimizer
10.	2020	[20]	The properties of the MPA and moth-flame optimization are combined in a hybrid SI-based strategy
11.	2020	[21]	Addressed the problem of dynamic clustering where the clusters cannot be specified in advance. A hybrid dynamic clustering method is proposed based on the MPA and the PSO algorithm.
12.	2020	[22]	The MPA is the version that has been updated to a novel metaheuristic algorithm.
13.	2021	[23]	The shape of SGCD ball surfaces is optimized using an EMPA.
14.	2021	[24]	The MPA is a modern bioinspired algorithm for optimization and for extracting the parameters of three solar cell PV models.
15.	2021	[25]	Increasing the convergence speed by solving the IEEE CEC'2020 benchmark questions.
16.	2021	[26]	A new MPA variation that incorporates a suggested LEO.
17.	2021	[27]	There are four MPA variations for solving multiobjective optimization problems.
18.	2021	[28]	To use a newly designed metaheuristic to explain the shape design of a vehicle bracket.

(Continued)

Table 10−1   (Continued)

No.	Years	References	Proposed
19.	2020	[29]	An innovative objective function with a strong and reliable optimization algorithm known as the MPA to give the ideal for three dimensions of PV arrays: 9 × 9, 16 × 16 and 25 × 25.
20.	2021	[30]	A new PV model based on the MPA that determines the best model parameters for solar cells or modules.
21.	2022	[31]	A hybrid MPA with SSA to find the optimal multilevel threshold for image segmentation called MPASSA.
22.	2022	[32]	An effective method for fusing medical images.
23.	2022	[33]	IMPOA was developed for tackling the combined power and heat economic dispatch problem.
24.	2022	[34]	An improved MPA for the best design of hybrid renewable energy systems.
25.	2022	[35]	ROBL-MPA to improve MPA in terms of reconnoitering a larger search field; it outperforms normal MPA.
26.	2022	[36]	The MPA is used as a learning algorithm to train the ANN for classification tasks.
27.	2022	[37]	MPA incorporates the principles of the memory perspective and the comprehensive learning strategy of fractional calculus.
28.	2022	[38]	MOEMPA to handle three objective functions aimed at decreasing operational costs and emissions while increasing the renewable component for optimal usage.
29.	2022	[39]	To improve the production of methane through steam gasification of PKS using coal bottom ash as a catalyst.
30.	2022	[40]	The FS approach is based on a recently updated version of the MPA.
31.	2022	[41]	MMPA for improving the performance of traditional MPA.
32.	2022	[42]	Multilayer perceptron neural network MLPNN and MPA to improve the problem of economic transmission of the microgrid system in Algeria.
33.	2023	[43]	A comprehensive review on K-means clustering with variant analysis and advances in the era of big data.
34.	2023	[44]	An SI-based metaheuristic algorithm for solving complex real world optimization problems.
35.	2022	[45]	The use of deep learning CNN for Artocarpus classification.
36.	2022	[46]	A generative adversarial network for synthetization of data to bridge the gap of insufficient data samples for training in deep learning models.
37.	2022	[47]	A metaheuristic optimization algorithm inspired by the effective propagation mechanism of Ebola virus disease.
38.	2022	[48]	An enhanced MapReduce a priori algorithm on the apache Hadoop cluster
39.	2022	[49]	The use of CNN and transfer learning technique in image processing identification.
40.	2022	[50]	Survey of clustering algorithm.
41.	2022	[51]	A nature-inspired metaheuristic algorithm inspired by Prairie dog behavior in their natural habitat.
42.	2022	[52]	A comprehensive review on differential evolution and its image processing applications and problems.
43.	2022	[53]	Big data classification technique for healthcare application based on SVM, RF, and J48.
44.	2022	[54]	A review of metaheuristic-based multiclass feature selection algorithms.
45.	2023	[55]	A modified version of the dwarf mongoose optimization algorithm for solving design problems in engineering.
46.	2023	[56]	Comparative study of initialization methods of population-based metaheuristic algorithms.
47.	2023	[57]	A population-based metaheuristic algorithm inspired by survival ability of gazelles in the predator-dominated environment.
48.	2023	[58]	A metaheuristic algorithm for solving CEC 2020 benchmark functions and continuous/discrete engineering problems.

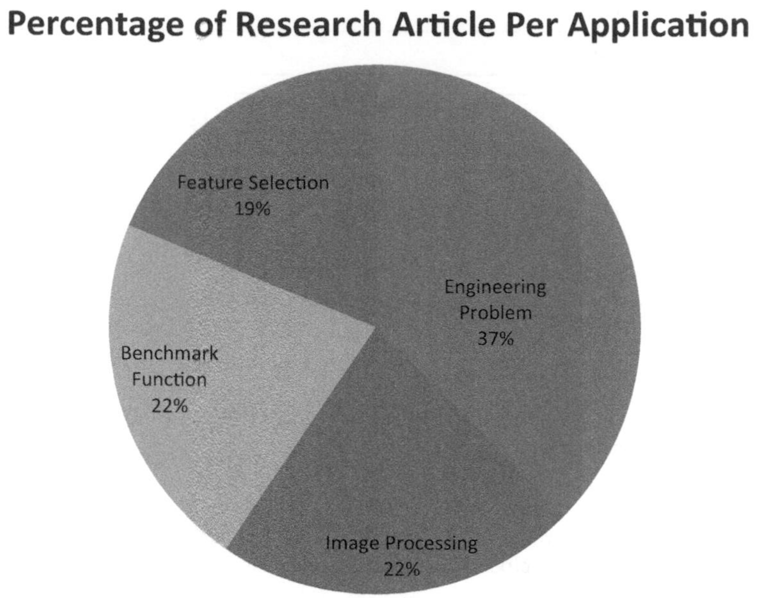

Percentage of Research Article Per Application

FIGURE 10–1 Percentage of research article per application.

This survey paper is arranged as follows: Section 10.2 explains the MPA, while Section 10.3 presents the related works for optimization algorithms. Section 10.4 discusses the optimization algorithms. Finally, Section 10.5 provides conclusion and discusses future work.

10.2 Marine Predator's Algorithm

In this section, the main MPA algorithm procedure is given. MPA simulates predator behaviors when hunting prey. MPA is defined as follows in mathematical terms:

$$Prey = X_{min} + r * (X_{max} - X_{min})$$

Minimum and Maximum vector are denoted by X_{min} and X_{max}, respectively. A vector random numeric value of 0 and $1 = r$.

The elite matrix shows the fitness value as well as the predator. The best fitness is chosen as the prime predator during the optimization phase.

The structure of this matrix is as follows:

$$E = \begin{bmatrix} À1.1 & À1.2 & À1.d \\ À2.1 & À2.2 & À2.d \\ \cdots & \cdots & \cdots \\ ÀN.1 & ÀN.2 & ÀN.d \end{bmatrix}$$

N is the individual numbers in the population. The top predator is denoted by A', and the dimension number is presented by d for each individual.

In the part of the process of optimization, the predators are then directed toward a prey matrix, prefixed and constructed as follows at random inside the search area:

$$Prey = \begin{bmatrix} A1.1 & A1.2 & \ldots & A1.d \\ A2.1 & A2.2 & \ldots & A2.d \\ \ldots & \ldots & \ldots & \ldots \\ AN.1 & AN.2 & \ldots & AN.d \end{bmatrix}$$

Three phases are an update of each prey during the optimization process, depending on the ratio of velocity between the prey and the predators, as shown in:

(1) High-velocity ratio, (2) Unit velocity ratio, (3). Low-velocity ratio.

Finally, fish aggregating devices (FADs) should be calculated mathematically using the formula:

$$Prey_i = \begin{cases} Prey_i + CF\left[\boldsymbol{X}_{min} + r_2(\boldsymbol{X}_{max} - \boldsymbol{X}_{min})\right] \otimes U & \text{if } r < \text{FADs} \\ Prey_i + \left\lceil \text{FADs}(1-r) + r \right\rceil \left(Prey_{r1} - Prey_{r2}\right) & \text{if } r \geq \text{FADs} \end{cases}$$

0 and 1 refer to r; they are random numbers. $(r2) = $ The index of prey chosen at random.

U denotes a vector of binary with 0 and 1 values. FAD = 0.2; it denotes the possibility of impacting FADs. $r1$ is the index of a prey chosen at random from the population [1].

10.3 Related Works

In this section, the recent related works are classified into four main parts as follows: engineering problems, image processing, benchmark function, and feature selection.

10.3.1 Engineering Problems

The economic status of countries is significantly influenced by the proper planning of electric power infrastructure [13]. The optimal reactive power dispatch (ORPD) is an important problem. ORPD is a continuous or noncontinuous, nonlinear, nonconvex optimization problem. The improved MPA and particle swarm optimization (IMPAPSO) technique is developed as a strong and adaptable optimization algorithm with the fewest modifiable parameters to deal with ORPD's nonlinearity.

MPA was tested with three different types of methods for optimization; CS, GSA, and SSA are relatively recent algorithms; GA and PSO are well-studied metaheuristics; while SHADE, CMA-ES, and LSHADE-cnEpSin are high-performance optimizers and IEEE CEC [14].

A logistic opposition-based learning (OBL) mechanism was proposed to increase population variety as well as create more precise solutions. On 23 classic benchmark functions, four real-world challenges, and CEC 2020 functions, the modified MPA's (MMPA) validity is verified [15].

Recently, several stochastic approaches have been developed to collect PV module/cell parameters [16]. In addition, some of these systems have limitations in terms of exploration and exploitation capabilities, either alone or in combination, due to their stochastic searching strategies [16]. MPA is merged with the Lambert W function named MPALW. The MPALW algorithm is assessed using real-world data from seven different sunlight and temperature settings. The MPALW can be employed in real-world engineering applications in smart grids, energy, and defect identification.

The proton exchange membrane fuel cells (PEMFCs) are being touted as a viable green energy option [17]. PEMFC models' unknown parameters have been evaluated using recent metaheuristic optimization methodologies. In addition to accurately extracting the nine parameters of the triple-diode PV (TDPV) model of the PV module, a new application of the MPA and a novel objective function were presented [18]. The MPA is used in this work to simplify the problem and obtain the TDPV MODEL's nine parameters for the PV model. As a result, they play an important part in grid-connected PV power simulation theories.

Moreover, a modified technique was proposed to improve the MPA named modified marine predator's optimizer (MMPO) [19]. MMPO is based on combining predatory strategies that consider the possibility of climatic and environmental variation. Improved marine predators' optimization algorithm (IMPOA) proved its effectiveness in solving the combined power and heat economic problem by providing optimal scheduling of power and heat generation supplies [33]. A wind turbine system, PV panels, battery storage devices, and a diesel engine are all part of a hybrid renewable energy microgrid system designed with Deep-MPA. The cost of energy is lowered by 6% of total usage when Deep-MPA is used [34]. The multiobjective optimization algorithm of the MPA (MOEMPA) is used for reducing operational costs and emissions by increasing the renewables factor for the effective use of energy resources. This approach ensures that the load is fed with a high profit [38].

However, to improve the production of methane from steam gasification of palm kernel shell (PKS) using coal bottom ash as a catalytic, the fuzzy logic method and MPA were employed. The results outperform the analysis of variance methods stated in the literature [39]. On the other hand, MMPA gave better results in improving the performance of traditional MPA by increasing the population's efficiency to achieve optimum fitness [41]. Using multilayer perceptron neural network (MLPNN) and MPA, the problem of economic transmission of the microgrid system in Algeria was solved. According to the findings, the integrated PV-BESS microgrid system reduced the daily operating costs by up to 34.5% [42].

10.3.2 Image Processing

Medical imaging methods are necessary for illness diagnostics and patient management. Image segmentation is among the most significant phases in medical image processing, and it has been employed in a variety of applications. An optimal solution for one of the fundamental problems of swarm intelligence (SI) approaches, that some may become stuck in local optima, must be determined [1,20].

Furthermore, a hybrid dynamic clustering solution based on the MPA and the PSO method was presented [21] to handle the dynamic clustering problem, in which the clusters cannot be determined. A new theory for dealing with image segmentation problems is also presented in [22] where MPA was modified using the quantum theory. The primary goal is to improve MPA's ability as well as to identify the best suitable threshold levels to improve the process of segmentation.

Furthermore, a new technique to enhance MPA was used to improve the shape of a shape-adjustable generalized cubic developable ball (SGCD ball) [23]. The ODMPA was proposed to increase population variety, while also improving its ability to jump out of local minima. The hybrid dynamic clustering method was based on both the MDA and PSO algorithm [21]. The current method is used to compensate for the lack of MPA in all global searches.

MPASSA, a hybrid of MPA and salp swarm algorithm (SSA) was proposed in [31]. MPASSA was applied to utilize several standard evaluation measures and benchmark images to identify the optimal multilevel threshold image segmentation. The findings revealed that the proposed MPASSA outperformed other well-known optimization methods in such a domain. An effective method for medical image fusion was presented. The current approach employs five of the most recent medical image fusion approaches as well as six picture quality metrics. According to the findings of the experiments, the proposed algorithm outperformed the most recent algorithms [32].

10.3.3 Benchmark Function

EMPA was developed to find unknown parameters in a variety of PV types, combining fixed (single-diode and double-diode) and dynamical PV models [2]. A differential evolution operator is added to the original MPA in EMPA. The root-mean-square error and standard deviation generated using the MPA are lower in this study [2].

In addition, on a vast range of theoretical and practical challenges, the effectiveness of the four variants is validated. The method and its modifications are shown to outperform a number of well-known multiobjective algorithms in all situations.

To handle all PV losses, a TDPV was developed [14]. The TDPV was modeled based on a nonlinear I-V behavior. The new application proposed MPA for extracting essential electrical parameters of the proposed module TDPV of a PV panel to achieve higher accurate models. The MPA was proposed as a new method for bioinspired optimization for extracting the parameters of three-PV models of solar cells [24]. Furthermore, OBL-dubbed MPA-OBL was proposed to enhance their retrieval performance and convergence [25]. Several experiments were published to assess the MPA-OBL. The results obtained showed the hybrid's influence.

In solving optimization problems, the proposed MPA exhibits competitive performance [26]. By using a local escaping operator (LEO), an improved variant of MPA was proposed. Lately, MPA is considered as a new as well as strong optimization algorithm [27]. Four variants of MPA were proposed to handle multiobjective problems of optimization.

The MPA SI technique was used as a learning algorithm to train the ANN for the classification task, specifically medical data classification. The results show that MPA outperforms other methods [36].

10.3.4 Feature Selection

The shape design of a vehicle bracket demonstrated by the eco geography-based optimization (EBO) method was developed [28]. The EBO employs newly created metaheuristic [59]. Recently, the PV reconfiguration strategy was established to achieve the highest harvested power [29]. Also, a novel function was presented to improve the effectiveness of the current algorithm. The findings show that the PV array power was enhanced by the MPA.

Based on multiple benchmark performance analysis tests, the addition of random OBL (ROBL) to the MPA improves its capacity to reconnoiter a larger search field and surpasses standard MPA [35]. With the goal of escaping from local solutions and avoiding immature convergence, the principle of the complete learning strategy and memory viewpoint of the fractional calculus have been introduced into MPA [37]. The feature selection (FS) technique is based on a recently updated version of the MPA. The sine and cosine algorithm (SCA) is used for the developed MPASCA model to optimize search ability. The performance of MPASCA was significant, and it outperformed classifying measures [40].

To predict the ideal model parameters of solar modules/cells, a new proposed PV model was based on MPA [30]. In addition, this model extracts single-, double-, and triple-diode model parameters. Thus, the best accuracy of results was found using the algorithm. An overview of the given survey is presented in Table 10−1.

10.4 Discussion

In this section, the theoretical features, assessment, and evaluation of the MPA are discussed.

MPA clearly has a good statistical analysis for higher and lower irradiance operating situations and also good convergence [24]. In terms of precision, the suggested ODMPA demonstrated superiority and efficiently solved optimization models [23]. Most statistical posthoc analysis revealed that the MPA-OBL produces the most accurate and efficient outcomes when compared to other rival algorithms [25]. A study enables both prey and predators to use an intelligence rate policy for interactions as well as an ideal foraging strategy [31].

On the other hand, candidates for the solution of the MPA were replaced with better candidates from the prior iteration, mimicking a memory of previously visited prey-rich regions [26]. MPA was also designed to deal with single-objective optimization issues, and it has the potential to significantly outperform other comparison algorithms [27]. Finally, the achieved simulation output shows the best improvement and also shows that MMPO is superior for DG allocation and simultaneous DNR [19].

The number of provides a higher is counted by DSEE. Those with a requirement to attain the objectives go through an exploitation phase, while those with a low dominance go

Table 10–2 The number of published research articles per application area.

Approach	Number of researches
Engineering problem	12
Image processing	7
Benchmark function	7
Feature selection	6

through a discovery phase. The 4th include such M-MMPA (M-MMPA-NMM) with the Nelder-Mead simplex approach at the beginning of the method for optimization to build a kind of nondominated solution that will aid M-MMPA in finding better effective results [2]. The findings of comparisons show that FOCLMPA is superior and stable in managing a series of tests with high quality [29].

The results of this survey show that 37% of the proposed search was concerned about an engineering problem, 22% with benchmarking, 22% with image processing, and 19% with feature selection, as shown in Fig. 10–1 and Table 10–2.

10.5 Conclusion and Future Work

In this survey, the recent related work of the MPA is presented. The primary goal is to review the recent work on the MPA algorithm and explain the procedure of MPA and give some of the applications that are used by MPA such as benchmark function, image processing, engineering, and other problems. In conclusion, several enhancements to MPA algorithms can be implemented by making different modifications based on problems' requirements to produce better outcomes. The results of this survey can also be used by researchers in this field.

In the future, this algorithm could be used to handle a lot of problems such as engineering problems, image processing, feature selection, image segmentation problem, parameter extraction problem, examination problems, systematic analysis, and task scheduling in cloud computing problems. Also, it can be used to solve the unsolved optimization problem by adapting the MPA algorithm.

References

[1] M. Abdel-Basset, R. Mohamed, M. Abouhawwash, Hybrid marine predators algorithm for image segmentation: Analysis and validations, Artif. Intell. Rev. 55 (4) (2022) 3315–3367. Available from: https://doi.org/10.1007/s10462-021-10086-0. Apr.

[2] M. Abd Elaziz, et al., Enhanced marine predators algorithm for identifying static and dynamic photovoltaic models parameters, Energy Convers. Manag. 236 (2021) 113971. Available from: https://doi.org/10.1016/j.enconman.2021.113971. May.

[3] G. Hu, Y. Zheng, L. Abualigah, A.G. Hussien, DETDO: An adaptive hybrid dandelion optimizer for engineering optimization, Adv. Eng. Inform. 57 (2023) 102004.

[4] D. Izci, S. Ekinci, S. Mirjalili, L. Abualigah, An intelligent tuning scheme with a master/slave approach for efficient control of the automatic voltage regulator, Neural Comput. Appl. (2023) 1−17.

[5] H. Jia, C. Lu, D. Wu, C. Wen, H. Rao, L. Abualigah, An improved reptile search algorithm with ghost opposition-based learning for global optimization problems, J. Comput. Des. Eng. (2023) qwad048.

[6] A.H. Alharbi, A.A. Abdelhamid, A. Ibrahim, S.K. Towfek, N. Khodadadi, L. Abualigah, et al., Improved dipper-throated optimization for forecasting metamaterial design bandwidth for engineering applications, Biomimetics 8 (2) (2023) 241.

[7] S. Nama, A.K. Saha, S. Chakraborty, A.H. Gandomi, L. Abualigah, Boosting particle swarm optimization by backtracking search algorithm for optimization problems, Swarm Evolut. Comput. 79 (2023) 101304.

[8] M. Zare, M. Ghasemi, A. Zahedi, K. Golalipour, S.K. Mohammadi, S. Mirjalili, et al., A global best-guided firefly algorithm for engineering problems, J. Bionic Eng. (2023) 1−30.

[9] D. Wu, C. Wen, H. Rao, H. Jia, Q. Liu, L. Abualigah, Modified reptile search algorithm with multi-hunting coordination strategy for global optimization problems, Math. Biosci. Eng. 20 (6) (2023) 10090−10134.

[10] S. Ekinci, D. Izci, L. Abualigah, R.A. Zitar, A modified oppositional chaotic local search strategy based aquila optimizer to design an effective controller for vehicle cruise control system, J. Bionic Eng. (2023) 1−24.

[11] L. Abualigah, D. Falcone, A. Forestiero, Swarm Intelligence to Face IoT Challenges, Comput. Intell. Neurosci. (2023) 2023.

[12] M. Hadni, H. Hassane, New model of feature selection based chaotic firefly algorithm for arabic text categorization, Int. Arab. J. Inf. Technol. 20 (3A) (2023) 461−468.

[13] M.A.M. Shaheen, D. Yousri, A. Fathy, H.M. Hasanien, A. Alkuhayli, S.M. Muyeen, A novel application of improved marine predators algorithm and particle swarm optimization for solving the ORPD problem, Energies 13 (21) (2020) 5679. Available from: https://doi.org/10.3390/en13215679. Oct.

[14] A. Faramarzi, M. Heidarinejad, S. Mirjalili, A.H. Gandomi, Marine predators algorithm: a nature-inspired metaheuristic, Expert. Syst. Appl. 152 (2020) 113377. Available from: https://doi.org/10.1016/j.eswa.2020.113377. Aug.

[15] Q. Fan, H. Huang, Q. Chen, L. Yao, K. Yang, D. Huang, A modified self-adaptive marine predators algorithm: framework and engineering applications, Eng. Comput. 38 (4) (2022) 3269−3294. Available from: https://doi.org/10.1007/s00366-021-01319-5. Aug.

[16] H.M. Ridha, Parameters extraction of single and double diodes photovoltaic models using marine predators algorithm and Lambert W function, Sol. Energy 209 (2020) 674−693. Available from: https://doi.org/10.1016/j.solener.2020.09.047. Oct.

[17] A.A.Z. Diab, M.A. Tolba, A.G.A. El-Magd, M.M. Zaky, A.M. El-Rifaie, Fuel cell parameters estimation via marine predators and political optimizers, IEEE Access. 8 (2020) 166998−167018. Available from: https://doi.org/10.1109/ACCESS.2020.3021754.

[18] M.A. Soliman, H.M. Hasanien, A. Alkuhayli, Marine predators algorithm for parameters identification of triple-diode photovoltaic models, IEEE Access. 8 (2020) 155832−155842. Available from: https://doi.org/10.1109/ACCESS.2020.3019244.

[19] A.M. Shaheen, A.M. Elsayed, R.A. El-Sehiemy, S. Kamel, S.S.M. Ghoneim, A modified marine predators optimization algorithm for simultaneous network reconfiguration and distributed generator allocation in distribution systems under different loading conditions, Eng. Optim. 54 (4) (2022) 687−708. Available from: https://doi.org/10.1080/0305215X.2021.1897799. Apr.

[20] M.A. Elaziz, et al., An improved marine predators algorithm with fuzzy entropy for multi-level thresholding: real world example of COVID-19 CT image segmentation, IEEE Access. 8 (2020) 125306−125330. Available from: https://doi.org/10.1109/ACCESS.2020.3007928.

[21] N. Wang, J.S. Wang, L.F. Zhu, H.Y. Wang, G. Wang, A novel dynamic clustering method by integrating marine predators algorithm and particle swarm optimization algorithm, IEEE Access. 9 (2021) 3557−3569. Available from: https://doi.org/10.1109/ACCESS.2020.3047819.

[22] M. Abd Elaziz, D. Mohammadi, D. Oliva, K. Salimifard, Quantum marine predators algorithm for addressing multilevel image segmentation, Appl. Soft Comput. 110 (2021) 107598. Available from: https://doi.org/10.1016/j.asoc.2021.107598. Oct.

[23] G. Hu, X. Zhu, G. Wei, C.-T. Chang, An improved marine predators algorithm for shape optimization of developable Ball surfaces, Eng. Appl. Artif. Intell. 105 (2021) 104417. Available from: https://doi.org/10.1016/j.engappai.2021.104417. Oct.

[24] A.S.A. Bayoumi, R.A. El-Sehiemy, A. Abaza, Effective PV parameter estimation algorithm based on marine predators optimizer considering normal and low radiation operating conditions, Arab. J. Sci. Eng. 47 (3) (2022) 3089−3104. Available from: https://doi.org/10.1007/s13369-021-06045-0. Mar.

[25] E.H. Houssein, et al., An improved opposition-based marine predators algorithm for global optimization and multilevel thresholding image segmentation, Knowl. Syst. 229 (2021) 107348. Available from: https://doi.org/10.1016/j.knosys.2021.107348. Oct.

[26] M. Oszust, Enhanced marine predators algorithm with local escaping operator for global optimization, Knowl. Syst. 232 (2021) 107467. Available from: https://doi.org/10.1016/j.knosys.2021.107467. Nov.

[27] M. Abdel-Basset, R. Mohamed, S. Mirjalili, R.K. Chakrabortty, M. Ryan, An efficient marine predators algorithm for solving multi-objective optimization problems: analysis and validations, IEEE Access. 9 (2021) 42817−42844. Available from: https://doi.org/10.1109/ACCESS.2021.3066323.

[28] B.S. Yıldız, V. Patel, N. Pholdee, S.M. Sait, S. Bureerat, A.R. Yıldız, Conceptual comparison of the ecogeography-based algorithm, equilibrium algorithm, marine predators algorithm and slime mold algorithm for optimal product design, Mater. Test. 63 (4) (2021) 336−340. Available from: https://doi.org/10.1515/mt-2020-0049. Apr.

[29] D. Yousri, T.S. Babu, E. Beshr, M.B. Eteiba, D. Allam, A robust strategy based on marine predators algorithm for large scale photovoltaic array reconfiguration to mitigate the partial shading effect on the performance of PV system, IEEE Access. 8 (2020) 112407−112426. Available from: https://doi.org/10.1109/ACCESS.2020.3000420.

[30] M.A. El Sattar, A. Al Sumaiti, H. Ali, A.A.Z. Diab, Marine predators algorithm for parameters estimation of photovoltaic modules considering various weather conditions, Neural Comput. Appl. 33 (18) (2021) 11799−11819. Available from: https://doi.org/10.1007/s00521-021-05822-0. Sep.

[31] L. Abualigah, N.K. Al-Okbi, M.A. Elaziz, E.H. Houssein, Boosting marine predators algorithm by salp swarm algorithm for multilevel thresholding image segmentation, Multimed. Tools Appl. 81 (12) (2022) 16707−16742. Available from: https://doi.org/10.1007/s11042-022-12001-3. May.

[32] P.-H. Dinh, An improved medical image synthesis approach based on marine predators algorithm and maximum Gabor energy, Neural Comput. Appl. 34 (6) (2022) 4367−4385. Available from: https://doi.org/10.1007/s00521-021-06577-4. Mar.

[33] A.M. Shaheen, A.M. Elsayed, A.R. Ginidi, R.A. EL-Sehiemy, M.M. Alharthi, S.S.M. Ghoneim, A novel improved marine predators algorithm for combined heat and power economic dispatch problem, Alex. Eng. J. 61 (3) (2022) 1834−1851. Available from: https://doi.org/10.1016/j.aej.2021.07.001. Mar.

[34] E.H. Houssein, I.E. Ibrahim, M. Kharrich, S. Kamel, "An improved marine predators algorithm for the optimal design of hybrid renewable energy systems, Eng. Appl. Artif. Intell. 110 (2022) 104722. Available from: https://doi.org/10.1016/j.engappai.2022.104722. Apr.

[35] K. Balakrishnan, R. Dhanalakshmi, U. Khaire, Excogitating marine predators algorithm based on random opposition-based learning for feature selection, Concurr. Comput. Pract. Exp., 34 4 (2022). Available from: https://doi.org/10.1002/cpe.6630. Feb.

[36] J. Bagchi, T. Si, Artificial neural network training using marine predators algorithm for medical data classification, 2022, pp. 137−148. Available from: https://doi.org/10.1007/978−981-16−3802-2_11.

[37] D. Yousri, M. Abd Elaziz, D. Oliva, A. Abraham, M.A. Alotaibi, M.A. Hossain, Fractional-order comprehensive learning marine predators algorithm for global optimization and feature selection, Knowl. Syst. 235 (2022) 107603. Available from: https://doi.org/10.1016/j.knosys.2021.107603. Jan.

[38] D. Yousri, et al., Managing the exchange of energy between microgrid elements based on multi-objective enhanced marine predators algorithm, Alex. Eng. J. 61 (11) (2022) 8487–8505. Available from: https://doi.org/10.1016/j.aej.2022.02.008. Nov.

[39] H. Rezk, A. Inayat, M.A. Abdelkareem, A.G. Olabi, A.M. Nassef, Optimal operating parameter determination based on fuzzy logic modeling and marine predators algorithm approaches to improve the methane production via biomass gasification, Energy 239 (2022) 122072. Available from: https://doi.org/10.1016/j.energy.2021.122072. Jan.

[40] M. Abd Elaziz, A.A. Ewees, D. Yousri, L. Abualigah, M.A.A. Al-qaness, Modified marine predators algorithm for feature selection: case study metabolomics, Knowl. Inf. Syst. 64 (1) (2022) 261–287. Available from: https://doi.org/10.1007/s10115-021-01641-w. Jan.

[41] M.H. Hassan, D. Yousri, S. Kamel, C. Rahmann, A modified marine predators algorithm for solving single- and multi-objective combined economic emission dispatch problems, Comput. Ind. Eng. 164 (2022) 107906. Available from: https://doi.org/10.1016/j.cie.2021.107906. Feb.

[42] A. Kheiter, S. Souag, A. Chaouch, A. Boukortt, B. Bekkouche, M. Guezgouz, Energy management strategy based on marine predators algorithm for grid-connected microgrid, Int. J. Renew. Energy Dev. 11 (3) (2022) 751–765. Available from: https://doi.org/10.14710/ijred.2022.42797. Aug.

[43] A.M. Ikotun, A.E. Ezugwu, L. Abualigah, B. Abuhaija, J. Heming, K-means clustering algorithms: a comprehensive review, variants analysis, and advances in the era of big data,", Inf. Sci. (Ny). 622 (2023) 178–210. Available from: https://doi.org/10.1016/j.ins.2022.11.139. Apr.

[44] S.K. Sahoo, et al., Moth flame optimization: theory, modifications, hybridizations, and applications, Arch. Comput. Methods Eng. 30 (1) (2023) 391–426. Available from: https://doi.org/10.1007/s11831-022-09801-z. Jan.

[45] L.Z. Pen et al., Artocarpus classification technique using deep learning based convolutional neural network, 2023, pp. 1–21. Available from: https://doi.org/10.1007/978-3-031–17576-3_1.

[46] O.N. Oyelade, A.E. Ezugwu, M.S. Almutairi, A.K. Saha, L. Abualigah, H. Chiroma, A generative adversarial network for synthetization of regions of interest based on digital mammograms, Sci. Rep. 12 (1) (2022) 6166. Available from: https://doi.org/10.1038/s41598-022-09929-9. Apr.

[47] O.N. Oyelade, A.E.-S. Ezugwu, T.I.A. Mohamed, L. Abualigah, Ebola optimization search algorithm: a new nature-inspired metaheuristic optimization algorithm, IEEE Access. 10 (2022) 16150–16177. Available from: https://doi.org/10.1109/ACCESS.2022.3147821.

[48] N. Milhem, L. Abualigah, M.H. Nadimi-Shahraki, H. Jia, A.E. Ezugwu, & A.G. Hussien, Enhanced MapReduce performance for the distributed parallel computing: application of the big data, 2023, pp. 191–203. Available from: https://doi.org/10.1007/978-3-031–17576-3_8.

[49] A. Khazalah et al., Image processing identification for sapodilla using convolution neural network (CNN) and transfer learning techniques, 2023, pp. 107–127. Available from: https://doi.org/10.1007/978-3-031–17576-3_5.

[50] A.E. Ezugwu, et al., A comprehensive survey of clustering algorithms: State-of-the-art machine learning applications, taxonomy, challenges, and future research prospects, Eng. Appl. Artif. Intell. 110 (2022) 104743. Available from: https://doi.org/10.1016/j.engappai.2022.104743. Apr.

[51] A.E. Ezugwu, J.O. Agushaka, L. Abualigah, S. Mirjalili, A.H. Gandomi, Prairie Dog optimization algorithm, Neural Comput. Appl. 34 (22) (2022) 20017–20065. Available from: https://doi.org/10.1007/s00521-022-07530-9. Nov.

[52] S. Chakraborty, A.K. Saha, A.E. Ezugwu, J.O. Agushaka, R.A. Zitar, L. Abualigah, Differential evolution and its applications in image processing problems: a comprehensive review, Arch. Comput. Methods Eng. 30 (2) (2023) 985–1040. Available from: https://doi.org/10.1007/s11831-022-09825-5. Mar.

[53] H. Al-Manaseer, L. Abualigah, A.R. Alsoud, R.A. Zitar, A.E. Ezugwu, & H. Jia, A novel big data classification technique for healthcare application using support vector machine, random forest and J48, 2023, pp. 205–215. Available from: https://doi.org/10.1007/978-3-031–17576-3_9.

[54] O.O. Akinola et al., Multiclass feature selection with metaheuristic optimization algorithms: a review, Available from: https://doi.org/10.1007/s00521-022-07705-4.

[55] J.O. Agushaka, A.E. Ezugwu, O.N. Olaide, O. Akinola, R.A. Zitar, L. Abualigah, Improved dwarf Mongoose optimization for constrained engineering design problems, J. Bionic Eng. (May 2022). Available from: https://doi.org/10.1007/s42235-022-00316-8.

[56] J.O. Agushaka, A.E. Ezugwu, L. Abualigah, S.K. Alharbi, H.A.E.-W. Khalifa, Efficient initialization methods for population-based metaheuristic algorithms: a comparative study, Arch. Comput. Methods Eng. 30 (3) (2023) 1727–1787. Available from: https://doi.org/10.1007/s11831-022-09850-4. Apr.

[57] J.O. Agushaka, A.E. Ezugwu, L. Abualigah, Gazelle optimization algorithm: a novel nature-inspired metaheuristic optimizer, Neural Comput. Appl. 35 (5) (2023) 4099–4131. Available from: https://doi.org/10.1007/s00521-022-07854-6. Feb.

[58] J.O. Agushaka, A.E. Ezugwu, L. Abualigah, Dwarf Mongoose optimization algorithm, Comput. Methods Appl. Mech. Eng. 391 (2022). Available from: https://doi.org/10.1016/j.cma.2022.114570. Mar.

[59] L. Abualigah, A. Diabat, C.L. Thanh, S. Khatir, Opposition-based Laplacian distribution with Prairie Dog optimization method for industrial engineering design problems, Comput. Methods Appl. Mech. Eng. 414 (2023) 116097.

11

Quantum approximate optimization algorithm: a review study and problems

Laith Abualigah[1,2,3,4,5,6,7], Saif AlNajdawi[4], Abiodun M. Ikotun[8],
Agostino Forestiero[9], Faiza Gul[10], Absalom E. Ezugwu[11], Heming Jia[12],
Mohsen Zare[13], Shubham Mahajan[14,15], Mohammad Alshinwan[16]

[1]HOURANI CENTER FOR APPLIED SCIENTIFIC RESEARCH, AL-AHLIYYA AMMAN UNIVERSITY, AMMAN, JORDAN [2]COMPUTER SCIENCE DEPARTMENT, AL AL-BAYT UNIVERSITY, MAFRAQ, JORDAN [3]MEU RESEARCH UNIT, MIDDLE EAST UNIVERSITY, AMMAN, JORDAN [4]SCHOOL OF COMPUTER SCIENCES, UNIVERSITI SAINS MALAYSIA, PULAU PINANG, MALAYSIA [5]SCHOOL OF ENGINEERING AND TECHNOLOGY, SUNWAY UNIVERSITY MALAYSIA, PETALING JAYA, MALAYSIA [6]DEPARTMENT OF ELECTRICAL AND COMPUTER ENGINEERING, LEBANESE AMERICAN UNIVERSITY, BYBLOS, LEBANON [7]ARTIFICIAL INTELLIGENCE AND SENSING TECHNOLOGIES (AIST) RESEARCH CENTER, UNIVERSITY OF TABUK, TABUK, SAUDI ARABIA [8]UNIVERSITY OF KWAZULU-NATAL, PIETERMARITZBURG CAMPUS, POTCHEFSTROOM, SOUTH AFRICA [9]INSTITUTE FOR HIGH PERFORMANCE COMPUTING AND NETWORKING, NATIONAL RESEARCH COUNCIL, RENDE, CS, ITALY [10]ELECTRICAL DEPARTMENT, AIR UNIVERSITY AEROSPACE AND AVIATION CAMPUS, KAMRA, PAKISTAN [11]UNIT FOR DATA SCIENCE AND COMPUTING, NORTH-WEST UNIVERSITY, POTCHEFSTROOM, SOUTH AFRICA [12]DEPARTMENT OF INFORMATION ENGINEERING, SANMING UNIVERSITY, FUJIAN, P.R.CHINA [13]DEPARTMENT OF ELECTRICAL ENGINEERING, FACULTY OF ENGINEERING, JAHROM UNIVERSITY, JAHROM, FRAS, IRAN [14]AJEENKYA DY PATIL UNIVERSITY, PUNE, MAHARASHTRA, INDIA [15]UNIVERSITY CENTER FOR RESEARCH & DEVELOPMENT (UCRD), CHANDIGARH UNIVERSITY, MOHALI, PUNJAB, INDIA [16]FACULTY OF INFORMATION TECHNOLOGY, APPLIED SCIENCE PRIVATE UNIVERSITY, AMMAN, JORDAN

11.1 Introduction

Quantum approximate optimization algorithm (QAOA) is a variant approach to solving the recurrent QAOA problem. In general, business cycle optimization is the task of identifying, from a limited number of options, the object that minimizes the cost function. Joint optimization is used to solve real-world problems such as reducing supply chain costs, vehicle routing, and work distribution [1].

QAOA is based on combinatorial optimized transformations by using a special variation of the T-wave method to obtain a ground-state approximation of the Hamiltonian. This method is described in terms and includes two values that require optimization using minimization techniques in classical machines [2]. Furthermore, QAOA is assumed to be the discrete time quantum annealing. The nonisothermal theorem ensures that quantum amplification gives a true ground state if the nonisothermal criterion is satisfied, thus providing at least one case where QAOA has an accurate answer. Also, QAOA has a subset, $p = 1$ [3]. Nonetheless, interest in QAOA has grown significantly in recent years. Normally, optimization methods can be used to deal with many problems in the sciences, as presented in refs [4−13].

This paper is divided as follows: Section 11.1 introduces the QAOA. Section 11.2 discusses methods of the fixed p algorithm, the ring of disagreeing, MaxCut on three graphs, relation to the quantum nonisothermal algorithm, and a variant of the algorithm. Section 11.3 reports the related works, while Section 11.4 reports the results. Section 11.5 presents the conclusion.

11.2 Methods

11.2.1 Fixed p algorithm

For a fixed p, the angle that maximizes FP (y, β) during preprocessing must be determined. This approach usually works, but it was demonstrated for one specific problem, the maximal cut of degree-bounded graphs. Suppose there is a graph of n values and an edge with a set of JK of size M, which is provided as input below.

$$C = \sum (JK)C(JK) \tag{11-1}$$

were

$$C<jk> = 12(-\sigma zj\sigma zk + 1), \tag{11-2}$$

Now

$$Fp(\gamma, \beta) = \sum <jk> <s|U\dagger(C,\gamma1)\cdots U\dagger(B,\beta p)C <jk> U(B,\beta p)\cdots U(C,\gamma1)|s>. \tag{11-3}$$

Assume that we have the method given below, which is associated with an edge

$$U\dagger(C,\gamma1)\cdots U\dagger(B,\beta p)C <jk> U(B,\beta p)\cdots U(C,\gamma1). \tag{11-4}$$

This applies to Site *S J* and *k*, as well as Site *S*. Consider the case where *P* is equal to 1, and the previous expression is:

$$U \dagger (C, \gamma 1) U \dagger (B, \beta 1) C <jk> U(B, \beta 1) U(C, \gamma 1). \tag{11-5}$$

The components within the operator $U (B, \beta 1)$ do not include SiteSpect$j$ or K through C (JK), and the following was obtained:

$$U \dagger (C, \gamma 1) e i \beta 1 (\sigma xj + \sigma xk) C <jk> e - i \beta 1 (\sigma xj + \sigma xk) U(C, \gamma 1) \tag{11-6}$$

Components that do not contain SiteSpect *j* or *k* in operator $U (C, \gamma 1)$ are replaced. So, the admin is in state (6) because it contains edges (JK) and edges adjacent to (JK) and SiteSpects on those edges. For each *p*, the analyst sees that the admin in (4) contains at most (JK) and the *p*-step edges that are missing in SiteSpect. Go back to the condition (3) and find the following:

$$|s> = |+ >1| + >2...| + >N \tag{11-7}$$

Confined to input charts of settled degree 3; for *P* = 1, there are as it were these conceivable subgraphs for the edge (JK):

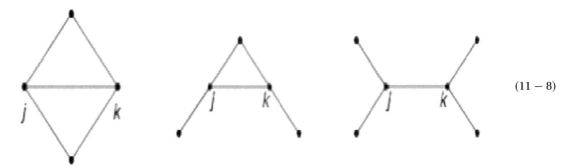

$$\tag{11-8}$$

as shown in this paper, the analysts will return to the case after. For any sub chart *G*, characterize the administrator *CG*, which is *C* confined to *G*

$$CG = \sum <ll' > \varrho GC < ll' > \tag{11-9}$$

and the related operation

$$U(CG, \gamma) = e - i\gamma \, CG. \tag{11-10}$$

Define

$$BG = \sum j\varrho G\sigma xj \tag{11-11}$$

and

$$U(BG, \beta) = e - i\beta BG. \tag{11-12}$$

Let the state (S, G) be

$$\{s, G\} = \prod l_Q G| + > l.$$

Return to condition number 3 over edge K within the whole, which is related to a subgraph (J, K) and makes a commitment to FP:

$$< s, g(j,k)|U \dagger (Cg(j,k), \gamma p) \cdots U \dagger (Bg(j,k), \beta 1)C \ <jk> \ U(Bg(j,k), \beta 1) \cdots U(Cg(j,k), \gamma p)|s, g(j,k) > \tag{11-13}$$

The researchers found that in (3), at that point, the comparing capacities of (γ, β) are the same. In this manner, the analysts can see 5 in (3) as a whole over subgraph types.
Define

$$fg(\gamma, \beta) = < s, g(j,k)|U \dagger (Cg(j,k), \gamma 1) \cdots U \dagger (Bg(j,k), \beta p)C \ <jk> \ U(Bg(j,x)\beta p) \cdots U(Cg(j,k), \gamma 1)|s, g(j,k) >, \tag{11-14}$$

where $G (J, K)$ is a subgraph of type g. Fp is then

$$Fp(\gamma, \beta) = \sum gwgfg(\gamma, \beta) \tag{11-15}$$

Here, WG is the number of events within the unique edge sum of subgraph g. Capacitance FG does not depend on N and M. It can be said that the correlations of n and m come from the weights WG, and these are fairly checked from the original graph. Note that the wish in (14) contains the site Spectin subgraph ordering g. For the graph with the highest height v, the site number is the pectin of this tree:

$$q \ tree = 2[(v - 1)p + 1 - 1(v - 1) - 1], \tag{11-16}$$

(or $2p + 2$ if $v = 2$), which is n- and m-independent. For each p, there are only finite subgraph types.

Using (14) FB (γ, β) in (15) allows for the evaluation of classical computers, whose power does not evolve with n. Each FG contains administrators and states in Hilbert space, whose measure is at most 2Q tree. In fact, for the big p, this can outperform the current classic innovation, but asset necessities do not develop quantum computation methods analysts first discover maximizing Fp (γ, β). This is dependent on n and m in the weights WG, which are evaluated effectively. Given the best (γ, β), the analyst turns to the quantum computer and produces the state (γ, β) given by Eq. (11-6). Analysts at this point are ranked within the assumptions of the calculation and receive the string z and rate C [14]. Rehashing produces a test of the value of C [14] between + m if the gray value is FP (γ, β). At least FP (γ, β)-1 results are obtained with a probability of $1-1/m$ with repeated placements of $m \log M$.

11.2.2 Concentration

Since they continue to use MaxCut in traditional charts as an example, it makes sense to request data on the propagation of C measured within the state (γ, β). If v is fixed and P is fixed (or if 6 gradually evolves with n), the proliferation of C [14] is focused on their cruelty. To check this, calculate:

$$< \gamma, \beta | C2 | \gamma, \beta > - < \gamma, \beta | C | \gamma, \beta > \qquad (11-17)$$

$$= \sum < jk > < j'k' > [< s | U \dagger (C, \gamma 1) \cdot \cdot \cdot U \dagger (B, \beta p) C < jk > C < j'k' > U(B, \beta p) \cdot \cdot \cdot U(C, \gamma 1) | s >] \qquad (11-18)$$

The subgraphs $G(J, K)$ and $G(J, K)$ do not contain a common qubit, and the sum of (18) is 0. Subgraphs $G(J, K)$ and $G(J, K)$ do not have a common site S, unless there is a path from (J, K) to (J, K) with a length of $2p + 1$ or less in the opportunity table. Replacing p from (16) with $2P + 1$, the analyst confirmed that there was a maximum for each (J, K).

$$2[(v - 1)2p + 2 - 1(v - 1) - 1] \qquad (11-19)$$

Edges (J, K) might contribute to the whole in (18) (or $4p + 4$ if $v = 2$) and therefore

$$< \gamma, \beta | C2 | \gamma, \beta > - < \gamma, \beta | C | \gamma, \beta > 262[(v - 1)2p + 2 - 1(v - 1) - 1] \cdot m \qquad (11-20)$$

This is because all standard addends have a maximum of 1. For V and p, the standard deviation of C [14] has been established to be up to about $\sqrt{m}$. This suggests that a cruel test of order $m2$ of C [14] is within 1 of FP (γ, β) with a probability of $1-1m$. The concentration of C [14] transmissions also means that the calculations shown are unlikely to produce C [14] strings that are much larger than FP (γ, β).

11.2.3 The ring of disagrees

Researchers analyzed and presented the execution of MaxCut's quantum computation on two regular graphs. A degree 2 standard (and related) means that the figure can be:

$$Mp = n(2p + 1)/(2p + 2)$$

Therefore, for every P, quantum calculus finds cuts greater than or equal to the estimated value $N(2P + 1)/(2P + 2) - 1$. Since the best cut is N, quantum computing can confidently generate an estimated ratio that can approach 1 by fully extending p and not including N. Two whole $(J + 1)$ methods C are used, where J is even and J is odd. Therefore, this calculation includes the depth of the N-independent circuit.

11.2.4 Maxcut on 3-regular graphs

Analysts also saw quantum surmised optimization calculation, and QAOA was performed on MaxCut on three (related) regular charts. The estimated ratio is C [14], where z is the yield of quantum computation separated by the extremum of C.

They initially appear to have the worst estimated ratio of 0.6924 for quantum computation when $P = 1$. Suppose a three-vertex regular graph (and preferably $3n/2$ edges) contains T subgraphs of frames, T "isolated triangles" and "intersecting squares":

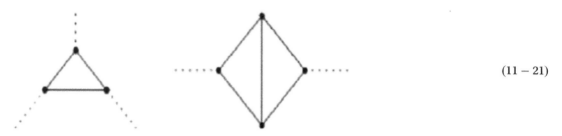

$$(11-21)$$

the mottled lines show the edges that contrast the bordered triangles with the intersecting squares. Separating the triangles means the three edges that separate the triangles near the vertices. At this point, the analyst has three regular charts separated by four nodes. In this unusual case (that is, the case where the following tests do not apply), the estimated ratio is higher than 0.6924. The common is $3T + 4S \leq n$ because squares that intersect different triangles cannot have common vertices.

$F1$ (γ, β) under condition (3) returns to the entire edge. For each intersecting square, there is an edge (J, K) where $G(J, K)$ is the main sort shown in (8). This subgraph type has four vertices, so we call it $g4$. Each intersecting square has four edges that raise the moment type subgraph shown in (8). This subgraph type is called $g5$ because it has five vertices. Since all three edges of each bounding triangle are subgraph type $g5$, there are $4S + 3T$ edges for subgraph type $G5$. All the remaining edges in the graph have a subgraph sort similar to the third edge shown in (8), and this subgraph sort is named $g6$. There are those $(3N/2 - 5S - 3T)$ and what they had:

$$F1(\gamma, \beta) = Sfg4(\gamma, \beta) + (4S + 3T)fg5(\gamma, \beta) + (3n2 - 5S - 3T)fg6(\gamma, \beta) \qquad (11-22)$$

The maximum of F1 is a function of N, S, and T,

$$1(n, S, T) = \max\gamma, \beta F1(\gamma, \beta). \qquad (11-23)$$

Given any three-normal chart, counting sand T is easy. At this point, you can directly calculate $M1$ (N, S, T) using a traditional computer. Manipulating the quantum computer at the maximization angles γ and β gives the current measured state (γ, β) within the calculation assumptions. N log place n iterations to find a string whose intersection is very close to or large for $M1$ (N, S, T). To derive the estimation part here, we need to know the finest cuts that can be obtained from the input plot. This is often not a fair task by S and T.

$$M1(n, S, T)(3n2 - S - T). \qquad (11-24)$$

It is helpful to scale out n from the best and foot of (24). Note that $M1/n$ which comes from $F1/N$ depends on $S/N \equiv s$ and $T/N \equiv t$. So that,

$$M1(1, s, t)(32 - s - t) \qquad (11-25)$$

where s, $t \geq 0$ and $4s + 3t \leq 1$. It is direct to numerically assess (25), and the analysts found that it accomplishes its least esteem at $s = t =$ and the esteem is 0.6924. On any 3-regular chart, the QAOA will continuously create a cut whose estimate is at least 0.69249 times the measure of the ideal cut. This $p = 1$ result on 3-regular charts is not as great as is known in the classical calculations [1]. It is conceivable to analyze the execution of the QAOA for $P = 2$ on 3-regular charts. Be that as it may, it is more complicated than the $p = 1$ case and it will present partial results. The subgraph with the frontline site S is this tree with 14 vertices.

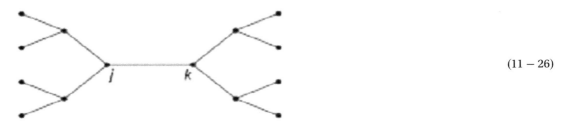

$$(11 - 26)$$

The numerical maximization of (14) by G given by (26) gives 0.7559. Consider the usual three graphs of n vertices with pentagons, squares, and triangles [15]. At this point, all edges except O [15] have (26) as a subgraph sort. A QAOA with $P = 2$ cannot tell if the figure is split in two, that is, if it is completely satisfactory, or if it contains many odd circles of length 7 or greater. If the plot is split into two parts, the estimated ratio is 0.7559, which is within the Lagan constraint. If the plot contains many odd circles (7 or longer in length), the percentage of guesses will be high.

11.2.5 Relation to the quantum adiabatic algorithm

Quantum adiabatic algorithm (QAA) [2] is designed to find the perfect approach, if it runs longer. Consider time-dependent Hamiltonian H [5] $= (1t/T)$ $B + (t/T)$ C. State S is B's most important and unsteady eigenstate with one analyst. Note that we tried to find high essence. Starting from S, we performed quantum adiabatic computation. If the execution time T is longer, the highest unsteady eigenstate of C can be found. Since B has a nonnegative off-diagonal component, the Peron−Frobenius theory states that there is an energy difference between the best and lower states. It shows that it is more important than t & lt; T, that is, enough sweep T triumph is processed. The course assumptions consist of a rotation of director $U(C, \gamma)$.

11.2.6 A variant of the algorithm

In this segment, analysts provide a basic calculation variant suitable for situations where the search space can be a complex subset of n-bit strings. Analysts use illustrations that outline the basic idea. Consider the problem of finding a comprehensive independent set in a particular graph with n vertices. A free set is a subset of vertices, with the characteristic that there is no edge between two vertices in the subset. There is a subset of vertices compared to the strings $z = z1, z2, \ldots, zn$, with each bit being 1 if the comparing vertex is within the subset and the bit is within the occasion when the vertex is not. The analysts were confined to strings, which were compared to free sets within the chart. The estimate of the free set is the Hamming weight of the string z, which it indicates by C [14]

$$C[4] = n\sum j = 1zj, \qquad (11-27)$$

In the Hilbert space of quantum computation, there is an orthonormal introduction (3, Z), where Z is any string that is compared to the independent set. In the case of charmed, the Hilbert space is not as large as 2N, but it estimates an exponentially large safe space. Hilbert space is not Cubit's unique tensor. Chair C is related to the dependent unit where γ is between and 2π because C has some eigenvalues. The certifier characterizes the quantum director B that connects the start state.

$$U(C, \gamma) = e - i\gamma C \qquad (11-28)$$

Note that B is the adjacency matrix of the hypercube restricted to the legal strings, that is, those that correspond to independent sets in the given graph. Now, in general, B does not have integer eigenvalues, so the researchers define

$$<z|B|z'> = \begin{cases} 1: z \text{ and } z' \text{ differ in one bit} \\ 0: \text{otherwise} \end{cases} \qquad (11-29)$$

$$U(B, b) = e - i - ibB \qquad (11-30)$$

where b is a real number.

For the beginning state of our calculation, take the simple step to develop state $(Z = 0)$ corresponding to the purge autonomous set, which has the least esteem of C. For $P \geq 1$, here, they have p genuine numbers ($b1$, $b2$.etc.). BP $\equiv$ band $p - 1$ angles ($\gamma1$, $\gamma2$, γ) as $P - 1 \equiv \gamma$. The quantum state:

$$|b, \gamma> = U(B, bp)U(C, \gamma p - 1) \cdots U(B, b1)|z = 0> \qquad (11-31)$$

They are what researchers obtained after the application of an alternation of the operators associated with B and C. Now they are defined as

$$Fp(b, \gamma) = <b, \gamma|C|b, \gamma> \qquad (11-32)$$

With the expectation of C in the state (b, γ), finally, they defined the maximum

$$Mp = maxb, \gamma Fp(b, \gamma). \qquad (11-33)$$

The maximization at $p - 1$ is the maximization at p with $bp = 0$ and $\gamma p - 1 = 0$, so they have

$$Mp \geq Mp - 1. \qquad (11-34)$$

Furthermore

$$\lim p \to \infty Mp = maxzlegalC[4]. \qquad (11-35)$$

Note that the initial state is the ground state of C to understand why (35) is justified. This is considered a condition with a very good eigenvalue of $-C$. The agent tries to reach the n-eigenstate of $+C$, which has the most anomalous eigenvalues. Since T becomes infinite, there is an adiabatic path (keeping pace with the whole run) of run time T that meets this. This path consists of two parts. In the beginning of the calculation, insert $-C$ between the starting Hamiltonian and Hamiltonian B:

$$H[5] = (1 - 2tT)(-C) + 2tTB, 0 \leq t \leq T2 \qquad (11-36)$$

The researchers evolve the initial state with this Hamiltonian for time $T/2$:

$$H[5] = (2 - 2tT)B + (2tT - 1)C, T2 \leq t \leq T \qquad (11-37)$$

Advance the quantum state provided fairly by time $T = T/2$ tot $= T$. Using the Perron–Frobenius hypothesis, as in the last segment number 6, analysts obtained the adiabatic hypothesis and the results are given in (35). Together, Eqs. (11−31) to (11−35) proposed quantum subroutines for the freest computations. Given p and given (B, γ), we generate (31) quantum state $|b, \gamma>$. A string z names a free set, whose degree is the Hamming weight of z. What is the order in the introduction of the calculation to activate? Continue with the same (b, γ) to facilitate the evaluation of FP (b, γ) in (32). This subroutine can be called from a program that aims to approach the MP given in (33). This comprehensive program can be tuned using either the techniques described in this document or the new techniques. If $p = 1$, the subroutine can be thought of as continuing its initial state $(z = 0)$ for time b at Hamilton's B. B is a series of large diagrams whose vertices can be compared to the free set of input diagrams and whose edges can be considered discrete (29). The prover sees this as a continuous-time quantum walk that enters a huge figure at a particular vertex [15]. In the rare case where the input graph has no edges, the Hilbert space estimate is 2N because all strings of length n communicate in a subset. In this case, B is the continuous order of Hyper Setting $b = \pi/2$, and the state (31) ($P = 1$, so to speak, uniform) is ($z = 11 \ldots 11$), maximizing the target work. In a more general case, (31) can be considered as a series of quantum walks interrupted by C's dependent unitization application to help the walk reach its goal. Calculations of past segments can be displayed as such, even if the initial state is not a single node.

11.3 Related works

This paper describes how Quantum Inexact Optimization Calculation will be improved, and it is compared with other QAOA calculations; settled p calculation, the ring of oppose this idea, MaxCut on 3-regular charts, horror and the connection to quantum adiabatic calculation in arrange to discover the finest execution among them. In this paper, a huge number of related works were referred when doing the comparison between QAOA calculations regarding optimization, and the list of these works are as follows:

Valuating QAOA: A case study. Egger et al. [16] discussed the noisy medium-sized quantum (NISQ) era. QAOA is one of the most promising quantum algorithms. It is critical to quantify the performance of QAOA in the near-term environment. In the low-to-medium depth regime, the researchers of this paper performed a largescale numerical analysis of the approximation ratios attainable by QAOA. The researchers of this paper evaluated 990 million 10qubit QAOA circuits to discover suitable QAOA settings. They found that as the depth grows, the approximation ratio increases only slightly, and the gains are countered by the growing difficulty of optimizing variational parameters. Researchers found that even within the same class of problem situations, QAOA achieves a variety of approach ratios.

A Quantum Approximation Optimization Algorithm. Farhi et al. [14] presented quantum computations. The calculation depends on the positive number p, and the quality of the estimation improves as p increases. The quantum circuit that performs the computation consists of a single door, which is the area of objective work that is the most extreme and requires optimization. The depth of the circuit increases the scope to P times the number of constraints (in the worst-case scenario). If p is fixed, that is, there is no input estimation, the calculation uses traditional productive preprocessing. If p evolves with the input measure, another method is suggested. The calculations related to MaxCut in regular charts are done, and the execution in fixed $p2$ and 3 standard charts is analyzed. For $p = 1$, the quantum computation continuously finds intersections on three normal plots that are at least 0.6924 times the ideal intersections.

Quantum advantages with QAOAs. Mills et al. [17] described a flat QAOA designed to run on a quantum computer with a gated model. It takes a combinatorial optimization problem as input and returns a string that fills most of the maximum number of phrases you can enter. For certain issues, the lowest QAOA version has a verifiable performance guarantee, but there are traditional algorithms with better guarantees. Here, QAOA argues that it can show quantum superiority beyond the calculated values that are possible. Based on the theoretical assumptions of reasonable complexity, even the flattest version of power distribution cannot be efficiently simulated with traditional devices. Compare this to sampling the output of a quantum computer running the quantum insulation algorithm (QADI). However, there is a warning that the evolutionary Hamiltonian is patchy and crouching. It can be observed that there is an oracle that allows for sampling from QADI, but even with this oracle, the polynomial hierarchy collapses if it can be sampled classically and efficiently from the output of QAOA. This shows that QAOA is suitable for short-term quantum computer operations, as it not only helps in optimization, but also has the potential to establish quantum advantages.

From the QAOA to a Quantum Alternating Operator Ansatz. The next few years will be exciting, with the advent of prototypes of universal quantum processors that allow for the implementation of a variety of algorithms. Of particular interest are quantum heuristics, whose evaluation requires experimentation with quantum hardware, which has the potential to significantly expand the range of applications in which quantum computers have established advantages. The main candidate is Farhi et al. QAOA by. It alternates between the cost function-based Hamiltonian operator and the mixed Hamiltonian operator. Now, researchers can extend this framework to switch between more common operator families. The essence of this extension, the quantum alternating operator approach, applies not only to time evolution under a fixed local Hamiltonian for the time specified by the parameter, but also to the general family of parameterized units. This approach supports the presentation of a variety of potentially beneficial conditions that are larger than the original formulation and can have long-term impact over a wide range of applications. If mixing is only needed within the desired subspace, readapting to the unitary instead of the Hamiltonian can implement the mixer more efficiently than was possible with the original framework. Such mixers are especially useful for optimization problems with hard constraints that must always be met to define a viable subspace and soft constraints that want to minimize violations. A more efficient implementation enables early experimental exploration of alternative operator approaches based on the spirit of quantum approximation optimization algorithms for various approximation optimizations, accurate optimizations, and sampling problems. In addition to the introduction of the quantum alternating operator approach, we define the design criteria for mixed operators, define detailed images of the eight problems, and give an overview including a brief description of the images of the various arrays [18].

Performance of QAOAs for Maximum Cut Problems QAOAs. They are promising for programming short-term gate-based hybrid quantum computers to find suitable approximate solutions for difficult combination problems. However, little is currently known about the capabilities of QAOA and the difficulty of optimizing the required parameters. Now, in the MaxCut combination optimization problem, researchers used Quantum Flow, a quantum circuit simulator implemented in TensorFlow, on a traditional computer with automatic differentiation and stochastic gradient descent. The quantum circuit was optimized. The QAOA performance was examined. We also found that optimizing many problem instances can recover training costs. QAOA outperforms traditional polynomial-time Goemans−Williamson algorithms at medium circuit depths, and performance at the fixed circuit depths is independent of problem size. In addition, MaxCut QAOA can be efficiently implemented in gate-based quantum computers with limited qubit connections using the qubit swap network.

These observations support the prospect that QAOA will be an effective way to solve interesting problems in quantum computers [18].

Quantum approximate optimization is computationally universal. The researchers of this paper discussed how QAOA applies two Hamiltonian operators alternately to a quantum system. The original goal of the algorithm was to bring the system closer to one of the ground states of the Hamiltonian operator. This paper shows that universal quantum computation can be performed using the same alternating procedure. The time when the Hamiltonian operator is applied can be programmed to generate computationally universal dynamics. The required Hamiltonian operator can be as simple as Pauli-X for a single qubit and the homogeneous sum of two local ZZ Hamiltonian operators on a one-dimensional qubit line [19].

Impact of Quantum Noise on QAOAs. Classic hybrid quantum algorithms are promising algorithms aimed at demonstrating the benefits of quantum in NISQ devices. When running such an algorithm, the effects of quantum noise are unavoidable. In our study, the researchers in this paper examined the well-known hybrid algorithm, the QAOA. The effect of typical quantum noise channels on QAOA was investigated, and some numerical results were produced. According to our research, the baseline fidelity is H. The cost function obtained from QAOA decreases exponentially with respect to the number of gates and noise intensity. Moreover, unless the noise is strong, the optimized parameters will not deviate from the ideal values. Our results show the effectiveness of the hybrid algorithm running on NISQ devices [15].

The QAOA Needs to See the Whole Graph: A Typical Case. In fact, the quantum approximation optimization algorithm may be applied to the combinatorial search problem of graphs. Quantum circuits have p units of unitary operators that respect the locality of the graph. For graphs of limited order where p is tiny enough, the distant qubit measurements of the QAOA state output give uncorrelated results. An outsized independent set in a very $dn/2$ edge random graph that fixes d and keeps n large must be found. Using the nearly optimal independent set overlap gap property of the random graph and the locality of QAOA, the researchers of this paper showed that QAOA is superior to the independent set if p is smaller than the dependent constant time log n. Find 0.854 times the optimal size for D large. The logarithm grows slowly, so even 1,000,000 SiteSpect can only show that the algorithm is blocked if p is within the single digit range. At higher PS, the algorithm "recognizes" the complete graph and has no indication that performance is restricted [20].

Counter adiabaticity and therefore the QAOA could be a short-term hybrid algorithm aimed toward solving combinatorial optimization problems like MaxCut. QAOA may be created to mimic an adiabatic scheme, and with the $p \to \infty$ limit, the ultimate state is the exact maximum eigenstate consistent with the adiabatic theorem. In this work, the link between QAOA and adiabatic properties is clarified by examining a regime with an outsized, but finite p. Counter diabetic QAOA (CDQAOA) mimics the antiinsulation scheme by fitting the Trotter's "error" term to approximate the insulation gage potential that suppresses adiabatic excitation at finite ramp velocities by combining QAOA with antiinsulation (CD) evolution. In our construction, these "error" terms are useful and do not harm QAOA. Combining QAOA with the QAA using this matching shows that the approximation ratio converges to 1, a minimum of $1 - C$ [5] to $1/p\mu$. The transfer of parameters between graphs and also the interpolation of the $p + 1$ angle for a specific p show that it is a natural byproduct of CDQAOA matching. Optimizing the CDQAOA angle is the same as optimizing the continual insulation schedule. Finally, using the variable adiabatic gage potential property, the researchers of this paper show that QAOA is not only adiabatic, but also a minimum of anti-insulation and is superior to adiabatic evolution during a finite time. They show this method using three examples: a two-level system, an Ising chain, and a MaxCut problem [21].

Policy gradient-based QAOA as a hybrid quantum/classical algorithm has received a lot of attention lately. QAOA may also be seen as a variational approach to quantum control. However, its direct application to new quantum technologies has additional physical limitations [15]. The state of the quantum system cannot be observed. Obtaining the derivative of the target function is computationally expensive or might not be accessible within the experiment. In the case of noisy subscale quanta, the worth of the target function is sensitive to varied sources of uncertainty NISQ. Taking these constraints into consideration, the researchers of this paper show that a policy gradient-based reinforcement learning [22] algorithm is suitable for optimizing QAOA variation parameters in an exceedingly noise-resistant manner for continuous quantum control. It paves the way for the event of RL methods. This is often advantageous for mitigating and monitoring the causes of doubtless unknown errors in modern quantum simulators. They also analyze the performance of algorithms for quantum state transfer problems in single and multicubit systems, betting on various noise sources like the error term of the Hamiltonian operator and the quantum uncertainty of the measurement process. It shows that in a very noisy setup, it can perform better than the most recent existing optimization algorithms [22].

QAOA for Continuous Problems: This paper presents the QAOA for continuous optimization. This algorithm is based on the dynamics of a quantum system that moves within the energy potential that encodes the objective function. By approximating the dynamics in finite time steps, the algorithm can be expressed as alternating evolution under two noncommuting Hamiltonian operators. This shows that each step of the algorithm updates the wavefunction in the direction of the local gradient with an additional momentum-dependent shift. Therefore, in the initial state of superimposing many points, this method can be interpreted as a coherent version of the steepest descent method. As "the steepest descent method," this approach can be used for both constrained and unconstrained optimizations. In terms of computational complexity, this paper shows how a variant of the algorithm can recover Glover's continuous search and how to duplicate a continuously variable quantum polynomial circuit in a single iteration. It also describes how to tune the algorithm to solve a discrete optimization problem. Finally, we test the algorithm through numerical simulation while optimizing the "StyblinskiTang" function [23].

Applying the QAOA to the Tail Assignment Problem: As explained by Vikstål et al. [24], airlines today face many major planning problems. One such issue is the tail allocation issue. It is often important to assign individual aircraft to flight sets to minimize overall costs. Each aircraft is identified by a tail number. In this chapter, researchers simulate a QAOA applied to an instance of this problem derived from real-world data. QAOA is a recently introduced variational hybrid classical quantum algorithm that can be run on short-term quantum devices. Instances are scaled down to accommodate 8, 15, and 25 qubit quantum devices. The mitigation method leaves only one possible solution per instance. This allows you to map tail mapping issues to accurate cover issues. Repeating QAOA for all instances shows a viable solution with a probability close to 1. Also, pay attention to the pattern of variable parameters so that you can apply an interpolation strategy that greatly simplifies normal optimization as part of QAOA. Finally, they also empirically find the relationship between the connectivity of the material graph and the single-shot probability of algorithm success.

The QAOA Needs to See the Whole Graph: Worst Case Examples. QAOA is applied to find problems in graphs that use cost functions. When using the stitch term, the unit quantity QAOA of depth p produces an operator that depends only on the subgraph consisting of the edges from the stitch in question to P. For very random regular graphs with fixed regular graphs with small constants d and p, most of them

Reachability Deficits in Quantum Approximate Optimization: The QAOA quickly became the premise for the fashionable development of quantum algorithms. Despite the growing scope of applications, few results are developed to know the final word limits of the algorithm. Here, the researchers of this paper report that QAOA strongly relies on the constraints of the matter instance for the ratio of variables. This problem density limits the power of the algorithm to reduce the corresponding objective function (and thus solve the optimization problem instance). These accessibility deficiencies act in the absence of barren plateaus and are outside the recently reported level 1 QAOA limits. These results are one in every of the primary to indicate strong limitations in optimizing variable quantum approximations [25].

Accelerating QAOA using Machine Learning: Willsch et al. [26] proposed a machine learning-based approach to accelerate the implementation of the QAOA, a promising quantum classical hybrid algorithm for proving what is called quantum superiority. In QAOA, parametric quantum circuits and classic optimizers iterate in an exceedingly closed-loop system to resolve difficult combinatorial optimization problems. The performance of QAOA improves because the number of steps (depth) of the quantum circuit increases. However, when a stage is added to a conventional optimizer, it introduces two new parameters that increase the amount of iterations of the optimization loop. It leverages it by determining the correlation between the parameters of low-depth and high-depth QAOA implementations and developing machine learning models to predict gate parameters that are near optimal values. As a result, the optimization loop converges with fewer iterations. Select the Graph MaxCut problem as a prototype to resolve with QAOA. Run feature extraction routines with 100 different QAOA instances and develop training datasets with 13,860 optimal parameters. The analysis of the four variants of the regression model and therefore the four variants of the classic optimizer is shown below. Finally, they show that the proposed approach can reduce the quantity of optimization iterations by a median of 44.9% (up to 65.7%) from analyses performed on 264 graphs.

Digitized-Counterdiabetic QAOA: The QAO set of rules has proved to be a robust classical-quantum set of rules serving a range of purposes, from fixing combinatorial optimization troubles to locating the ground country of many-frame quantum systems. Since QAOA is an ansatz-established set of rules, there is constantly a need to layout ansatz for higher optimization. To that end, the researchers of this paper advocate a digitized model of

QAOA more suitable through the usage of shortcuts to adiabaticity. Specifically, they also use a CD using time to layout a better ansatz, along with the Hamiltonian and mixing terms, improving the worldwide performance. In addition, they need our digitized-CD QAOA for icing models, classical optimization troubles, and the *P*-spin model, demonstrating that it outperforms widespread QAOA in all the instances they study [27].

QAO of nonplanar graph problems on a planar superconducting Faster combinatorial optimization algorithm can revolutionize various areas like logistics, finance, and machine learning. Therefore, the chance of quantum-enhanced optimization has aroused great interest in quantum technology. Here is a way to apply Google Sycamore's superconducting qubit processor to combinatorial optimization problems using the QAOA. Like in previous QAOA experiments, the performance of the matter defined within the hardware's native planar connection graph was examined. However, QAOA also applies to the Sherrington–Kirkpatrick model and MaxCut. This is often a nonnative issue that needs extensive compilation to implement. For hardware-related problems which will be solved classically and efficiently on the average, get a size-independent approximation ratio and see that performance improves with the circuit depth. For problems that need compilation, performance degrades with the scale of the matter. Circuits with thousands of gates are better than random rates, but not better than some efficient traditional algorithms. Our results suggest that short-term implementations of QAOA make it difficult to scale problems with nonnative graphs. These figures are near real-world instances, so it is advisable to pay more attention to those issues when benchmarking quantum processors using QAOA [23].

An Efficient Circuit Compilation Flow for QAOA: The QAOA is a promising quantum-classical hybrid algorithm for solving hard combinatorial optimization problems. The 2 qubit gates employed in QAOA quantum circuits are commutative. The order of the gates is often changed without changing the logical output. This relocation runs more gates in parallel, reducing the number of additional gates and compiling the QAOA circuit. This reduces the depth of the circuit and the number of gates, which is advantageous in terms of circuit execution time and noise. A little number of gates means less accumulation of gate errors, and a smaller circuit depth means less time for qubit deco-healing (state loss). However, the researchers of this paper found that the optimal reordered circuit may be a difficult problem and cannot cope well with the circuit size. This report describes a compilation procedure that uses three approaches to search the simplest sort of circuit with the reduced gate depth and number. Our approach can reduce the number of gates by up to 23.21% and the depth of the circuit by up to 53.65%. Our approach is compiler-independent, integrates with the existing compilers, and is scalable [23].

Quantum Approximate Optimization with Parallelizable Gates: The QAOA was introduced as a heuristic digital quantum computing scheme for locating approximate solutions to combinatorial optimization problems. This paper presents a scheme to parallelize this approach to problem graphs connected from all to any or all in an exceeding layout of quantum bits (qubits) with nearest neighbor interactions. The protocol consists of individual qubit operations that encode the optimization problem, but the interaction may be a per-pair CNOT gate that is independent of the matter between the closest neighbors. This enables parallelizable implementations in quantum components using planar lattice geometry. This proposal relies on a grid model that also introduces QAOA's additional parameters and protocols to boost efficiency [28].

11.4 Result

The results of this paper show high-level analysis. Using fermion representations, the evolution of the system under QAOA is transformed into quantum control of a population of independent spins. This process allows us to obtain an analytical expression for the performance of any p QAOA. It also greatly simplifies the numerical search for optimal parameter values. By examining the symmetry, this paper identifies the low-dimensional submanifolds of interest, which can be reduced. This analysis also describes the symmetry observed with the optimal parameter values. In addition, it examines the parameter landscape numerically and shows that it is simple, in the sense that there is no local optimization.

11.5 Discussion

This paper presents a variational classical method for simulating QAOA. This is a hybrid quantum classical approach to solve combinatorial optimization with the prospect of quantum acceleration in short-term devices. We use a self-contained approximation simulator based on the fixed p algorithm borrowed from many-body quantum physics, which deviates from the traditional accurate simulation of this class of quantum circuits.

The performance of the method near the optimal QAOA angle was the best; it was able to successfully explore areas previously unreachable in the QAOA parameter space. Model limitations are explained in terms of reduced accuracy in the reproduction of suboptimal quantum states. Due to these different application areas and relatively low computational effort, this method has been introduced as a supplement to the established numerical method of classical simulation of quantum circuits. The classical variational simulation of the quantum algorithm provides a natural way to evaluate and understand the limitations of quantum hardware soon. In terms of algorithms, this paper's approach helps to answer fundamentally unanswered questions in this area, that is, whether QAOA is superior to classical optimization algorithms or quantum-inspired classical algorithms based on other QAOA algorithms.

11.6 Conclusion

The researchers advanced a quantum technique for approximation combinatorial optimization that is supported by an integer parameter known as P. The center is an n-bit example with a sum of m nearby phrases goal characteristic C. The goal is to identify a string z that C (z) tactics C's international maximum. Each name to the quantum pc inside the simple set of rules makes use of a set of 2P angles (,) to create the state. This is frequently accompanied with the aid of using a dimension inside the computational foundation, yielding a string z

with a related price $C(z)$. Repeated calls to the quantum *pc* will yield a first-rate estimate. Running the set of rules calls for a method for choosing a series of units of angles with the aim of making *gFp* massive and viable. They gave numerous viable techniques for finding a sincere set of angles. In segment 1.2, the researchers targeted a constant *p*, and consequently, the case in which every bit is in now no longer pretty a hard and fast wide variety of clauses. In the course of this scenario, a fast classical technique is hired to identify the most beneficial set of angles, which are then entered into the quantum *pc*. Only the only set of angles is hired to run the quantum *pc* here. It is well worth noting that the "efficient" classical method that evaluates (25) using (24) might also additionally call for an area in p that is two times as large. Making a couple of calls to the quantum *pc* with specific units of angles is an alternative to using a classical preprocessor for the training session of the only angles. When p does not increase with n, one approach is to attract a quality grid at the compact set [0,2] *p* [0,] *p*, with the kind of factors that are handiest polynomials in *n* and *m*. This works due to the fact the characteristic FP does not have peaks which might be so slim that they are now no longer visible without the aid of the grid. The QAOA could be run on a quantum *pc* with *p* being developed with n if there is a method for deciding on units of angles. Perhaps for some combinatorial optimization problems, the exact angles can be determined before. The quantum PC is frequently known as *G*, FP (γ, β); the expectancy of *C* inside the state is $\beta >$. This name is frequently used as a subroutine with the aid of using a classical set of rules that seeks the maximum of the smooth characteristic FP (γ, β). The researchers wish that both the *p* constant and slow development with n are going to be sufficient to make this quantum set of rules be of use to find answers to combinatorial troubles beyond what classical algorithms can do.

References

[1] L.T. Brady, C.L. Baldwin, A. Bapat, Y. Kharkov, A.V. Gorshkov, Optimal protocols in quantum annealing and quantum approximate optimization algorithm problems, Phys. Rev. Lett. 126 (7) (2021)070505. Available from: https://doi.org/10.1103/PhysRevLett.126.070505.

[2] S.H. Sack, M. Serbyn, Quantum annealing initialization of the quantum approximate optimization algorithm, Quantum 5 (2021)491. Available from: https://doi.org/10.22331/q-2021-07-01-491.

[3] J.C. Aguma, An upper bound on the universality of the quantum approximate optimization algorithm, Apr. 2021.

[4] L. Abualigah, A. Diabat, C.L. Thanh, S. Khatir, Opposition-based Laplacian distribution with Prairie Dog optimization method for industrial engineering design problems, Comput. Methods Appl. Mech. Eng. 414 (2023) 116097.

[5] G. Hu, Y. Zheng, L. Abualigah, A.G. Hussien, DETDO: an adaptive hybrid dandelion optimizer for engineering optimization, Adv. Eng. Inform. 57 (2023) 102004.

[6] D. Izci, S. Ekinci, S. Mirjalili, L. Abualigah, An intelligent tuning scheme with a master/slave approach for efficient control of the automatic voltage regulator, Neur. Comput. Appl. (2023) 1−17.

[7] H. Jia, C. Lu, D. Wu, C. Wen, H. Rao, L. Abualigah, An improved reptile search algorithm with ghost opposition-based learning for global optimization problems, J. Comput. Design Eng. (2023). qwad048.

[8] A.H. Alharbi, A.A. Abdelhamid, A. Ibrahim, S.K. Towfek, N. Khodadadi, L. Abualigah, et al., Improved dipper-throated optimization for forecasting metamaterial design bandwidth for engineering applications, Biomimetics 8 (2) (2023) 241.

[9] S. Nama, A.K. Saha, S. Chakraborty, A.H. Gandomi, L. Abualigah, Boosting particle swarm optimization by backtracking search algorithm for optimization problems, Swarm Evol. Comput. 79 (2023) 101304.

[10] M. Zare, M. Ghasemi, A. Zahedi, K. Golalipour, S.K. Mohammadi, S. Mirjalili, et al., A global best-guided firefly algorithm for engineering problems, J. Bionic Eng. (2023) 1−30.

[11] D. Wu, C. Wen, H. Rao, H. Jia, Q. Liu, L. Abualigah, Modified reptile search algorithm with multi-hunting coordination strategy for global optimization problems, Math. Biosc. Eng. 20 (6) (2023) 10090−10134.

[12] S. Ekinci, D. Izci, L. Abualigah, R.A. Zitar, A modified oppositional chaotic local search strategy based aquila optimizer to design an effective controller for vehicle cruise control system, J. Bionic Eng. (2023) 1−24.

[13] L. Abualigah, D. Falcone, A. Forestiero, Swarm intelligence to face IoT challenges, Comput. Intell. Neurosci. (2023) 2023.

[14] E. Farhi, J. Goldstone, S. Gutmann, L. Zhou, The quantum approximate optimization algorithm and the Sherrington-Kirkpatrick model at infinite size, Quantum 6 (2022)759. Available from: https://doi.org/10.22331/q-2022-07-07-759.

[15] B.T. Kiani, G. De Palma, M. Marvian, Z.-W. Liu, S. Lloyd, Learning quantum data with the quantum earth mover's distance, Quant. Sci. Technol. 7 (4) (2022) 045002. Available from: https://doi.org/10.1088/2058-9565/ac79c9.

[16] D.J. Egger, et al., Quantum computing for finance: State-of-the-art and future prospects, IEEE Trans. Quant. Eng. 1 (2020) 1−24. Available from: https://doi.org/10.1109/TQE.2020.3030314.

[17] D. Mills, S. Sivarajah, T.L. Scholten, R. Duncan, Application-motivated, holistic benchmarking of a full quantum computing stack, Quantum 5 (2021)415. Available from: https://doi.org/10.22331/q-2021-03-22-415.

[18] V. Kremenetski, T. Hogg, S. Hadfield, S.J. Cotton, N.M. Tubman, Quantum alternating operator ansatz (QAOA) phase diagrams and applications for quantum chemistry, August 2021, [Online]. < http://arxiv.org/abs/2108.13056>.

[19] P.C. Lotshaw, T.S. Humble, R. Herrman, J. Ostrowski, G. Siopsis, Empirical performance bounds for quantum approximate optimization, Quant. Inf. Process. 20 (12) (2021) 403. Available from: https://doi.org/10.1007/s11128-021-03342-3.

[20] R. Shaydulin, S. Hadfield, T. Hogg, I. Safro, Classical symmetries and the quantum approximate optimization algorithm, Quant. Inf. Process. 20 (11) (2021) 359. Available from: https://doi.org/10.1007/s11128-021-03298-4.

[21] J. Wurtz, P.J. Love, Counterdiabaticity and the quantum approximate optimization algorithm, Quantum 6 (2022) 635. Available from: https://doi.org/10.22331/q-2022-01-27-635.

[22] M. Medvidović, G. Carleo, Classical variational simulation of the quantum approximate optimization algorithm, Npj Quant. Inf 7 (1) (2021)101. Available from: https://doi.org/10.1038/s41534-021-00440-z.

[23] M.P. Harrigan, et al., Quantum approximate optimization of non-planar graph problems on a planar superconducting processor, Nat. Phys. 17 (3) (2021) 332−336. Available from: https://doi.org/10.1038/s41567-020-01105-y.

[24] P. Vikstål, M. Grönkvist, M. Svensson, M. Andersson, G. Johansson, G. Ferrini, Applying the quantum approximate optimization algorithm to the tail-assignment problem, Phys. Rev. Appl. 14 (3) (2020) 034009. Available from: https://doi.org/10.1103/PhysRevApplied.14.034009.

[25] V. Akshay, H. Philathong, I. Zacharov, J. Biamonte, Reachability deficits in quantum approximate optimization of graph problems, Quantum 5 (2021)532. Available from: https://doi.org/10.22331/q-2021-08-30-532.

[26] D. Willsch, M. Willsch, F. Jin, K. Michielsen, H. De Raedt, GPU-accelerated simulations of quantum annealing and the quantum approximate optimization algorithm, Comput. Phys. Commun. 278 (2022) 108411. Available from: https://doi.org/10.1016/j.cpc.2022.108411.

[27] P. Chandarana, et al., Digitized-counterdiabatic quantum approximate optimization algorithm, Phys. Rev. Res. 4 (1) (2022)013141. Available from: https://doi.org/10.1103/PhysRevResearch.4.013141.

[28] M. Fellner, K. Ender, R. ter Hoeven, W. Lechner, Parity quantum optimization: benchmarks, Quantum 7 (2023) 952. Available from: https://doi.org/10.22331/q-2023-03-17-952.

12

Crow search algorithm: a survey of novel optimizer and its recent applications

Laith Abualigah[1,2,3,4,5,6,7], Sabreen Faweer[7], Ali Raza[8], Faiza Gul[9], Absalom E. Ezugwu[10], Mohammad Alshinwan[11], Mohammad Rustom Al Nasar[12], Ala Mughaid[13], Shadi AlZu'bi[14]

[1]ARTIFICIAL INTELLIGENCE AND SENSING TECHNOLOGIES (AIST) RESEARCH CENTER, UNIVERSITY OF TABUK, TABUK, SAUDI ARABIA [2]HOURANI CENTER FOR APPLIED SCIENTIFIC RESEARCH, AL-AHLIYYA AMMAN UNIVERSITY, AMMAN, JORDAN [3]MEU RESEARCH UNIT, MIDDLE EAST UNIVERSITY, AMMAN, JORDAN [4]SCHOOL OF COMPUTER SCIENCES, UNIVERSITI SAINS MALAYSIA, PULAU PINANG, MALAYSIA [5]SCHOOL OF ENGINEERING AND TECHNOLOGY, SUNWAY UNIVERSITY MALAYSIA, PETALING JAYA, MALAYSIA [6]DEPARTMENT OF ELECTRICAL AND COMPUTER ENGINEERING, LEBANESE AMERICAN UNIVERSITY, BYBLOS, LEBANON [7]COMPUTER SCIENCE DEPARTMENT, AL AL-BAYT UNIVERSITY, MAFRAQ, JORDAN [8]INSTITUTE OF COMPUTER SCIENCE, KHWAJA FAREED UNIVERSITY OF ENGINEERING AND INFORMATION TECHNOLOGY, RAHIM YAR KHAN, PAKISTAN [9]ELECTRICAL DEPARTMENT, AIR UNIVERSITY AEROSPACE AND AVIATION CAMPUS, KAMRA, PAKISTAN [10]UNIT FOR DATA SCIENCE AND COMPUTING, NORTH-WEST UNIVERSITY, POTCHEFSTROOM, SOUTH AFRICA [11]FACULTY OF INFORMATION TECHNOLOGY, APPLIED SCIENCE PRIVATE UNIVERSITY, AMMAN, JORDAN [12]DEPARTMENT OF INFORMATION TECHNOLOGY MANAGEMENT, COLLEGE OF COMPUTER INFORMATION TECHNOLOGY (CCIT), AMERICAN UNIVERSITY IN THE EMIRATES (AUE), ACADEMIC CITY, DUBAI, UNITED ARAB EMIRATES [13]DEPARTMENT OF INFORMATION TECHNOLOGY, FACULTY OF PRINCE AL-HUSSIEN BIN ABDULLAH II FOR IT, THE HASHEMITE UNIVERSITY, ZARQA, JORDAN [14]FACULTY OF SCIENCE AND IT, AL-ZAYTOONAH UNIVERSITY OF JORDAN, AMMAN, JORDAN

12.1 Introduction

Optimization is becoming one of the most significant and hotly debated subjects in the scientific community. It may be found in almost every discipline [1], including engineering,

Metaheuristic Optimization Algorithms. DOI: https://doi.org/10.1016/B978-0-443-13925-3.00004-2

science, energy, and computer science. Since the complexity of real-world scientific and engineering problems has increased, optimization has become a major concern in soft computing. Mathematical problems may be difficult to answer and handle using traditional approaches. With the metaheuristics algorithm (MA), real-time solutions to certain nondeterministic polynomial problems may be found. Easy implementation, avoiding local optima, and flexibility and adaptability have made these algorithms very popular. One or more objectives may be specified, and the solution may be limited or unconstrained and continuous or discontinuous [2]. They can be seen as black boxes.

Single-based/individual-based algorithms and population-based algorithms are two broad categories. TS, GLS, and PS are examples of single-based algorithms, and particle swarm optimization (PSO) and gray wolf optimizer are examples of population-based algorithms [2−4].

Alireza Askarzadeh created the crow search algorithm (CSA) in 2016, a new algorithm that mimics the crow's food storage and retrieval behavior [5]. When CSA first appeared, it was used for a broad range of optimization problems, including those in chemical engineering, medical technology, and power generation. These articles are essential since they offer and debate the most current research. Numerous studies have been conducted on MAs, such as the firefly algorithm and gravitational search. The Krill herd and gray wolf optimizer are also discussed in the literature.

Normally, optimization methods can be used to deal with many problems in the sciences, as presented in [6−15]. To the best of our knowledge, there is no study in the literature that covers or lists all CSA aspects, variants, and applications. This study aims to review all CSA aspects and how scientists/researchers are motivated to use this algorithm to solve different real-world optimization problems. Besides, this review collects and summarizes all modifications and variants of CSA to overcome its drawbacks.

12.2 Crow search algorithm

This section discusses the continuous CSA's biological inspiration, mathematical theory, and pseudocode.

12.2.1 Inspiration

Crows (family Corvidae) are very clever birds. Numerous investigations, including the size of their brains, their intellect, their conduct while using tools, and their success on self-recognition tests using mirrors, have shown their superior intelligence. These birds have a substantially bigger brain than other species, with a high brain-to-body ratio and a brain that is proportionately superior to that of a chimp. The New Caledonian crow, for instance, is the only nonhuman species known to make hooked tools in the wild. Their intellect is rich, proving that they are incredibly hungry birds and strategists, since they conceal food and are able to retrieve it months later; they monitor where other birds store their food in order to take it; and they also protect themselves from being future victims.

12.2.2 Continuous crow search algorithm

The CSA is a population-based approach for simulating some of the abovementioned intelligent behaviors in order to solve optimization issues. The algorithm's functioning, in general, mimics a group of crows flying across a particular area, concealing food, learning and defending caches, and following one another in search of a better food source. From this vantage point, the crows are indeed the seekers (researchers), the surroundings are the search space, each position in the atmosphere corresponds to a workable alternative, the performance of the food source is the result of applying the objective function to that position (fitness), and the best food source in the environment is the global solution to the problem. Consider a *d*-dimensional ecosystem with *N* crows (flock size) traveling across space in search of the optimum food source at a particular time (*t*) (generation). A vector can be used to specify the location of the same crow within this generation *t*. Eq. (12−1) illustrates that [16]:

$$x^{i,t} = \left[x_1^{i,t}, x_2^{i,t}, \ldots, x_d^{i,t} \right] \tag{12-1}$$

where *i* ranges from 1 to *N* and *t* spans the range from 1 to t_{max} (maximum number of generations) [16].

As previously stated, crows also recall their optimal position, which really is the position of their preferred food source. The best location of crow I thus far is also defined in the generation process by a vector denoted by [16]:

$$m^{i,t} = \left[m_1^{i,t}, m_2^{i,t}, \ldots, m_d^{i,t} \right] \tag{12-2}$$

This algorithm may update the location of crows in two distinct ways in the following scenario: at a certain iteration *t*, crow j is flying about its hiding site (*m7*, *z*), and crow I chooses to follow it in order to determine its greatest source of food, which it subsequently steals. Two things may occur in this case:

Case 1: Crow J is unaware that Crow I is pursuing it. Simultaneously, crow I reaches crow j, and crow i's new position is updated by [16]:

$$x^{i,t+1} = x^{i,t} + r_j \times fl^{i,t} \times \left(m^{j,t} - x^{i,t} \right) \tag{12-3}$$

where *rj* is a random value produced with a uniform distribution among (0,1) and awareness probability (AP), *t*, which denotes the likelihood of crow J becoming aware in generation *t*.

Case 2: Crow J is aware because Crow I is pursuing it. As a result, crow j seeks to divert crow i's attention by moving somewhere else in the search region to preserve its hiding location. Crow's new position is determined at random. Additionally, the two situations may be represented using the following expression:

$$x^{i,t+1} = \begin{cases} x^{i,t} + r_j \times fl^{i,t} \times (m^{j,t} - x^{i,t}) & r_j \geq AP^{j,t} \\ a \quad \text{random} \quad \text{position} & \text{otherwise} \end{cases} \tag{12-4}$$

Where *rj* is a random value produced with a uniform distribution among (0,1) and AP, *t*, which denotes the likelihood of crow j becoming aware in generation *t*.

It is essential to attend to the two primary components of any metaheuristic, diversity and intensification, or alternatively, exploitation and exploration, in order to attain a global optimum.

Diversification entails developing numerous solutions in order to thoroughly investigate the search space on a worldwide scale, while intensification entails concentrating the search on a limited location, certain that a suitable solution will be discovered there. A suitable balance between intensification and diversity must be struck throughout the solution selection process in order to increase the algorithms' convergence rate.

In CSA, the primary parameter influencing diversity and intensity is the crows' AP. When tiny values for AP are employed, the algorithm often leads to a local search, increasing its intensity. On the other hand, when the AP value grows, the algorithm prefers to explore the search space globally, increasing the search space's diversity. Algorithm 12−1 contains the pseudocode for the traditional CSA algorithm.

The pseudocode for the traditional CSA algorithm is provided [16].

Although CSA is a relatively recent development, it has shown promise for a variety of optimization algorithms, including restricted design process, capacitor location in distribution

Algorithm 12−1:　Crow search algorithm

1: **begin**
2: Randomly initialize the position of a flock of N crows
3: Evaluate the position of the crows
4: Initialize the memory of each crow
5: **while** maximum generation is not reached, **do**
6:　**for** $i = 1: N$ (all N crows of the flock)
7:　　Randomly choose one of the crows to follow
8:　　Define an awareness probability
9:　　**if** $r_j > AP^{j,t}$
10:　　　$x^{i,t+1} = x^{i,t} + r_j \times fl^{i,t} \times \left(m^{j,t} - x^{i,t} \right)$
11:　　**else**
12:　　　$x^{i,t+1} = $ a random position of search space
13:　　**end if**
14:　**end for**
15:　Check the feasibility of new positions
16:　Evaluate the new position of the crows
17:　Update the memory of crows
18: **end while**
19: **end**

networks, tidal current estimation, multiobjective optimization, and electromagnetic optimization. Below is a short summary of each of these CSA applications:

The CSA's creator initially applied it to a set of five test functions and six restricted engineering design problems with varying goal functions, restrictions, and decision variables. The simulation findings indicate that CSA may provide more promising outcomes than the other methods. On the collection of benchmark problems, it is noticed that, despite its reputation as a rapid population-based method, PSO is surpassed by CSA. Other researches advocated using CSA to determine the ideal capacitor location in a distribution system. Power electronics are often used in electricity distribution networks to compensate for reactive power. Simulated findings from the case studies reveal that CSA generates more precise findings than the other search techniques examined. A three-phase adjustment strategy is suggested for increasing crow population variety while maintaining an appropriate balance between local and global searches in a unique hybrid approach premised on support vector regression for forecasting tidal current direction and speed. The first phase modification used the Levy plane to increase the algorithm's diversity; the second phase modification directed the crow flock toward the crow with the best fitness function, using the population's mean value; and the third phase modification proposed a new dynamic equation for the participation probability. On real data, the suggested hybrid model was very accurate and outperformed previous techniques.

In this case, Satpathy [17] and his team used CSA to solve a problem with cloud data center virtual machine allocation. Proper simulation has been conducted, and the results indicate that CSA outperforms other algorithms in terms of server utilization, power usage, and resource waste. Coelho et al. used a modified version of the CSA method to change both the probability of being conscious and the length of the flight. They used demographic diversity information and a truncated and reduced Gaussian distribution in the range (0, 1). This improved CSA was used for the Loney's solenoid design challenge, a well-known electromagnetic benchmark. The creation of random sequences using Gaussian distributions to change the control parameters of optimization metaheuristics led to a big improvement in the conventional algorithm's convergence rate.

12.3 Related work

De Souza et al. [18] contributed to the development of the V-shaped binary CSA (BCSA) for selecting features. The instance presented here demonstrates feature selection (FS), which is the process of finding and distinguishing significant features in a dataset in order to find the optimal solution to a pattern classification or regression issue [19]. The primary advantages of FS also include accurate classification models, easier model interpretation, and a decrease in classification processing time where wrappers are a common technique in FS. In this strategy, features are chosen depending on the results of a classification algorithm's assessment. The CSA has been presented as an optimized bioinspired evolutionary algorithm based on the cognitive behavior of crows. Besides, CSA is based on the premise that crows hide surplus food and recover it when it is required. The primary reasons for utilizing CSA are its ease of implementation, the small number of control parameters that must be adjusted, the rapid convergence speed, and its high efficiency. To further improve the efficiency of the standard CSA technique, De Souza suggested a novel wrapper based on the CSA's "v-shaped" binarization. The wrapper, dubbed BCSA in this paper, is deployed on six benchmark functions. The paper analyzes and evaluates the suggested technique's benefits and drawbacks with respect to classification accuracy, the number of chosen characteristics, and computational cost in comparison to other classical and state-of-the-art methods. The findings were positive, demonstrating that BCSA produced an excellent accuracy rate and also efficiently picked subsets with a modest number of characteristics.

Bhullar et al. [20] suggested an improved CSA (I-CSA) for numerical and real-world engineering issues. The suggested strategy is novel in four ways: (1) incorporating an archive component into the standard CSA to account for prior expertise in solution discovery; (2) terminology of nonhideout position such that the crow remains close to its hideout position; (3) application of Rechenberg's 1/5th rule to change the flight length (rather than keeping it constant) to accelerate the optimization process; and (4) regulation of AP to establish a trade-off among both local and global exploration. The proposed technique's performance is evaluated against 23 benchmark functions, including unimodal, multimodal, and fixed-dimension multimodal benchmarking functions. I-CSA's performance is compared to that of other government metaheuristic algorithms, and I-CSA outperforms them in the majority of benchmark functions. Additionally, to confirm the suggested method's efficacy, I-CSA was utilized to optimize a proportional−integral−derivative (PID) controller. I-CSA−PID results were compared to those of traditional CSA and other state-of-the-art approaches such as Ziegler−Nichols (Z−N), Kitamori, ACO, multiobjective ACO, multiobjective GA, and fuzzy and space gravitational optimization algorithms. The suggested method is applied to the AVR system, and its resilience is evaluated under a variety of scenarios. The consistency of the findings on benchmark systems and their variations, as well as on the AVR system and its modifications, demonstrates the suggested method's resilience. Additionally, the suggested approach outperforms current strategies in terms of performance.

Khalilpourazari et al. [21] suggested a new hybrid algorithm called the sine−cosine CSA that combines the benefits of two recently developed algorithms, namely, CSA and the sine−cosine algorithm. Their suggested algorithm's exploratory and exploitative capabilities have been significantly enhanced. The performance of the so-called SCCSA was tested utilizing robust metrics in unimodal, multimodal, fixed-dimensional multimodal, and composite benchmark functions. The research found that when compared to other algorithms that are already used, the proposed method might give good results.

Eligüzel and Zceylan [22] presented the improved CSA (I-CSA), a modified version of the CSA. CSA is a novel metaheuristic optimization technique inspired by nature. I-CSA is different from CSA because it can be used to solve a single problem that is P-median and because it encourages faster convergence to an optimal or near-optimal solution. Local searches give improvements by enabling escape from optimization algorithms or convergence to the optimum solution; elitism improves intensification by picking the most frequent centers that occurred in concealing better sites for local searches on the P-median issue. The I-CSA application process is divided into three sections. The first step analyzes and optimizes I-CSA settings using well-known data tests. To demonstrate the efficacy and applicability of I-CSA on the P-median issue, test datasets were acquired from the OR-library. The second step involves solving 40-pmed test items from the library using I-CSA and comparing the results to the known optimum solutions and previously recorded findings from other metaheuristic methodologies. Additionally, the Wilcoxon signed-rank test is used to assess the performance of I-CSA against that of well-known methods. When compared to the conventional CSA of other metaheuristic techniques, the suggested method displayed a quicker convergence rate and a superior solution in the majority of situations. Finally, the suggested I-CSA technique is evaluated on a real-world case study in Tunceli, Turkey, including 2121 nodes. Obtaining ideal outcomes in a fair amount of time demonstrates that the I-CSA's potential is promising. In summary, this chapter discusses a modification of CSA and analyzes its effectiveness in a three-phase test method.

Majhi et al. [23] investigated in swarm-based algorithms, which perform better when they can maintain an optimal balance between exploration and exploitation processes and converge quicker by effectively avoiding entrapment in local optima. In recent years, the CSA has been created as a swarm-based algorithm inspired by nature. It is capable of resolving continuous, nonlinear, and difficult optimization issues encountered in daily life. As is the case with many other optimization techniques, CSA suffers from local stagnation. This study provided an updated version of the CSA algorithm that utilizes opposing learning and mutation operators to enhance the performance of the previous CSA method. The suggested algorithm is denoted by the acronym OBL-CSA-MO. The OBL-CSA-MO improves the capacity for exploration and exploitation in the search space and effectively avoids entrapment in local optima. The IEEE CEC 2017 standard benchmark function set is used to assess the OBL-CSA-MO. The suggested OBL-CSA-MO's efficiency and robustness are evaluated utilizing performance indicators, following consequences, and statistical evidence. The suggested technique for developing fractional order PID controllers is shown using a real-world situation. To accomplish this, the FOPID design incorporates first and higher-level plants through the proposed OBL-CSA-MO. Analysis and experiments show that the proposed OBL-CSA-MO algorithm is good at solving optimization problems.

Montoya et al. [24] approached the issue of parametric estimate in photovoltaic (PV) modules with regard to manufacturer information from the standpoint of combinatorial optimization. A nonlinear, nonconvex optimization problem is developed using the data sheet given by the PV manufacturer. The data sheet provides information about the maximum power, open-circuit, and short-circuit locations. After the three parameters of the PV model (i.e., the idealist diode factor [a] and the parallel and series resistances [Rp and Rs]) have been estimated, the CSA is used, in which a metaheuristic optimization technique inspired by the behavior of crows searches for food deposits. Through a simple evolution rule adapted from the standard PSO approach, the CSA enables the exploration and exploitation of the solution space. Numerical simulations demonstrate the CSA's efficacy and resilience in estimating these parameters when the objective function is smaller than 1 in 1028 and the processing time is less than 2 seconds. All of the numerical simulations were done in MATLAB® 2020a and compared to sine-cosine and vortex search methods that have been done before.

12.4 Conclusion and future work

In conclusion, this chapter provides a comprehensive overview of the CSA and its various applications in optimization problems. It also highlights the strengths, weaknesses, and potential improvements of the CSA, making it a valuable resource for researchers and practitioners in the field of optimization. It begins by introducing the CSA and explaining its inspiration from the foraging behavior of crows. It explores the key components of the algorithm, including the initialization process, the search operator, and the update mechanism. It also discusses the advantages of the CSA, such as its simplicity, fast convergence, and ability to handle both continuous and discrete optimization problems.

Furthermore, this chapter presents a detailed analysis of the applications of the CSA in various domains, such as engineering design, data mining, image processing, and machine learning. It provides specific examples and case studies to illustrate the effectiveness of the CSA in solving complex optimization problems in these domains. These examples demonstrate the versatility of the CSA and its potential to outperform other optimization algorithms in certain scenarios.

While this chapter provides a comprehensive overview of the CSA and its applications, there are several directions for future work that can further enhance and expand the algorithm's capabilities. Some of these directions include:

- Algorithm enhancements: Researchers can explore modifications and extensions to the CSA to improve its performance. This could involve incorporating adaptive parameters, hybridizing the CSA with other optimization techniques, or introducing local search strategies to overcome stagnation and improve exploration−exploitation trade-offs.
- Theoretical analysis: Conducting a more in-depth theoretical analysis of the CSA can provide a better understanding of its convergence properties, convergence rates, and robustness. Theoretical insights can guide algorithmic improvements and shed light on the behavior of the algorithm in different problem settings.
- Benchmarking and comparative studies: Conducting rigorous benchmarking experiments and comparative studies with other state-of-the-art optimization algorithms can provide further insights into the strengths and weaknesses of the CSA. This can help researchers identify specific problem domains or scenarios where the CSA excels and where it may need further improvements.
- Real-world applications: While this chapter covers several application domains, there is still a need for more real-world case studies and applications of the CSA. Applying the CSA to complex, practical problems can provide valuable insights into its performance and highlight its practical utility.

- Parameter tuning and sensitivity analysis: Investigating the sensitivity of the CSA to its parameters and conducting parameter tuning studies can help researchers understand the impact of different parameter settings on the algorithm's performance. This can lead to recommendations for parameter selection guidelines or even automated parameter tuning methods.

Overall, future works should focus on refining and expanding the CSA to make it even more efficient, robust, and applicable to a wide range of optimization problems. By addressing the challenges and limitations identified in the survey, researchers can further enhance the algorithm's performance and promote its adoption in practical applications.

References

[1] J. Gholami, F. Mardukhi, H.M. Zawbaa, An improved crow search algorithm for solving numerical optimization functions, Soft Comput. 25 (14) (2021) 9441−9454. Available from: https://doi.org/10.1007/s00500-021-05827-w.

[2] P.G. Panah, M. Bornapour, R. Hemmati, J.M. Guerrero, Charging station stochastic programming for hydrogen/battery electric buses using multi-criteria crow search algorithm, Renew. Sustain. Energy Rev. 144 (2021) 111046. Available from: https://doi.org/10.1016/j.rser.2021.111046. Jul.

[3] J.O. Agushaka, A.E. Ezugwu, L. Abualigah, Dwarf Mongoose optimization algorithm, Comput. Methods Appl. Mech. Eng. 391 (2022). Available from: https://doi.org/10.1016/j.cma.2022.114570. Mar.

[4] J.O. Agushaka, A.E. Ezugwu, L. Abualigah, Gazelle optimization algorithm: a novel nature-inspired metaheuristic optimizer, Neural Comput. Appl. 35 (5) (2023) 4099−4131. Available from: https://doi.org/10.1007/s00521-022-07854-6.

[5] S. Ouadfel, M. Abd Elaziz, Enhanced crow search algorithm for feature selection, Expert. Syst. Appl. 159 (2020) 113572. Available from: https://doi.org/10.1016/j.eswa.2020.113572. Nov.

[6] L. Abualigah, A. Diabat, C.L. Thanh, S. Khatir, Opposition-based Laplacian distribution with Prairie Dog optimization method for industrial engineering design problems, Comput. Methods Appl. Mech. Eng. 414 (2023) 116097.

[7] G. Hu, Y. Zheng, L. Abualigah, A.G. Hussien, DETDO: an adaptive hybrid dandelion optimizer for engineering optimization, Adv. Eng. Inform. 57 (2023) 102004.

[8] D. Izci, S. Ekinci, S. Mirjalili, L. Abualigah, An intelligent tuning scheme with a master/slave approach for efficient control of the automatic voltage regulator, Neural Comput. Appl. (2023) 1−17.

[9] H. Jia, C. Lu, D. Wu, C. Wen, H. Rao, L. Abualigah, An Improved reptile search algorithm with ghost opposition-based learning for global optimization problems, J. Comput. Des. Eng. (2023). qwad048.

[10] A.H. Alharbi, A.A. Abdelhamid, A. Ibrahim, S.K. Towfek, N. Khodadadi, L. Abualigah, et al., Improved dipper-throated optimization for forecasting metamaterial design bandwidth for engineering applications, Biomimetics 8 (2) (2023) 241.

[11] S. Nama, A.K. Saha, S. Chakraborty, A.H. Gandomi, L. Abualigah, Boosting particle swarm optimization by backtracking search algorithm for optimization problems, Swarm Evolut. Computation 79 (2023) 101304.

[12] M. Zare, M. Ghasemi, A. Zahedi, K. Golalipour, S.K. Mohammadi, S. Mirjalili, et al., A global best-guided firefly algorithm for engineering problems, J. Bionic Eng. (2023) 1−30.

[13] D. Wu, C. Wen, H. Rao, H. Jia, Q. Liu, L. Abualigah, Modified reptile search algorithm with multi-hunting coordination strategy for global optimization problems, Math. Biosci. Eng. 20 (6) (2023) 10090−10134.

[14] S. Ekinci, D. Izci, L. Abualigah, R.A. Zitar, A modified oppositional chaotic local search strategy based aquila optimizer to design an effective controller for vehicle cruise control system, J. Bionic Eng. (2023) 1−24.

[15] L. Abualigah, D. Falcone, A. Forestiero, Swarm intelligence to face IoT challenges, Comput. Intell. Neurosci. 2023 (2023).

[16] Y. Meraihi, A.B. Gabis, A. Ramdane-Cherif, D. Acheli, A comprehensive survey of crow search algorithm and its applications, Artif. Intell. Rev. 54 (4) (2021) 2669−2716. Available from: https://doi.org/10.1007/s10462-020-09911-9.

[17] A. Satpathy, S.K. Addya, A.K. Turuk, B. Majhi, G. Sahoo, Crow search based virtual machine placement strategy in cloud data centers with live migration, Comput. Electr. Eng. 69 (2018) 334−350. Available from: https://doi.org/10.1016/j.compeleceng.2017.12.032. Jul.

[18] R.C. T. De Souza, L.D. S. Coelho, C.A. De Macedo, & J. Pierezan, A V-shaped binary crow search algorithm for feature selection, in: 2018 IEEE Congress on Evolutionary Computation (CEC), July 2018, pp. 1−8. Available from: https://doi.org/10.1109/CEC.2018.8477975.

[19] O.O. Akinola et al., Multiclass feature selection with metaheuristic optimization algorithms: a review, Available from: https://doi.org/10.1007/s00521-022-07705-4.

[20] A.K. Bhullar, R. Kaur, S. Sondhi, Enhanced crow search algorithm for AVR optimization, Soft Comput. 24 (16) (2020) 11957−11987. Available from: https://doi.org/10.1007/s00500-019-04640-w.

[21] S. Khalilpourazari, S.H.R. Pasandideh, Sine−cosine crow search algorithm: theory and applications, Neural Comput. Appl. 32 (12) (2020) 7725−7742. Available from: https://doi.org/10.1007/s00521-019-04530-0.

[22] İ.M. Eligüzel, E. Özceylan, Application of an improved discrete crow search algorithm with local search and elitism on a humanitarian relief case, Artif. Intell. Rev. 54 (6) (2021) 4591−4617. Available from: https://doi.org/10.1007/s10462-021-10006-2.

[23] S.K. Majhi, M. Sahoo, R. Pradhan, Oppositional crow search algorithm with mutation operator for global optimization and application in designing FOPID controller, Evol. Syst. 12 (2) (2021) 463−488. Available from: https://doi.org/10.1007/s12530-019-09305-5.

[24] O.D. Montoya, C.A. Ramírez-Vanegas, L.F. Grisales-Noreña, Parametric estimation in photovoltaic modules using the crow search algorithm, Int. J. Electr. Comput. Eng. 12 (1) (2022) 82. Available from: https://doi.org/10.11591/ijece.v12i1.pp82-91.

13

A review of Henry gas solubility optimization algorithm: a robust optimizer and applications

Laith Abualigah[1,2,3,4,5,6,7], Ghada Al-Hilo[8], Ali Raza[9],
Absalom E. Ezugwu[8], Mohammad Rustom Al Nasar[10],
Ala Mughaid[11], Shadi AlZu'bi[12], Khaled Aldiabat[13],
Mofleh Al-diabat[1]

[1]ARTIFICIAL INTELLIGENCE AND SENSING TECHNOLOGIES (AIST) RESEARCH CENTER, UNIVERSITY OF TABUK, TABUK, SAUDI ARABIA [2]HOURANI CENTER FOR APPLIED SCIENTIFIC RESEARCH, AL-AHLIYYA AMMAN UNIVERSITY, AMMAN, JORDAN [3]MEU RESEARCH UNIT, MIDDLE EAST UNIVERSITY, AMMAN, JORDAN [4]SCHOOL OF COMPUTER SCIENCES, UNIVERSITI SAINS MALAYSIA, PULAU PINANG, MALAYSIA [5]SCHOOL OF ENGINEERING AND TECHNOLOGY, SUNWAY UNIVERSITY MALAYSIA, PETALING JAYA, MALAYSIA [6]COMPUTER SCIENCE DEPARTMENT, AL AL-BAYT UNIVERSITY, MAFRAQ, JORDAN [7]DEPARTMENT OF ELECTRICAL AND COMPUTER ENGINEERING, LEBANESE AMERICAN UNIVERSITY, BYBLOS, LEBANON [8]UNIT FOR DATA SCIENCE AND COMPUTING, NORTH-WEST UNIVERSITY, POTCHEFSTROOM, SOUTH AFRICA [9]INSTITUTE OF COMPUTER SCIENCE, KHWAJA FAREED UNIVERSITY OF ENGINEERING AND INFORMATION TECHNOLOGY, RAHIM YAR KHAN, PAKISTAN [10]DEPARTMENT OF INFORMATION TECHNOLOGY MANAGEMENT, COLLEGE OF COMPUTER INFORMATION TECHNOLOGY (CCIT), AMERICAN UNIVERSITY IN THE EMIRATES (AUE), ACADEMIC CITY, DUBAI, UNITED ARAB EMIRATES [11]DEPARTMENT OF INFORMATION TECHNOLOGY, FACULTY OF PRINCE AL-HUSSIEN BIN ABDULLAH II FOR IT, THE HASHEMITE UNIVERSITY, ZARQA, JORDAN [12]FACULTY OF SCIENCE AND IT, AL-ZAYTOONAH UNIVERSITY OF JORDAN, AMMAN, JORDAN [13]DEPARTMENT OF MANAGEMENT INFORMATION SYSTEMS, AJLOUN NATIONAL UNIVERSITY, AJLOUN, JORDAN

13.1 Introduction

Optimization issues are relevant in both industrial and scientific applications. There are two sorts of optimization algorithms: deterministic mathematical programming methods and

Metaheuristic Optimization Algorithms. DOI: https://doi.org/10.1016/B978-0-443-13925-3.00013-3

metaheuristic algorithms, which is an intuitive or experimentally constructed method that can provide a practical solution to the cost issue (in terms of computing time and space) [1].

Metaheuristic algorithms have been effectively employed to handle a range of optimization issues newly, including scheduling, image segmentation, feature selection, economic load dispatch, and a variety of other engineering applications. There are four different categories of optimization algorithms: [1] evolutionary-based, [2] physics-based [2] like simulated annealing (SA) which is a nonlinear technique for solving inverse problems [3] human-based, [4] swarm intelligence-based [2] like Particle swarm optimization (PSO) which is a popular optimization algorithm to solve path planning problems [4] gravitational search algorithm (GSA) is a population-based algorithm based on physical laws [5] cuckoo search algorithm (CS) which is qualified of solving complex nonlinear optimization problems [6] gray wolf optimizer (GWO) inspired by wild gray wolves' natural foraging behaviors and leadership hierarchy [7], whale optimization algorithm (WOA) which emulates the sociable manners of humpback whales. They are based on the bubble-net hunting technique [8], elephant herding algorithm (EHO) for solving the problems of static drone location [9], and simulated annealing (SA) which is a single-solution metaheuristic approach inspired by the metallurgical annealing process [10]. One of the most recent metaheuristic methods is Henry gas solubility optimization (HGSO) [11] It is a physics-based algorithm that emulates the process of gas solubility in liquid changing with temperature. It is based on Henry's Law [12], which states that the amount of gas soluble in a specified volume of solvent at a constant temperature is presently balanced to the partisan pressure of the gas in its balance state with the solvent [12]. Henry's law has an effect on our daily lives in the form of carbonated beverage cans [13]. It also corresponds to the solubility of materials. This law controls the conduct of the algorithm [14]. HGSO successfully simulates Henry's law-governed gas behavior on a variety of test suites, benchmark functions, and three real-world optimization issues. Also, it was utilized to solve the challenge of motif discovery (MD) [15]. Henry's law is a basic gas law that represents how much of a given gas liquefies in a distinct kind and amount of fluid at a specific temperature. The solubility of low solubility gases in fluids can be specified using Henry's law. Furthermore, temperature and pressure are two major elements that have a primary effect on solubility. Solids become more soluble as temperature rises; gases, on the other hand, have a lower likelihood of becoming soluble. According to the pressure, raising the amount of pressure increased the gas's ability to dissolve in liquids [16].

Normally, optimization methods can be used to deal with many problems in the sciences, as presented in refs [17–26]. A new population-based metaheuristic optimization algorithm based on physics principles is proposed [27]. The major aim of this chapter is to classify and examine the optimization algorithms currently in use. The general procedures of HGSO, its modifications, applications, and outcomes compared to other similar algorithms were the subject of this chapter. It also discusses the benefits and drawbacks of HGSO, as well as prospective future research avenues for those interested. Researchers will be able to completely comprehend the design and operation of the HGSO algorithm after reading this chapter.

The rest of this chapter is arranged as follows: The HGSO algorithm developed in this study is explained in Section 2. Section 3 includes a literature review. Section 4 presents discussion of the HGSO evaluation. Section 5 outlines the key findings and proposed extensions for future research.

13.2 Henry gas solubility optimization

This section contains the stimulus for HGSO, which is based on Henry's law's manners.

13.2.1 Henry's law

In 1803, Henry's law was developed by William Henry [28]. It implies that the quantity of a specific gas that melts in a specific kind and amount of fluid is balanced to the partisan pressure of that gas' instability with that fluid at a fixed temperature. Thus, the temperature has a big impact on Henry's law [19]. The following equation expresses it:

$$S_g = H \times P_g \tag{13-1}$$

H is a constant, which is unique per gas solvent variety at each temperature, P_g is the partisan pressure of the gas, and the solubility of a gas is S_g. The influence of temperature dependency on Henry's law constants must also be considered. The van't Hoff formula can be used to show how Henry's law constants modify with changes in a system's temperature:

$$\frac{d \ln H}{d(1/T)} = \frac{-\nabla_{sol}E}{R} \tag{13-2}$$

where $-\nabla_{sol}E$ is the dissolution enthalpy, R is a gas constant, and A and B are variables for T's reliance on H. Thus, Eq. (13–1) can be implemented in the following way:

$$H(T) = \exp(B/T) \times A \tag{13-3}$$

H is a product of A and B. A and B are variables for T's reliance on H. Otherwise, at the temperature $T = 298.15$ K, a statement based on H can be formed.

$$H(T) = H^\theta \times \exp\left(\frac{-\nabla_{sol}E}{R}\left(1/T - 1/T^\theta\right)\right) \tag{13-4}$$

When $(-\nabla_{sol}E)$ is a constant, the van't Hoff formula is suitable; thus, Eq. (13–4) can be rewritten as follows:

$$H(T) = H^\theta \times \exp(-C \times (1/T - 1/T^\theta)) \tag{13-5}$$

13.2.2 Inspiration source

The conduct of Henry's law inspired HGSO. It can be employed to define the solubility of low-solubility gases in fluids using the aforementioned Eq. (13−1) through (13−5).

13.2.3 Henry gas solubility optimization mathematical model

The following are the mathematical stages:

Stage 1: Initialization procedure: The following equation is used to calculate the number of gases (inhabitants size N) and their locations:

$$X_i(t+1) = X_{\min} + r \times (x_{\max} - X_{\min}) \qquad (13-6)$$

X_i is the location of the ith gas in inhabitants N, and r is a numeral between 0 and 1 that is chosen at random. The problem's boundaries are $X_{\min}$ and $X_{\max}$, and t is the numeral of iterations.

Henry's constant values of kind $j(H_j(t))$ are set up with the following formula:

$$H_j = l_1 \times rand(0,1), P_{i,j} = l_2 \times rand(0,1), C_j = l_3 \times rand(0,1) \qquad (13-7)$$

where i is the amount of gas, $P_{i,j}$ is the partisan pressure of gas i in group j, $\frac{\nabla_{sol}E}{R}$ constant value of type $j(C_i)$, the constants (l_1, l_2, l_3) are defined as 5E − 02, 100, and 1E − 02 in that order.

Stage 2: Clustering: The agents in the population are split into equivalent clusters. The numeral of gas kinds equals the numeral of clusters. Because the gases in each cluster are similar, the Henry's constant (H_j) is the same for all of them.

Stage 3: Evaluation: Each cluster (j) is analyzed to determine which gas reaches the maximum stability state among those of its category. The gases are then organized to find the best gas for the whole group.

Stage 4: Update Henry's factor: The following equation is used to update Henry's factor:

$$H_j(t+1) = H_j(t) \times \exp\big(-C_j \times \big(1/T(t) - 1/T^\theta\big)\big), T(t) = \exp(-t/\text{iter}) \qquad (13-8)$$

H_j is Henry's factor for cluster j, T is the temperature, T^θ is a constant equivalent to 298.15, and the whole computational time is $iter$.

Stage 5: Update solubility: The following equation is employed to update the solubility:

$$S_{i,j}(t) = K \times H_j(t+1) \times P_{i,j}(t) \qquad (13-9)$$

In cluster j, the solubility of gas i is $(S_{i,j})$; $(P_{i,j})$ is the partisan pressure on gas i in cluster j and K is a constant.

Stage 6: Modify location: The following is a formula to modify the location:

$$X_{(i,j)}(t+1) = X_{(i,j)}(t) + F \times r \times \gamma \times \left(X_{(i,best)}(t) - X_{(i,j)}(t) \right) + F \times r \times \alpha \times (S_{(i,j)}(t) \times X_{best}(t) - X_{(i,j)}(t))$$

$$\gamma = \beta \times \exp\left(-\frac{F_{best}(t) + \varepsilon}{F_{(i,j)}(t) + \varepsilon} \right), \varepsilon = 0.05 \qquad (13-10)$$

In cluster j, $X_{(i,j)}$ is the location of gas i, r is a constant that is a randomly number, and t is the computational time. $X_{(i,best)}$ and X_{best} are parameters relevant for counteracting the exploration and exploitation capacities. $X_{(i,best)}$ is the best gas i in the cluster j, while X_{best} is the best gas in the group. Furthermore, γ represents the power of gas j in cluster i to cooperate with the gases in its cluster, α represents the effect of other gases on gas i in cluster j and equivalent to 1, and β represents a constant. $F_{i,j}$ represents the appropriateness of gas i in cluster j, whereas F_{best} represents the suitability of the best gas throughout the system. The flag F guides the search agent in a different direction, resulting in diversity $= \pm$.

Stage 7: Exit from local optimum: This stage is utilized to get out of a local optimal situation. The following equation is to organize and pick the numeral of the worst agents N_w:

$$N_w = N \times (r \ and(C_2 - C_1) + C_1), C_1 = 0.1 \text{ and } C_2 = 0.2 \qquad (13-11)$$

Where the numeral of search agents is N.

Stage 8: Modify the location of the worst agents:

$$G_{(i,j)} = G_{min(i,j)} + r \times (G_{max(i,j)} - G_{min(i,j)}) \qquad (13-12)$$

$G_{(i,j)}$ is the location of gas i in cluster j, r represents a random number, *and* G_{min} and G_{max} are the boundaries of the situation.

13.2.4 Exploration and exploitation phases

Through an iteration of the search procedure, the dimension-wise variety was assessed as follows:

$$\frac{1}{Div_j} = \frac{1}{N} \sum_{i=1}^{N} median\left(X^j\right) - x_i^j \; ; Div^t = \frac{1}{N} \sum_{i=1}^{D} Div_j \qquad (13-13)$$

where x_i^j is j^{th} measurement of ith individual population, and *median*$\left(X^j\right)$ is the middle value of jth measurement of the entire population with size N. Div_j means the variety value measures for dimension j. For iteration t ($t = 1, 2, 3, ..., iter$), this dimentional variety is then averaged Div^t across all D dimensions.

The following equation can be used to calculate the exploration/exploitation percentage:

$$\text{Exploration}\% = \frac{Div^t}{Div_{\max}} \times 100; \text{Exploitation}\% = \frac{\left|Div^t - Div_{\max}\right|}{Div_{\max}} \times 100 \qquad (13-14)$$

where Div^t is population variety of tth iteration, and the maximum variety discovered in all t iterations is $Div_{\max}$. Algorithm 13−1 presents the procedure of the HGSO algorithm.

Algorithm 13−1   HGSO algorithm pseudocode:

1. **begin**
2.   Initialize population $X_i(i = 1, 2, 3, \ldots, N)$, number of gas kinds $(i, H_i, P_i, C_j, l_1, l_2$ and $l_3)$.
3.   split the population agents into clusters that all have the exact Henry's constant
4.   Assess every cluster j.
5.   Obtain the best gas $X_{(i,best)}$ in every cluster, and the best search agent X_{best}.
6.   **while** (Stopping criteria not met (t < maximum iteration time) do)
7.   **for** every search agent **do**
8.   renew the location of every search agents by utilizing Eq. (13.10).
9.   **end for**
10.   Modify Henry's factor of every gas kind utilizing Eq. (13.8).
11.   Modify the solubility per gas utilizing Eq. (13.9).
12.   Organize and pick the numeral of worst agents utilizing Eq. (13.11).
13.   Modify the worst agents location utilizing Eq. (13.12).
14.   Modify the best gas $X_{(i,best)}$, and the best search agent X_{best}.
15.   **end while**
16. $t = t + 1$
17. **return** X_{best}
18. **end**

13.3 Related works

HGSO has been successfully utilized to resolve a variety of optimization issues in a variety of domains, including benchmark functions, data mining, engineering design problems, and others. This section examines and categorizes real-world applications found in HGSO into discrete and continuous applications.

13.3.1 Data mining

A novel technique was proposed for dimensionality reduction by selecting relevant features using the HGSO algorithm to improve classification accuracy. The suggested method is compared to popular metaheuristic algorithms for example the WOA, GOA, SSA, GWO, DA, and others using some datasets with a diverse selection of feature sizes, from small to huge. To analyze the selected feature set, an expert system is used like support vector machine (SVM) and k-nearest neighbor [13].

13.3.2 Genome biology (motif discovery problems)

The problem of DNA MD is the most difficult in genome biology, and its relevance grows in lockstep with the advancement of sequencing tools. MD is important in the recognition of transcript issue binding sites, which aids in the understanding of gene regulation mechanisms. Metaheuristic algorithms are talented strategies for extracting motif from DNA genomic sequences; however, they are frequently unsuccessful to prove reliable efficiency by overpowering the intrinsic challenges of complicated gene sequences, making the search domain for optimization techniques particularly nonconvex. A new modified HGSO (MHGSO) algorithm for motif detection in DNA genomic sequences was introduced, which produces a functional motif. A new stage in this method captures the essential properties of motifs in DNA sequences, and MHGSO mimics these features for precise target motif detection. Both simulated and actual datasets are utilized to validate the MHGSO algorithm's achievement [29].

13.3.3 Engineering problems

13.3.3.1 Solar energy

HGO is used to offer a unique maximum power point tracking (MPPT) technique. Traditional MPPT approaches generate random oscillation in PV systems and partial shading causes power loss. The HGO-based MPPT method can properly manage both of these problems. The existing MPPT techniques such as dragonfly optimization algorithm, PSO, CSA, perturb and observe, and grasshopper optimization are compared to the suggested HGO-based MPPT method. The outcomes show that the HGO-based MPPT method is capable of solving the two primary MPPT difficulties and outperforms existing MPPT strategies. Furthermore, a study was conducted utilizing the area of atmospheric data to evaluate the influence on energy yield during various seasons of the year [12].

A combined heat and power plant (CHPP) approach was employed to undertake multiobjective optimization (MOO) of an exergy, energy, and economic (3E) analysis. The HGSO algorithm is used in a CHPP base case condition to perform MOO.

One of the most recent population-based techniques is HGSO. Henry's law of physics influenced this algorithm. To assess a novel algorithm's performance, it must be used in a combination of problems.

The optimization of proportional integral derivative (PID) achieves capacity in a nuclear power plant (NPP); on the other hand, it is an excellent challenge for evaluating the performance of HGSO. The energy control of a pressurized water reactor is studied using a point kinetics model with six levels of delayed neutron precursors. Any optimization issue employing metaheuristic techniques requires an efficient objective function. As a result, in steady-state operations, the HGSO objective (cost) function is the integral of the time-weighted square error performance index, which is controlled by a stability requirement. This stability is ensured by using a Lyapunov method. The results show that this strategy outperforms an empirically adjusted PID regulator with the smallest amount of errors. In comparison to a known GA-tuned PID controller, it also performs with good accuracy [11].

13.3.3.2 Cloud computing task scheduling

For optimum task scheduling, a modified HGSO is proposed, which is derived from the comprehensive opposition-based learning (COBL) and WOA. The suggested method is called HGSWC. WOA is used as a local search technique in the proposed HGSWC to increase solution goodness, while COBL is used to enhance the poorest solution by calculating their inverse solutions and after that choosing the superior one between them. HGSWC is compared to standard HGSO and WOA and validated on a group of 36 optimization benchmark functions. It has been demonstrated that the suggested HGSWC outperforms comparison algorithms. Furthermore, HGSWC has also been tried via its paces on a variety of artificial and real-world demands, including 15 different job scheduling challenges. The findings of simulation trials show that HGSWC outperforms six well-known metaheuristic algorithms and finds near-optimal solutions with no computing overhead [30].

Newly, metaheuristic techniques have been frequently applied for the optimum structure of vehicle components, with positive outcomes reported. The HGSO technique, a newly invented optimization approach, is utilized to resolve the form optimization of a car brake pedal to demonstrate how HGSO can be employed to tackle form optimization problems [31].

A novel metaheuristic based on combining chaotic maps into HGSO is proposed. Chaotic HGSO (CHGSO) is the name of the new algorithm. The hybridization aims to improve the authentic HGSO's convergence rate for handling real-world engineering optimization issues. This hybridization produces an optimization technique that is independent of the problem. Various standard restrained optimization problems, such as a welded beam issue and a cantilever beam issue, are used to assess the CHGSO's performance. Both manufacturing and diaphragm spring structure concerns from the automotive sector are used to investigate the CHGSO's performance. The results of using CHGSO to solve various restricted test cases are compared to several selected and recently devised metaheuristics algorithms. The CHGSO is a strong optimization strategy for getting the best factors in the mechanistic design and simulating optimization issues when using an appropriate chaotic map, according to the results [32].

An enhancement to the HGSO metaheuristic method was presented [16], which simulates Henry's gas law and was newly advanced. It is called quantum HGSO (QHGSO). The proposed enhancements improved HGSO's capacity to strike a balance between exploitation and exploration, allowing for a more thorough analysis of the solution area.

A new method adapts the current HGSO with multiple objectives to present a novel multiobjective evolutionary algorithm. The proposed MOHGSO compares solutions using the Pareto dominance relation and includes two kinds of archives: a favored archive for storing Pareto solutions discovered throughout the evolutionary process and external archives for storing local best solutions fitting to each cluster. Furthermore, to direct the population toward the genuine Pareto front, efficient archiving and director choosing procedures based on the crowding space calculation are given [33].

13.3.4 Benchmark functions

To enhance the effectiveness of the random vector functional link (RVFL) network, the HGSO method has been integrated into a novel hybrid artificial neural network technique. The HGSO-RVFL model was created using four characteristics: welding speed, rotational speed, pin profile, and tilt angle. The force of the model was explored, and it was discovered that the HGSO-RVFL model is a good tool for forecasting the UTS of friction stir welded joints. The impacts of procedure variables on the UTS of welded joints were also investigated, with a signed concurrence between practical and expected results, confirming the model's strong performance in predicting the best welding parameters for optimal UTS [34].

An enhanced HGSO based on the Harris Hawk optimization (HHO-HGSO) was proposed [12]. Through the iteration, the algorithm uses the HHO algorithm's escaping energy function as an indication and determines a point; when the value of the escape energy function exceeds the point, the algorithm employs the HGSO search technique, and when it is less than the point, it uses the four Harris Hawk exploitation techniques.

13.3.5 Automatic voltage regulator

The suggested method was employed to get the best FOPID settings by reducing a time-scope objective function. To prove the efficacy of the proposed technique, the phase graph and convergence analyses were performed. Transient and frequency response evaluations were used to assess the effectiveness of the HGSO-based FOPID controller (HGSO-FOPID) with enhanced kidney algorithm-based PID (IKA-PID), salp swarm algorithm-based FOPID (SSA-FOPID), and stochastic fractal search algorithm-based PID (SFS-PID) controllers [15].

13.3.6 Optimization tasks

With dynamical obverse learning, converting probability, interval compaction approach, and sine cosine factor, a higher performance, enhanced HGSO is proposed to resolve some complex optimization issues [1].

13.3.7 Prediction of soil shear force

A new hybrid type is optimized using the HGSO technique, often known as HGSO-adaptive neuro-fuzzy interface system (ANFIS), for resolving a nonlinear and difficult problem involving the prediction of soil shear strength [14].

13.3.8 Autonomous vehicle management system

To improve the vehicle's sturdiness, a convolution neural network opposition-based HGSO (CNN-OHGS) technique was developed for an independent vehicle management system. At the same time, the assailants tried to implant incorrect data into the independent vehicle's sensor readings in order to disrupt the appropriate spacing between the automated vehicles. The CNN-OHGS algorithm is used to decrease vehicle distance variance, assuring safety and optimal distance variance [35].

13.3.9 Software engineering problems

A development of hybrid HGSO (HHGSO) is proposed in this research. HHGSO is a mixture of HGSO with four newly discovered metaheuristic algorithms: owl search algorithm, butterfly optimization algorithm, sooty tern optimization algorithm, and jaya algorithm. Each algorithm's specific mapping is made dynamic using penalized and reward-adaptive probability. A well-known search-based software engineering scenario requiring team creation is used to compare the performance of HHGSO with the aforementioned techniques. Furthermore, the specified hybridization strategy was used as a hybridization template for addressing the combinatorial test generation problem using the same metaheuristic algorithm combinations [36].

13.3.10 Machine learning

One of the most significant copper resources is porphyry copper deposits (PCDs), and one of the numerous essential difficulties is determining the copper grade. To evaluate the copper grade in PCDs, researchers used the ANFIS and multilayer perceptron (MLP). The MLP and ANFIS models' parameters were established using HGSO, moth flame optimization (MFO), and weed algorithm (WA) [37].

13.3.11 Image processing

A computerized image category technique established on a bag-of-features framework is evaluated to manage soil images. AlexNet is employed in the attributes extraction stage in the suggested method. The effectiveness of the coding design stage is enhanced by HGSO by choosing the best visual works [38].

13.3.12 Optimal power system

HGSO is evaluated for its practicality in achieving finest parameters for a power system stabilizer (PSS). To achieve this, the format issue was recast as an optimization issue with an essential time reproduced total error objective function. To optimize the PSS settings and enhance the control system's dynamic implementation, this goal function was minimized. It has been demonstrated that the proposed HGSO strategy for setting PSS parameters suppresses electromechanical oscillations and improves statistical performance and convergence ratio [39] (Table 13−1).

Table 13–1 shows a summary of the provided related works.

No.	Years	Authors	References	Method names	Proposed
1.	2020	Naggaz et al.	[13]	HGSO	Proposed a new technique for dimensionality reduction by selecting relevant features using HGSO algorithm to advance classification accuracy.
2.	2020	Yildiz et al.	[31]	HGSO	To address the form optimization of an automobile brake pedal, a new optimization approach is used.
3.	2020	Mirza et al.	[12]	HGO-based MPPT	Proposed a new MPPT technique based on HGO to gather a huge amount of solar energy in PV systems.
4.	2020	Hashim et al.	[29]	MHGSO	Suggested a new modified HGO algorithm named MHGSO algorithm for motif finding, which produces a practical pattern in DNA genomic arrangements.
5.	2021	AbdElaziz and Ibrahim	[30]	HGSWC	Proposed a MHGSO derived from the WOA and COBL for the best job scheduling.
6.	2021	Yildiz et al.	[32]	CHGSO	Proposed a new metaheuristic based on combining chaotic maps into the HGSO algorithm to solve various restricted test cases.
7.	2020	Shehabe deen et al.	[34]	HGSO-RVFL	A new technique was developed to forecast procedure factors and mechanical impacts of AA6061-T6 aluminum alloy joints (UTS).
8.	2020	Xie et al.		HHO-HGSO	The HHO algorithm's escape energy function value is employed in an upgraded algorithm that predicts if the agent should use the HGSO or one of HHO's four local movement strategies.
9.	2020	Ekinci et al.	[15]	HGSO-FOPID	A proposed technique was used to get optimal FOPID setting by minimizing a time domain objective function.
10.	2021	Bi and Young Zhang	[1]	HGSO	Higher performance and enhanced HGSO is proposed to resolve some complex optimization issues.
11.	2021	Ding et al.	[14]	HGSO-ANFIS	A new hybrid model is optimized using HGSO technique, often known as HGSO-ANFIS for resolving a nonlinear and difficult problem involving the prediction of soil shear strength.
12.	2021	Mohammadi et al.	[16]	QHGSO	Proposed enhancements method that improved HGSO's capacity to strike a balance between exploitation and exploration.
13.	2021	Ravikumar and Kavitha	[35]	CNN-HGSO	Proposed a new algorithm that used to reduce vehicle distance variations, assuring safety and optimal distance variation.
14.	2021	Zamli et al.	[36]	HHGSO	A development of HHGSO is proposed for addressing the combinatorial test generation problem using the same metaheuristic algorithm combinations.
15.	2022	Kahloul et al.	[33]	MHGSO	A new method adapts the current HGSO with multiple objectives to present a new multiobjective evolutionary algorithm.
16.	2021	Abbaszadeh et al.	[37]	PCD	The MLP and ANFIS models' parameters were established using the HGSO, WA, and MFO.

(Continued)

Table 13−1 (Continued)

No.	Years	Authors	References	Method names	Proposed
17.	2022	Agarwal and Shekhawat	[38]	AlexNet, HGSO	The effectiveness of the codebook design phase is enhanced using HGSO by selecting the optimal visual works.
18.	2021	Sukpancharoen and Prasartkaew	[40]	MOO-HGSO	Employed the CHPP approach to undertake MOO of 3E analysis. The HGSO algorithm is used in a CHPP base case condition to perform MOO.
19.	2021	Ekinci, Izci, and Hekimoğlu	[39]	PSS	HGSO is evaluated for its practicality in achieving the best parameters for a PSS.
20.	2021	Mousakazemi	[11]	HGSO, PID, and NPP	The optimization of PID achieves capacity in a NPP is an excellent challenge for evaluating the performance of HGSO.
21	2022	Ezugwu et al.	[41]		A comprehensive survey of clustering algorithm.
22	2022	Khazala et al.	[42]		The use of CNN and transfer learning technique in image processing identification.
23	2022	Milhem et al.	[43]		An enhanced MapReduce Apriori algorithm on the apache Hadoop cluster.
24	2022	Oyelade et al.	[44]		A metaheuristic optimization algorithm inspired by the effective propagation mechanism of Ebola virus disease.
25	2022	Oyelade et al.	[45]		A generative adversarial network for synthetization of data to bridge the gap of insufficient data samples for training in deep learning models.
26	2022	Pen et al.	[46]		The use of deep learning CNN for Artocarpus classification.
27	2023	Sahoo et al.	[47]		A swarm intelligence-based metaheuristic algorithm for solving complex real-world optimization problems.
28	2023	Ikotun et al.	[48]		A comprehensive review on K-means clustering with variant analysis and advances in the era of big data.
29	2023	Agushaka, Ezugwu, and Abualigah	[49]		A metaheuristic algorithm for solving CEC 2020 benchmark functions and continuous/ discrete engineering problems.
30	2023	Agushaka et al.	[50]		A population-based metaheuristic algorithm inspired by survival ability of gazelles in a predator-dominated environment.
31	2023	Agushaka et al.	[51]		Comparative study of initialization methods of population-based metaheuristic algorithms.
32	2023	Agushaka, Ezugwu, and Abualigah	[52]		A modified version of the dwarf mongoose optimization algorithm for solving design problems in engineering.
33	2022	Akinola et al.	[53]		A review on metaheuristic-based multiclass feature selection algorithms.
34	2022	Al-Manaseer et al.	[54]		Big data classification technique for healthcare applications based on SVM, RF, and J48.
35	2022	Chakraborty et al.	[55]		A comprehensive review on differential evolution and its image processing applications and problems.
36	2022	Ezugwu et al.	[56]		A nature-inspired metaheuristic algorithm inspired by prairie dog behavior in its natural habitat.

13.4 Discussion

HGSO is a physics-based optimization technique that has been applied to various optimization issues. The proposed HGSO method which is founded on Henry's law was executed in MATLAB® version R2016a. It is worth mentioning that the provided algorithm heavily relies on the capacity to hover exploration and exploitation. HGSO is well suited to handle complicated optimization issues with numerous local best solutions because it holds inhabitants of solutions and analyzes a vast space to identify the finest international solution. The numeric effectiveness of HGSO was assessed in this study by solving several standard benchmark functions and engineering issues. SA, WOA, EHO, GWO, CS, GSA, and PSO were used to compare the performance of the proposed HGSO to those of seven state-of-the-art optimization techniques. The results suggest that HGSO has a great exploitation capacity when analogized to the other competitor algorithms and that it also has good exploration ability. In general, the HGSO algorithm was the most effective in most benchmark trial functions; it showed good performance on unimodal analysis functions, which measure algorithm exploitation and convergence speed, and exhibited excellent behavior on multimodal analysis functions, which include a significant number of local solutions and necessitate the inclusion of proper methods to avoid them in an algorithm.

13.5 Conclusion and future works

Over 20 research publications were collected, reviewed, and analyzed in this review study to highlight the benefits and drawbacks of HGSO for academics interested in metaheuristic optimization algorithms. HGSO is a new physics-based algorithm that simulates Henry's law's behavior. The goal of HGSO is to equilibrium the exploration and exploitation capabilities of the search domain and avert regional optima. In most circumstances, the results achieved by HGSO are better than those obtained by other popular and new metaheuristics algorithms like SA, WOA, EHO, GWO, CS, GSA, and PSO. The HGSO algorithm ought to be used in future research to resolve problems including image processing, data mining, and real-world optimization. In addition, HGSO will be modified to resolve other real-scale optimization challenges, like binary and multiobjective capabilities and introducing chaotic maps.

References

[1] J. Bi, Y. Zhang, An improved Henry gas solubility optimization for optimization tasks, Appl. Intell. 52 (6) (2022) 5966–6006.

[2] Y. Meraihi, A.B. Gabis, A. Ramdane-Cherif, D. Acheli, A comprehensive survey of crow search algorithm and its applications, Artif. Intell. Rev. 54 (4) (2021) 2669–2716.

[3] S. Nayeri, R. Tavakkoli-Moghaddam, Z. Sazvar, J. Heydari, A heuristic-based simulated annealing algorithm for the scheduling of relief teams in natural disasters, Soft Comput. 26 (4) (2022) 1825–1843.

[4]   H. Huang, C. Jin, A novel particle swarm optimization algorithm based on reinforcement learning mech-anism for AUV path planning, Complexity 2021 (2021) 1−13.

[5]   X. Li, H. Yang, J. Li, Y. Wang, S. Gao, A novel distributed gravitational search algorithm with multi-layered information Interaction, IEEE Access. 9 (2021) 166552−166565.

[6]   J. Ding, Q. Wang, Q. Zhang, Q. Ye, Y. Ma, A hybrid particle swarm optimization-cuckoo search algorithm and its engineering applications, Math. Probl. Eng. 2019 (2019) 1−12.

[7]   E. Uzlu, Estimates of greenhouse gas emission in Turkey with grey wolf optimizer algorithm-optimized artificial neural networks, Neural Comput. Appl. 33 (20) (2021) 13567−13585.

[8]   S. Mirjalili, A. Lewis, The whale optimization algorithm, Adv. Eng. Softw. 95 (2016) 51−67.

[9]   I. Strumberger, N. Bacanin, S. Tomic, M. Beko, M. Tuba, Static drone placement by elephant herding optimization algorithm, 25th Telecommunication Forum (TELFOR), 2017, IEEE, 2017, pp. 1−4.

[10] B. Morales-Castañeda, D. Zaldívar, E. Cuevas, O. Maciel-Castillo, I. Aranguren, F. Fausto, An improved simulated annealing algorithm based on ancient metallurgy techniques, Appl. Soft Comput. 84 (2019) 105761.

[11] S.M.H. Mousakazemi, Henry gas solubility optimization for control of a nuclear reactor: a case study, Nucl. Eng. Technol. 54 (3) (2022) 940−947.

[12] A.F. Mirza, M. Mansoor, Q. Ling, A novel MPPT technique based on Henry gas solubility optimization, Energy Convers. Manag. 225 (2020)113409.

[13] N. Neggaz, E.H. Houssein, K. Hussain, An efficient Henry gas solubility optimization for feature selec-tion, Expert. Syst. Appl. 152 (2020)113364.

[14] W. Ding, M.D. Nguyen, A. Salih Mohammed, D.J. Armaghani, M. Hasanipanah, L.Van Bui, et al., A new development of ANFIS-Based Henry gas solubility optimization technique for prediction of soil shear strength, Transp. Geotech. 29 (2021)100579.

[15] S. Ekinci, D. Izci, B. Hekimoglu, Henry gas solubility optimization algorithm based FOPID controller design for automatic voltage regulator, International Conference on Electrical, Communication, and Computer Engineering (ICECCE), 2020, IEEE, 2020, pp. 1−6.

[16] D. Mohammadi, M. Abd Elaziz, R. Moghdani, E. Demir, S. Mirjalili, Quantum Henry gas solubility opti-mization algorithm for global optimization, Eng. Comput. 38 (S3) (2022) 2329−2348.

[17] L. Abualigah, A. Diabat, C.L. Thanh, S. Khatir, Opposition-based Laplacian distribution with Prairie Dog optimization method for industrial engineering design problems, Comput Methods Appl. Mech. Eng. 414 (2023) 116097.

[18] G. Hu, Y. Zheng, L. Abualigah, A.G. Hussien, DETDO: an adaptive hybrid dandelion optimizer for engi-neering optimization, Adv. Eng. Inform. 57 (2023) 102004.

[19] D. Izci, S. Ekinci, S. Mirjalili, L. Abualigah, An intelligent tuning scheme with a master/slave approach for efficient control of the automatic voltage regulator, Neural Comput. Appl. (2023) 1−17.

[20] H. Jia, C. Lu, D. Wu, C. Wen, H. Rao, & L. Abualigah, An improved reptile search algorithm with ghost opposition-based learning for global optimization problems, J. Comput. Design Eng. (2023) qwad048.

[21] A.H. Alharbi, A.A. Abdelhamid, A. Ibrahim, S.K. Towfek, N. Khodadadi, L. Abualigah, A.E. Ahmed, Improved dipper-throated optimization for forecasting metamaterial design bandwidth for engineering applications, Biomimetics 8 (2) (2023) 241.

[22] S. Nama, A.K. Saha, S. Chakraborty, A.H. Gandomi, L. Abualigah, Boosting particle swarm optimization by backtracking search algorithm for optimization problems, Swarm Evolut. Comput. 79 (2023) 101304.

[23] M. Zare, M. Ghasemi, A. Zahedi, K. Golalipour, S.K. Mohammadi, S. Mirjalili, L. Abualigah, A global best-guided firefly algorithm for engineering problems, J. Bionic Eng. (2023) 1−30.

[24] D. Wu, C. Wen, H. Rao, H. Jia, Q. Liu, L. Abualigah, Modified reptile search algorithm with multi-hunting coordination strategy for global optimization problems, Math. Biosci. Eng. 20 (6) (2023) 10090−10134.

[25] S. Ekinci, D. Izci,, L. Abualigah, & R.A. Zitar, (2023). A modified oppositional chaotic local search strategy based aquila optimizer to design an effective controller for vehicle cruise control system, J. Bionic Eng. 1–24.

[26] L. Abualigah, D. Falcone, A. Forestiero, Swarm intelligence to face IoT challenges, Comput. Intell. Neurosci. 2023 (2023).

[27] F.A. Hashim, E.H. Houssein, M.S. Mabrouk, W. Al-Atabany, S. Mirjalili, Henry gas solubility optimization: a novel physics-based algorithm, Futur. Gener. Comput. Syst. 101 (2019) 646–667.

[28] Y. Li, W. Zhang, L. Wang, F. Zhao, W. Han, G. Chen, Henry's law and accumulation of weak source for crust-derived helium: a case study of Weihe Basin, China, J. Nat. Gas. Geosci. 2 (5–6) (2017) 333–339.

[29] F.A. Hashim, E.H. Houssein, K. Hussain, M.S. Mabrouk, W. Al-Atabany, A modified Henry gas solubility optimization for solving motif discovery problem, Neural Comput. Appl. 32 (14) (2020) 10759–10771.

[30] M. Abd Elaziz, I. Attiya, An improved Henry gas solubility optimization algorithm for task scheduling in cloud computing, Artif. Intell. Rev. 54 (5) (2021) 3599–3637.

[31] B.S. Yıldız, A.R. Yıldız, N. Pholdee, S. Bureerat, S.M. Sait, V. Patel, The Henry gas solubility optimization algorithm for optimum structural design of automobile brake components, Mater. Test. 62 (3) (2020) 261–264.

[32] B.S. Yıldız, N. Pholdee, N. Panagant, S. Bureerat, A.R. Yildiz, S.M. Sait, A novel chaotic Henry gas solubility optimization algorithm for solving real-world engineering problems, Eng. Comput. 38 (S2) (2022) 871–883.

[33] S. Kahloul, D. Zouache, B. Brahmi, A. Got, A multi-external archive-guided Henry gas solubility optimization algorithm for solving multi-objective optimization problems, Eng. Appl. Artif. Intell. 109 (2022) 104588.

[34] T.A. Shehabeldeen, M.A. Elaziz, A.H. Elsheikh, O.F. Hassan, Y. Yin, X. Ji, et al., A novel method for predicting tensile strength of friction stir welded AA6061 aluminium alloy joints based on hybrid random vector functional link and henry gas solubility optimization, IEEE Access. 8 (2020) 79896–79907.

[35] S. Ravikumar, D. Kavitha, CNN-OHGS: CNN-oppositional-based Henry gas solubility optimization model for autonomous vehicle control system, J. F. Robot. 38 (7) (2021) 967–979.

[36] K.Z. Zamli, M.A. Kader, S. Azad, B.S. Ahmed, Hybrid Henry gas solubility optimization algorithm with dynamic cluster-to-algorithm mapping, Neural Comput. Appl. 33 (14) (2021) 8389–8416.

[37] M. Abbaszadeh, M. Ehteram, A.N. Ahmed, V.P. Singh, A. Elshafie, The copper grade estimation of porphyry deposits using machine learning algorithms and Henry gas solubility optimization, Earth Sci. Inform. 14 (4) (2021) 2049–2075.

[38] R. Agarwal, N.S. Shekhawat, enhanced bag of features using alexnet and henry gas solubility optimization for soil image classification, 2022, pp. 493–503.

[39] S. Ekinci, D. Izci, B. Hekimoglu, Implementing the Henry gas solubility optimization algorithm for optimal power system stabilizer design, Electrica 21 (2) (2021) 250–258.

[40] S. Sukpancharoen, B. Prasartkaew, Combined heat and power plant using a multi-objective Henry gas solubility optimization algorithm: a thermodynamic investigation of energy, exergy, and economic (3E) analysis, Heliyon 7 (9) (2021)e08003.

[41] A.E. Ezugwu, A.M. Ikotun, O.O. Oyelade, L. Abualigah, J.O. Agushaka, C.I. Eke, et al., A comprehensive survey of clustering algorithms: state-of-the-art machine learning applications, taxonomy, challenges, and future research prospects, Eng. Appl. Artif. Intell. 110 (2022)104743.

[42] A. Khazalah, B. Prasanthi, D. Thomas, N. Vello, S. Jayaprakasam, P. Sumari et al., Image processing identification for sapodilla using convolution neural network (CNN) and transfer learning techniques, 2023, pp. 107–27.

[43] N. Milhem, L. Abualigah, M.H. Nadimi-Shahraki, H. Jia, A.E. Ezugwu, A.G. Hussien, Enhanced MapReduce performance for the distributed parallel computing: application of the big data, 2023, pp. 191–203.

[44] O.N. Oyelade, A.E.-S. Ezugwu, T.I.A. Mohamed, L. Abualigah, Ebola optimization search algorithm: a new nature-inspired metaheuristic optimization algorithm, IEEE Access. 10 (2022) 16150−16177.

[45] O.N. Oyelade, A.E. Ezugwu, M.S. Almutairi, A.K. Saha, L. Abualigah, H. Chiroma, A generative adversarial network for synthetization of regions of interest based on digital mammograms, Sci. Rep. 12 (1) (2022)6166.

[46] L.Z. Pen, K. Xian Xian, C.F. Yew, O.S. Hau, P. Sumari, L. Abualigah et al., Artocarpus classification technique using deep learning based convolutional neural network, 2023, pp. 1−21.

[47] S.K. Sahoo, A.K. Saha, A.E. Ezugwu, J.O. Agushaka, B. Abuhaija, A.R. Alsoud, et al., Moth flame optimization: theory, modifications, hybridizations, and applications, Arch. Comput. Methods Eng. 30 (1) (2023) 391−426.

[48] A.M. Ikotun, A.E. Ezugwu, L. Abualigah, B. Abuhaija, J. Heming, K-means clustering algorithms: a comprehensive review, variants analysis, and advances in the era of big data, Inf. Sci. (Ny.) 622 (2023) 178−210.

[49] J.O. Agushaka, A.E. Ezugwu, L. Abualigah, Dwarf Mongoose optimization algorithm, Comput. Methods Appl. Mech. Eng. 391 (2022).

[50] J.O. Agushaka, A.E. Ezugwu, L. Abualigah, Gazelle optimization algorithm: a novel nature-inspired metaheuristic optimizer, Neural Comput. Appl. 35 (5) (2023) 4099−4131.

[51] J.O. Agushaka, A.E. Ezugwu, L. Abualigah, S.K. Alharbi, H.A.E.-W. Khalifa, Efficient initialization methods for population-based metaheuristic algorithms: a comparative study, Arch. Comput. Methods Eng. 30 (3) (2023) 1727−1787.

[52] J.O. Agushaka, A.E. Ezugwu, O.N. Olaide, O. Akinola, R.A. Zitar, L. Abualigah, Improved dwarf Mongoose optimization for constrained engineering design problems, J. Bionic Eng. (2022).

[53] O.O. Akinola, E. Absalom, A. Ezugwu, J.O. Raed, A. Zitar et al., Multiclass feature selection with metaheuristic optimization algorithms: a review. <https://doi.org/10.1007/s00521-022-07705-4>.

[54] H. Al-Manaseer, L. Abualigah, A.R. Alsoud, R.A. Zitar, A.E. Ezugwu, H. Jia, A novel big data classification technique for healthcare application using support vector machine, random forest and J48, 2023, pp. 205−215.

[55] S. Chakraborty, A.K. Saha, A.E. Ezugwu, J.O. Agushaka, R.A. Zitar, L. Abualigah, Differential evolution and its applications in image processing problems: a comprehensive review, Arch. Comput. Methods Eng. 30 (2) (2023) 985−1040.

[56] A.E. Ezugwu, J.O. Agushaka, L. Abualigah, S. Mirjalili, A.H. Gandomi, Prairie Dog optimization algorithm, Neural Comput. Appl. 34 (22) (2022) 20017−20065.

14

A survey of the manta ray foraging optimization algorithm

Laith Abualigah[1,2,3,4,5,6,7], Farah Mahadeen[8], Absalom E. Ezugwu[9], Khaled Aldiabat[10], Mofleh Al-diabat[6], Davut Izci[11], Ahmad MohdAziz Hussein[8], Peiying Zhang[12,13], Canan Batur Şahin[14]

[1]ARTIFICIAL INTELLIGENCE AND SENSING TECHNOLOGIES (AIST) RESEARCH CENTER, UNIVERSITY OF TABUK, TABUK, SAUDI ARABIA [2]HOURANI CENTER FOR APPLIED SCIENTIFIC RESEARCH, AL-AHLIYYA AMMAN UNIVERSITY, AMMAN, JORDAN [3]MEU RESEARCH UNIT, MIDDLE EAST UNIVERSITY, AMMAN, JORDAN [4]SCHOOL OF COMPUTER SCIENCES, UNIVERSITI SAINS MALAYSIA, PULAU PINANG, MALAYSIA [5]SCHOOL OF ENGINEERING AND TECHNOLOGY, SUNWAY UNIVERSITY MALAYSIA, PETALING JAYA, MALAYSIA [6]COMPUTER SCIENCE DEPARTMENT, AL AL-BAYT UNIVERSITY, MAFRAQ, JORDAN [7]DEPARTMENT OF ELECTRICAL AND COMPUTER ENGINEERING, LEBANESE AMERICAN UNIVERSITY, BYBLOS, LEBANON [8]DEANSHIP OF E-LEARNING AND DISTANCE EDUCATION, UMM AL-QURA UNIVERSITY, MAKKAH, SAUDI ARABIA [9]UNIT FOR DATA SCIENCE AND COMPUTING, NORTH-WEST UNIVERSITY, POTCHEFSTROOM, SOUTH AFRICA [10]DEPARTMENT OF MANAGEMENT INFORMATION SYSTEMS, AJLOUN NATIONAL UNIVERSITY, AJLOUN, JORDAN [11]DEPARTMENT OF COMPUTER ENGINEERING, BATMAN UNIVERSITY, BATMAN, TURKEY [12]COLLEGE OF COMPUTER SCIENCE AND TECHNOLOGY, CHINA UNIVERSITY OF PETROLEUM (EAST CHINA), QINGDAO, P.R. CHINA [13]STATE KEY LABORATORY OF INTEGRATED SERVICES NETWORKS, XIDIAN UNIVERSITY, XI'AN, P.R. CHINA [14]FACULTY OF ENGINEERING AND NATURAL SCIENCES, MALATYA TURGUT OZAL UNIVERSITY, MALATYA, TURKEY

14.1 Introduction

Firstly, iterative optimization is a time-consuming procedure that entails completing a comprehensive search is among trial solution possibilities to identify the optimum solution to a certain problem. To provide the best solution to the problem, an optimum solution vector is chosen that can minimize or maximize the considered objective [1].

This study describes MRFO [2], a new metaheuristic algorithm that models manta ray foraging habits. There are three foraging operators in this algorithm: sequential search, spiral search, and forage somersault. The performance of the MRFO is assessed using a 31 test

Metaheuristic Optimization Algorithms. DOI: https://doi.org/10.1016/B978-0-443-13925-3.00005-4

functions and 8 engineering issues. The test results suggest that the proposed technique out-performs established descriptive qualities significantly.

A full-scale wastewater treatment plant using an activated sludge treatment method was forecasted using a new predictive model [3]. The suggested model consists of random vector functional link (RVFL) networks that have been integrated with the MRFO. RVFL is a complex artificial neural network (ANN) that avoids overfitting and other common ANN difficulties. To improve the model's prediction accuracy, MRFO is utilized to find the best RVFL parameters.

Optimization algorithms are a rapidly growing technique. The MRFO is used in this study to minimize power losses by sizing and allocating DG type I integrated into radial distribution networks [4].

Normally, optimization methods can be used to deal with many problems in the sciences, as presented in refs [5−14]. This chapter is a review of the previously released MRFO algorithm papers. Twenty research papers are analyzed and categorized based on how the MRFO algorithm is applied (neural networks, feature selection, and data clustering). The core technique of the MRFO algorithm is presented. The results provided in this survey can be used as a baseline for future study on the MRFO and MRFO applications.

This chapter is organized as follows: firstly, a detailed explanation of the subject in provided in Section 14.1; main models are presented in Section 14.2; and Section 14.3 of the presentation includes related work and applications. The discussion based on the literature is given in Section 14.4. Section 14.5 provides the conclusion and future works.

14.2 Manta ray foraging optimization

We mathematically analyze these foraging patterns to undertake a global optimization and develop a new metaheuristic algorithm named MRFO [2].

In this section, we display the behavior of the MRFO algorithm.

14.2.1 Chain foraging

Manta rays form a foraging chain by connecting their heads and tails in a straight line. According to MRFO, the ideal option is a larger concentration of plankton, which is the main food source for manta rays. While the first person goes only in search of food, the others move not just in search of food but also in search of individuals in the foraging chain ahead of them [15] (Fig. 14−1).

The following is a mathematical model of chain foraging:

$$x_i^{t+1} \begin{cases} x_i^t + r_1.(x_{best}^t - x_i^t) \\ \quad + \alpha.\left(x_{best}^t - x_i^t\right), \ i=1 \\ x_i^t + r_2.(x_{i-1}^t - x_i^t) \\ \quad + \alpha.\left(x_{best}^t - x_i^t\right), \ i=2,3,\ldots NP \end{cases}$$

$$\alpha = 2.r_3\sqrt{|\log(r_4)|}$$

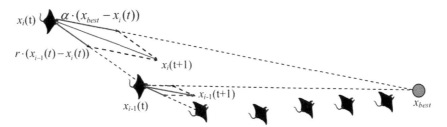

FIGURE 14–1 Chain foraging behavior in a 2D space [2].

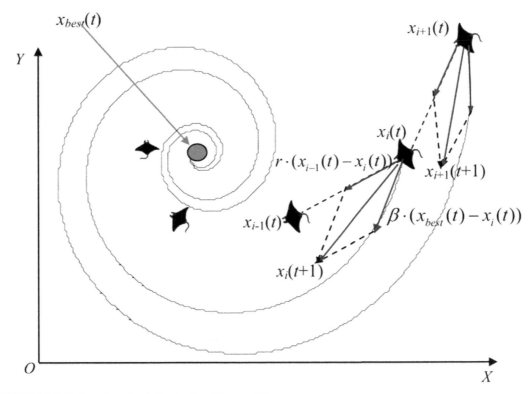

FIGURE 14–2 Cyclone foraging behavior in a 2D space [2].

14.2.2 Cyclone foraging

When manta rays come upon a large concentration of plankton, they will travel in a spiral pattern while also forming a chain [16].

During this stage, manta rays travel forward in a spiral pattern. Unlike the WOA's spiral foraging strategy, each individual not only swims forward in a spiral pattern toward its goal, but also adjusts to the positions of the current and previous best agents [16] (Fig. 14–2).

This spiral model can be expressed mathematically as follows:

$$x_i(k+1) = \int \begin{array}{c} x_{best} + r_2(x_{rand} - x_i(k) \\ + \beta(x_{best} - x_i \quad (k))), \quad i = 1 \\ x_{best} + r_2(x_{i-1}(k) - x_i(k) \\ + \beta(x_{best} - x_i(k))), \quad i = 2, 3, \ldots, n \end{array}$$

where $\beta = 2e^{r_2 \frac{k_{max}+1}{k_{max}}} \sin(2\pi r_2)$

14.2.3 Somersault foraging

Somersault feeding is always done in the opposite direction. When there is a lot of prey, the manta ray does a backward feeding somersault, completing a loop that is smaller than its body width. When the prey is concentrated at the surface, this sort of feeding is employed to limit the prey's movement and increase feeding efficiency. While somersault feeding, they expand their mouths wide and place their fins in front of their lower jaws [17].

The mathematical model can be created in the following manner:

$$x_i^d(t+1) = x_i^d(t) + S.\left[r_2.x_{best}^d(t) - r_3.x_i^d(t)\right]$$

$$i = 1, 2, \ldots N,$$

where S stands for the somersault factor, which indicates the range of each flip. The parameter is set to MRFO 2. $r2$ and $r3$ are both random numbers within (0,1) (Fig. 14−3).

14.3 Related works

14.3.1 Machine learning

The initial MRFO algorithm is prone to being stuck in local optima, necessitating further research and exploitation. As a result, during the MRFO's starting stage, we used opposition-based learning (OBL) to increase the diversity of the population in the search space.

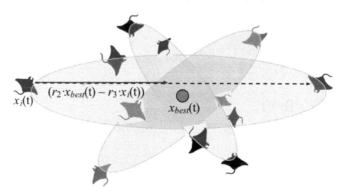

FIGURE 14–3 *Somersault* foraging behavior in a 2D space [2].

Using multilayer thresholding, the MRFO-OBL algorithm can address the problem of image segmentation. Using Otsu's method, the suggested MRFO-OBL is compared to six metaheuristic algorithms on COVID-19 CT scans [18].

This work introduces a quasi-reflected opposition technique that extends MRFO. The manta ray, a cartilaginous fish, was the inspiration for the creation of MRFO [19].

Chew et al. looked at the design, experimentation, and prototype testing of a propulsion system for the robot manta ray. The robot manta ray's propulsive system and pectoral fins were based on some of the hydrodynamic concepts of manta ray movement. The designs are straightforward, relying on passive flexibility to provide significant forward thrust while conserving energy. Fin materials of various thicknesses were used in experiments to investigate the effect of flexibility on the fins. Experiments were also carried out to see how different flapping amplitudes and frequencies affected the results. A prototype of the robot manta ray was made to evaluate the swimming ability of the propulsion mechanism [20].

14.3.2 Engineering application

For global optimization issues, engineering design optimization challenges and multithreshold segmentation, this chapter presents a novel form of the manta ray foraging optimizer. The proposed strategy is as follows: to improve manta ray movement in the exploitation phase by leveraging FC's history dependency to boost exploitation of the optimal solutions by sharing past knowledge during the optimization process using the fractional calculus (FC) with the Caputo fractional differ-sum operator. To avoid early convergence, the somersault factor has also been modified adaptively [21].

In this work, the proposed algorithm is applied to structural design problems such as four-bar truss design, speed reduction design, welded beam design, and disk brake design, and it is tested on five bi-objective and seven three-objective test functions. Four well-known multiobjective metaheuristics are used to compare the algorithm. The MOMRFO algorithm outperforms the selected multiobjective metaheuristics in terms of convergence behavior and solution diversity, according to the results of the trials [22].

Magnetorheological (Mr) dampers are important components in a variety of engineering systems, and determining it has become difficult without any prior knowledge of the control settings of Mr damper models. An improved MRFO (IMRFO) is created to more precisely discover the control parameters of Mr damper models. The new algorithm creates a searching control factor based on MRFO's limited exploration ability, thus increasing the algorithm's overall exploration [23].

The MRFO optimizer is investigated in this study in order to build a novel method for solving multiobjective engineering design issues; to do so, an external archive incorporated within the traditional MRFO is employed to use the elitism notion to save the collection of Pareto solutions. In order to govern the convergence and variety of manta ray populations, this archive also serves as a repository from which a search agent is picked depending on its density degree. The efficiency of our approach is first confirmed through extensive tests on 10 test functions, with nearly all of the results being quite satisfying in terms of convergence and variety. The algorithm is then used to solve four multiobjective engineering issues, and it shows promise in tackling real-world problems with multiple objectives [24].

The inaccuracies of selecting parameters for a single-phase transformer are examined in this chapter. Furthermore, based on newly published optimization techniques and an objective function, this study presents two unique transformer parameter estimation algorithms to optimize the estimate process and remove errors and parameter mismatches with real transformer parameters. To estimate transformer parameters, the suggested algorithms use MRFO and chaotic MRFO techniques [25].

This chapter presents the IMRFO as a solution to OPF in electric power systems with and without new VSC station technology. As a result of the planned IMRFO, total fuel prices, total greenhouse gas emissions, and total electricity losses are all predicted to reduce. The MRFO is a simulation of manta ray foraging behavior. By introducing an external store individuals who are not controlled by Pareto, MRFO is strengthened to enable multiobjectives. Iteratively adjusting the weights of the fitness function changes the shape of the fitness function. To extract a suitable operational point from the resulting Pareto set, the TOPSIS algorithm is used to prioritize orders based on their resemblance to the ideal answer [26].

14.3.3 Network problems

In a smart environment, the MRFO algorithm is used to propose optimum power planning and allocating production resources as a distributed generation system with a timetable capability (DGSC) with the purpose of reducing losses and improving the voltage profile. Resources that can be planned and generated based on network requirements are also known as DGSCs. The major goal of this study is to improve the efficiency of smart and traditional distribution networks by intelligently scheduling and distributing DGSCs [27].

This work proposes a spectrum sensing approach that works together based on the MRFO. The fusion center is where MRFO is employed to optimize the weighting vector. The range of possibilities is vast. Allocated for secondary users, the best weight vector is used. The suggested study's purpose is to figure out what the best possibility of detection is. The detection probability is crucial in spectrum sensing. The primary users' presence or absence on the channel must be identified. If the likelihood of detection is increased, the channel utilization efficiency will improve. Other state-of-the-art methods are compared to the proposed method. According to the findings, cognitive radios may be able to successfully use MRFO for spectrum sharing [28].

Saleh et al. [29] looked at how a virtual inertia control concept for frequency control might improve the dynamic security of an islanded microgrid. The proportional–integral (PI) controller in the virtual inertia control loop was optimized using the MRFO technique. The performance of the PI controller based on MRFO was good compared to further examples of evolutionary optimization algorithm-based PI controllers under various operating situations. Actual wind and solar power statistics, as well as random load variations, were used to produce realistic simulation circumstances. The results reveal that the MRFO-based PI controller outperforms the other optimization approaches in terms of frequency disturbance reduction and reference frequency tracking.

14.3.4 Optimization problem

The MRFO is utilized to solve the EDCS problem in this chapter, which includes both wind power and valve point implications. To find the most possible and ideal operating locations for the EDCS issue, the MRF optimizer employs adaptive penalty functions [30].

In this chapter, MRFO is a technique for optimizing filtering equipment internal capacitance distribution in a substation with renewable energy integration, with the purpose of lowering the imbalanced current generated by the notified capacitance and protecting the equipment. To that purpose, this research develops an internal capacitor H-bridge model, which is based on measured data from the 500 kV Yunnan Luquan Converter Station. The original information is then evaluated to the data that has been optimized using the MRFO, genetic algorithm, and particle swarm optimization. Finally, the MRFO algorithm is shown to have a greater convergence rate and higher quality outputs [31].

This study compares the upgraded method's behavior with the optimization problem to that of the initial algorithm as well as other re-sent algorithms. The assessment procedure is carried out using several assessment approaches for precision and statistical analysis for resiliency, such as root mean square error. QMRFO's outcomes are more precise than MRFOs and other optimization techniques procedures that have been investigated [32].

The model proton exchange membrane fuel cells (PEMFCs) with unknown characteristics are extracted in a reliable and exact manner using a recently designed bioinspired foraging optimizer for manta rays MRFO in this work. The estimate of parameters problem is described as a constraint-based a challenge of nonlinear optimization. The astonishing progress and revolution of computation heuristic-based approaches prompted the authors to tackle this constrained optimization problem by using MRFO, yielding a precise PEMFC model. Ballard type Mark V, NedStack type PS6, and Horizon type H-12 are examples of typical field PEMFC stacks. Using a variety of I to V datasets, MRFO's performance is compared to that of other current optimizers available in the literature [33].

14.3.5 Image processing

Ouyang et al. [34] attempted to optimize the K-means algorithm for picture segmentation using the MRFO algorithm. The initial clustering center of K-means is determined by applying MRFO features to the problem of K-means being easily affected by noise and falling into a local optimal solution [35]. MATLAB® is used to simulate K-means and MRFO image segmentation, and the image segmentation performance is assessed using three standard image segmentation metrics: PSNR, SSIM, and FSIM. Experiments demonstrate that optimizing the K-means clustering algorithm with the MRFO algorithm can result in good image segmentation results.

In this chapter, IMRFO improves individual manta ray flexibility via Lévy flight and then employs studying on a whim to keep the algorithm from sliding into the local best-case scenario Finally, the particle swarm optimization learning concept is introduced increase the algorithm's precision of convergence, which successfully improves the algorithm's global and local optimization capacity at the same time. The optimized K-means have greater stability since the likelihood of reaching a local optimum decrease [36]. Seven fundamental algorithms and four variation algorithms are compared to IMRFO inside the 12 common test functions. The statistical test and the optimization index results suggest that IMRFO has superior enhancement capabilities. For the experiment, 8 underwater photographs were chosen and compared to 11 algorithms [37].

This study introduces MantaRayWmark, a novel picture watermarking that adapts a system that leverages MRFO to balance imperceptibility and resilience by optimizing locally appropriate multiple embedding strengths (MES). A bi-directional ELM (B-ELM) was used to train for a sequence of images; the time-consuming MRFO-based optimization is done only once. To get approximation coefficients, each training picture is treated to a four-level DTCWT. The approximation coefficients are used as input features for B-ELM training, while the MES values are used as goal outputs (obtained using MRFO with as an optimization criterion, imperceptibility, and robustness). Using the previously trained model, the B-ELM is then used to forecast the optimal MES for a new image. An image is converted with four-level DTCWT for watermark embedding, and the resulting approximation subband matrix is decomposed with SVD to obtain the principal component matrix [38].

14.3.6 Other applications

The electric power requirement in this study will be met by a renewable-based microgrid because distributed generators (DGs)' operating costs are mostly dictated by load dispatch, which has a variety of types. It been used to examine the working environment costs of various DGs functioning within their corresponding constraints. To discover the optimum way to decrease the total operating cost, MRFO was employed. The MRFO is a recently developed metaheuristic way to finding food in the ocean that is inspired by manta ray behavior and foraging strategies. The MRFO's usefulness has been established by comparing it to other existing strategies mentioned in the literature [39].

14.4 Discussion

Speed reducers, disk-clutch brakes, tension springs, pressure vessels, welded beams, Belleville spring design, and PEMFCs have all been used to solve reference optimization problems and real-world engineering difficulties using the MRFO process [40]. MRFO has a wide range of applications that have been recorded in a number of different sectors. MRFO has been used to overcome a variety of difficulties, including performance optimization and real-world problems.

14.5 Conclusion and future work

For this study, approximately 20 articles were gathered, reviewed, and analyzed in order to highlight the robustness, weaknesses, benefits, and drawbacks of MRFO for researchers interested in using the method. From 2015 to the present, this review compiles a thorough list of references. The majority of these articles discussed the multinational force's applications in various disciplines. Data collection, medical research, picture processing, and engineering design are just a few examples. MRFO is a vast and promising algorithm that has been used to solve a variety of problems. We intend to present an embedded FS technique in the future, which will combine binary MRFO with a filter that is a compatible mechanism. We could also combine MRFO with another metaheuristic FS approach. Furthermore, because the suggested FS MRFO's version is a universal strategy, it can be simply extended to other common classification of pattern issues involving a significant feature vector dimensions [41]. The binary MRFO may be offered in future works to cope with complex discrete situations. Multiobjective optimization could likewise be addressed with the expanded MRFO [2].

References

[1] O.E. Turgut, A novel chaotic manta-ray foraging optimization algorithm for thermo-economic design optimization of an air-fin cooler, SN Appl. Sci. 3 (1) (2021) 3.

[2] W. Zhao, Z. Zhang, L. Wang, Manta ray foraging optimization: an effective bio-inspired optimizer for engineering applications, Eng. Appl. Artif. Intell. 87 (2020) 103300. Jan.

[3] K. Elmaadawy, M.A. Elaziz, A.H. Elsheikh, A. Moawad, B. Liu, S. Lu, Utilization of random vector functional link integrated with manta ray foraging optimization for effluent prediction of wastewater treatment plant, J. Env. Manage 298 (2021) 113520. Nov.

[4] M.G. Hemeida, A.A. Ibrahim, A.-A.A. Mohamed, S. Alkhalaf, A.M.B. El-Dine, Optimal allocation of distributed generators DG based manta ray foraging optimization algorithm (MRFO), Ain Shams Eng. J. 12 (1) (2021) 609–619.

[5] L. Abualigah, A. Diabat, C.L. Thanh, S. Khatir, Opposition-based Laplacian distribution with Prairie Dog optimization method for industrial engineering design problems, Comput. Methods Appl. Mech. Eng. 414 (2023) 116097.

[6] G. Hu, Y. Zheng, L. Abualigah, A.G. Hussien, DETDO: an adaptive hybrid dandelion optimizer for engineering optimization, Adv. Eng. Inform. 57 (2023) 102004.

[7] D. Izci, S. Ekinci, S. Mirjalili, L. Abualigah, An intelligent tuning scheme with a master/slave approach for efficient control of the automatic voltage regulator, Neural Comput. Appl. (2023) 1–17.

[8] H. Jia, C. Lu, D. Wu, C. Wen, H. Rao, L. Abualigah, An improved reptile search algorithm with ghost opposition-based learning for global optimization problems, J. Comput. Des. Eng. 10 (2023) 1390–1422.

[9] A.H. Alharbi, A.A. Abdelhamid, A. Ibrahim, S.K. Towfek, N. Khodadadi, L. Abualigah, et al., Improved dipper-throated optimization for forecasting metamaterial design bandwidth for engineering applications, Biomimetics 8 (2) (2023) 241.

[10] S. Nama, A.K. Saha, S. Chakraborty, A.H. Gandomi, L. Abualigah, Boosting particle swarm optimization by backtracking search algorithm for optimization problems, Swarm Evolut. Computation 79 (2023) 101304.

[11] M. Zare, M. Ghasemi, A. Zahedi, K. Golalipour, S.K. Mohammadi, S. Mirjalili, et al., A global best-guided firefly algorithm for engineering problems, J. Bionic Eng. (2023) 1−30.

[12] D. Wu, C. Wen, H. Rao, H. Jia, Q. Liu, L. Abualigah, Modified reptile search algorithm with multi-hunting coordination strategy for global optimization problems, Math. Biosci. Eng. 20 (6) (2023) 10090−10134.

[13] S. Ekinci, D. Izci, L. Abualigah, R.A. Zitar, A modified oppositional chaotic local search strategy based aquila optimizer to design an effective controller for vehicle cruise control system, J. Bionic Eng. (2023) 1−24.

[14] L. Abualigah, D. Falcone, A. Forestiero, Swarm intelligence to face IoT challenges, Comput. Intell. Neurosci. (2023) 2023.

[15] A. Tang, H. Zhou, T. Han, L. Xie, A modified manta ray foraging optimization for global optimization problems, IEEE Access. 9 (2021) 128702−128721.

[16] Y. Duan, C. Liu, S. Li, X. Guo, C. Yang, Manta ray foraging and Gaussian mutation-based elephant herding optimization for global optimization, Eng. Comput. 39 (2) (2023) 1085−1125.

[17] M.G. Hemeida, S. Alkhalaf, A.-A.A. Mohamed, A.A. Ibrahim, T. Senjyu, Distributed generators optimization based on multi-objective functions using manta rays foraging optimization algorithm (MRFO), Energies 13 (15) (2020) 3847.

[18] E.H. Houssein, M.M. Emam, A.A. Ali, Improved manta ray foraging optimization for multi-level thresholding using COVID-19 CT images, Neural Comput. Appl. 33 (24) (2021) 16899−16919.

[19] A.A. Abdul Razak, A.N.K. Nasir, N.M. Abdul Ghani, M.F. Mat Jusof, Manta ray foraging optimization with quasi-reflected opposition strategy for global optimization, 2022. pp. 477−85.

[20] C.-M. Chew, Q.-Y. Lim, K.S. Yeo, Development of propulsion mechanism for robot manta ray, IEEE International Conference on Robotics and Biomimetics (ROBIO), 2015, IEEE, 2015, pp. 1918−1923.

[21] D. Yousri, A.M. AbdelAty, M.A.A. Al-qaness, A.A. Ewees, A.G. Radwan, M. Abd Elaziz, Discrete fractional-order Caputo method to overcome trapping in local optima: manta ray foraging optimizer as a case study, Expert. Syst. Appl. 192 (2022) 116355. Apr.

[22] D. Zouache, F. Ben Abdelaziz, Guided manta ray foraging optimization using epsilon dominance for multi-objective optimization in engineering design, Expert. Syst. Appl. 189 (2022) 116126. Mar.

[23] Y. Liao, W. Zhao, L. Wang, Improved manta ray foraging optimization for parameters identification of magnetorheological dampers, Mathematics 9 (18) (2021) 2230.

[24] A. Got, D. Zouache, A. Moussaoui, MOMRFO: multi-objective manta ray foraging optimizer for handling engineering design problems, Knowl. Syst. 237 (2022) 107880. Feb.

[25] M. Calasan, A. Jovanovic, V. Rubezic, D. Mujicic, A. Deriszadeh, Notes on parameter estimation for single-phase transformer, IEEE Trans. Ind. Appl. (2020) 1−1.

[26] E.E. Elattar, A.M. Shaheen, A.M. Elsayed, R.A. El-Sehiemy, Optimal power flow with emerged technologies of voltage source converter stations in meshed power systems, IEEE Access. 8 (2020) 166963−166979.

[27] M. Zahedi Vahid, Z.M. Ali, E. Seifi Najmi, A. Ahmadi, F.H. Gandoman, S.H.E.A. Aleem, Optimal allocation and planning of distributed power generation resources in a smart distribution network using the manta ray foraging optimization algorithm, Energies 14 (16) (2021) 4856.

[28] K.K. Singh, P. Yadav, A. Singh, G. Dhiman, K. Cengiz, Cooperative spectrum sensing optimization for cognitive radio in 6 G networks, Comput. Electr. Eng. 95 (2021) 107378. Oct.

[29] A. Saleh, W.A. Omran, H.M. Hasanien, M. Tostado-Véliz, A. Alkuhayli, F. Jurado, Manta ray foraging optimization for the virtual inertia control of islanded microgrids including renewable energy sources, Sustainability 14 (7) (2022) 4189.

[30] A.M. Shaheen, A.R. Ginidi, R.A. El-Sehiemy, E.E. Elattar, Optimal economic power and heat dispatch in cogeneration systems including wind power, Energy 225 (2021) 120263. Jun.

[31] J. Wei, J. Lan, P. Jiang, W. Mao, K. Zeng, B. Yang, MRFO based optimal filter capacitors configuration in substations with renewable energy integration, 4th Asia Energy and Electrical Engineering Symposium (AEEES), 2022, IEEE, 2022, pp. 328−333.

[32] A. Ramadan, S. Kamel, F. Jurado, Parameter extraction of three diode solar photovoltaic model using quantum manta ray foraging optimization algorithm, IEEE CHILEAN Conference on Electrical, Electronics Engineering, Information and Communication Technologies (CHILECON), 2021, IEEE, 2021, pp. 1−6.

[33] S.I. Selem, H.M. Hasanien, A.A. El-Fergany, Parameters extraction of PEMFC's model using manta rays foraging optimizer, Int. J. Energy Res. 44 (6) (2020) 4629−4640.

[34] C.T. Ouyang, S.K. Liao, Z.W. Huang, Y.K. Gong, Optimization of K-means image segmentation based on manta ray foraging algorithm, 3rd International Conference on Electronic Communication and Artificial Intelligence (IWECAI), 2022, IEEE, 2022, pp. 151−155.

[35] A.M. Ikotun, A.E. Ezugwu, L. Abualigah, B. Abuhaija, J. Heming, K-means clustering algorithms: A comprehensive review, variants analysis, and advances in the era of big data, Inf. Sci. (Ny.) 622 (2023) 178−210. Apr.

[36] A.M. Ikotun, A.E. Ezugwu, Boosting k-means clustering with symbiotic organisms search for automatic clustering problems, PLoS One 17 (8) (2022) e0272861.

[37] D. Zhu, L. Xie, C. Zhou, K-means segmentation of underwater image based on improved manta ray algorithm, Comput. Intell. Neurosci. 2022 (2022) 1−26. Mar 16.

[38] N.K. Sharma, S. Kumar, A. Rajpal, N. Kumar, MantaRayWmark: an image adaptive multiple embedding strength optimization based watermarking using manta ray foraging and bi-directional ELM, Expert. Syst. Appl. 200 (2022) 116860. Aug.

[39] V. Tiwari, H.M. Dubey, M. Pandit, Economic dispatch in renewable energy based microgrid using manta ray foraging optimization, IEEE 2nd International Conference On Electrical Power and Energy Systems (ICEPES), 2021, IEEE, 2021, pp. 1−6.

[40] U.C. Ben, A.E. Akpan, C.C. Mbonu, E.D. Ebong, Novel methodology for interpretation of magnetic anomalies due to two-dimensional dipping dikes using the manta ray foraging optimization, J. Appl. Geophys. 192 (2021) 104405. Sep.

[41] K.K. Ghosh, R. Guha, S.K. Bera, N. Kumar, R. Sarkar, S-shaped versus V-shaped transfer functions for binary manta ray foraging optimization in feature selection problem, Neural Comput. Appl. 33 (17) (2021) 11027−11041.

15

A review of mothflame optimization algorithm: analysis and applications

Laith Abualigah[1,2,3,4,5,6,7], Laheeb Al-Abadi[7], Abiodun M. Ikotun[8], Faisal AL-Saqqar[7], Davut Izci[9], Peiying Zhang[10,11], Canan Batur Şahin[12], Mohammad El-Bashir[7], Putra Sumari[4]

[1]ARTIFICIAL INTELLIGENCE AND SENSING TECHNOLOGIES (AIST) RESEARCH CENTER, UNIVERSITY OF TABUK, TABUK, SAUDI ARABIA [2]HOURANI CENTER FOR APPLIED SCIENTIFIC RESEARCH, AL-AHLIYYA AMMAN UNIVERSITY, AMMAN, JORDAN [3]MEU RESEARCH UNIT, MIDDLE EAST UNIVERSITY, AMMAN, JORDAN [4]SCHOOL OF COMPUTER SCIENCES, UNIVERSITI SAINS MALAYSIA, PULAU PINANG, MALAYSIA [5]SCHOOL OF ENGINEERING AND TECHNOLOGY, SUNWAY UNIVERSITY MALAYSIA, PETALING JAYA, MALAYSIA [6]DEPARTMENT OF ELECTRICAL AND COMPUTER ENGINEERING, LEBANESE AMERICAN UNIVERSITY, BYBLOS, LEBANON [7]COMPUTER SCIENCE DEPARTMENT, AL AL-BAYT UNIVERSITY, MAFRAQ, JORDAN [8]UNIVERSITY OF KWAZULU-NATAL, PIETERMARITZBURG CAMPUS, POTCHEFSTROOM, SOUTH AFRICA [9]DEPARTMENT OF COMPUTER ENGINEERING, BATMAN UNIVERSITY, BATMAN, TURKEY [10]COLLEGE OF COMPUTER SCIENCE AND TECHNOLOGY, CHINA UNIVERSITY OF PETROLEUM (EAST CHINA), QINGDAO, P.R. CHINA [11]STATE KEY LABORATORY OF INTEGRATED SERVICES NETWORKS, XIDIAN UNIVERSITY, XI'AN, P.R. CHINA [12]FACULTY OF ENGINEERING AND NATURAL SCIENCES, MALATYA TURGUT OZAL UNIVERSITY, MALATYA, TURKEY

15.1 Introduction

The process of discovering the best potential solution(s) to a given problem is known as optimization [1]. The need for novel optimization strategies has grown more apparent in recent decades as the complexity of issues has increased. Prior to the introduction of heuristic optimization approaches, techniques were the only tools for solving issues. Local optima entrapment is a serious difficulty in mathematical optimization approaches, which are mainly deterministic [2]. Gradient-based algorithms, for example, necessitate the derivation of the search space. As a result, they are inept at solving real-world issues.

Insects can fly at a fixed angle for a remote light source, such as the moon, thanks to a technique known as the transdirection [3]. Fig. 15−1 depicts the transverse direction as a conceptual model [4]. This aids in their straight-line flight. Unnatural sources of light, such as a bulb, are too

Metaheuristic Optimization Algorithms. DOI: https://doi.org/10.1016/B978-0-443-13925-3.00006-6

FIGURE 15–1 The direction of the moth is transverse.

close together, causing significant angular variations in the light source's angular interaction with the direction of flight. Insects would describe a spiral flight toward the light bulb illustrated in Fig. 15−2 by intuitively attempting to maintain the angle of their direction of flight constant [4].

Normally, optimization methods can be used to deal with many problems in the sciences, as presented in [5−14]. This chapter presents a comprehensive review that studied the papers that have been published on moth flame optimization (MFO). We classified them into several categories like benchmark functions, chemical and economical applications, image processing, medical, and machine learning.

This review is organized as follows: MFO and its framework are covered in Section 2. Section 3 discusses application enhancements in specific fields, Section 4 illustrates the assessment of the multinational force and observers, and finally, Section 5 concludes with a list of potential study topics.

15.2 Moth Flame Optimization Algorithm

15.2.1 Origin

Moths are beautiful insects that are very similar to butterflies. In nature, there are many different species of this insect. The most fascinating thing about moths is their unique night

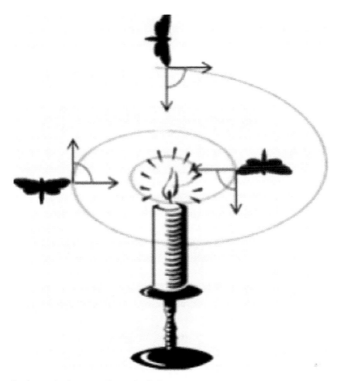

FIGURE 15–2 Flying path that spirals around nearby light sources.

navigation routes. With the help of moonlight, they evolved to fly at night. They used a mechanism called transverse direction to move. In this strategy, the moth flies by maintaining a constant angle with the moon, a particularly successful mechanism for traversing long distances in a straight line.

Fig. 15–1 depicts a transverse direction conceptual model. This mechanism ensures that the moth will fly in a straight line because the moon is far away. Humans can use the same mobility strategy. Let us imagine you want to travel east and the moon is on the south side of the sky. If the moon is on his left side while you walk, you will be able to walk in a straight line eastward.

Despite the efficiency of the transverse direction, the mites usually fly in a spiral around the lights. Artificial lights, in fact, deceive the mites and cause them to behave in this way. This is because the transverse direction is ineffective because it is only beneficial when the light source is too far away to travel in a straight direction When the mite recognizes artificial light, it strives to fly in a straight line by keeping a comparable angle to the light.

Because of the moon's closeness, maintaining the same angle to the light source results in a futile or fatal spiral fly route. Fig. 15–2 [4] depicts a conceptual representation of this behavior.

15.2.2 Moth Flame Optimization Algorithm

The proposed MFO begins by randomly producing moths within the solution space and then calculating the fitness values for each moth and marking the optimal place by flame, as shown

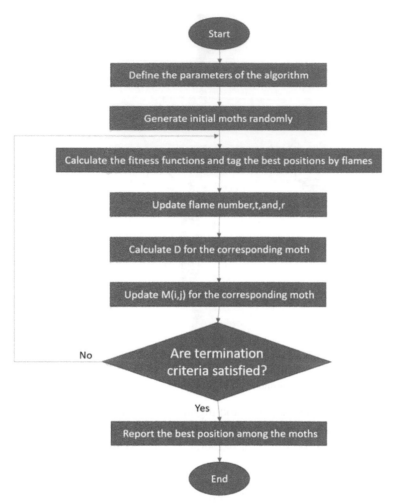

FIGURE 15–3 The moth flame optimization algorithm's flowchart.

in Fig. 15–3. The moth positions are then updated to better flame-tagged positions using the spiral motion function, the new best individual positions are updated, and the procedure is repeated until the termination criteria are met. Fig. 15–3 shows the MFO algorithm's flowchart.

15.2.3 Establishing a Moth Population

Mirjalili [15] believed that each moth could fly in space 1D, 2D, 3D, or hyperdimensional space. The moth group can be expressed as follows:

$$M = \begin{bmatrix} x_{1,1} & x_{1,2} & \cdots & x_{1,d} \\ x_{2,1} & x_{2,2} & \cdots & x_{2,d} \\ \vdots & \vdots & & \vdots \\ \vdots & \vdots & & \vdots \\ x_{n,1} & x_{2,1} & \cdots & x_{n,d} \end{bmatrix} \quad (15-1)$$

In addition, n denotes the number of moths, and d is the number of dimensions in the solution space. The fitness values of each moth are saved in the following array:

$$OM = \begin{bmatrix} O_{M1} \\ O_{M2} \\ \cdot \\ \cdot \\ \cdot \\ O_{Mn} \\ \cdot \end{bmatrix} \qquad (15-2)$$

Flames make up the remaining components of the MFO algorithm.

The flames in space D-dimensions, along with the fitness function vector, appear in the matrix below:

$$F = \begin{bmatrix} A_{1,1} & A_{1,2} & \cdots & A_{1,d} \\ A_{2,1} & A_{2,2} & \cdots & A_{2,d} \\ \vdots & \vdots & & \vdots \\ \vdots & \vdots & & \vdots \\ A_{n,1} & A_{2,1} & \cdots & A_{n,d} \end{bmatrix} \qquad (15-3)$$

$$OF = \begin{bmatrix} O_{A1} \\ O_{A2} \\ \cdot \\ \cdot \\ O_{nd} \end{bmatrix} \qquad (15-4)$$

15.2.4 Updating the Moths' Positions

For convergence of global optimization problems, Rhea uses three separate functions. Given below are definitions of these functions:

$$MFO = (R'S'E) \qquad (15-5)$$

S refers to the movement of moths in the search space ($S: M \longrightarrow M$), and E refers to the end of the research process ($E: M \longrightarrow$ true; false).

The function R, which is used to perform randomization, is represented by the following equation.

$$M(i,j) = (\mathrm{ub}(i) - \mathrm{lb}(j)) * \mathrm{rand}() + \mathrm{lb}(i) \qquad (15-6)$$

The lower and upper boundaries of variables are denoted by lb and ub, respectively.

15.3 The Growth of the Moth Flame Optimization Algorithm in the Literature

There have been numerous publications on the multinational force and observers. In this review, the keyword "moth-flame optimization" is used to collect articles.

Fig. 15−4 illustrates the number of MFO articles released by well-known publishers between 2015 and 2020 (magazines and conferences).

15.3.1 Variants

The several variants of MFO were developed to overcome persistent variable issues. This approach used the Sini function to translate the continuous field into the binary field in order to solve bilateral problems [16]. Single-purpose issues can be resolved using both continuous and dual MFO. Many scientists have tried to build a multipurpose version of this method as a result of this [17].

A nondominant multigoal MFO was offered in a report [16]. An archive was used in a similar study to force MFO to solve multigoal problems [18]. A change in the multinational force, in which many sanction functions were used to solve limited problems using multinational force and observers, was proposed [1,19].

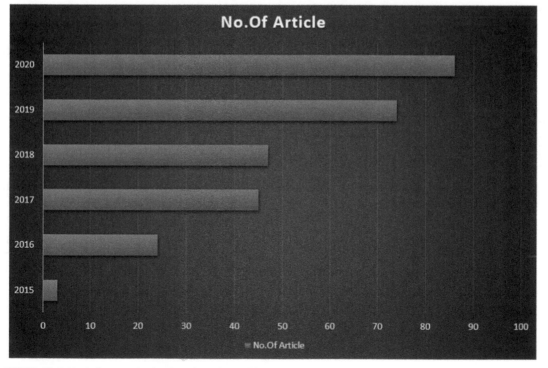

FIGURE 15–4 Moth flame opitmization algorithm publications.

There are also a number of studies in the literature aimed at promoting the exploration and/or exploitation of the multinational force and observers. During the improvement phase, an opposition-based educational several of MFO was proposed [20], which took into account the site opposing moths. Three papers [21,22] use messy maps to modify different MFO organization parameters in order to improve their performance. Many Levi's trips are also used to make efficient the exploration of the MFO algorithm and avoid local optimization [23,24].

15.4 Application

MFO has been used in a wide range of applications in many areas. Fig. 15−5 depicts the MFO's publishing distribution in these domains [3,4]. The following is a list of a few of them:

15.4.1 Benchmark Functions

Bhesdadiya et al. [1] developed the MFO algorithm to deal with inequality and equality-constrained improvement, as well as real-world planning problems, using a navigation strategy. In the universe, the travel approach is called episodic direction moths a highly effective

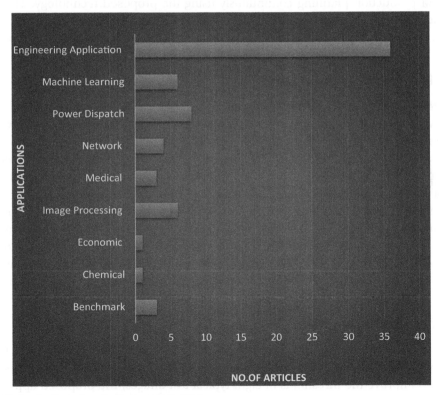

FIGURE 15–5 Application of moth flame optimization.

technique to cover this long distance in a straight line. On the other hand, real challenge limitations have been presented as an improvement strategy in the presence of actual restrictions on selected variables [25].

MFO is one of the most promising nature-inspired improvement methods that has a direct impact on the problem of improvement. On the other hand, slow convergence is one of the main flaws of the multinational force. MFO has been modified to deal with this problem using 10 messy maps to discover top prospectors and speed up the procedure for determining the most appropriate solutions. This method was developed in order to overcome the limitations of the current test methods [26]. Simulations suggest that chaotic maps aid the MFO's convergence speed performance. In addition, simulation tests show that pocket maps significantly enhance MFO performance.

15.4.2 Chemical Applications

Chauhan and Kutisha [27] proposed an approach to improving the efficiency of single-level production planning using evolutionary algorithms. The multinational force and observers demonstrate the effectiveness of the strategy and assist in assessing the performance of the proposed technique. The multinational force and observers have been shown to solve the problem of production planning continuously using the proposed technology. The multinational and magnetic force in the chemical industry has proven to be useful in production planning, but can be applied in a variety of industries to find the best production portfolio.

15.4.3 Economical Applications

Pasandideh and Khalil Porzari [28] proposed a multiitem model for the multiitem economic demand with the cost of maintaining a nonlinear unit and partial predemand. Several technical, strategic, and material restrictions, such as the entire cost of detention, warehouse capacity, available budget, and total acceptable late order cost limits, were considered while designing a feasible model [28]. The key contribution is determining the lengths of inventory cycles, in which inventory levels rise and fall as the overall inventory costs fall.

Furthermore, the rate of late orders for each product during periods of shortage is a change in choice in order to drastically reduce total inventory costs. The RIA algorithm and the inner point approach are used to optimize the model in multiple sizes due to the proposed model's nonlinearity and complexity. Finally, the execution of the proposed approaches is statistically compared using three metrics to determine the best way to solve them.

15.4.4 Image Processing

Zhou et al. [25] reported the problem of increasing thresholds through the ideal threshold, and a multithreshold technique to picture segmentation based on MNF was proposed as a solution. To improve the thresholds of eight typical test images, the proposed approach used the Kapoor entropy method. Image segmentation data and numerical experiment results were used to generate simulation results. The proposed algorithm is superior to previous modern algorithms in terms of effectiveness and durability.

Happy et al. [29] suggested a successful solution for liver fragmentation based on the MNF algorithm. The image of the abdomen is compiled using this approach.

The desired combinations were captured by the user exposing the liver to obtain the initial segmented image in this technique. Subsequently, morphological processes were used to create the final segmented liver. A total of 70 magnetic resonance imaging scans were used to evaluate the proposed approach and liver division. Empirical results show that the proposed method is generally 95.66% accurate.

Muangkot et al. [30] proposed it to improve the MNF image segmentation algorithm in order to optimize the best multilevel threshold for satellite images effectively. In terms of image segmentation, the multilevel threshold is commonly used because it is easy to build and works well in processing. However, as the number of threshold values grows, it becomes more cost-effective mathematically. To determine the appropriate multilevel threshold in image segmentation, Azizi et al. [31] compared two methods of improvement inspired by nature (MNF and WWA). Using the image graph, the presented algorithms were created and candidate solutions were considered. Then, based on the characteristics of each algorithm, the status was updated.

15.4.5 Medical Applications

Plant diseases are one of the most important issues in agricultural production, with serious economic consequences. These effects can be mitigated if disorders like these can be detected spontaneously [32]. For automatic infection detection systems, a common pretreatment step known as feature identification is used. It is a critical measure in the sector to identify and process acute, redundant, and irrelevant data in order to maximize detection performance. An improved moth flame technology was introduced [31] to automatically detect tomato problems.

Alzheimer's disease (AD) is one of the most frequent forms of dementia and typically affects people starting at the age of 65. According to current studies, the most important factor for identifying AD is that it takes a long time and is inconvenient. As a result, Sayed et al. [2] suggested an automated system for diagnosing AD. The basic concepts of MFO as a choice-building technique, as well as an adaptive SVM classifier, are used to distinguish three types of categories: normal, AD, and cognitive impairment.

Wang et al. [33] suggested a new machine for learning an approach based on the moth optimization strategy and anarchist flame (kmvo) (Kelm). Optimization parameters and the selection method used by cmvo were used in this algorithm. The proposed scheme methodology is compared to other Kelm schemes that use genetic algorithms, improve particle swarm, and improve moth and flame. Breast cancer and Parkinson's disease are used for screening.

In addition, the proposed scheme was used in realistic medical diagnostic cases. The proposed strategy works best with a subset of reduced features, according to the results of the experiment. Cmfs-Kelm also becomes a useful and effective computer-assisted tool in medical diagnostics.

15.4.5.1 Breast Cancer Detection

Breast cancer is the most common cancer among women and the second largest cause of cancer-related death. As a result, detecting a breast tumor early, before it develops and spreads to nearby cells, may lower mortality [34]. Breast cancer, on the other hand, is a diverse disease, which makes early identification a great therapeutic issue. There are various imaging techniques available in the realm of early breast cancer detection. The gold standard, currently known as X-ray mammography [35,36], is the most commonly used procedure.

Other alternatives to breast testing are available that are more effective and safer.

Thermal imaging, also called infrared imaging, is a noncontact, noninvasive method of measuring body temperature that detects infrared radiation emitted by the skin [37]. Other, more effective methods of breast testing are available. Since 1960, digital infrared imaging has been utilized in medical diagnosis, and in 1982, the US Food and Drug Administration approved it as an addition to breast cancer diagnostics [34,38].

Since then, more emphasis has been placed on improving the sensitivity of infrared imaging technology. Thermal imaging, often known as thermal imaging, is now thought to be a better way to detect breast cancer [39]. The concept behind thermal imaging is that the ERT camera detects any differences in body heat resulting from irregularities in blood flow found on the surface of diseased tissue. Breast cancer can be detected via thermal imaging because malignant tumors have increased blood supply and cell proliferation.

15.4.5.2 Alzheimer's Disease Diagnosis

AD is the most frequent type of dementia in adults over 65. The traditional criteria for identifying AD are time-consuming and tiresome. A method for AD disease has been proposed. The feature selection approach is based on the MFO theory. To distinguish between three classes, a support vector machine classifier is utilized: normal, AD, and cognitive impairment [2].

15.4.6 Machine Learning

Recent developments in computer technologies and databases have led to data accumulation at a rate that exceeds human data processing capacity. Machine learning curricula (such as selecting, assembling, and classifying features) are able to efficiently handle data mountains [40].

MFO-AHLR, a new MFO-based strategy to improve AHLR accuracy with minimal features, was introduced by Aziz, Ewees, and Hassanien [31]. In MFO-AHLR technology, three steps were used: (i) triviality and noise removal, (ii) extraction features, and (iii) classification. It should be noted that the multinational force and observers were used as a landmark before the classification step.

Alzaqebah et al. [41] used multinational force and observers to develop the best set of features (i.e., locate the smallest number of features) and rating performance to the maximum (i.e., improve rating accuracy). MFO performance was assessed using 18 different data sets from the UCI Machine Learning Library.

15.5 Discussion

Since its introduction in 2015, the multinational force has been widely used to address a variety of challenges in a variety of sectors. The success of MNF is due to its simplicity, flexibility, and ease of implementation, just like many other metaheuristic algorithms. Moreover, the multinational force has its own set of benefits. For example, the transition from exploration to exploitation at a very early stage allows for very rapid convergence. As a result, MNF's efficiency has been enhanced for applications like classifications that require a speedy response [2].

The multinational force, on the other hand, has many limitations and downsides. There are no free lunch theories for improvement, as far as we know. As a result, MNF shares this restriction with all optimization algorithms, which means that no optimization method can solve all optimization problems [2].

As a result, the multinational force may require certain changes in order to address different types of improvement issues. MNF has a special disadvantage, in that it is difficult to implement due to a large number of parameters compared to other methods [42,43]. The performance of the MNF fits into the problem of community detection. However, the performance of MNF in large networks is inefficient and may decrease when compared to other community discovery methods. MNF only accepts new solutions that outperform the current global best. As a result, the number of fires that can be found in the search area may be limited [44]. Moreover, since the method diverges to the stage of exploitation by adjusting the amount of flame, the inefficiency of the MNF culminates in stagnation after the first stage [45]. It also has slow speed convergence, causing it to become stuck in the local optima [46].

15.6 Concluding Remarks

For this study, approximately 37 articles were gathered, reviewed, and analyzed in order to emphasize the robustness, weaknesses, benefits, and drawbacks of MNF for researchers interested in using this technique. This review collects a comprehensive list of references from 2015 to the present. Most of these articles described the applications of the multinational force in various fields, for example, data collection, medical research, robotics, image processing, and engineering design. MFO is a large and promising algorithm that has already been applied to several problems [3,30].

It has a number of advantages over other optimization techniques, including simplicity, search speed, and ease of hybridization. However, because the multinational force and observers are focused on exploitation rather than exploration, they are optimally trapped in a terrible local area.

As a result, it is important to investigate and propose improved algorithms to improve swarm intelligence in order to enhance algorithmic performance and expand its field of application. Finally, we make several recommendations for future multinational force and observer research. To improve performance, PA and MFA can be paired at [16] relatively low as fitness function. The calculation time of the feature selection model increases when using the proportional reduction of feature selection. As a result, new computational techniques, such as parallel calculations, must be integrated in order to shorten the processing time. Several hybridization procedures are described [47,48], which can be applied to the BA to increase its performance. Two strategies were described for creating new businesses [49,50]: foundational research on how to tackle multigoal optimization issues and the application of momfo's to real-world industry settings. Various selection procedures are used to improve MNF performance, such as linear ranking selection, exponential ranking selection, tournament selection, and so on.

References

[1] R.H. Bhesdadiya, I.N. Trivedi, P. Jangir,N. Jangir, Moth-flame optimizer method for solving constrained engineering optimization problems, 2018, pp. 61−68. Available from: https://doi.org/10.1007/978−981-10−3773-3_7.

[2] G.I. Sayed, A.E. Hassanien, T.M. Nassef, J.-S. Pan, alzheimer's disease diagnosis based on moth flame optimization, 2017, pp. 298−305. Available from: https://doi.org/10.1007/978-3-319−48490-7_35.

[3] S.K. Sahoo, et al., Moth flame optimization: theory, modifications, hybridizations, and applications, Arch. Comput. Methods Eng. 30 (1) (2023) 391−426. Available from: https://doi.org/10.1007/s11831-022-09801-z.

[4] M. Shehab, L. Abualigah, H. Al Hamad, H. Alabool, M. Alshinwan, A.M. Khasawneh, Moth−flame optimization algorithm: variants and applications, Neural Comput. Appl. 32 (14) (2020) 9859−9884. Available from: https://doi.org/10.1007/s00521-019-04570-6.

[5] L. Abualigah, A. Diabat, C.L. Thanh, S. Khatir, Opposition-based Laplacian distribution with Prairie Dog optimization method for industrial engineering design problems, Comput. Methods Appl. Mech. Eng. 414 (2023) 116097.

[6] G. Hu, Y. Zheng, L. Abualigah, A.G. Hussien, DETDO: An adaptive hybrid dandelion optimizer for engineering optimization, Adv. Eng. Inform. 57 (2023) 102004.

[7] D. Izci, S. Ekinci, S. Mirjalili, L. Abualigah, An intelligent tuning scheme with a master/slave approach for efficient control of the automatic voltage regulator, Neural Comput. Appl. (2023) 1−17.

[8] H. Jia, C. Lu, D. Wu, C. Wen, H. Rao, L. Abualigah, An improved reptile search algorithm with ghost opposition-based learning for global optimization problems, J. Comput. Des. Eng. (2023). qwad048.

[9] A.H. Alharbi, A.A. Abdelhamid, A. Ibrahim, S.K. Towfek, N. Khodadadi, L. Abualigah, et al., Improved dipper-throated optimization for forecasting metamaterial design bandwidth for engineering applications, Biomimetics 8 (2) (2023) 241.

[10] S. Nama, A.K. Saha, S. Chakraborty, A.H. Gandomi, L. Abualigah, Boosting particle swarm optimization by backtracking search algorithm for optimization problems, Swarm Evolut. Comput. 79 (2023) 101304.

[11] M. Zare, M. Ghasemi, A. Zahedi, K. Golalipour, S.K. Mohammadi, S. Mirjalili, et al., A global best-guided firefly algorithm for engineering problems, J. Bionic Eng. (2023) 1−30.

[12] D. Wu, C. Wen, H. Rao, H. Jia, Q. Liu, L. Abualigah, Modified reptile search algorithm with multi-hunting coordination strategy for global optimization problems, Math. Biosci. Eng. 20 (6) (2023) 10090−10134.

[13] S. Ekinci, D. Izci, L. Abualigah, R.A. Zitar, A modified oppositional chaotic local search strategy based aquila optimizer to design an effective controller for vehicle cruise control system, J. Bionic Eng. (2023) 1−24.

[14] L. Abualigah, D. Falcone, A. Forestiero, Swarm intelligence to face IoT challenges, Comput. Intell. Neurosci. 2023 (2023).

[15] S. Mirjalili, Moth-flame optimization algorithm: a novel nature-inspired heuristic paradigm, Knowl. Syst. 89 (2015) 228−249. Available from: https://doi.org/10.1016/j.knosys.2015.07.006.

[16] S.R. K, L.K. Panwar, B.K. Panigrahi, R. Kumar, Solution to unit commitment in power system operation planning using binary coded modified moth flame optimization algorithm (BMMFOA): a flame selection based computational technique, J. Comput. Sci. 25 (2018) 298–317. Available from: https://doi.org/10.1016/j.jocs.2017.04.011.

[17] V. Savsani, M.A. Tawhid, Non-dominated sorting moth flame optimization (NS-MFO) for multi-objective problems, Eng. Appl. Artif. Intell. 63 (2017) 20–32. Available from: https://doi.org/10.1016/j.engappai.2017.04.018.

[18] Vikas, S.J. Nanda, Multi-objective moth flame optimization, in: 2016 International Conference on Advances in Computing, Communications and Informatics (ICACCI), September 2016, pp. 2470–2476. Available from: https://doi.org/10.1109/ICACCI.2016.7732428.

[19] N. Jangir, M.H. Pandya, I.N. Trivedi, R.H. Bhesdadiya, P. Jangir,A. Kumar, Moth-flame optimization algorithm for solving real challenging constrained engineering optimization problems, in: 2016 IEEE Students' Conference on Electrical, Electronics and Computer Science (SCEECS), March 2016, pp. 1–5. Available from: https://doi.org/10.1109/SCEECS.2016.7509293.

[20] W. Apinantanakon, K. Sunat, OMFO: A new opposition-based moth-flame optimization algorithm for solving unconstrained optimization problems, 2018, pp. 22–31. Available from: https://doi.org/10.1007/978-3-319-60663-7_3.

[21] E. Emary, H.M. Zawbaa, Impact of chaos functions on modern swarm optimizers, PLoS One 11 (7) (2016) e0158738. Available from: https://doi.org/10.1371/journal.pone.0158738.

[22] S.H. H. Mehne, S. Mirjalili, Moth-flame optimization algorithm: theory, literature review, and application in optimal nonlinear feedback control design, 2020, pp. 143–166. Available from: https://doi.org/10.1007/978-3-030-12127-3_9.

[23] P. Jangir et al., Implementation of meta-heuristic levy flight moth-flame optimizer for solving real challenging constrained engineering optimization problems single and multi-objective constraint environment economic dispatch (CEED/MOCEED) view project implementation of meta-heuristic levy flight moth-flame optimizer for solving real challenging constrained engineering optimization problems. Available from: https://doi.org/10.13140/RG.2.1.4211.4960.

[24] Z. Li, Y. Zhou, S. Zhang, J. Song, Lévy-flight moth-flame algorithm for function optimization and engineering design problems, Math. Probl. Eng. 2016 (2016) 1–22. Available from: https://doi.org/10.1155/2016/1423930.

[25] Y. Zhou, X. Yang, Y. Ling, J. Zhang, Meta-heuristic moth swarm algorithm for multilevel thresholding image segmentation, Multimed. Tools Appl. 77 (18) (2018) 23699–23727. Available from: https://doi.org/10.1007/s11042-018-5637-x.

[26] U. Guvenc, S. Duman, Y. Hinislioglu, Chaotic moth swarm algorithm, in: 2017 IEEE International Conference on Innovations in Intelligent Systems and applications (INISTA), July 2017, pp. 90–95. Available from: https://doi.org/10.1109/INISTA.2017.8001138.

[27] S.S. Chauhan, P. Kotecha, Single level production planning in petrochemical industries using Moth-flame optimization, in: 2016 IEEE Region 10 Conference (TENCON), November 2016, pp. 263–266. Available from: https://doi.org/10.1109/TENCON.2016.7848003.

[28] S. Khalilpourazari, S.H.R. Pasandideh, Multi-item EOQ model with nonlinear unit holding cost and partial backordering: moth-flame optimization algorithm, J. Ind. Prod. Eng. 34 (1) (2017) 42–51. Available from: https://doi.org/10.1080/21681015.2016.1192068.

[29] S. Said, A. Mostafa, E.H. Houssein, A.E. Hassanien, H. Hefny, Moth-flame optimization based segmentation for MRI liver images, 2018, pp. 320–330. Available from: https://doi.org/10.1007/978-3-319-64861-3_30.

[30] N. Muangkote, K. Sunat, S. Chiewchanwattana, Multilevel thresholding for satellite image segmentation with moth-flame based optimization, in: 2016 13th International Joint Conference on Computer Science and Software Engineering (JCSSE), July 2016, pp. 1–6. Available from: https://doi.org/10.1109/JCSSE.2016.7748919.

[31] M.A. El Aziz, A.A. Ewees, A.E. Hassanien, Whale optimization algorithm and moth-flame optimization for multilevel thresholding image segmentation, Expert. Syst. Appl. 83 (2017) 242–256. Available from: https://doi.org/10.1016/j.eswa.2017.04.023.

[32] L.Z. Pen et al., Artocarpus classification technique using deep learning based convolutional neural network, 2023, pp. 1–21. Available from: https://doi.org/10.1007/978-3-031–17576-3_1.

[33] M. Wang, et al., Toward an optimal kernel extreme learning machine using a chaotic moth-flame optimization strategy with applications in medical diagnoses, Neurocomputing 267 (2017) 69–84. Available from: https://doi.org/10.1016/j.neucom.2017.04.060.

[34] O.N. Oyelade, A.E. Ezugwu, M.S. Almutairi, A.K. Saha, L. Abualigah, H. Chiroma, A generative adversarial network for synthetization of regions of interest based on digital mammograms, Sci. Rep. 12 (1) (2022) 6166. Available from: https://doi.org/10.1038/s41598-022-09929-9.

[35] U.R. Gogoi, G. Majumdar, M.K. Bhowmik, A.K. Ghosh, D. Bhattacharjee, Breast abnormality detection through statistical feature analysis using infrared thermograms, in: 2015 International Symposium on Advanced Computing and Communication (ISACC), September 2015, pp. 258–265. Available from: https://doi.org/10.1109/ISACC.2015.7377351.

[36] S. Pramanik, D. Bhattacharjee, M. Nasipuri, Wavelet based thermogram analysis for breast cancer detection, in: 2015 International Symposium on Advanced Computing and Communication (ISACC), September 2015, pp. 205–212. Available from: https://doi.org/10.1109/ISACC.2015.7377343.

[37] M. Milosevic, D. Jankovic, A. Peulic, Comparative analysis of breast cancer detection in mammograms and thermograms, Biomed. Eng. / Biomed. Tech. 60 (1) (2015). Available from: https://doi.org/10.1515/bmt-2014-0047.

[38] N. Arora, et al., Effectiveness of a noninvasive digital infrared thermal imaging system in the detection of breast cancer, Am. J. Surg. 196 (4) (2008) 523–526. Available from: https://doi.org/10.1016/j.amjsurg.2008.06.015.

[39] F.J. González, Non-invasive estimation of the metabolic heat production of breast tumors using digital infrared imaging, Quant. Infrared Thermogr. J. 8 (2) (2011) 139–148. Available from: https://doi.org/10.3166/qirt.8.139-148.

[40] A.E. Ezugwu, O.N. Oyelade, A.M. Ikotun, J.O. Agushaka, Y.-S. Ho, Machine learning research trends in africa: a 30 years overview with bibliometric analysis review, Arch. Comput. Methods Eng. (2023). Available from: https://doi.org/10.1007/s11831-023-09930-z.

[41] M. Alzaqebah, N. Alrefai, E.A.E. Ahmed, S. Jawarneh, M.K. Alsmadi, Neighborhood search methods with moth optimization algorithm as a wrapper method for feature selection problems, Int. J. Electr. Comput. Eng. 10 (4) (2020) 3672. Available from: https://doi.org/10.11591/ijece.v10i4.pp3672-3684.

[42] J. Luo, H. Chen, Q. zhang, Y. Xu, H. Huang, X. Zhao, An improved grasshopper optimization algorithm with application to financial stress prediction, Appl. Math. Model. 64 (2018) 654–668. Available from: https://doi.org/10.1016/j.apm.2018.07.044.

[43] G.I. Sayed, M. Soliman, A.E. Hassanien, Bio-inspired swarm techniques for thermogram breast cancer detection, 2016, pp. 487–506. Available from: https://doi.org/10.1007/978-3-319-33793-7_21.

[44] A.A. Saleh, A.-A.A. Mohamed, A.M. Hemeida, A.A. Ibrahim, Comparison of different optimization techniques for optimal allocation of multiple distribution generation, in: 2018 International Conference on Innovative Trends in Computer Engineering (ITCE), Februry 2018, pp. 317–323. Available from: https://doi.org/10.1109/ITCE.2018.8316644.

[45] E. Mostafa, M. Abdel-Nasser, K. Mahmoud, Performance evaluation of metaheuristic optimization methods with mutation operators for combined economic and emission dispatch, in: 2017 Nineteenth International Middle East Power Systems Conference (MEPCON), December 2017, pp. 1004–1009. Available from: https://doi.org/10.1109/MEPCON.2017.8301304.

[46] X. Lai, D. Qiao, Y. Zheng, L. Zhou, A fuzzy state-of-charge estimation algorithm combining ampere-hour and an extended Kalman filter for li-ion batteries based on multi-model global identification, Appl. Sci. 8 (11) (2018) 2028. Available from: https://doi.org/10.3390/app8112028.

[47] L.M. Abualigah, A.T. Khader, E.S. Hanandeh, A hybrid strategy for krill herd algorithm with harmony search algorithm to improve the data clustering, Intell. Decis. Technol. 12 (1) (2018) 3−14. Available from: https://doi.org/10.3233/IDT-170318.

[48] L.M. Abualigah, A.T. Khader, E.S. Hanandeh, A.H. Gandomi, A novel hybridization strategy for krill herd algorithm applied to clustering techniques, Appl. Soft Comput. 60 (2017) 423−435. Available from: https://doi.org/10.1016/j.asoc.2017.06.059.

[49] L.M. Abualigah, A.T. Khader, E.S. Hanandeh, A combination of objective functions and hybrid krill herd algorithm for text document clustering analysis, Eng. Appl. Artif. Intell. 73 (2018) 111−125. Available from: https://doi.org/10.1016/j.engappai.2018.05.003.

[50] M. Shehab, A.T. Khader, M. Al-Betar, New selection schemes for particle swarm optimization, IEEJ Trans. Electron. Inf. Syst. 136 (12) (2016) 1706−1711. Available from: https://doi.org/10.1541/ieejeiss.136.1706.

16

Gradient-based optimizer: analysis and application of the Berry software product

Laith Abualigah[1,2,3,4,5,6,7], Laith Elkhalaifa[4], Abiodun M. Ikotun[8],
Faisal AL-Saqqar[2], Mohammad El-Bashir[2], Putra Sumari[4],
Mohammad Shehab[9], Diaa Salama Abd Elminaam[10,11],
Absalom E. Ezugwu[12]

*[1]HOURANI CENTER FOR APPLIED SCIENTIFIC RESEARCH, AL-AHLIYYA AMMAN
UNIVERSITY, AMMAN, JORDAN [2]COMPUTER SCIENCE DEPARTMENT, AL AL-BAYT
UNIVERSITY, MAFRAQ, JORDAN [3]MEU RESEARCH UNIT, MIDDLE EAST UNIVERSITY,
AMMAN, JORDAN [4]SCHOOL OF COMPUTER SCIENCES, UNIVERSITI SAINS MALAYSIA,
PULAU PINANG, MALAYSIA [5]SCHOOL OF ENGINEERING AND TECHNOLOGY, SUNWAY
UNIVERSITY MALAYSIA, PETALING JAYA, MALAYSIA [6]ARTIFICIAL INTELLIGENCE AND
SENSING TECHNOLOGIES (AIST) RESEARCH CENTER, UNIVERSITY OF TABUK, TABUK,
SAUDI ARABIA [7]DEPARTMENT OF ELECTRICAL AND COMPUTER ENGINEERING,
LEBANESE AMERICAN UNIVERSITY, BYBLOS, LEBANON [8]UNIVERSITY OF KWAZULU-
NATAL, PIETERMARITZBURG CAMPUS, POTCHEFSTROOM, SOUTH AFRICA [9]COLLEGE OF
COMPUTER SCIENCES AND INFORMATICS, AMMAN ARAB UNIVERSITY, AMMAN,
JORDAN [10]INFORMATION SYSTEMS DEPARTMENT, FACULTY OF COMPUTERS AND
ARTIFICIAL INTELLIGENCE, BENHA UNIVERSITY, BENHA, EGYPT [11]COMPUTER SCIENCE
DEPARTMENT, FACULTY OF COMPUTER SCIENCE, MISR INTERNATIONAL UNIVERSITY,
CAIRO, EGYPT [12]UNIT FOR DATA SCIENCE AND COMPUTING, NORTH-WEST UNIVERSITY,
POTCHEFSTROOM, SOUTH AFRICA*

16.1 Introduction

Among the most essential problems in software applied research is software test suite optimization. One of the most time-consuming and expensive phases of the software development process is software testing [1]. It takes a long time and accounts for 55% of the cost of software development [1,2]. It takes hard work to design test automation technologies that can minimize software development cost and time. To create appropriate test data from unsuitable data, a

Metaheuristic Optimization Algorithms. DOI: https://doi.org/10.1016/B978-0-443-13925-3.00002-9

testing system is required. A system for comparing the outputs on a given set of outputs is all that testing a software application entails [3]. The software testing method does not guarantee that the product is fault-free, but it does assure that the error is satisfactory.

Software engineering is a branch of computer science that focuses on the creation, operation, modification, and maintenance of software components. Software engineering is separated into several subdisciplines. It is a critical component of software quality [4]. Errors and defects are discovered via testing. Testing is a procedure that is both static and dynamic. Unit testing, black-box testing, white-box testing, system testing, and other types of testing are all types of testing [5]. The key steps are software creation, verification, and validation. The primary goal of the verification is to ensure that the system is meeting expectations. The goal of validation is to see if the system operates as expected by the client. Selecting test inputs, running the inputs through the program for testing, and assessing the validity of the expected outputs are all part of software testing. Throughout the software development life cycle, software testing is performed to find faults as early as possible and to guarantee that current software does not break the program.

The two main answers to the problem of test case optimization are selection and prioritizing of test cases. Any selection algorithm can be used for prioritization. The selection of the smallest subset of test cases is known as test suite reduction [2]. To make the quality assurance work parallel with automation testing, gradient-based optimization (GBO) will be utilized to determine the expected failed test cases by heuristic mechanisms from the start of the execution run. In the case of Berry software testing process, GBO will save time, effort, and resources compared to the current process (sequence test casing execution).

16.2 Literature review

16.2.1 Gradient-based optimization

16.2.1.1 Theoretical background

Normally, optimization methods can be used to deal with many problems in the sciences, as presented in [6−14]. In general, optimization approaches can be classified into two parts: approaches based on gradients, such as the LM algorithm [15], gradient descent [16], and Newton's method [17], and genetic algorithms, as well as current nongradient-based approaches (i.e., metaheuristic algorithms (MAs) [18], simulated annealing [19], water evaporation optimization [20], teaching−learning-based optimization [21], self-defense mechanism of plants algorithm [22], Henry gas solubility optimization [23], and Harris hawks optimization [24]. To solve optimization problems, gradient-based approaches have been widely used. Using gradient-based approaches to discover the best solution, it is necessary to locate an extreme point when the gradient is equal to zero. The conjugate direction is one of the gradient approaches [25]. This is the foundation of Newton's approach. In most other optimization approaches, including gradient methods, a search direction is chosen and the search proceeds in that direction in pursuit of the best solution [26]. In order to investigate the search directions in these approaches, the derivatives of the objective function as well as the restrictions must be determined. The following are the two main drawbacks of this form of optimization:

(1) The convergence rate is really sluggish.
(2) There is no assurance that the right idea will be found [27]

Some initial points (i.e., initial population) are randomly created in the second group nullI. There is a search direction for each point. This is defined by data gathered from prior outcomes. The search parameters must be updated to continue the optimization technique until the convergence condition is fulfilled. Various engineering issues have been improved using such optimization approaches (i.e., MAs such as Dwarf Mongoose Optimization Algorithm [28], Grasshopper Optimisation Algorithm [29], Improved Dwarf Mongoose Optimization Algorithm [30], and Prairie Dog Optimization Algorithm [31]). While gradient-based approaches tend to converge into local optima, MAs give greater robustness in finding global optima. Nongradient-based approaches, on the other hand, necessitate greater processing power, particularly for situations involving strong solution space. As a result, developing an optimization method that uses a gradient method to skip impossible points and advance toward the possible area while also taking advantage of the characteristics of population-based optimization methods will be worthwhile. As a result, one of the study's distinctive aspects is that it combines the concepts of gradient-based and population-based methods to create an optimized and effective algorithm that addresses the shortcomings of earlier methods.

16.2.1.2 Gradient-based optimization

Within the proposed GBO, gradient- and population-based approaches are integrated. Newton's technique of exploring the search area using a collection of vectors and two primary operators [i.e., gradient search rule [GSR] and localized fleeing operators] specifies the search direction. In optimization issues, the objective function minimization is taken into account.

16.2.1.2.1 Initialization
A set of decision variables is used in an optimization problem, restrictions, and a goal-oriented function. A parameter for transitioning from exploration to exploitation (x) and a probability rate are among the GBO's control parameters. Depending on the problem difficulty, the number of iterations and population size are determined. Each member of the population is referred to as a "vector" in the proposed algorithm. As a result, in a D-dimensional search space, the GBO includes N vectors. As a result, a vector may be written as

$$y_{a,b} = [y_{a,1}, y_{a,2}, \ldots, y_{a,b}], \quad a = 1, 2, \ldots, A, \quad b = 1, 2, \ldots, B \tag{16-1}$$

In most cases, the GBO's starting vectors are produced at random in the D-dimensional solution space, which is specified as:

$$y_a = y_{\min} + r \, and_{(0,1)} \times (y_{\max} - y_{\min}) \tag{16-2}$$

where $y_{\min}$ and $y_{\max}$ are the bounds of variabley, $and \, r \, and_{(0,1)}$ is a random number in[0, 1].

16.2.1.2.2 Gradient search rule

The movement of vectors is regulated in the GSR to effectively search in the possible range and get better locations. With the goal of increasing investigation and speeding rate of convergence of the GBO, the GSR is a suggested approach based on the gradient-based technique [17].

Most optimization problems are not distinguishable; hence, as an alternative to direct function derivation, a numerical gradient approach is used. In general, the gradient-based technique starts with a predicted initial guess and advances across a gradient-specified direction to the next place. The GSR can be calculated using

$$y_{n+1} = y_n - \frac{f(y_n)}{f'(y_n)} \tag{16-3}$$

The Taylor series must be used to calculate the very first differential.

The Taylor series for functions $f(y + \Delta y)$ and $f(y - \Delta y)$ can be respectively expressed as

$$f(y + \Delta y) = f(y) + f'(y_0)\Delta y + \frac{f''(y_0)\Delta y^2}{2!} + \frac{f^{(3)}(y_0)\Delta y^3}{3!} + \ldots \tag{16-4}$$

$$f(y - \Delta y) = f(y) - f^1(y_0)\Delta y + \frac{f^2(y_0)\Delta y^2}{2!} - \frac{f^3(y_0)\Delta y^3}{3!} + \ldots \tag{16-5}$$

From the simplified Eqs. (16–4) and (16–5), the following central differencing formula yields the first-order derivative [32]:

$$f'(y) = \frac{f(y + \Delta y) - f(y - \Delta y)}{2\Delta y} \tag{16-6}$$

Based on Eqs. (16–3) and (16–6), the new position (y_{n+1}) is specified as follows:

$$y_{n+1} = y_n - \frac{2\Delta y \times f(y_n)}{f(y_n + \Delta y) - f(y_n - \Delta y)} \tag{16-7}$$

Because the GSR is the core component of the suggested algorithm to accommodate the population-based search, several changes are required. Concerning Eq. (16–7), the nearby places of y_n are $y_n + \Delta y$ and $y_n - \Delta y$, as shown in Fig. 16–1. Two more places (vectors) in the population are used to replace these adjacent positions in the GBO. Because $f(y)$ is a problem of minimization, as shown in Fig. 16–1, position $y_n + \Delta y$ has a worse fitness than y_n, while $y_n - \Delta y$ is better than y_n.

As a result, the GBO algorithm replaces position $y_n - \Delta y$ with y_{worst}; this is a worse situation in the vicinity of y_n. Furthermore, the suggested technique makes use of the position (y_n), rather than its fitness $(f(y_n))$, because using the fitness of a position in the computation takes longer. After that, the suggested GSR is written as follows:

$$GSR = randa \times \frac{2\Delta y \times y_a}{(y_{worst} - y_{best} + \varepsilon)} \tag{16-8}$$

where $randn$ is a randomly generated number with a normal curve, and ε is a tiny number in the [0, 0.1] range. During the optimization process, the best and worst option are y_{worst} and y_{best}.

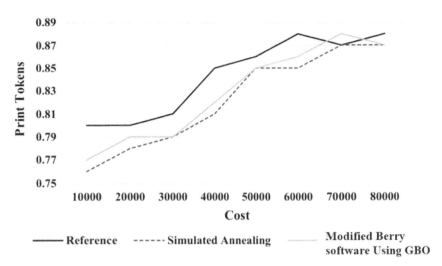

FIGURE 16–1 Print tokens for Berry software using gradient-based optimization.

Eq. (16−8) can aid in updating the present solution's position. To increase the projected GBO's search ability and find a middle ground between global exploration and exploitation (local), the GSR is altered by the addition of a random parameter ρ_1 in Eq. (16−8), as specified below.

In general, an optimization algorithm is required to balance global exploration with local exploitation in order to discover interesting areas in the dimensional search space and correlated positively on the optimal point.

16.3 Results and discussion

The effectiveness of the GBO algorithm is assessed using eight mathematical functions that have been used extensively in earlier research. Unimodal functions (f1−f6) and multimodal functions (f7−f8) may be found. Table 16−1 provides a quick overview of all functions. It is worth noting that optimizing hybrid and composite mathematical functions is more difficult and time-consuming than optimizing unimodal and multimodal functions. As a result, it is more appropriate to assess the algorithms' skills in tackling complicated real-world optimization issues. Therefore, in the case of software test suite optimization, GBO was utilized to determine the expected failed test cases by heuristic mechanisms from the start of the execution run. In the case of the Berry software testing process, experiments cost between $10,000 and $80,000. GBO showed that it saves time, effort, and resources compared to the current process (sequence test casing execution). Table 16−2 shows the test suites used in Berry software in terms of size, tokens, and space, correspondingly.

When comparing the modified Berry software using GBO to the standard one, it can be shown that the modified Berry software has higher print tokens by 1.31% for 10,000 dollars, no change for 30,000 dollars, no change for 50,000 dollars, and 1.14% for 70,000 dollars. When compared to the reference, the modified Software has reduced print tokens by 3.82% for 10,000 dollars, 2.5% for 30,000 dollars, 1.17% for 50,000 dollars, and 1.14% for 70,000 dollars. Please refer to Fig. 16−1.

Table 16–1 Print tokens for modified Berry software using gradient-based optimization.

Cost	Reference	Standard	Using GBO
10,000	0.8	0.76	0.77
20,000	0.8	0.78	0.79
30,000	0.81	0.79	0.79
40,000	0.85	0.81	0.82
50,000	0.86	0.85	0.85
60,000	0.88	0.85	0.86
70,000	0.87	0.87	0.88
80,000	0.88	0.87	0.87

Table 16–2 Space for modified Berry software using gradient-based optimization.

Cost	Reference	Standard	Using GBO
10,000	0.77	0.76	0.76
20,000	0.78	0.76	0.76
30,000	0.8	0.77	0.77
40,000	0.82	0.81	0.81
50,000	0.84	0.82	0.82
60,000	0.86	0.84	0.85
70,000	0.86	0.84	0.84
80,000	0.87	0.86	0.86

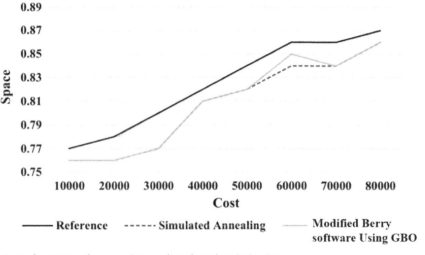

FIGURE 16–2 Space for Berry software using gradient-based optimization.

As shown in Fig. 16–2, when comparing the modified Berry software using GBO to the standard one, it can be seen that the modified Berry software has the same space for 10,000, 30,000, 50,000, and 70,000 dollars, respectively. When compared to the reference, the modified Berry software using GBO saves 1.31% for 10,000 dollars, 3.82% for 30,000 dollars, 2.41% for 50,000 dollars, and 2.35% for 70,000 dollars.

16.4 Conclusion

The selection of test cases is a reverting back testing approach that aims to pick a fresh batch of test cases based on the criteria of interest. The approach will be used to reduce the size of the test suite. GBO tries to choose a subset of tests in order to eliminate redundant or undesired test data and increase problem identification. The GBO is reformulated as a multiobjective problem in this chapter, with the cost of execution and code coverage as objective functions. For upgrading the Berry software, a hybrid approach based on GBO and high gradient descent is suggested. When compared to the standard Berry software, the updated Berry software has a greater number of print tokens by around 1.31% for 10,000 dollars, no difference for 30,000 dollars, no change for 50,000 dollars, and about 1.14% for 70,000 dollars. When opposed to the reference, the modified Berry program has a reduced number of print tokens by 3.82% for 10,000 dollars, around 2.5% for 30,000 dollars, about 1.17% for 50,000 dollars, and finally about 1.14% for 70,000 dollars.

References

[1] P. Thakur, T. Varma, A survey on test case selection using optimization techniques in software testing, Int. J. Innov. Sci. Eng. Technol. (2015) 593−596.

[2] T.M. Nithya, S. Chitra, Soft computing-based semi-automated test case selection using gradient-based techniques, Soft Comput. 24 (17) (2020) 12981−12987. Available from: https://doi.org/10.1007/s00500-020-04719-9.

[3] I. Ahmadianfar, O. Bozorg-Haddad, X. Chu, Gradient-based optimizer: a new metaheuristic optimization algorithm, Inf. Sci. (Ny). 540 (2020) 131−159. Available from: https://doi.org/10.1016/j.ins.2020.06.037.

[4] K. Pei, Y. Cao, J. Yang, S. Jana, DeepXplore: automated whitebox testing of deep learning systems, Proceedings of the 26th Symposium Operating Syst. Princ. (2017) 1−18. Available from: https://doi.org/10.1145/3132747.3132785.

[5] Y. Kim, J. Yoon, MaxAFL: maximizing code coverage with a gradient-based optimization technique, Electronics 10 (1) (2020) 11. Available from: https://doi.org/10.3390/electronics10010011.

[6] L. Abualigah, A. Diabat, C.L. Thanh, S. Khatir, Opposition-based Laplacian distribution with Prairie Dog optimization method for industrial engineering design problems, Comput. Methods Appl. Mech. Eng. 414 (2023) 116097.

[7] G. Hu, Y. Zheng, L. Abualigah, A.G. Hussien, DETDO: an adaptive hybrid dandelion optimizer for engineering optimization, Adv. Eng. Inform. 57 (2023) 102004.

[8] D. Izci, S. Ekinci, S. Mirjalili, L. Abualigah, An intelligent tuning scheme with a master/slave approach for efficient control of the automatic voltage regulator, Neural Comput. Appl. (2023) 1−17.

[9] H. Jia, C. Lu, D. Wu, C. Wen, H. Rao, L. Abualigah, An improved reptile search algorithm with ghost opposition-based learning for global optimization problems, J. Comput. Des. Eng. 10 (2023).

[10] A.H. Alharbi, A.A. Abdelhamid, A. Ibrahim, S.K. Towfek, N. Khodadadi, L. Abualigah, et al., Improved dipper-throated optimization for forecasting metamaterial design bandwidth for engineering applications, Biomimetics 8 (2) (2023) 241.

[11] S. Nama, A.K. Saha, S. Chakraborty, A.H. Gandomi, L. Abualigah, Boosting particle swarm optimization by backtracking search algorithm for optimization problems, Swarm Evolut. Comput. 79 (2023) 101304.

[12] M. Zare, M. Ghasemi, A. Zahedi, K. Golalipour, S.K. Mohammadi, S. Mirjalili, et al., A global best-guided firefly algorithm for engineering problems, J. Bionic Eng. (2023) 1−30.

[13] D. Wu, C. Wen, H. Rao, H. Jia, Q. Liu, L. Abualigah, Modified reptile search algorithm with multi-hunting coordination strategy for global optimization problems, Math. Biosci. Eng. 20 (6) (2023) 10090−10134.

[14] L. Abualigah, D. Falcone, A. Forestiero, Swarm intelligence to Face IoT challenges, Comput. Intell. Neurosci. (2023) 2023.

[15] J.J. Moré, The Levenberg-Marquardt Algorithm: Implementation and Theory (1978) 105−116. Available from: https://doi.org/10.1007/BFb0067700.

[16] S.O.H. Madgwick, A.J.L. Harrison, R. Vaidyanathan, Estimation of IMU and MARG orientation using a gradient descent algorithm, 2011 IEEE International Conference on Rehabilitation Robotics (2011) 1−7. Available from: https://doi.org/10.1109/ICORR.2011.5975346.

[17] T.J. Ypma, Historical development of the Newton−Raphson method, SIAM Rev. 37 (4) (1995) 531−551. Available from: https://doi.org/10.1137/1037125.

[18] J.H. Holland, Genetic Algorithms 267 (1) (1992) 66−73. Available from: https://doi.org/10.2307/24939139.

[19] E. Aarts, J. Korst, and W. Michiels, Simulated annealing, in: Search Methodologies, Boston, MA: Springer US, pp. 187−210. Available form: https://doi.org/10.1007/0-387-28356-0_7.

[20] A. Kaveh, T. Bakhshpoori, Water evaporation optimization: a novel physically inspired optimization algorithm, Comput. Struct. 167 (2016) 69−85. Available from: https://doi.org/10.1016/j.compstruc.2016.01.008.

[21] R.V. Rao, V.J. Savsani, D.P. Vakharia, Teaching−learning-based optimization: A novel method for constrained mechanical design optimization problems, Comput. Des. 43 (3) (2011) 303−315. Available from: https://doi.org/10.1016/j.cad.2010.12.015.

[22] C. Caraveo, F. Valdez, O. Castillo, A new optimization meta-heuristic algorithm based on self-defense mechanism of the plants with three reproduction operators, Soft Comput. 22 (15) (2018) 4907−4920. Available from: https://doi.org/10.1007/s00500-018-3188-8.

[23] F.A. Hashim, E.H. Houssein, M.S. Mabrouk, W. Al-Atabany, S. Mirjalili, Henry gas solubility optimization: a novel physics-based algorithm, Futur. Gener. Comput. Syst. 101 (2019) 646−667. Available from: https://doi.org/10.1016/j.future.2019.07.015.

[24] A.A. Heidari, S. Mirjalili, H. Faris, I. Aljarah, M. Mafarja, H. Chen, Harris hawks optimization: algorithm and applications, Futur. Gener. Comput. Syst. 97 (2019) 849−872. Available from: https://doi.org/10.1016/j.future.2019.02.028.

[25] C.C. Aggarwal, P.S. Yu, J. Han, J. Wang, A framework for clustering evolving data streams, Proc. 2003 VLDB Conf. 29th Int. Conf. Very Large Databases (2003) 81−92. Available from: https://doi.org/10.1016/B978-012722442-8/50016-1.

[26] N. Shahidi, H. Esmaeilzadeh, M. Abdollahi, E. Ebrahimi, C. Lucas, Self-adaptive memetic algorithm: an adaptive conjugate gradient approach, IEEE Conf. Cybern. Intell. Syst. (2004) 6−11. Available from: https://doi.org/10.1109/ICCIS.2004.1460378.

[27] F. Salajegheh, E. Salajegheh, PSOG: enhanced particle swarm optimization by a unit vector of first and second order gradient directions, Swarm EComput. 46 (2019) 28−51. Available from: https://doi.org/10.1016/j.swevo.2019.01.010.

[28] J.O. Agushaka, A.E. Ezugwu, L. Abualigah, Dwarf Mongoose optimization algorithm, Comput. Methods Appl. Mech. Eng. 391 (2022). Available from: https://doi.org/10.1016/j.cma.2022.114570.

[29] J.O. Agushaka, A.E. Ezugwu, L. Abualigah, Gazelle optimization algorithm: a novel nature-inspired meta-heuristic optimizer, Neural Comput. Appl. 35 (5) (2023) 4099−4131. Available from: https://doi.org/10.1007/s00521-022-07854-6.

[30] J.O. Agushaka, A.E. Ezugwu, O.N. Olaide, O. Akinola, R.A. Zitar, L. Abualigah, Improved Dwarf Mongoose optimization for constrained engineering design problems, J. Bionic Eng. (2022). Available from: https://doi.org/10.1007/s42235-022-00316-8.

[31] A.E. Ezugwu, J.O. Agushaka, L. Abualigah, S. Mirjalili, A.H. Gandomi, Prairie Dog optimization algorithm, Neural Comput. Appl. 34 (22) (2022) 20017−20065. Available from: https://doi.org/10.1007/s00521-022-07530-9.

[32] F. Osuský, Š. Čerba, J. Lüley, B. Vrban, G. Farkas, V. Slugeň, Multi-group transient numerical analysis of slab nuclear reactor.

17

A review of krill herd algorithm: optimization and its applications

Laith Abualigah[1,2,3,4,5,6,7], Mohammad Al-Zyod[8], Abiodun M. Ikotun[9], Mohammad Shehab[8], Mohammed Otair[10], Absalom E. Ezugwu[11], Essam Said Hanandeh[12], Ali Raza[13], El-Sayed M. El-kenawy[14]

[1]*ARTIFICIAL INTELLIGENCE AND SENSING TECHNOLOGIES (AIST) RESEARCH CENTER, UNIVERSITY OF TABUK, TABUK, SAUDI ARABIA* [2]*HOURANI CENTER FOR APPLIED SCIENTIFIC RESEARCH, AL-AHLIYYA AMMAN UNIVERSITY, AMMAN, JORDAN* [3]*MEU RESEARCH UNIT, MIDDLE EAST UNIVERSITY, AMMAN, JORDAN* [4]*SCHOOL OF COMPUTER SCIENCES, UNIVERSITI SAINS MALAYSIA, PULAU PINANG, MALAYSIA* [5]*SCHOOL OF ENGINEERING AND TECHNOLOGY, SUNWAY UNIVERSITY MALAYSIA, PETALING JAYA, MALAYSIA* [6]*COMPUTER SCIENCE DEPARTMENT, AL AL-BAYT UNIVERSITY, MAFRAQ, JORDAN* [7]*DEPARTMENT OF ELECTRICAL AND COMPUTER ENGINEERING, LEBANESE AMERICAN UNIVERSITY, BYBLOS, LEBANON* [8]*COLLEGE OF COMPUTER SCIENCES AND INFORMATICS, AMMAN ARAB UNIVERSITY, AMMAN, JORDAN* [9]*UNIVERSITY OF KWAZULU-NATAL, PIETERMARITZBURG CAMPUS, POTCHEFSTROOM, SOUTH AFRICA* [10]*KHAWARIZMI UNIVERSITY TECHNICAL COLLEGE, AMMAN, JORDAN* [11]*UNIT FOR DATA SCIENCE AND COMPUTING, NORTH-WEST UNIVERSITY, POTCHEFSTROOM, SOUTH AFRICA* [12]*DEPARTMENT OF COMPUTER INFORMATION SYSTEM, ZARQA UNIVERSITY, ZARQA, JORDAN* [13]*INSTITUTE OF COMPUTER SCIENCE, KHWAJA FAREED UNIVERSITY OF ENGINEERING AND INFORMATION TECHNOLOGY, RAHIM YAR KHAN, PAKISTAN* [14]*DEPARTMENT OF COMMUNICATIONS AND ELECTRONICS, DELTA HIGHER INSTITUTE OF ENGINEERING AND TECHNOLOGY, MANSOURA, EGYPT*

17.1 Introduction

The objective function used in global optimization issues as often as possible features a big computing complexity, conditionality, and a nonclear scene. Such jobs are immensely useful, and a variety of methodologies have been proposed as a foundation for solving them. Heuristic optimization and decision-making approaches are actively developing bioinspired algorithms. New bioinspired algorithms that take into account information about the search

Metaheuristic Optimization Algorithms. DOI: https://doi.org/10.1016/B978-0-443-13925-3.00017-0

that is the problem-oriented region for the best results, as well as the search history, are currently the most promising direction [1].

An optimization technique inspired by nature called the krill herd (KH) has been successfully employed to solve a range of hard optimization issues. The performance of the KH algorithm can be impacted by its weak exploration (diversification) ability on an irregular basis [2].

Normally, optimization methods can be used to deal with many problems in the sciences, as presented in refs [3–12]. This study is a survey of the publications on the krill heard optimization algorithm; seven publications were analyzed and classified into three categories (medical, network, classification and electric power, image segmentation, and data intelligence).

The remainder of this chapter is organized as follows: Section 17.2 presents the KH algorithm procedure, and Section 17.3 summarizes related work. The final result and some future work are discussed in Section 17.4.

17.2 Krill herd algorithm procedure

17.2.1 Krill swarms herding behavior

Diverse marine animal species form clumps that are underdispersed and nonrandomly formed. A great number of researches have been attempted to understand the fundamental mechanisms that drive the generation of these structures. Feeding abilities, improved reproduction, predator protection, and environmental variables are among the key mechanisms recognized. Some mathematical models have been built based on experimental results to examine the relative contributions of various systems.

One of the most well-studied marine organisms is Antarctic krill. On times of hours to days, and in space, KHs are aggregations with no parallel direction dimensions of 10 to 100 seconds of meters. This species' propensity to generate enormous swarms is one of its most distinguishing features.

Several researches have been undertaken over the last three decades to learn about krill ecology and distribution. Although the mechanisms that control KH dispersal remain a mystery, to explain how KHs form, conceptual models have been proposed.

Krill swarms are the species' primary unit of organization, according to the findings of such conceptual frameworks. In order to know the development of krill swarms, as well as the proximate causes and elements that constitute it, it is important to separate the adaptive benefits of aggregation formation (ultimate impacts). When predators attack krill, like as seals, penguins, or seagulls, they take individual krill with them, increasing the density of krill and obtaining food. This mechanism was taken into account in the current study to offer a new metaheuristic algorithm for tackling global optimization issues. The krill's density-dependent attraction (growing density) and the search for food (high-food-concentration zones) were employed as goals, leading to the krill herding around the global minima. If a krill seeks for the highest density and food in this process, it travels toward the best solution. That is, the goal function decreases the separation between foods, the high density grows as the distance between the meal, and the high density grows. In general, when adopting for a single target, multiobjective herding behavior, some coefficients should be computed. The coefficients in this study were based on specialist experiments on krill behavior reviewed in the literature as well as a trial investigation.

17.2.2 Standard of krill herd

17.2.2.1 Movement induced by other instances (Krill)

$$\frac{dX_i}{dt} = N_i + F_i + D_i$$

where N_i indicates the movement caused by other krills, F_i indicates foraging movement, and D_i denotes physical dissemination of the krill.

17.2.2.2 Foraging activity

$$N_i^{\text{new}} = N^{\text{max}} \alpha_i + \omega_n N_i^{\text{old}}$$

where

$$\alpha_i = \alpha_i^{\text{local}} + \alpha_i^{\text{target}}$$

In addition, N^{max} represents the induced maximum speed. ω_n is the mass of inertia caused by the movement in the interval ([0, 1)]. N_i^{old} is the most recent movement that has been caused, α_i^{local} is the effect that neighbors have on the local area, and α_i^{target} is the effect of the best krill person on the desired direction

$$\alpha_i^{\text{local}} = \sum_{J=1}^{NN} \hat{k}_{IJ} \hat{X}_{IJ}$$

$$\hat{X}_{ij} = \frac{X_j - X_i}{\|X_j - X_i\| + \varepsilon}$$

$$pc\hat{K}_{ij} = \frac{K_i - K_j}{K^{\text{worst}} - K^{\text{best}}}$$

where $K^{\text{worst}} - K^{\text{best}}$ is the krill individuals' highest and poorest fitness values so far; Ki reflects the value of fitness or objective function of a krill; K_j is the *j*th ($j = 1, 2, \ldots, NN$) neighbor's fitness, X depicts the locations that are linked; and NN stands for the number of neighbors.

A positive number is not too large. It is used to avoid singularities.

$$d_{s.i} = \frac{1}{5N} \sum_{j=1}^{N} \|X_i - X_j\|$$

where $d_{s,i}$ is the ith krill individual's sensing distance and N is the total count of krill individuals.

$$\propto_i^{\text{target}} = C^{\text{best}} \hat{K}_{i,\text{best}} \hat{X}_{i,\text{best}}$$

where C^{best} is the krill with the best physical condition to the ith krill individual is effective degree is the ith krill individual.

$$C^{\text{best}} = 2\left(rand + \frac{1}{I_{\text{max}}}\right)$$

The actual iteration number is I, while rand is a random value between 0 and 1 that is utilized to improve the view, and I_{max} is the number of iterations that can be performed.

$$F_i = V_F \beta_i + \omega_F F_i^{\text{old}}$$

where

$$\beta_i = \beta_i^{\text{food}} + \beta_i^{\text{best}}$$

V_F is the rate of foraging in the final foraging movement, ω_F is the foraging motion's inertia weight in the range [0,1], β_i^{food} represents food appealing, and β_i^{best} is the consequence of the ith krill's most fit condition as yet.

$$X^{food} = \frac{\sum_{i=1}^{N} \frac{i}{k_i} X_i}{\sum_{i=1}^{N} \frac{1}{K_i}}$$

$$\beta_i^{\text{food}} = C^{food} \hat{K}_{i,food} \hat{X}_{i,food}$$

where C^{food} is the coefficient of food. The impact of food on krill herding diminishes over time.

$$C^{food} = 2\left(1 - \frac{1}{I_{\text{max}}}\right) \beta_i^{\text{best}} = \hat{K}_{i,\text{best}} \hat{X}_{i,\text{best}}$$

where $\hat{K}_{i,\text{best}}$ is the ith krill individual's best previously visited position

$$D_i = D^{\text{max}\delta}$$

where D^{max} is the greatest rate of diffusion, and δ is a directional vector at random with arrays of random values ranging from -1 to 1.

$$D_i = D^{\text{max}}\left(1 - \frac{1}{I_{\text{max}}}\right)^{\delta} X_i(t + \Delta t) = X_i(t) + \Delta t \frac{dX_i}{dt} \Delta t = C_t \sum_{j=1}^{NV} (UB_j - LB_j)$$

The number of variables in total is NV, and LB_j and UB_j are top and bottom boundaries, respectively, of the jth variable ($j = 1, 2, \ldots,$ and NV). As a result, the search space is revealed by the absolute of their subtraction.

$$X_{i,m} = \begin{cases} X_{r,m} rand_{i,m} & {}^{< Cr} \\ X_{i,m} & else \end{cases} Cr = 0.2 \hat{K}_{i,best}$$

where $r \, \varepsilon$ is the crossover expectation. With this, new zero is the global best. At crossover probability, it climbs as fitness drops.

$$X_{i,m} = \begin{cases} X_{gbes,m + \mu(X_{p,m} - X_{q,m}) rand_{i,m}} & {}^{< Mu} \\ X_{i.m} & else \end{cases} Mu = 0.05 / \hat{K}_{i,best}$$

where p, q, and μ are numbers between 0 and 1 [13].

17.2.3 Krill herd algorithm

The KH algorithm is shown in Fig. 17−1.

17.3 Related work

For detecting breast problems on a regular basis, parameters of the profound belief system improved using the chaotic KH optimization (KHO) algorithm are used to categorize breast masses:

The masses in mammography pictures are classified using a variety of deep-learning approaches [14]. However, the current approach is insufficiently precise. This publication provides an effective framework for breast and cancer picture classification based on the deep belief network (DBN) and the chaotic KHO method for the categorization of breast lumps in mammography pictures for the categorization of masses in mammography images. To remove undesirable noise and artifacts, the input mammography pictures were first pre-processed using the adjusted dynamic range compression with phase preservation method; these preprocessed images were then utilized to determine if the lump in mammography images was normal, benign, or malignant using the DBN.

When compared to the existing methods such as the flame optimization for moths [15], an extreme learning machine classifier is created. The salp swarm algorithm is a chaotic algorithm with kernel extreme learning machine classifier and a fruit fly optimization strategy for an extreme learning machine classifier. The krill swarm DBN optimization algorithm achieves a high precision of 44.5%, 33.42%, 55.23%, and 62.35% [16].

Optimization of the BP neural network model by the chaotic KH algorithm: The kidney bean was chosen as the study's subject. As experimental parameters, row spacing, fertilizer treatment, and planting density were used, production was used as a response indicator. The KH algorithm and chaos theory were BP's neural network, which was given a boost. The minimum training error was chosen as a goal. Variables were weight and threshold in the BP

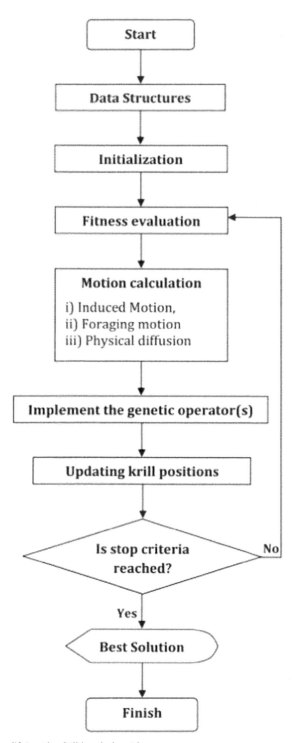

FIGURE 17–1 Flowchart simplifying the frill herd algorithm.

neural network optimization model. The BP neural network prediction model was developed by using the KH algorithm, which is chaotic. The outcomes of this study can be used to create a new strategy for predicting and optimizing comparable grain production models [17].

For sentiment text analytics, using the KH algorithm, a fuzzy rough set nearest neighbor classification model is optimized. In recent years, social networks such as Facebook have grown in popularity, allowing users to communicate their emotions and opinions. The emotions are classified. Displayed content on social media is useful in a variety of fields, including politics, e-commerce, and social good. Several studies concentrating on sentiment and emotion analysis have been undertaken previously. These studies mostly focused on single-label classification, ignoring the relationship between distinct emotions displayed by a person. The simulation findings revealed that the suggested FRSNN-KH algorithm outperformed the other approaches in numerous dimensions [18].

Fuzzy extended KHO with a quantum bat algorithm for cluster-based outing in mobile adhoc networks: MANET is made up of a collection of self-contained mobile nodes that move about and communicate via wireless networks. Clustering [19] and routing are two common energy-saving approaches that can viewed as an NP-hard issue that can solved using computational intelligence algorithms. The nodes' mobility causes frequent link failures and low energy efficiency. This research introduces cluster-based routing; a novel fuzzy extended KHO method based on quantum bat (FEKHO-QBA) was developed. MANETs are used to achieve excellent energy efficiency and network connectivity. A series of experiments were conducted to determine the FEKHO-QBA algorithm's efficacy in terms of several performance measures, and the results revealed the algorithm's superiority over the comparison approaches [20].

Using the stud KH method through a radial distribution system, an optimum multiobjective optimization location and scale of many distributed generation (DG) deployments are determined. In this study, the KH algorithm was utilized to discover the right size and location for DG units in a radial distribution system. In recent years, DG in the electric power industry has grown increasingly significant. At various load levels, the approach has been evaluated with DG placement radial systems IEEE 33, 69, and 94 bus routes. The simulation results were compared to those produced using different approaches. According to the comparison, the proposed method gives a better solution for optimal DG quicker convergence placement in the radial distribution system [21].

Multilevel thresholding for image segmentation using the KHO algorithm: For solving the picture segmentation problem, a novel multilevel thresholding approach based on a metaheuristic KHO algorithm was proposed in this study. The ideal threshold values are established by applying the KHO technique to maximize Kapoor's or Otsu's objective function. The proposed method minimizes the amount of time it takes to calculate the best multilevel thresholds. Various benchmark photos were used to demonstrate the applicability and computing efficiency of the KHO-based multilevel thresholding. To demonstrate the superior performance of the proposed method, a detailed comparison with the other existing bioinspired techniques based on multilevel thresholding techniques such as bacterial foraging, particle swarm optimization, genetic algorithm, and moth flame optimization was performed [22].

For the estimation of daily pan evaporation, the MLP-KH model, an integrated data-intelligence model based on multilayer perceptron (MLP) and KHO, was proposed [23]. The suggested model's potential compared to that of classical MLP and support vector machine models was determined using daily climatological data obtained from two meteorological stations in Iran's northern area. Different error and goodness-of-fit measures were used to evaluate the integrated and classical models. When compared to traditional models, the quantitative findings demonstrated the suggested MLP-KH model's ability to forecast daily pan evaporation. The integrated model produced the lowest root mean square error (RMSE) values of 0.725 and 0.855 mm/d for both weather stations, while the RMSE values for MLP were 1.088 and 1.197 [23].

17.4 Conclusion

We have discussed the KH, an ecologically inspired approach, to solve optimization difficulties. Based on an emulation of individual krill herding behavior, the KH algorithm was created. The shortest distances between individual krills and the herd's densest population establish the target function for krill migration. The approach now includes two adaptive genetic operators for a more detailed modeling of krill behavior, and the proposed technique validated using numerous benchmark issues was frequently utilized in the optimization area.

KH presented a swarm intelligence approach for optimization tasks by idealizing krill swarm behavior. The objective function employed in KH for krill movement is determined by the least distances between food and the largest herd density. One of the advantages of the KH algorithm over other algorithms is that it requires just a few control variables to govern.

In general, KH successfully and efficiently traverses the search space, although it may not always be able to avoid some local optima. As a result, it falls short of fully implementing global search in a particular decision space. KH's search is mostly reliant on random walks; as a result, it does not always converge to an acceptable solution [24].

KH can be applied in many problems in many domains such as machine language, clustering, energy, and task scheduling to obtain the best solution.

References

[1] R. Damaševičius, R. Maskeliūnas, Agent state flipping based hybridization of heuristic optimization algorithms: a case of bat algorithm and krill herd hybrid algorithm, Algorithms 14 (12) (2021) 358.

[2] L.M. Abualigah, A.T. Khader, E.S. Hanandeh, A.H. Gandomi, A novel hybridization strategy for krill herd algorithm applied to clustering techniques, Appl. Soft Comput. 60 (2017) 423–435.

[3] L. Abualigah, A. Diabat, C.L. Thanh, S. Khatir, Opposition-based Laplacian distribution with Prairie Dog optimization method for industrial engineering design problems, Comput. Methods Appl. Mech. Eng. 414 (2023) 116097.

[4] G. Hu, Y. Zheng, L. Abualigah, A.G. Hussien, DETDO: an adaptive hybrid dandelion optimizer for engineering optimization, Adv. Eng. Inform. 57 (2023) 102004.

[5] D. Izci, S. Ekinci, S. Mirjalili, L. Abualigah, An intelligent tuning scheme with a master/slave approach for efficient control of the automatic voltage regulator, Neural Comput. Appl. (2023) 1−17.

[6] H. Jia, C. Lu, D. Wu, C. Wen, H. Rao, L. Abualigah, An improved reptile search algorithm with ghost opposition-based learning for global optimization problems, J. Comput. Des. Eng. (2023). qwad048.

[7] A.H. Alharbi, A.A. Abdelhamid, A. Ibrahim, S.K. Towfek, N. Khodadadi, L. Abualigah, et al., Improved dipper-throated optimization for forecasting metamaterial design bandwidth for engineering applications, Biomimetics 8 (2) (2023) 241.

[8] S. Nama, A.K. Saha, S. Chakraborty, A.H. Gandomi, L. Abualigah, Boosting particle swarm optimization by backtracking search algorithm for optimization problems, Swarm Evolut. Comput. 79 (2023) 101304.

[9] M. Zare, M. Ghasemi, A. Zahedi, K. Golalipour, S.K. Mohammadi, S. Mirjalili, et al., A global best-guided firefly algorithm for engineering problems, J. Bionic Eng. (2023) 1−30.

[10] D. Wu, C. Wen, H. Rao, H. Jia, Q. Liu, L. Abualigah, Modified reptile search algorithm with multi-hunting coordination strategy for global optimization problems, Math. Biosci. Eng. 20 (6) (2023) 10090−10134.

[11] S. Ekinci, D. Izci, L. Abualigah, R.A. Zitar, A modified oppositional chaotic local search strategy based aquila optimizer to design an effective controller for vehicle cruise control system, J. Bionic Eng. (2023) 1−24.

[12] L. Abualigah, D. Falcone, A. Forestiero, Swarm intelligence to face IoT challenges, Comput. Intell. Neurosci. (2023) 2023.

[13] A.H. Gandomi, A.H. Alavi, Krill herd: a new bio-inspired optimization algorithm, Commun. Nonlinear Sci. Numer. Simul. 17 (12) (2012) 4831−4845.

[14] O.N. Oyelade, A.E. Ezugwu, M.S. Almutairi, A.K. Saha, L. Abualigah, H. Chiroma, A generative adversarial network for synthetization of regions of interest based on digital mammograms, Sci. Rep. 12 (1) (2022) 6166.

[15] S.K. Sahoo, A.K. Saha, A.E. Ezugwu, J.O. Agushaka, B. Abuhaija, A.R. Alsoud, et al., Moth flame optimization: theory, modifications, hybridizations, and applications, Arch. Comput. Methods Eng. 30 (1) (2023) 391−426.

[16] Akinola O.O., Absalom, Ezugwu E., Agushaka J.O., Raed, Zitar A., et al. Multiclass feature selection with metaheuristic optimization algorithms: a review. https://doi.org/10.1007/s00521-022-07705-4.

[17] L. Yu, L. Xie, C. Liu, S. Yu, Y. Guo, K. Yang, Optimization of BP neural network model by chaotic krill herd algorithm, Alex. Eng. J. 61 (12) (2022) 9769−9777.

[18] Krishanmoorthy S., Chai Y., Du Y., Zhou X., Zhang H., Liu H., et al. An optimization of fuzzy rough set nearest neighbor classification model using krill herd algorithm for sentiment text analytics, 2022, pp. 3−21.

[19] A.E. Ezugwu, A.M. Ikotun, O.O. Oyelade, L. Abualigah, J.O. Agushaka, C.I. Eke, et al., A comprehensive survey of clustering algorithms: state-of-the-art machine learning applications, taxonomy, challenges, and future research prospects, Eng. Appl. Artif. Intell. 110 (2022) 104743. Apr.

[20] M. Srinivas, M.R. Patnaik, Fuzzy extended krill herd optimization with quantum bat algorithm for cluster based routing in mobile adhoc networks, J. Appl. Sci. Eng. 25 (4) (2021) 733−740.

[21] S.A. Chithra Devi, K. Yamuna, M. Sornalatha, Multi-objective optimization of optimal placement and sizing of multiple DG placements in radial distribution system using stud krill herd algorithm, Neural Comput. Appl. 33 (20) (2021) 13619−13634.

[22] K.P. Baby Resma, M.S. Nair, Multilevel thresholding for image segmentation using krill herd optimization algorithm, J. King Saud. Univ. - Comput. Inf. Sci. 33 (5) (2021) 528−541.

[23] A. Ashrafzadeh, M.A. Ghorbani, S.M. Biazar, Z.M. Yaseen, Evaporation process modelling over northern Iran: application of an integrative data-intelligence model with the krill herd optimization algorithm, Hydrol. Sci. J. 64 (15) (2019) 1843−1856.

[24] G.-G. Wang, A.H. Gandomi, A.H. Alavi, An effective krill herd algorithm with migration operator in biogeography-based optimization, Appl. Math. Model. 38 (9−10) (2014) 2454−2462.

18

Salp swarm algorithm: survey, analysis, and new applications

Laith Abualigah[1,2,3,4,5,6,7], Worod Hawamdeh[8], Raed Abu Zitar[8], Shadi AlZu'bi[9], Ala Mughaid[10], Essam Said Hanandeh[11], Anas Ratib Alsoud[2], El-Sayed M. El-kenawy[12]

[1]ARTIFICIAL INTELLIGENCE AND SENSING TECHNOLOGIES (AIST) RESEARCH CENTER, UNIVERSITY OF TABUK, TABUK, SAUDI ARABIA [2]HOURANI CENTER FOR APPLIED SCIENTIFIC RESEARCH, AL-AHLIYYA AMMAN UNIVERSITY, AMMAN, JORDAN [3]MEU RESEARCH UNIT, MIDDLE EAST UNIVERSITY, AMMAN, JORDAN [4]SCHOOL OF COMPUTER SCIENCES, UNIVERSITI SAINS MALAYSIA, PULAU PINANG, MALAYSIA [5]SCHOOL OF ENGINEERING AND TECHNOLOGY, SUNWAY UNIVERSITY MALAYSIA, PETALING JAYA, MALAYSIA [6]COMPUTER SCIENCE DEPARTMENT, AL AL-BAYT UNIVERSITY, MAFRAQ, JORDAN [7]DEPARTMENT OF ELECTRICAL AND COMPUTER ENGINEERING, LEBANESE AMERICAN UNIVERSITY, BYBLOS, LEBANON [8]SORBONNE CENTER OF ARTIFICIAL INTELLIGENCE, SORBONNE UNIVERSITY-ABU DHABI, ABU DHABI, UNITED ARAB EMIRATES [9]FACULTY OF SCIENCE AND IT, AL-ZAYTOONAH UNIVERSITY OF JORDAN, AMMAN, JORDAN [10]DEPARTMENT OF INFORMATION TECHNOLOGY, FACULTY OF PRINCE AL-HUSSIEN BIN ABDULLAH II FOR IT, THE HASHEMITE UNIVERSITY, ZARQA, JORDAN [11]DEPARTMENT OF COMPUTER INFORMATION SYSTEM, ZARQA UNIVERSITY, ZARQA, JORDAN [12]DEPARTMENT OF COMMUNICATIONS AND ELECTRONICS, DELTA HIGHER INSTITUTE OF ENGINEERING AND TECHNOLOGY, MANSOURA, EGYPT

18.1 Introduction

Computer science and the coding and data fields are highly dependent on, and somewhat influenced by, the field of improvement. The area of improvement is based on the use of a variety of techniques. There are quite a few optimization solutions. However, there are areas for further improvement to lead the new algorithms to better results. In addition, some optimization methods are suitable for specific problems, and others work better for other types. As a result, while presenting a novel improvement strategy to focus on the quality of solutions when dealing with a variety of situations, strengths and weaknesses should be tested.

In recent years, because of their high efficiency and power in exploring and utilizing the field of search space, nature-inspired algorithms have been widely used to solve polynomial

Metaheuristic Optimization Algorithms. DOI: https://doi.org/10.1016/B978-0-443-13925-3.00009-1

(NP-hard) issues to advance mathematics and geometry (NP-hard). Among the methods inspired by nature, evolutionary algorithms (EAs) and swarm intelligence properties were most effectively applied to various challenging real-world domains and challenges. EAs approach the research process by adopting the breeding, intersection, and mutation factors of natural evolution, while swarm intelligence keeps pace with the collective intelligence of a group of organisms from nature such as ant colonies, bees, flock of birds, and school of fish, and these methods belong to the group of techniques improving artificial intelligence [1].

The stages of exploitation or exploration are preferred in the field of swarm exploration, as the basic and true capabilities of the swarm characteristics are done through the hybridization process, as it depends on merging the original algorithm with another algorithm that has better characteristics to reach better solutions in the next stages, and because of its robustness, simplicity, and ease of implementation, sea salmon-associated polyp (SALP) swarm algorithm (SSA) was chosen by the authors, and they suggested modifications for more precise tuning.

Because of the vast amount of data available and the processing capability of computer devices, there has been an interaction between metaheuristics inspired by machine learning and nature, which is one of the domains of artificial intelligence and a vital tool for data science. Machine learning models can be used to more efficiently detect patterns and generate predictions. Often, large numbers of unnecessary and redundant data are stored, which negatively affects the quality of machine learning performance and affects its accuracy and computational complexity. This phenomenon is usually known as the curse of the dimension phenomenon. Therefore, finding the important information that exists among a large set of data is very important and known as the challenge of reducing the dimension, as it is usually used in the preprocessing stage of data in machine learning, which is represented in two parts: the first section includes data extraction and it is derived from the raw data derivation of new variables, and the second section includes feature selection, which is done by selecting task variables only to reach additional use. The goal of feature selection is to find the subset of high-dimensional data by removing features that are useless and thus improving the accuracy in classification and improvement of prediction for the machine learning model.

Feature identification methods are divided into three basic groups: filter, envelope, and built-in. One of the most efficient methods is convolutional learning algorithms to evaluate the subset of features, which is done by training the model, but one of the disadvantages is that it requires more requirements from the computational point of view. Other filtering methods apply a scale to assign a score to subsets of features, that is, they do not depend on a training system and are characterized by being less computationally costly than the cover group or family, but they are based on creating a global group that is not set on a specific predictive model because it is not based on training the model. Finally, feature selection is implemented during model training by inline methods as part of the model-building process. The built-in methods are just as quick as the filter methods, but they are more accurate. The built-in methods fall in between wrappers and filters in terms of computational difficulty.

The science of investigative analysis of swarm intelligence is based on the application of algorithms inspired by nature, so that the success of aggregate methods for selecting features in machine learning, the intersection of machine learning, and metaheuristics at one point. If there are nf features in the data set, then the total number of 2nf subsets is present, and since nf is a large number of high dimensional data sets, this challenge is considered a difficult NP. Thus, concerning the fact that swarm intelligence has proven to be a powerful and effective enhancer for solving NP-hard challenges, its application as a cover feature selection method is straightforward.

Although current literature sources reveal various applications of swarm intelligence to feature selection, given the no free lunch theory, there is still potential for advancement in this field. For all datasets, no strategy effectively overcomes feature selection difficulties. The literature supports the necessity to focus on improving or proposing new algorithms to handle numerous challenges, including the feature selection challenge. Normally, optimization methods can be used to deal with many problems in the sciences, as presented in [2–12].

The goal of this research is to improve and enhance feature selection in machine learning using an optimized negative SSA, which is improved by including an additional mechanism and hybridization with metaanalysis of other known swarm intelligence. SSA is part of the metaheuristics intelligence family. Mirjalili et al. proposed the swarm in 2017. The suggested SSA is tested and assessed on a recognized hard-case test base for 30-Dimensional Functions of Congress on Evolutionary Computing 2013 (CEC2013), allowing for simple comparison of the obtained findings with the output of the Congress on Evolutionary Computing 2013 (CEC2013). After that, a shell-based method to feature selection and validation is used to adapt a wide range of state-of-the-art metaheuristics. Collective algorithms such as GA, ant colony optimization (ACO), PSO, DE, and ES are among the most well-known available today. The SSA and multipurpose SSA (MSSA) and their processes were studied for the optimization for engineering difficulties; the results of 20 different investigations were compiled and summarized. Metaheuristic optimization techniques like SSA may be used for a broad variety of optimization problems, from machine learning to engineering design to wireless networking to image processing [13].

In Section 18.2, we will discuss the mechanism that is associated with the algorithm. In Section 18.3, several ideas and a scientific model that has been suggested are presented. Additionally, suggestions for the SSA and the multiobjective SSA are included in this section.

In Section 18.4, we will show and analyze the qualitative and numerical results obtained by applying both approaches to a variety of benchmark functions. In Section 18.5, SSA and MSSA are combined to address a variety of challenging problems that occur in the real world.

18.2 Related work procedure of the algorithm

18.2.1 Single-objective optimization problems

Single-objective optimization (SOO) is the maximization or minimization of an objective function based on a single variable in the presence of a constraint or an uncontrolled condition. In the given objective function for SOO issues, there is only one variable. The function may change depending on the value of that variable. The function may have one or both of the following properties: (i) relative or local minimum, (ii) relative or local maximum, (iii) global or absolute minimum, (iv) global or absolute maximum. SOO's applicability is limited to less complicated real-time situations. However, small-scale optimization is also required.

18.2.2 Single-objective optimization procedures

Optimization algorithms may be classified as either deterministic or stochastic. For any given issue, deterministic algorithms will always arrive to the same solution, since they start from the same place. Because these algorithms always come up with a solution in each iteration, they are a major benefit. This is a drawback since these algorithms are incapable of solving optimization problems with unpredictable behavior. The second type of optimization technique relies on stochastic approaches. So, even if the starting point stays constant, multiple explanations may be discovered, making stochastic algorithms less reliable than deterministic ones. Algorithms for optimizing data have been classified as stochastic or deterministic anonymous behavior in the literature.

To prevent local optima, stochastic algorithms have the benefit of predictable anonymous behavior. More runs and better tweaking may help improve stochastic algorithms' reliability. It is important to note that stochastic optimization techniques may be divided into individualist and collective algorithms. The simplest stochastic algorithms start with a single answer and work their way up to more complex ones through optimization. Random changes and improvements are made for a defined number of phases. For as long as a specific outcome is achieved, the TS family of algorithms is perhaps the most well-known [14,15], besides hill climbing [16], ILS [17], and SA. The low computational cost and the necessity for a small number of function evaluations are two benefits of this group.

🔳🔳🔳 ━━━━━━━━━━━━━━━━━━━━━━━━━━━━━

Initialize the salp population x_i (i = 1, 2,..., n) considering ub and lb
while (end condition is not satisfied)
Calculate the fitness of each search agent (salp)
F = the best search agent
Update c_1 by *Eq. (3.2)*
for each salp (xi)
  if (i == 1)
   Update the position of the leading salp by Eq. (3.1)
  else
   Update the position of the follower salp by Eq. (3.4)
  end
end
 Amend the salps based on the upper and lower bounds of variables
 end
return F

━━━━━━━━━━━━━━━━━━━━━━━━━━━━━ 🔳🔳🔳

18.2.3 Multiobjective optimization problems

In multiobjective (or multicriteria or multiattribute) optimization (MOO), two or more conflicting objectives are optimized simultaneously with respect to a set of constraints. However, in real-world situations, achieving one aim may necessitate the sacrifice of another. MOO can be used for a variety of tasks, including network analysis, aircraft design, bioinformatics, the oil and gas industry, car design, product and process design, and more. To summarize, optimization problems include the following characteristics 18

- A variety of decision options are available.
- Additional limits reduce the number of decision options available.
- Each decision alternative has a different impact on the evaluation criteria.

18.2.4 Multiobjective optimization procedures

Two ways for tackling multiobjective issues are the a priori methodology and the a posteriori method [19]. The multiobjective issue is initially reduced to a single-objective problem by aggregating all of the goals. An expert-determined weighting system is used to provide a value to each of the goals, and this is how it all comes together. After the goals have been aggregated, the best solution may be found using a single-objective optimizer. The primary drawback of this approach is that the Pareto optimum set and front may be obtained by rerunning the algorithm with various weights.

Ad- dative weights in such approaches make it impossible to determine the concave areas of Pareto's optimum front [20,21].

▯▯▯ ━━━━━━━━━━━━━━━━━━━━━━━━━━━━━━━━━━━

Initialize the salp population x_i $(i = 1,2,..., n)$ considering ub and Ib
while *(end criterion is not met)*
  Calculate the fitness of each search agent (salp)
  Determine the nondominated salps
  Update the repository considering the obtained nondominated salps
  if *the repository becomes full*
    Call the repository maintenance procedure to remove one repository resident
    Add the nondominated salp to the repository
  end
  Choose a source of food from repository: F = SelectFood (repository)
  Update c by Eq. (3.2)
  for each salp (x_i)
    if *(i = − 1)*
      Update the position of the leading salp by Eq. (3.1)
    else
      Update the position of the follower salp by Eq. (3.4)
    end
  end
    Amend the salps based on the upper and lower bounds of variables
end
return repository

━━━━━━━━━━━━━━━━━━━━━━━━━━━━━━━ ▯▯▯

Since the first problem was addressed, several runs are required to identify more than one Pareto optimum solution. Despite this, there have been notable advances [21]. The multiobjective structure of the issue is kept intact by the a posteriori method. The fact that the Pareto optimum set may be obtained in a single run is the primary benefit of this method [22]. In addition, any Pareto optimal front may be estimated, and the weight does not need to be provided by specialists in the field. This approach would present decision-makers with a wider variety of choices as compared to other strategies that have been used in the past. On the other hand, one of the most significant drawbacks is that one is required to manage several objectives and use novel approaches in order to determine the Pareto optimum set and front. As a direct consequence of this, carrying out an a posteriori optimization becomes a task that is both more challenging and time-consuming. When weighed against techniques based on previous knowledge, optimization based on a posteriori data has advantages that exceed the drawbacks.

It is not possible to utilize relational operatives to do a comparison of the responses given because of the nature of the challenges. This is because there are many different criteria that are used to evaluate different solutions. When we make use of relational operators, we are in a position to definitively state if one solution is superior to another; but, when we have a large number of goals, we are required to make use of additional operator(s). When comparing two solutions with several objectives, the Pareto optimum dominance is the primary operator that is used, and it may be defined as follows:

Definition 1 Pareto domination:

Taking into account the following two vectors, $x = (x_1, x_2, \ldots, x_k)$ and $y = (y_1, y_2, \ldots, y_k)$, it is possible to regard a solution to be superior than others if it satisfies the goals in the same or at least in one more way than the additional one does. In this scenario, one option is said to determine the viability of the other. The Pareto optimal solutions, also known as nondominated solutions, are those in which this is not the case for both of the solutions. The best answers to multiobjective issues are those that include nondominated solutions. Pareto optimality is also crucial in multiobjective optimization, where it plays the following role:

Definition 2 Pareto optimality:

Considering that x is less than X, x is a Pareto-optimal answer only if the following conditions are met:

There is a collection of Pareto optimum solutions that may be found for each multiobjective issue. These solutions reflect the best possible trade-offs between the different goals. This is referred to as the Pareto optimum set in the optimization field. The Pareto optimal front is the projection of Pareto optimum solutions in the objective space. This is sometimes referred to as the optimal front. The following is a rundown of the two sets:

Definition 3 Pareto optimal set:

A set that contains all of the Pareto optimum solutions is known as the Pareto set.

Definition 4 Pareto optimal front:

This set consists of the objective values for the Pareto solutions set's solutions:

Solutions to multiobjective issues may be readily compared using these four descriptions of the problem. A search landscape is defined by a collection of variables, objectives, and restrictions. The main distinction between a multiobjective search space and a single-objective search space is the presence of several goals in the former. It is difficult to illustrate the search area for problems with more than three goals. Researchers generally divide their search into bound and objective areas while performing their studies.

18.2.5 Research and studies related to the subject of the study

This part focuses on the current status of stochastic optimization research. Among the various subfields in this discipline are the following: single-objective, multiobjective, limited, dynamic, surrogate-aided, and many-objective. It is in this part that the reader will find information on issues relating to single- and MOO as well as associated research. Just as in any other classification problem, feature quality has a significant impact on classification performance in the detection of modulations. Minimum distance (MD) and other instance-based machine learning algorithms benefit from a feature weighting strategy, which increases the accuracy of their distance measurements. For the sake of improving the feature weights in an MD classifier, we provide improved SSA (ISSA).

A blind digital modulation detection methodology is used by a digital modulation detection method to improve performance. The majority of the SSA's advancements are based on the opposition-based learning technique. The ISSA beats both the SSA and the algorithms that are built on it, according to simulations. When the ISSA is properly executed, it is most effective [23].

The SSA is investigated and explained in this study. SSA is a cutting-edge metaheuristic optimization approach that has been effectively applied to a wide range of optimization issues, including machine learning, engineering design, wireless networking, image processing, and energy management. The findings are followed by applications, evaluation, and assessment, which focus on the existing SSA research and identify potential study subjects for future research [24].

SSA and MSSA are two new optimization methods developed in this paper for conducting optimization problems with one or more goals. The SALP's swarming habit when moving and foraging in water influenced the SSA and MSSA's development. The efficiency of these two strategies is examined using a broad variety of mathematical optimization functions. These calculations show that SSA is capable of improving on the random answers and combining the best response. A great degree of convergence and coverage of Pareto optimum solutions may be achieved using MSSA. A broad variety of computationally costly and technically challenging engineering design problems are being studied using SSA and MSSA in this study (e.g., airfoil design and marine propeller design). Real-world case examples illustrate the strategy's usefulness [25].

As the name suggests, this metaheuristic utilizes swarming behavior SALPs. Since its inception, SSA has shown to be effective in a broad variety of applications. SSA may also be used to improve the extreme learning machine and overcome the drawbacks of its standard training technique, which is investigated further. The technique is put to test against two other well-known confirmation methods on 10 benchmark datasets. According to the findings, SSA-based training techniques outperform other training approaches in terms of accuracy and confidence [26].

A smooth balance between exploration and exploitation is achieved by the use of a swarm-based method, which effectively avoids local optimal constraints. Based on the SALP's predation behavior, the SALP SSA is capable of solving complex daily life optimization issues in nature. There are also problems with local stagnation and sluggish convergence in SSA. Using the chaotic sequence start approach and symmetric adaptive population division, this study presents an improved SSA. In addition, a simulated annealing strategy based on symmetric perturbation is used to improve the algorithm's local jumping capabilities. The new algorithm's name is SASSA. Using CEC standard benchmark functions, the SASSA's efficiency is evaluated, and the results show that it has better global search capabilities. SASSA may also be used to solve engineering optimization challenges. Experimentation has been shown to be beneficial in this study [27].

It is standard practice to use metaheuristic techniques to solve global optimization issues. This study provides a novel hybrid method based on the perturbation weight mechanism to improve on the core SSA's poor real-time performance and low accuracy. For large-scale issue solving, the perturbation weight SALP swarm method provides a wide range of search options and a good balance of exploration and exploitation while maintaining a low computational cost. The underlying SALP swarm method is given a new coefficient factor, and new update tactics for the leader and followers are added during the search phase. Iteration is aided by the new leader 0position update technique's limited scope and strong search performance. The new follower update method maintains a wide range of possible outcomes while reducing the amount of processing time required. This chapter describes how the suggested approach may be used to solve low-dimensional problems [28].

The SALP swarm technique (SSA) is an innovative optimization algorithm that has recently seen broad use in the process of solving engineering issues. This study offers a more effective SSA that is built on the concept of quantum computing. Concepts from quantum computing, such as qubits and quantum states, are included into the first version of the SSA in order to readily circumvent the flaw of being trapped in a local optimum. Altering the quantum angle that is linked with the quantum state rather than changing the SALP location is done to enhance the variety of quantum states. The enhanced SSA that was developed is put through its paces by testing it with two different multidimensional benchmark functions; the results imply that using quantum computing may be able to effectively prevent the SSA from approaching the local optimum and boost accuracy [28].

Invoked by the swarming behavior of SALPs while feeding and navigating in the water, the SSA is an unique and uncomplicated swarm-based metaheuristic optimization approach. However, SSA has major issues, including erratic exploration and exploitation and sluggish convergence. As a result, this study gives a better form of SSA known as OOSSA to increase the basic method's overall performance.

Using an optical lens imaging principle-based opposition learning approach, we have devised an orthogonal lens opposition-based learning strategy to assist the general population in breaking out of the local optimal. The adaptively altering number of systems is then used to enhance global exploration capacity and convergence speed. Adding a dynamic learning mechanism to traditional training methods enhances students' ability to commit crimes such as child abuse [29].

This study uses a modified SSA to construct a multithreshold picture segmentation system (SSA). The multithreshold technique offers excellent segmentation results, but as the threshold number increases, the segmentation accuracy decreases. SSA is used to identify the ideal parameters for the fitting function, and Lévy flight is used to fine-tune the SSA to avoid the issues mentioned above. During the optimization process, the appropriateness functions of Kapoor's entropy, Otsu entropy, and Renyi entropy are employed to evaluate the solutions. It is determined whether the proposed method outperforms competing algorithms using a large number of reference photographs. Best fitness values, peak signal to noise ratios, and feature similarity indices were all used to examine the data. Experiments show that the proposed method is superior to the existing algorithms in addressing complicated issues [30].

In the busy field of bioinspired population-based metaheuristics, the SSO technique just debuted and has immediately acquired popularity. This strategy is likely to work effectively since it is based on the unusual spatial organization of SALP colonies, which form long chains following a leader. There were several conceptual and mathematical faults in the original study, which impacted all subsequent attempts on the topic. SSO is subjected to a rigorous evaluation in this paper, which highlights all of the issues raised in the literature and the negative effects they have on the optimization process. ASSO is a mathematically sound SSO that solves all of the issues highlighted. ASSO outperformed the original SSO in a series of benchmark tests that we developed to measure its performance. Finally, we staged a performance [31].

A new metainspired optimization method (SSA) has revolutionized the field. We chose this strategy because of the swarming habits of SALPs during ocean migration and foraging. This algorithm has previously proved its capacity to solve a broad variety of engineering design problems. The simplex technique-based SALP algorithm used in this work is an improved version of the original SSA.

The simplex approach is a stochastic variation strategy that enhances the algorithm's local search capabilities by boosting population diversity. It improves the SSA's trade-off between exploration and exploitation capabilities while also increasing the SSA's resilience and agility. The suggested method is compared to four other metainspired algorithms on four benchmark functions. It is also tested in a real-world limited engineering design problem. Studies show that MSSSA performs better than the alternative [24].

A metaheuristic optimization approach (SSA) has been effectively used in a broad range of optimization issues in a number of industries. An algorithm's exploratory and exploitation skills were found to be challenging to balance over the course of the study. Researchers want to develop an algorithm that can successfully balance exploration and exploitation skills. After further investigation, it was discovered that the sine and cosine functions and the SALP foraging trajectory share a high degree of mathematical resemblance, enhancing the algorithm's optimization capabilities. As a further benefit, a variable neighborhood technique has the ability to greatly expand the algorithm's optimal range of values. Finally, this study proposes a new SALP swarm with variable neighborhood search, which is the outcome of this research [32].

A unique and effective maximum power point (MPP) tracking method for maximizing solar power from high-efficiency photovoltaic is presented in this work (PSC). With excellent tracking efficiency and a speedy convergence to the global MPP (GMPP), the proposed method predicts the GMPP. Similar to the whale optimization algorithm and grey wolf optimization (GWO), SSO reduces computational costs. MATLAB®/Simulink software was used to simulate and assess the SSO approach's efficacy in finding the MPP during PSCs. It exhibits more than 95% tracking efficiency at a quicker convergence rate than the current SSO method, according to the simulation findings. The SSO is a group of individuals who collaborate to accomplish a common goal [33].

SSA is a revolutionary metaheuristic technique for solving particular optimization issues. As the problem becomes increasingly complex to solve, the SSA technique's accuracy and stability diminish (e.g., multimodal, high-dimensional). As a solution for the limits, the swarm algorithm with crossover and Lévy flight (SSACL) is proposed. The crossover scheme and the Lévy flight strategy are utilized to improve the movement patterns of the SALP leader and its followers. There have been studies on unimodal, multimodal, and composite test functions. The proposed SSACL approach outperforms more complex algorithms in terms of accuracy, stability, and efficiency. Furthermore, the Wilcoxon rank-sum test statistically and significantly confirms the advantages of the proposed strategy [34].

Metered premise cloud computing can process and use efficient resources. This is an essential research subject since it offers cloud customers with a high quality of service (QoS).

In order to verify QoS, this research aims to utilize the least amount of resources feasible. At every level, cloud service providers should be able to self-provide resources. Cloud resource management has received a wide range of recommendations and model-based techniques.

Methods: SLA and QoS criteria are used in conjunction with the SSA to determine how many virtual machines should be placed in a limited data center.

Results: For optimization, first fit, greedy crow search (GCS), and HCS are all acceptable solutions. When it comes to identifying the greatest potential match, the combination of the traveling salesman problem (TSP) and the crow search (CS) algorithm is more efficient than the first fit, GCS, and TSPCS [35].

Data science and data mining face high-dimensionality challenges as a consequence of the massive quantity of data available. Traditional machine learning algorithms provide drab results when dealing with large, multidimensional datasets. Data may be reduced in dimensionality by removing irrelevant information from a dataset using feature selection.

SSA, a population-based metaheuristic optimization approach built on sea SALP's swarming, has just been suggested. SSA failed to converge random initial solutions to the global optimum because it relied only on the number of iterations in the exploration and exploitation phase. The suggested ISSA aims to increase its ability to explore different locations by randomly updating SALP's position. An increase in the model's exploitation potential may be achieved by applying Lévy flight to randomize the SALP's location. ISSA's performance is evaluated via six tests.

In order to solve a broad variety of optimization issues, the SSA was developed and implemented. There are a number of algorithms in the swarm intelligence family to which the SSA algorithm belongs. Social activity resulting from swarm intelligence is decentralized and self-organized. Birds, fish, and social insects like bees and termites are all examples of swarms that may best be linked to this kind of behavior. The SSA method was introduced in this work. Mathematical examples, as well as the traditional SSA method pseudocode and source code in two programming languages (Mat lab and C++), were offered to assist academics in understanding the SSA task and process [36].

For early detection of prostate cancer, transrectal ultrasound (TRUS) imaging is the best option. It is difficult to distinguish between normal and pathological prostate lesions in TRUS pictures because of speckle noise, tracking, and low dissimilarity. Misdiagnosis or delayed diagnosis might lead to unneeded biopsies being performed. For radiologists, the use of computer-based categorization methods gives another perspective. A collection of measurable characteristics is used to represent objects in pattern recognition. As a result of the feature selection strategy, data visualization is reduced and classification efficiency is increased while maintaining high accuracy. Enhancement of ultrasound pictures is achieved by ACO methods, which is followed by a boundary complete recurrent neural network algorithm to identify the region of interest (ROI). VGG-19 transfer learning algorithms are then used to extract the features from ROI. Researchers used an optimization-based method for optimizing feature sets [37].

Cloud computing in data centers may host a broad variety of virtual machines and offer several assistances over conventional data centers, including flexibility, security, support, and even enhanced maintenance.

Numerous difficulties must be handled, such as improving energy utilization, resource efficiency, lowering time consumption, and optimizing virtual machine placement. As a consequence of this study, a novel MOP approach for virtual machine placement that combines the SALP swarm and sine-cosine algorithms is provided. It tries to raise the mean time before a host shutdown, minimize power consumption, and eliminate service level agreement violations. The suggested approach enhances the SALP swarm and SCA by adopting the MOP technique. The SCA boosts the performance of the classic SSA by adopting a local search strategy to prevent getting stuck in a loop [38].

SSA has been introduced as a novel approach to optimization. The multiobjective SSA is introduced to tackle multiobjective situations. A variety of mathematical optimization approaches are used to put both algorithms through their paces. The design of airfoils and marine propellers are two technical challenges that have been solved. SSA and MSSA are successful, as shown by the qualitative and quantitative findings. Two new methods for solving optimization problems with single and multiple goals have been developed in this study: SSA and MSSA. They were created in response to SALPs' tendency to gather in large groups to hunt and move in water. Tests on various mathematical optimization functions demonstrate the efficiency of these two strategies in dealing with issue optimization. Results from the mathematical functions show that the SSA method is able to outperform and combine the best random solutions [34].

The table given below shows a presentation of the most important previous studies related to the subject of the study, arranged from the most recent to the oldest:

No.	Years	Authors	Ref.	Method Names	Proposed
1.	2022	Castelli et al.	[24]	ASSO	The experimental results, which show that SSO cannot outperform common metaheuristics, suggest that the scientific community can safely discard SSO.
2.	2021	Duan et al.	[29]	SASSA	The experimental results showed that the proposed swarm SALP algorithm in this study has the ability to improve the mining and exploration properties, and it also has the ability to improve better and more stability when dealing with engineering optimization problems.
3.	2021	Chaabane et al.	[16]	ISSA	Computer simulations have shown that ISSA outperforms SSA and its derived algorithms and offers ISSA better performance once applied to feature weighting
4.	2019	Abualigah et al.	[13]	SSA	This study focuses on the most relevant advantages and disadvantages of SSA for academics interested in optimization algorithms, and it was based on a review of more than 70 research articles. SSA applications are shown in many disciplines such as engineering (controlling and scheduling in power systems and renewable energy systems), image processing, and machine learning for alterations, hybridization, chaotic, and multiobjective (through feature selection and training of neural networks).

Through previous studies, it can be concluded that the proposed and improved algorithms show better and more accurate results than the original algorithm. Among the most prominent weaknesses and disadvantages of the original algorithm is that it has a weak exploration ability and works poorly on the multimodal target functions and its inability to unfairly balance exploration and exploitation. However, one of its most prominent advantages is that it has a simple structure and speed of processing, and it can achieve important results in specific objective functions with fewer options.

At the same time, there was a need to find and develop improved algorithms from the original algorithm, such as SAASA and ISSA, in order to address the weaknesses and shortcomings of the original algorithm reported in a recent research.

18.3 Methods

18.3.1 Stimulation

The scientific investigation of this creature is still in its preliminary stages since obtaining their native habitats and maintaining them in laboratory settings are both exceedingly demanding tasks. As a result, the investigation is still in its preliminary stages. The swarming performance of SALPs, which is discussed in the study, is one of the most amazing aspects of these organisms. In the ocean's depths, SALPs typically congregate into groups that are referred to as SALP chains. Some experts believe that this behavior is carried out in order to increase mobility via the use of quick coordinated alterations and foraging, despite the fact that the specific rationale for this activity is unknown.

18.3.2 Mathematical model

The swarming behavior of SALPs, as well as their population, is not well represented by many mathematical models. Swarms of bees, ants, and fish have all been thoroughly researched and utilized to solve challenging optimization problems, but there is no mathematical model for SALP swarms.

18.3.3 Single-objective SALP swarm algorithm

It should come as no surprise that the mathematical model for SALP chains cannot be used to solve optimization problems directly. The leader SALP is followed by a group of follower SALPs in the SSA swarm model. The SALP chain will automatically move closer and closer to the global ideal if the food supply is replenished. The food supply will be replenished during the optimization process, as it is likely that the SALP chain will discover a better solution by exploring and utilizing the space surrounding it. Apart from the fact that the SALP chain can track a shifting food source, the SALP chain may eventually reach a global optimum, which may change over time. It needs to be seen how effective the SALP chain model and the SSA approach for addressing optimization problems are.

18.3.4 Multiobjective SALP Swarm algorithm

If you have several goals, the best option is called the Pareto optimum set.

SALPs can be routed to a food supply using the SSA algorithm, which can be tweaked over time. This technique cannot be utilized to address multiobjective problems because of the following two issues: SSA can only save one option as the best solution to a multiobjective problem; hence, several answers to a multiobjective problem cannot be saved. Multiobjective issues, on the other hand, do not have a single best solution. In each iteration, SSA refreshes the food source with the best reaction so far.

To guarantee that the algorithm's nondominant answers are always saved, these limitations might be applied to the source. When the repository is full, a SALP is no longer dominating in comparison to the repository's inhabitants. Removing one of the repository's nondominated solutions is preferred.

18.4 Results

In order to determine if SSA is better to other algorithms of its kind, a set of metrics are utilized to do so. A second objective is to collect data that may be used to compare the SSA to other systems. Finally, the MSSA approach has been linked to a slew of previously published algorithms. Many demanding single- and multiobjective benchmarks are included in this section.

18.4.1 Qualitative results of SALP swarm algorithm and discussion

Visualization approaches have a huge role in qualitative results. It is common to see convergence curves in SOO. Each iteration of an algorithm is often measured by drawing a line from its current best answer, which researchers use to determine how well it improves its approximation of the global optimum with each passing cycle. SSA's ability to deal with a variety of challenges is examined in this research via a number of additional qualitative outcomes.

The search histories of SSA search agents throughout time provide the earliest qualitative findings. Searching history statistics generally display the location history of all agents during optimization. Examining a search history diagram allows us to identify whether and how an algorithm explores and exploits the search space.

18.4.2 Quantitative results of SALP swarm algorithm and discussion

A thorough analysis and exploitation of the SSA algorithm was shown; however, the qualitative outcomes failed to support the method's efficacy. The SSA technique is evaluated and compared to other similar methods in this section using two performance criteria. First, the SSA algorithm's performance on average is measured, and then the algorithm's stability is measured. Each test function's best algorithm is selected and compared to other algorithms for the statistical test. If SSA is the optimal technique, then a pairwise comparison between SSA and PSO, SSA, and GSA, and so on may be made.

18.4.3 On the CEC-BBOB-2015 test functions, SALP swarm algorithm, and harmony search

The most recent test suite, CEC-BBOB-2015, which includes noiseless and noisy functions, should be used to evaluate the SSA method.

On the majority of noiseless and noisy test functions in the CEC-BBOB-2015 test suite, the proposed SSA technique outperforms competing algorithms.

18.4.4 Scalability analysis

Test functions are run 30 times with various sets of variables, and their averaged results are shown. This experiment has a total of 200 solutions and 500 iterations. In the CEC-BBOB-2015 test suite, the proposed SSA method outperforms previous algorithms on a wide range of calm and noisy test functions. Both noisy and nonnoisy test functions can be successfully solved using the approach proposed in this paper.

According to this section's findings and research, the SSA algorithm may be sophisticated enough to solve real-world problems using novel search locations.

SSA's dominance was predicated on this explanation, which emerged as a consequence of the adaptive process. SSA outperforms other swarm-based approaches due to its increased exploration during optimization. The SSA method prevents solutions from becoming too localized. As previously shown, SSA can handle a broad variety of challenging scenarios, but the next section covers a number of real-world issues to showcase the SSA algorithm's ability in action. The SSA needs a strategy for coping with limitations. Because it is beyond the scope of his study to examine and pick an appropriate constraint treatment technique for SSA, the most basic constraint management strategy is used, in which a penalty function punishes search agents with enormous goals.

18.4.5 Results of multipurpose SALP swarm algorithm and discussion

Many common tests may be used for evaluating both single-objective and multiobjective optimization. In order to evaluate MSSA's effectiveness, Zitzler et al. provided five stringent test functions. The mathematical models for these benchmark functions are provided. ZDT1 to ZDT3 are the first three benchmark functions, which should be remembered. In order to carry out a variety of testing activities, modified ZDT1 and ZDT2 models with linear or three-objective fronts are used. MOPSO and NSGA-II, two of the most widely used MOO techniques, are used to verify the findings. Due to their complexity, multiobjective test functions need a higher maximum number of iterations. IGD creates and offers quantitative findings after 30 runs of each strategy. The maximum archive size supported by MSSA and MOPSO is the same, which should be noted. Using ZDT1, the fourth case study, is simple since the front of the algorithm is linear. The NSGA-II results show once again that it does not converge to a real Pareto optimal solution. When compared to MOPSO's metrics, convergence and coverage metrics are obviously better than those of MOPSO's.

In contrast to NSGA, MOPSO's ideals are viable and superior. As these results demonstrate, MSSA successfully distributes SALPs along a real Pareto optimum front in a variety of locations. There are two goals in four experiments, and the findings show that MSSA is very useful in addressing these issues. Only a tiny area of the front is covered by this approach, as seen by the MOPSO data. Following these discoveries, MSSA is able to calculate the true Pareto optimal fronts.

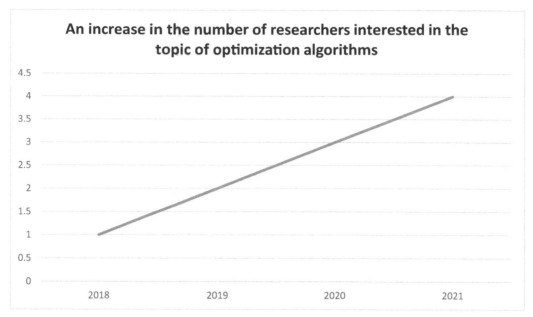

FIGURE 18–1 The number of interested researchers in SSA.

It was also shown through the results in Fig. 18−1 and by reviewing the literature and previous studies that there is an increase in the number of researchers interested in the topic of optimization algorithms in order to reach better solutions to problems, enhance strengths, and try to find a remedy for weaknesses by introducing new algorithms and improvements to them.

18.5 Conclusion

The typical swarming behavior of SALP was shown in this work. Using two mathematical models, the point of the leading and subsequent SALPs was modified. Swarm simulations in two and three dimensions have shown that the model is capable of investigating both fixed and mobile food sources. SALP has relied on SSA as its primary food source for the time being. The performance of ISSA is compared to four different nature-inspired algorithms, PSO, GA, ALO, and GWO, using small, medium, and large datasets. The fundamental SSA method is also put to test. Classification accuracy was greater for a suggested optimizer, despite it being the second quickest and selecting a smaller number of features. The inertia weight parameter improves the SSA method's performance, according to the results.

A repository for the nondominant solutions generated so far was constructed via the MSSA approach. When there was an abundance of solutions in highly inhabited regions, nondominant solutions in sparsely populated areas were tapped for food supplies. It started with search history and trajectory analysis and moved on to average fitness and the convergence curve.

It is clear that SSA-based approaches outperform other techniques in terms of accuracy and prediction stability when compared to others. Three constrained engineering optimization projects are used to assess ESSA's ability to meet real-world engineering application difficulties. That SSA is capable of examining the most promising areas of a search area has been observed and demonstrated. The study also recommends the need to pay attention to research and studies that help develop algorithms in order to avoid weaknesses and enhance their strengths to help apply them on the ground and in practical life and in a variety of different fields.

References

[1] C. Blum, X. Li, Swarm intelligence in optimization, Swarm Intelligence, Springer, 2008, pp. 43−85.

[2] L. Abualigah, A. Diabat, C.L. Thanh, S. Khatir, Opposition-based Laplacian distribution with Prairie Dog optimization method for industrial engineering design problems, Comput. Methods Appl. Mech. Eng. 414 (2023) 116097.

[3] G. Hu, Y. Zheng, L. Abualigah, A.G. Hussien, DETDO: An adaptive hybrid dandelion optimizer for engineering optimization, Adv. Eng. Inform. 57 (2023) 102004.

[4] D. Izci, S. Ekinci, S. Mirjalili, L. Abualigah, An intelligent tuning scheme with a master/slave approach for efficient control of the automatic voltage regulator, Neural Comput. Appl. (2023) 1−17.

[5] H. Jia, C. Lu, D. Wu, C. Wen, H. Rao, L. Abualigah, An improved reptile search algorithm with ghost opposition-based learning for global optimization problems, J. Comput. Des. Eng. (2023). qwad048.

[6] A.H. Alharbi, A.A. Abdelhamid, A. Ibrahim, S.K. Towfek, N. Khodadadi, L. Abualigah, et al., Improved dipper-throated optimization for forecasting metamaterial design bandwidth for engineering applications, Biomimetics 8 (2) (2023) 241.

[7] S. Nama, A.K. Saha, S. Chakraborty, A.H. Gandomi, L. Abualigah, Boosting particle swarm optimization by backtracking search algorithm for optimization problems, Swarm Evolut. Comput. 79 (2023) 101304.

[8] M. Zare, M. Ghasemi, A. Zahedi, K. Golalipour, S.K. Mohammadi, S. Mirjalili, et al., A global best-guided firefly algorithm for engineering problems, J. Bionic Eng. (2023) 1−30.

[9] D. Wu, C. Wen, H. Rao, H. Jia, Q. Liu, L. Abualigah, Modified reptile search algorithm with multi-hunting coordination strategy for global optimization problems, Math. Biosci. Eng. 20 (6) (2023) 10090−10134.

[10] S. Ekinci, D. Izci, L. Abualigah, R.A. Zitar, A modified oppositional chaotic local search strategy based aquila optimizer to design an effective controller for vehicle cruise control system, J. Bionic Eng. (2023) 1−24.

[11] L. Abualigah, D. Falcone, A. Forestiero, Swarm intelligence to face IoT challenges, Comput. Intell. Neurosci. 2023 (2023).

[12] M. Hadni, H. Hassane, New model of feature selection based chaotic firefly algorithm for arabic text categorization, Int. Arab. J. Inf. Technol. 20 (3A) (2023) 461−468.

[13] L. Abualigah, M. Shehab, M. Alshinwan, H. Alabool, SALP swarm algorithm: a comprehensive survey, Neural Comput. Appl. 32 (15) (2020) 11195−11215.

[14] Y. Fan, J. Shao, G. Sun, X. Shao, A modified SALP swarm algorithm based on the perturbation weight for global optimization problems, Complexity (2020).

[15] D.B. Fogel, Artificial Intelligence Through Simulated Evolution, Wiley-IEEE Press, 1998.

[16] S.B. Chaabane, A. Belazi, S. Kharbech, A. Bouallegue, & L. Clavier, improved SALP swarm optimization algorithm: application in feature weighting for blind modulation identification, 2021.

[17] I.Y. Kim, O.L. De Weck, Adaptive weighted-sum method for bi-objective optimization: Pareto front generation, Struct. Multidiscip. Optim. 29 (2) (2005) 149−158.

[18] K.E. Parsopoulos, M.N. Vrahatis, Particle swarm optimization method in multiobjective problems, Proc. 2002 ACM Symposium Appl. Comput. (2002).

[19] J. Branke, T. Kaußler, H. Schmeck, Guidance in evolutionary multi-objective optimization, Adv. Eng. Softw. 32 (6) (2001) 499−507.

[20] E.H. Houssein, I.E. Mohamed, A.E. Hassanien, SALP Swarm Algorithm: Modification and Application, in Swarm Intelligence Algorithms, CRC Press, 2020, pp. 285−299.

[21] H. Jia, C. Lang, SALP swarm algorithm with crossover scheme and Lévy flight for global optimization, J. Intell. & Fuzzy Syst. (2021) 1−12. Preprint.

[22] D.K. Mathi, R. Chinthamalla, A hybrid global maximum power point tracking of partially shaded PV system under load variation by using adaptive SALP swarm and differential evolution−perturb & observe technique, Energy Sources, Part. A: Recovery, Utilization, Environ. Eff. 43 (20) (2021) 2471−2495.

[23] S. Mirjalili, A.H. Gandomi, S.Z. Mirjalili, S. Saremi, H. Faris, S.M. Mirjalili, SALP swarm algorithm: a bio-inspired optimizer for engineering design problems, Adv. Eng. Softw. 114 (2017) 163−191.

[24] M. Castelli, L. Manzoni, L. Mariot, M.S. Nobile, A. Tangherloni, SALP swarm optimization: a critical review, Expert. Syst. Appl. 189 (2022)116029.

[25] R. Aswani, S. Ghrera, & S. Chandra, A novel approach to outlier detection using modified grey wolf optimization and k-nearest neighbors algorithm, 2016.

[26] A. Messac, C.A. Mattson, Generating well-distributed sets of Pareto points for engineering design using physical programming, Optim. Eng. 3 (4) (2002) 431−450.

[27] I. Aljarah, M. Habib, H. Faris, N. Al-Madi, Mafarja, M. AbdElaziz, et al., A dynamic locality multi-objective SALP swarm algorithm for feature selection, Comput. Ind. Eng. 147 (2020) 106628.

[28] L. Davis, Bit-climbing, representational bias, and test suit design, in:, Proceedings of the Intlernational Conference on Genetic Algorithm (1991) 1991.

[29] Q. Duan, l Wang, H. Kang, Y. Shen, X. Sun, Q. Chen, Improved SALP swarm algorithm with simulated annealing for solving engineering optimization problems, Symmetry. 13 (6) (2021) 1092.

[30] S. Wang, H. Jia, X. Peng, Modified SALP swarm algorithm based multilevel thresholding for color image segmentation, Math. Biosci. Eng. 17 (1) (2020) 700−724.

[31] D. Wang, J. Shengqi, & X. Liu, A Simplex method-based SALP swarm algorithm for numerical and engineering optimization, in: Proceedings of the 10th IFIP TC 12 International Conference, IIP 2018, Nanning, China, October 19−22, 2018, pp. 150−159.

[32] F. Tian, H. Wei, X. Li, M. Lv, P. Wang, An improved SALP optimization algorithm inspired by quantum computing, Journal of Physics: Conference Series, IOP Publishing, 2020. 2020.

[33] Z. Wang, H. Ding, Z. Yang, B. Li, Z. Guan, L. Bao, Rank-driven SALP swarm algorithm with orthogonal opposition-based learning for global optimization, Appl. Intell: (2021) 1−43.

[34] H.R. Lourenç o, O.C. Martin, T. Stützle, Iterated local search, Handbook of Metaheuristics, Springer, 2003, pp. 320−353.

[35] R. Jaganathan, Hybrid of SALP swarm optimization algorithm and grasshopper optimization algorithm (SSOAGOA) for feature selection, Int. J. Grid Distrib. Comput. 14 (2021) 1350−1366.

[36] K. Balakrishnan, R. Dhanalakshmi, U.M. Khaire, Improved SALP swarm algorithm based on the levy flight for feature selection, J. Supercomputing (2021) 1−21.

[37] F. Glover, Future paths for integer programming and links to artificial intelligence, Comput. Oper. Res. 13 (5) (1986) 533−549.

[38] D. Indraneel, Normal-boundary inersection: a new method for generating the pareto surface in nonlinear multicriteria optimization problems, Soc. Ind. Appl. Math. 8 (3) (1998) 631−657.

Index

Note: Page numbers followed by "*f*" and "*t*" refer to figures and tables, respectively.